DIGITAL LAWYERING

In today's rapidly changing legal landscape, becoming a digital lawyer is vital to success within the legal profession. This textbook provides an accessible and thorough introduction to digital lawyering, present and future, and a toolkit for gaining the key attributes and skills required to utilise technology within legal practice effectively.

Digital technologies have already begun a radical transformation of the legal profession and the justice system. *Digital Lawyering* introduces students to key topics, from the role of blockchain to the use of digital evidence in courtrooms, supported by contemporary case studies and integrated, interactive activities. The book considers specific forms of technology, such as Big Data, analytics and artificial intelligence, but also broader issues including regulation, privacy and ethics. It encourages students to explore the impact of digital lawyering upon professional identity, and to consider the emerging skills and competencies employers now require. Using this textbook will allow students to identify, discuss and reflect on emerging issues and trends within digital lawyering in a critical and informed manner, drawing on both its theoretical basis and accounts of its use in legal practice.

Digital Lawyering is ideal for use as a main textbook on modules focused on technology and law, and as a supplementary textbook on modules covering lawyering and legal skills more generally.

Emma Jones is a senior lecturer in law and Director of Wellbeing at the University of Sheffield's School of Law. Her research interests focus upon emotions and wellbeing in legal education and the legal profession, and digital lawyering. She teaches modules on digital lawyering.

Francine Ryan is a senior lecturer in law, Co-director of the Open Justice Centre at The Open University in the UK, and a qualified solicitor. Her teaching and research interests are clinical legal education with a particular focus on technology and innovation enhanced learning.

Ann Thanaraj leads the digital transformation of learning and teaching at Teesside University. Her scholarly work focuses on raising the significance of law degrees in preparing for the Fourth Industrial Revolution. She has developed models of digital lawyering to transform law degrees.

Terry Wong is a technologist and entrepreneur based in Hong Kong. Born, raised and educated in the United States, he holds degrees in architecture and management from the Massachusetts Institute of Technology. Terry leads a global team of technologists and designers building and actively investing in technology-led businesses, with interests in legal and financial services.

DIGITAL LAWYERING

Technology and Legal Practice in the 21st Century

EMMA JONES,
FRANCINE RYAN,
ANN THANARAJ
AND TERRY WONG

Routledge
Taylor & Francis Group
LONDON AND NEW YORK

First published 2022
by Routledge
2 Park Square, Milton Park, Abingdon, Oxon OX14 4RN

and by Routledge
605 Third Avenue, New York, NY 10158

Routledge is an imprint of the Taylor & Francis Group, an informa business

British Library Cataloguing-in-Publication Data
A catalogue record for this book is available from the British Library

Library of Congress Cataloging-in-Publication Data
A catalog record for this book has been requested

ISBN: 978-1-032-12216-8 (hbk)
ISBN: 978-0-367-26078-1 (pbk)
ISBN: 978-0-429-29821-9 (ebk)

DOI: 10.4324/9780429298219

Typeset in Galliard
by Apex CoVantage, LLC

DEDICATION

To the educators past, present and future who inspire learning and innovation.

CONTENTS

ILLUSTRATIONS

FIGURES

MIND MAPS

IMAGES

ACKNOWLEDGEMENTS

Thank you to Chris Sykes, Lead Designer of BPP Law School, UK, for introducing Emma, Francine and Ann to Terry.

Thank you to Dr. Graeme Horsman for co-authoring Chapter 7. Dr. Horsman is a digital forensics analyst and former EnCase Certified Examiner and Computer Certified Examiner (EnCE) and Certified Computer Examiner (CCE). He teachers in computer/digital forensics at Teesside University, UK. With a PhD in digital forensic triage and a graduate diploma in law, master's of jurisprudence and postgraduate certificate in higher education practice, Dr. Horsman focuses his research on digital forensic examination techniques, methods for forensically investigating mobile devices, systems for improving digital forensic examinations and evidence, and testing and validation in digital forensics. You can keep up to date on developments in digital forensics and law enforcement as part of your ongoing digital lawyering journey by following Dr. Horsman at @GraemeHorsman on Twitter.

Thank you to Kieron Metcalf for his substantial contribution to Chapter 8. Kieron is a Fellow of the Higher Education Academy recognised for his teaching at the University of Cumbria, UK. Having worked previously in the legal aid sector in Cumbria, specialising in employment law, social security law and housing law, appearing in district court and tribunal hearings, Kieron now leads on the Lawyering in a Digital Age module. The module was designed by Ann Thanaraj in 2015 as part of a body of theory to accompany the Virtual Law Clinic built as an experiential tool for students to practise professional and lawyering skills online. It was the first module in the country that began preparing students for the digital delivery of legal services, unique in its balance of focusing on technology and practical skills. The module tackles a lot of the issues focused on in Chapter 8 and has helped students to think of legal practice and the administration of justice in a different light. Since 2019, Kieron took over the design and delivery of this module, and it has become even more relevant since March

2020, when the effects of the COVID-19 pandemic were felt on the legal system. Students have been at the forefront of understanding the changes made to our court services in response to the pandemic. Students build on skills, knowledge and aptitude necessary for a competent digital professional to represent a client in a manner that is consistent with the rules of the profession.

Terry would like to thank his wife Jean for her love and support throughout this journey, and his parents and teachers for all the advantages they gave him. He would also like to thank Frances Hsieh, Rebecca Martin, Cabrini Pak and Amelia Sitou for reading his working drafts and providing valuable feedback and advice.

1 INTRODUCTION

DEFINING DIGITAL LAWYERING

Emma Jones, Francine Ryan, Ann Thanaraj and Terry Wong

WELCOME TO DIGITAL LAWYERING IN THE 21ST CENTURY

This textbook is designed to introduce you to the dynamic, innovative, complex and fascinating world of digital lawyering—in other words, the use of digital technology within the legal profession. It will give you the opportunity to understand what digital lawyering is, how it has developed and what role it now plays within legal practice and the delivery of legal services. It will also encourage you to reflect upon your own knowledge and skills and how these can be applied within the digital world. Mind Map 1.1 shows the key topics we will cover, using the title of each chapter.

In exploring digital lawyering, this textbook will take a range of perspectives and approaches, drawing on the viewpoints of its four authors (all of whom wrote this chapter and the conclusion). This includes:

- *A legal perspective*—looking at how laws and regulations have had to, or may have to, adapt to reflect the changes in digital technology and the legal profession.
- *A technical perspective*—looking at the functions and capabilities of technology.
- *A sociological perspective*—looking at the impact digital lawyering has upon the profession and wider society.
- *An educational and reflective perspective*—encouraging you to reflect upon your digital and educational experiences and your skills development going forward.

DOI: 10.4324/9780429298219-1

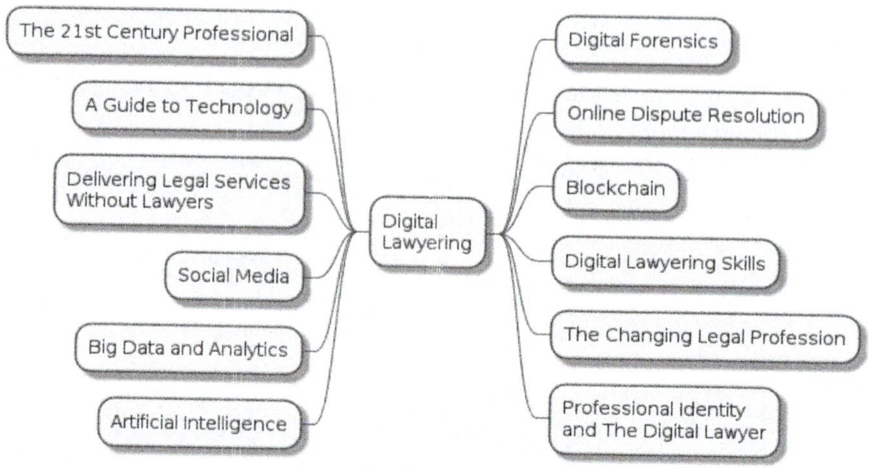

Mind Map 1.1 Topics of chapters

As the four authors, we each have different but equally valuable perspectives, which we will introduce you to later in this chapter. That is the reason that the authors names are strictly in alphabetical order on the cover!

In this chapter, we will begin by thinking about the role of digital technology within society, definitions of digital technology and digital lawyering, and the relevance of ethics and legal education. We will then move on to explain the way the rest of this book will work. The chapter will finish by explaining the authors' journeys into and within digital lawyering. This will help put each of the chapters we have written in context as you work through the rest of the textbook. Let us begin by considering the role of technology within society.

TECHNOLOGY AND SOCIETY

Technology plays a critical role in shaping our society. It impacts on the way individuals communicate, interact and think. The advancement of technology has had both positive and negative effects on our lives. It is hard to imagine our existence without access to the Internet and smartphones, but we need to be aware of the pervasive effect of technology on our lives too. Technology brings opportunities for innovation and change, but it also brings risk, distrust and concern. Throughout this textbook, it is important to consider to what extent technological development is a good thing for our society and for our legal system. This may be a good opportunity for you to reflect on your own experiences of technology to help you understand in more depth the issues raised in this textbook.

Technology is now commonplace in our lives. According to Statista, between 2016 and 2021 the number of global smartphone users increased by 40%, and by 2023 mobile devices users will increase to 7.33 billion.[1] The highest number of smartphone users are in China, the United States and India. Social media reach and adoption is growing in popularity too. Two billion users use WhatsApp monthly, and 53.6% of the world's population uses social media.[2] More people are accessing the Internet via smartphones and using tablets for activities such as online shopping, watching TV and films, and engaging in social media. Social media, email and apps are used by governments to engage with their citizens. We now have online services for many aspects of our lives. If you want to apply for a driving licence, file your taxes or start divorce proceedings, all of this can be done online. The United Nations states that there has been a "sharp rise in the number of countries that are using e-government to provide public services online through one-stop-platforms".[3]

In terms of the workplace, in 2014 the UK House of Lords Select Committee on Digital Skills urged that, for the country to stay competitive globally, "the UK must ensure it has the necessary pool of (highly) digitally skilled graduates and others . . . to support and drive research and innovation throughout the whole economy".[4] A wider initiative by the European Commission has given priority to digital literacy as a major component of the EU's Europe 2020 strategic plan

1 Statista, 'Number of Smartphone Users Worldwide from 2016 to 2023' (undated) <https://www.statista.com/statistics/330695/number-of-smartphone-users-worldwide/> accessed 12 May 2021.

2 Statista, 'Social Media—Statistics and Facts' (undated) <https://www.statista.com/topics/1164/social-networks/#dossierSummary> accessed 12 May 2021.

3 United Nations, 'UN E-Government Survey 2016' (2016) <https://publicadministration.un.org/egovkb/en-us/reports/un-e-government-survey-2016> accessed 12 May 2021.

4 House of Lords Select Committee on Digital Skills, *Make or Break: The UK's Digital Future* (February 2015), Chapter 3.

through its Digital Agenda for Europe, defining it in terms of "the skills required to achieve digital competence, the confident and critical use of ICT for work, leisure, learning and communication".[5] The effective and critical use of technology is "so fundamental that, like writing once did, it permeates all forms of communication, presentation and reference".[6] The term "Fourth Industrial Revolution" is now commonly used to refer to the way in which new technologies are currently reshaping industries, professions and society generally.

Technology has become an integral part of our working lives and it features in many jobs. Digital technologies enabled many people to work from home during the COVID-19 pandemic, which allowed many businesses to keep functioning. The pandemic demonstrated that flexible working is possible and that productivity is not lost. As a result, we are seeing significant shifts in patterns of work, with flexible working becoming commonplace and workers splitting their time between home and the office. Companies are readjusting to new ways of working, and this is going to change how businesses operate and evolve in the future. All this demonstrates that technology is now firmly embedded in our lives.

However, not everyone is able to participate in the digital world. Many people struggle to access and use the Internet. There are many parts of our society without the skills, knowledge or access to be able to engage effectively with technology. Economically disadvantaged groups cannot afford a computer or a smartphone or the cost of mobile data or Wi-Fi. It is estimated that there are six million people in the UK who are classified as socially and digitally excluded.[7] Low levels of literacy make engaging online very challenging. A lack of confidence or people to ask for help makes many people reluctant to use technology. The global digital divide is even greater, as half of the

5 European Parliament, 'Digital Agenda For Europe' (2008) <https://www.europarl.europa.eu/registre/docs_autres_institutions/commission_europeenne/sec/2008/2629/COM_SEC(2008)2629_EN.pdf>; <https://ec.europa.eu/digital-single-market/en/europe-2020-strategy>

6 Jisc, 'Developing Digital Literacies' (2014).

7 Royal Geographical Society, 'Digital Divide in the UK' (Royal Geographical Society, n.d.) <https://21stcenturychallenges.org/what-is-the-digital-divide/> accessed 28 April 2021.

world's population does not have access to the Internet.[8] Policies on investment infrastructure, improved regulation and skills development are required to close the digital divide, because if not addressed it will lead to further inequality and exclusion of marginalised and vulnerable groups.

WHAT IS DIGITAL TECHNOLOGY?

Technology can be understood as the practice of making and using tools to achieve specific practical goals. Writing implements—from a stylus for inscribing a stone tablet with the Code of Hammurabi, to the quills used to draft and sign the Magna Carta, to the gel ink rollerball pens of today—are all examples of the slow evolution of writing technology. A field of continuous and discrete marks can be put on a writing surface. Incisions, shades of tone, or smooth curved lines can be seen by human eyes, processed in the language centres of human brains, and recognised as writing, representing items of information. These can be referred to as analogue technology. This is a term which defines technology that does not involve processing letters, numbers or other information electronically. Another common example of analogue technology you may have come across is a watch or clock with a numbered clock face and two hands that show and measure the passage of time.

In contrast, digital technology entails the use of electricity and electronic devices to create, process, transmit and store information. It is distinct from analogue technology in that it uses a discrete, regular representation of information in sequences of binary values (ones or zeros). Unlike with analogue technology, there are absolutely no in-between values or states, no shades or tones or gradations; there are only two values in the base unit of expression. Using our example of a watch or clock, if you read the time from your smartphone or tablet it is represented by a set of numbers, such as 19:00, rather than as a form of continuous measurement.

8 World Bank Live, 'Closing the Digital Divide' (*World Bank*, 2020) <https://live.worldbank.org/closing-the-digital-divide> accessed 28 April 2021.

The constraint on the expressiveness of the fundamental element (in other words, the fact there are no in-between values or states) may seem like an impediment to building anything useful. In fact, as we will see in this textbook, this constraint is the basis of computing systems that exploit the physical properties of certain electrical devices connected in specific combinations and configurations that yield the results of concrete calculations, or operations that manipulate data represented in ones and zeros. Layering these fundamental building blocks over time in assemblies, and advances in materials, processes and miniaturisation, have led to the complex web of high-speed computation and high-resolution media and communication that we experience in our daily environment, powered by digital technology.

You should note that throughout this book the terms "technology" and "digital technology" may be used interchangeably, depending on the context.

WHAT IS DIGITAL LAWYERING?

There is no single simple definition of digital lawyering, and it is likely that you will develop your own definition as you work through the textbook. Overall, digital lawyering is a broad term encompassing both practical and theoretical elements. It can be used to refer to the practical ways in which individual lawyers, and the legal profession more generally, have begun to use and adapt to digital technologies. It also refers to a body of theory which begins to identify and explain the sorts of learning that are required for law students and future professionals to thrive in a digital age. It encapsulates an understanding of some of the complex and disruptive changes brought about by technologically mediated practices, including:

- Their impact on current and future legal practice, questioning what is required for a law graduate, trainee or lawyer to thrive in a modern practice.
- Their impact on the sorts of knowledge that make up a law degree, exploring what interdisciplinary knowledge and awareness can equip a law student to be future-ready.

Professor Richard Susskind, IT Adviser to the Lord Chief Justice in the UK, has discussed the impact that digitalisation and technology have had on legal services. In his book *The End of Lawyers? Rethinking the Nature of Legal Services*,[9] he advised that enhancements in technology leading to improved, sustained and advanced methods of legal services delivery are inevitable and that, consequently, lawyers should change the way they work. As the legal profession undergoes its digital transformation, reshaping how we practice as lawyers and the nature of how legal services are delivered, learning about digital lawyering can help in developing a necessary understanding of core technologies, their features and functionalities, how they are being utilised and the impact of these technologies on the role of legal professionals. Digital lawyering theory also assists in highlighting gaps within the profession and demonstrating the opportunities to merge law with technology to create hybrid roles within the legal sector. It can also be used to explore limitations and gaps in the existing law and how it can be interpreted more broadly to capture both the physical and digital worlds. This raises much wider questions about the intersection between technology, law and society. For example, as a society how should we balance the sharing of information online with people's right to privacy? How can we protect the right to privacy while preserving the right to free speech? How can we protect the more vulnerable members of society?

Looking at these aspects of digital lawyering encourages law students and existing legal professionals to prepare for the changing legal profession. Examples of legal practice embracing digital technologies include advances in artificial intelligence (AI) and Big Data for decision-making, the automation of a range of previously manual processes, in the revolutionising of the execution of wills and in the areas of property and probate laws, the use of blockchain technologies for executing contractual agreements, changes to the delivery of legal services including practising law through virtual law firms, and the use of online court systems for dispute resolution and small civil claims. As the legal profession and the delivery of legal services undergo a journey of digital transformation, this creates new opportunities for lawyers and law students to explore new areas of practice. All these topics are discussed within subsequent chapters of this textbook.

The use of these types of technology, while novel in many respects, still requires lawyers to exercise the traditionally required knowledge, skills and aptitude for the purpose of collaborating, advising clients, undertaking dispute resolution and other forms of advocacy, and

9 Richard Susskind, *The End of Lawyers? Rethinking the Nature of Legal Services* (Oxford, Oxford University Press, 2010).

processing legal transactions. The technologies used in legal practice are not, as yet, capable of replacing our human and intellectual faculties, such as legal reasoning, the art of persuasion and the process of interpreting information in the context of the realities of our world today. However, other transformative changes, such as the emergence of alternative business structures, unbundling of services, digitalisation of services through legal platforms, off-the-shelf solutions, automation of procedural work and machine learning impacting technical legal expertise, are all affecting the identity of the legal professional.[10] Looking at digital lawyering enables us to explore what legal professionals require to thrive in a contemporary legal practice. It affords a richness of awareness of the relevance of this digital transformation of the profession and its linkage with our own digital understanding, and raises questions around the intersection of law, legal theory, legal practice and technology. Our exploration of digital lawyering will also highlight that digital lawyers must not only be aware of emerging technologies but also have an understanding of the way in which technology works in order to appreciate the impact that technology has on the practice of law. It will also emphasise that digital lawyering is not about requiring lawyers to be IT professionals. Instead, it is about having enough knowledge to understand where law and technology intersect, being aware of the implications of technology and becoming digitally literate so that you can leverage the benefits of technology in your work.

With the seamless integration of the digital and physical worlds in so many aspects of our lives, clients will also require advice on regulations governing the use of technology and associated issues such as digital assets, digital evidence, property ownership, privacy and intellectual property protection. There is a significant body of writing and research upon these issues (often referred to as "law and technology" issues), and it is important to be aware of such topics. However, we will not be exploring these in detail in this textbook. Instead, our particular focus is upon the relationship between digital technology and the legal profession. In other words, this is about the ways in which lawyers can appropriately, safely and effectively use online technological innovations and techniques within the delivery of legal services, often through secure and authentic online law platforms. It is not a technology or law and technology textbook.

10 Solicitors Regulation Authority, 'Technology and Legal Services' (2018) <https://www.sra.org.uk/risk/resources/technology-legal-services.page>

DIGITAL LAWYERING AND ETHICS

This textbook explores how we prepare law students for the practice of law in a technologically enhanced world, and it considers some of the knowledge, skills and competencies that digital lawyers require. However, as referred to previously, digital lawyering is not separate to the conventional practice of law, and we cannot consider it in isolation. The role of a lawyer is changing, and with the emergence of new technologies, law firms are being challenged to rethink how legal services are delivered. When we think about the future of legal practice, technology will be harnessed further to support innovation. Although online communications, paperless offices and cloud services are all integral features of digital lawyering, technology only serves to facilitate the practice of law. What we want to instil is an understanding of how technology impacts on legal practice and give you the opportunity to reflect on this new reality. Ethical issues are varied, and exposing you to some of these potential issues will help you develop your own approach to the use of technology within law.

An understanding of ethics is an essential component of legal education, and ethics is an integral part of being a lawyer. Throughout your law degree you will have opportunities to explore ethics in many different contexts and engage in ethical debates. Many fundamental ethical issues arise with the development of new technologies, legal practice and the delivery of legal services in a digital environment. In this textbook we discuss ethics through the lens of technology to give you a flavour of some of the ethical issues that technology may raise. If you understand technology and become tech-savvy, then you will be able to consider some of the potential ethical dilemmas that arise at the intersection of law and technology. If you are advanced digitally, you will have an awareness of technology-related ethical issues, and this will enable you to leverage that knowledge and understanding in your career.

In this textbook we discuss some specific technologies, such as AI in Chapter 7 and some of the ethical issues which can arise from it. For example, there are increasing concerns about the ethical implications of the use of predictive analytics in relation to judicial decision-making (using technology to predict the likely decision of a judge in a case). In addition, the use of AI does not just impact on the administration of law; it is also changing the way lawyers practice law. Technology-assisted reviews are an example of the application of AI in legal practice and involve training a machine to review documents. Several law firms are using ROSS, which is a robot lawyer that provides legal research.[11] In Chapter 4 we discuss legal bots, which use AI to automate interactions between the user and the bot. They are being developed by law firms and in the not-for-profit sector to help people who would otherwise struggle to access legal information and advice. All of this can create ethical issues, from ensuring individual lawyers understand its use sufficiently to meet their professional obligations to act competently, to meeting their requirements to supervise its use appropriately.

In addition to thinking about ethical issues which may arise for you personally, it is important that you are aware of the ethical implications of technology because you may be in a position in the future where you have to advise on ethical challenges that face your client and your law firm. If you have a greater understanding of how technology is transforming the practice of law, then you are going to be better prepared to enter the workplace. You need to be ethically driven from the start and have the confidence to be able to recognise ethical issues, evaluate the options and make sound decisions.

DIGITAL LAWYERING AND LEGAL EDUCATION

Now is an exciting time in the legal profession as it adapts to and leverages the affordances of digital transformation in its delivery of services. This means it is equally an exciting time to be a law student who is preparing to embark on this digital transformation journey and work in new and creative ways with the law and in the practice of law. For legal academics, this is also an important time to consider how to create opportunities for learning and to prepare students for the digital change in the profession.

Although not all law students will go on to (or want to go on to) become legal professionals, a significant number do so. Often law schools work with law firms and other stakeholders within the legal profession to develop their offerings and provide extracurricular activities for their students. This means that changes within the legal profession will usually also filter through to legal education. More generally, most law schools and universities are keen that their students should be able to gain employment after they graduate, so they will try to equip

11 <https://www.rossintelligence.com>

their students with skills they feel are necessary or desirable within the workplace.

As a result of this, digital lawyering has already begun to impact on legal education. This will be explored further in Chapters 11 and 13, but one example is the increased number of law schools that offer modules, courses or programmes with a focus on digital lawyering. Other students will be given extracurricular opportunities involving digital technology, such as volunteering to develop a smartphone app or online legal resources. More broadly, all students have to develop their digital skills to ensure that they can cope with the demands of the law degree, from completing word processed assignments and submitting them online to using online databases for legal research.

Digital lawyering is multifaceted in that it encompasses knowledge, skills, attributes and professional rules into a mindset and professional way of being. As such, it asks students to consider and develop their own impressions on how they, using the law, can contribute towards the challenges of digital transformation of the workplace and the role the law plays in innovations and in regulating the digital world. Digital lawyering cannot be studied as a single discipline. It impacts all knowledge and skills and extends its boundaries beyond the components of subjects and modules that make up a law degree, drawing on a broad range of knowledge and awareness that can equip a law student to be future-ready. This may sound daunting as an understanding of digital lawyering cannot be easily learnt or acquired simply through a series of lectures or a one-off project. However, it also means that students can draw upon their own existing knowledge, experience, skills and attributes to develop their understanding and insight. We hope this textbook will help you in identifying and developing how you can best do this.

HOW TO USE THIS TEXTBOOK

Each chapter in this textbook can stand alone, or they can be read in order, cover to cover. If you are using this textbook to accompany a course or module, your instructor may ask you to read specific chapters, depending on the focus. In all cases, Chapters 1–3 are recommended as core readings.

Each chapter will have a number of features that students and instructors will find helpful:

- *Hot spots.* At the beginning of each chapter are a number of key questions that you should keep in mind as you read the chapter text. When you have completed a chapter, you should return to those questions and review them to see if you feel able to provide an answer to each one. If there are any questions you find difficult to answer, you may want to reread sections of the chapter or undertake some wider reading on the topics. Underneath the key questions for each chapter there is also space for you to write some additional questions. These may be focused on queries or issues that you think of when you read the chapter title, or those that arise during your reading of the chapter. At the end of the chapter, you should check whether these have been answered or consider undertaking some wider research and reading.
- *Mind maps.* Each chapter contains a mind map summarising its key themes to help you navigate the content. These are also summarised in the conclusion to the textbook.
- *Syncs.* Each chapter includes a number of syncs, interactive exercises of varying length and complexity. These are designed to help you think about and understand what you have read, for example, by asking you to apply some of the concepts presented in the chapter or to perform a limited amount of research on a topic to see real-life illustrations.
- *Skills boxes.* Most chapters highlight key skills that a digital lawyer should be sure to acquire and practice.
- *Additional resources.* Each chapter lists a number of additional resources for learning, to enrich the information presented, or to highlight additional paths for skills and knowledge acquisition relevant to the topic at hand.
- *Glossary.* Legal and technological terms that are important for you to understand are listed and defined in the glossary included at the end of the textbook.

We recommend that you read actively, with a notebook or note-taking application at the ready to use your favourite note-taking method, whether it be outlining, mind mapping or a more structured method such as the Cornell Method. Traditional annotation in the margins of the purchased paper edition, or using note-taking features of your reader application in the case of an e-book edition, is warmly recommended, if possible, given the density and range of topics we will present.

As you read, try to take occasional breaks during reading or after your sync activities to summarise in note form your impressions and write down any questions that occur based on your work in that chapter to that point. Being active in your reading, pausing and taking stock of questions are practices that serve the traditional lawyer well and will surely bear fruit for the rising digital lawyer.

A NOTE ON SOURCES

One of the reasons we chose to write this textbook was because there was a lack of books, particularly aimed at students, which explored digital lawyering. Although there are a range of academic articles on the topic, these are often very jurisdiction specific; for example, some focus on the specific requirements placed on lawyers in the United States when dealing with technology. They can also appear dated quite quickly; for example, you will find older articles which discuss the implications of introducing computerised databases or email systems into law firms! Although these are interesting historical snapshots of the development of digital lawyering, they are unlikely to be very helpful to a contemporary researcher.

As a result of this, you may find that you are relying more heavily upon non-academic sources than you would usually do when studying law. For example, there are a wide range of websites, blogs and podcasts devoted to digital lawyering and related issues. The benefit of this is it means you can access a diverse range of perspectives on relevant topics. You can also read commentary on very recent innovations or challenges that have arisen. However, it also means that you have to be very careful to assess the validity and persuasiveness of your sources. A good starting point is to check who the author is: Are they known for a particular viewpoint? Do they have a vested interest in the topic? For example, someone who works for a company developing AI for law firms is unlikely to argue that AI is a danger to the future of the legal profession! You will also need to check the date to ensure technological developments have not overtaken its content.

In terms of the content itself, think about whether the points the author makes are supported by evidence. What sources have they used? How reliable are they? It is important to try and separate out personal opinion from factual information and well-evidenced arguments. You should also try and think about any counterarguments that the author has ignored or disregarded to assess their validity for yourself.

This may sound like extra work, but approaching your research and reading in this way will in itself assist you in developing valuable skills. You will be practising active reading and applying critical thinking, both of which are crucial for digital lawyers.

OUR JOURNEYS INTO DIGITAL LAWYERING

Having introduced you to digital lawyering and the structure of this book, we now want to introduce you to ourselves as authors. The previous section emphasised that when reading a piece of writing, you should think about the position of the author and how that may affect their perspective. Hearing a little about our journeys will help you to understand and evaluate our perspectives as you read through the

Image 1.1 Emma Jones

subsequent chapters. In the conclusion to this textbook, we will also give you our personal visions of digital lawyering 30 years into the future, which are again influenced by our experiences to date.

EMMA JONES

I began my working life as a solicitor, specialising in construction law. During my training in the late 1990s, at a large firm in London, I spent a lot of time photocopying paperwork and hand delivering documents to the nearby court and sets of barristers' chambers. Although we did have access to email, it was not particularly well used, and there was still a large emphasis on speaking to the clients by telephone or sending documents via the direct exchange system (a kind of postal service for law firms). When I qualified as a solicitor, I worked at two large regional firms in Manchester, and during that time there was definitely a growing focus on digital technology, for example, using electronic templates when drafting construction contracts and conducting legal research using electronic databases. However, a lot of the work was still conducted fairly traditionally and there was an emphasis on face-to-face and telephone interactions with clients.

From working as a solicitor, I eventually moved into academia via owning a bookshop, being a baby massage instructor and teaching 16- to 18-year-olds! At that point I became very interested in the role of emotions and wellbeing in legal education and the legal profession. It seemed to me to be something that had never really been discussed at my law school or during my time in legal practice. As a result, I began researching that area. During my research, digital technology was quite often referred to in relation to legal professionals as something that could potentially impact negatively on their wellbeing. In particular, the sense of emails and mobile telephones meaning clients assumed they were available 24/7. Of course, there were also some positives mentioned. In particular, my research around wellbeing during the COVID-19 pandemic suggests that legal professionals really valued the opportunities which digital technology gave them to work from home and in a flexible manner.

My research has also led me to study concepts like professional identity and professionalism in detail. When doing so, it has become clear that digital technology is impacting on many facets of legal life. It is not simply about making processes faster and/or more effective; it also influences how people perceive themselves and their work and has the potential to alter key concepts which define who and what a legal professional is.

Image 1.2 Francine Ryan

FRANCINE RYAN

I qualified as a solicitor in 1996 at a large regional law firm in Manchester specialised in complex disease litigation. It might be hard to imagine, but when I started as a trainee there was no computer on my desk, there was no email and if you were lucky enough to have a mobile phone, it looked like a brick! In those days, lawyers dictated letters which were typed by secretaries; the telephone and the fax machine were the other main forms of communication. During my career, I saw how technology was transforming the practice of law. The case management system emerged, along with access to the Internet, email and smartphones, all of which have had a significant impact on the way in which law firms operate. During my career I learned how technology could assist and redesign the practice of law. I developed new skills to help me navigate these changes and when I left legal practice, it had been transformed beyond recognition.

In 2010 I moved from legal practice into academia, and in 2014 I became a lecturer in law at The Open University. The Open

University is the UK's largest university and has pioneered distance learning for over 50 years. Technology and pedagogy are symbiotic at The Open University: They go hand in hand to deliver the learning experience to our students. In the law school we have been exploring how we can use new and emerging technologies to develop practical legal activities for students. We created a virtual law clinic, which is open to anyone with an Internet connection. All the work is carried out through our case management system, and we conduct virtual interviews. Our virtual law clinic was modelled on a virtual law firm.[12] Virtual law firms operate through a digital infrastructure and are gathering momentum.

I am also passionate about access to justice and how we can leverage technology to provide information and advice to people via smartphones and the Internet.[13] I have been involved in developing a digital justice project where students design chatbots to give legal information and advice on a variety of different areas of law. I have also had the opportunity to explore the use of virtual reality in my teaching.[14] We use smartphone-based virtual reality to provide students with an immersive environment to practice and develop their presentation skills. This project is being expanded with the development of a virtual courtroom.

My research explores technology-enhanced learning and innovation in clinical legal education. I am particularly interested in graduate attributes and skills. I am leading a research project that involves legal academics, law firms, and trainee and newly qualified solicitors to explore what graduates need to successfully transition into legal practice. The data is showing the importance of students developing digital skills and competencies that are required for legal practice. I think it is an exciting time to be studying law: There are many new opportunities emerging that go beyond a career as a lawyer.

12 Francine Ryan, 'A Virtual Law Clinic: A Realist Evaluation of What Works for Whom, Why, How and in What Circumstances?' (2020) 54 (2) *The Law Teacher* 237–48.

13 Hugh McFaul, Elizabeth FitzGerald, David Byrne and Francine Ryan, 'A Mobile App for Public Legal Education: A Case Study of Co-designing with Students' (2020) 28 *Research in Learning Technology*.

14 Hugh McFaul and Elizabeth FitzGerald, 'A Realist Evaluation of Student Use of a Virtual Reality Smartphone Application in Undergraduate Legal Education' (2020) 51 (3) *British Journal of Educational Technology* 572, 589.

Image 1.3 Ann Thanaraj

ANN THANARAJ

I started teaching law at the University of Cumbria. I specialised in land law, equity and trusts, and employment law. I always created opportunities that encouraged curiosity and inspired students to learn. Eager to expand the learning ecosystem into courtrooms, I developed a new module which I called Lawyers' Skills. It focused on preparing students for the real world of legal practice, coaching and mentoring them with the confidence to thrive in the professional world of practice, combining a sense of adventure and realism. The craft of advocacy, courtroom skills and client interviews featured heavily in this module, supported by a body of professional and legal ethics.

In 2014, as I took on the role of head of a law school, industries and professions began to embark on a digital transformation journey, I wondered what the direction of the legal profession would be: Would technology be of interest to the way the profession operated? Would it change what we do? What would that mean for my students? My reflections led to some scholarly work which has been at the epicentre of developing my future-focused thinking of how curricula can be shaped to address the changing legal profession. To me it was more than just skills to use pieces of technologies; beyond that, it involved developing the art and craft of creativity in learners, to become resilient, adaptable and communicate in a variety of novel ways using digital solutions and other ways that are accessible. It was also about reimagining law modules so that they captured learning that seamlessly integrated the physical and digital worlds and the adequacy of laws to protect and regulate.

I set out to invest time to support students to develop digital literacies within the law curriculum within this module. I designed the Virtual Law Clinic (VLC), a novel approach that allows real-world legal transactions to take place online in partnership between students, supervising tutors and pro bono solicitors in practice. Shifting to a virtual clinic allowed me to take practical learning to a digital landscape, giving students a realistic view of the impact of technologies redefining the role of legal professionals. As a learning and teaching tool, the VLC was showcased in several countries, profiled by the Higher Education Academy in its *Handbook of Teaching and Learning: Teaching in the Disciplines* and identified as a best practice in learning and teaching (L+T) by the Solicitors Regulation Authority for its transformation of practical legal education. To accompany the practical hands-on digital lawyering experiences in the VLC, I began to build "digital lawyering" as a new body of theory within legal education. The impact on learning comes through the redesign of how students study law. I passionately advocate for an interdisciplinary law curriculum, weaving subjects from humanities, science, ethics, technology and philosophy into the study of law to bring to life and prepare students to address societal, technological and regulatory challenges in a technologically mediated world. This puts students at the forefront of shaping innovation and thinking beyond legal doctrine—as real-world problems are multidimensional—and futureproofing themselves for the reshaping of the world of work.

To spearhead a growing field of tech law in legal education, I founded Lawyering in a Digital Age, an international conference (now annual) born out of my conviction that committed and enthusiastic people interested in legal education could contribute to global excellence in L+T in the discipline. It has led to an extensive reach of a collaborative interdisciplinary and global audience sharing the value in preparing students with the creativity, digital skill set, design concepts and systems thinking through interdisciplinarity.

As I continue to advocate strongly for modern models of legal education that encompasses digital literacies and interdisciplinary learning, I now lead the digital transformation of learning and teaching across Teesside University in my present role as assistant academic registrar. The past few years of research, curriculum design and advocacy on digital lawyering has been a catalyst for me to commence Teesside University's Education 4.0 ambitions and setting the sector standard for driving excellence in university-wide course design and delivery. There is much more for me to learn, and much more I'd love to share. I continue my search to understand how best students learn, particularly in becoming future-ready for dynamic technology-mediated practices and how teaching practitioners from across disciplines can be supported better to design excellent learning experiences to educate law students and others for the Fourth Industrial Revolution. I am also a principal fellow of the Higher Education Academy. You can connect with me via LinkedIn.

Image 1.4 Terry Wong

TERRY WONG

I remember vividly the day I arrived at secondary school in a quiet town in central Connecticut in the United States. I walked into our campus computing centre and sat down at a terminal, beginning a journey that has taken me through most of my education and professional life to this day. It was a privilege in those days to access and use without limitation what was a then state-of-the-art minicomputer, the Digital Equipment VAX 11–750 running UNIX. It was a large, powerful, versatile machine occupying most of the floor space in a constantly air-conditioned room of 9 square metres with specialised electrical outlets and fail-safes. This sort of power was usually reserved for university research or running advanced automated operations in manufacturing plants, *not* the study tool and occasional playground of a little gang of curious teenagers with a predilection for hacking. As we will see, the same computer power can be found today in the widely popular education and maker computer platform, the Raspberry Pi from the UK's Raspberry Pi foundation.

Graphics-rich word processors like today's Microsoft Word were not widely available. Most publishing was still done with analogue tools like phototypesetting systems. One of the tasks that the minicomputer class of UNIX computers I had at my disposal did better than nearly any other was text processing and digital typesetting. Precursors to the programs that now produce the Portable Document Format (PDF) files all lawyers and businesspeople handle every day were first created and used on those machines. Working not only on our school news publications but also on reports and personal publishing projects, I learned the concepts and intricacies of document structure, indexing, typesetting software, and other foundation knowledge needed to support large-scale creation and management of electronic documents at a young age.

My early professional life was as a consultant working in Boston with Andersen Consulting LLP, the firm that would become Accenture. I was chosen by the firm's leadership to be the technology lead in a specially formed unit that took emerging Internet technologies and made them understandable and, more importantly, strategically useful to our clients and consultants. This role led naturally to my ongoing involvement since then in a continuous series of roles in new technology-enabled ventures, with a focus on leading teams to integrate promising new technologies in the construction of innovative, scalable systems for consumers and the companies that serve them.

A group of investors and entrepreneurs in Hong Kong approached me in 2014 to serve as the chief technology officer (CTO) on the founding team of a legal technology venture dedicated to making the process of drafting legal documents more consistent, reliable and, most importantly, accessible and affordable for the everyday small businessperson. My team did so with a novel combination of automation, expert systems technology and an innovative online subscription service delivery model that had not yet been attempted in Asia—or indeed in many parts of the world. Interest in the venture and in our technology led to speaking and lecturing opportunities for me, and wonderful opportunities to engage practising lawyers and firm leaders, other entrepreneurs and, perhaps most rewarding, students who always asked tough questions I could not have anticipated.

Today I continue with Cydeas, my current software development and investment business. I lead a team of professionals developing and operating a portfolio of technology-enabled businesses serving needs in a range of industries, including human resources, financial technology and, of course, legal technology. In the process I have had the good fortune to be introduced by a good friend and former colleague, Chris Sykes, to my co-authors, who all impressed upon me the need and important opportunity to share a legal technologist's views as we offer this text on *Digital Lawyering*. I hope my presentation of some of the more involved technology concepts is accessible and useful, and that it might help some of you along your path in the legal profession, but perhaps in this exciting interdisciplinary area of digital lawyering, where there is sure to be much action and new directions in the coming decades.

Conclusion

As you read this book you will see there are many ways students can get involved in digital lawyering and start to develop the skills required for a transforming workplace. It is also important to remember that the whole world of work is changing. The future of work is going to look different across all industries and professions. It will revolve around how we use technology to remove boundaries, connect securely and collaborate to achieve productive and meaningful interactions. Whatever your career plans, you need to be open to learning because as new digital technology is adopted, the skills required will change. This means you will need to become a lifelong learner, continuing to invest the time in building the skills that are going to be required for the next stage of your career.

ADDITIONAL RESOURCES

To start or continue your digital lawyering learning journey, here are some useful additional resources:

Hackathons <https://bryter.io/decision-automation/why-hackathons-are-great-for-lawyers/>
Society for Computers and Law <https://www.scl.org>
Cisco Academy <https://www.netacad.com>
Future Learn <https://www.futurelearn.com/subjects/it-and-computer-science-courses>
LinkedIn <https://www.linkedin.com> Join one of the many legal technology groups including Legal Hackers, Legal Design Special Interest Group, and Social Media and Digital Technology: Opportunities and Challenges.
Law Lab Showcase <https://lawlabshowcase.org>

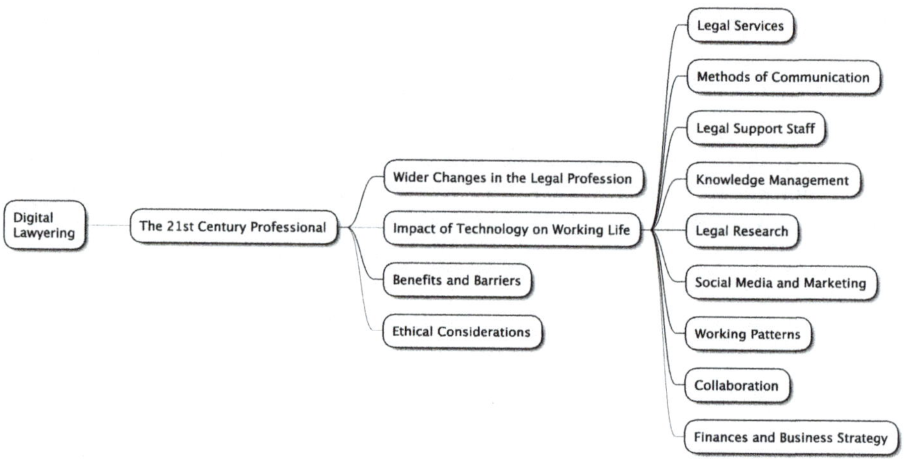

Mind Map 2.1 Chapter topics

2

THE 21ST-CENTURY LEGAL PROFESSIONAL

Emma Jones

INTRODUCTION

This chapter begins by considering the various developments and changes which have shaped the contemporary role and work of the legal profession. It looks at the ways in which technology is impacting on, and in some cases transforming, everyday legal practice. It explores the opportunities and challenges that arise, with a particular emphasis on day-to-day workings of law firms and other legal providers. It concludes by considering how this will shape the lawyer of the future.

Chapter hot spots

When reading this chapter, questions to think about include:

- To what extent has (and is) technology driving change in the legal profession?
- How does technology interact with other factors influencing the legal profession?
- How is technology changing the relationships between legal professionals and their clients?
- What does the lawyer of the future do?

Having read the title and introduction, you can add any other questions you want to explore here:

DOI: 10.4324/9780429298219-2

THE CHANGING LEGAL PROFESSION

In recent years, the legal profession has experienced a significant level of transformation. It is important to understand the key changes involved to put the role of technology in context (Figure 2.1). These include the following:

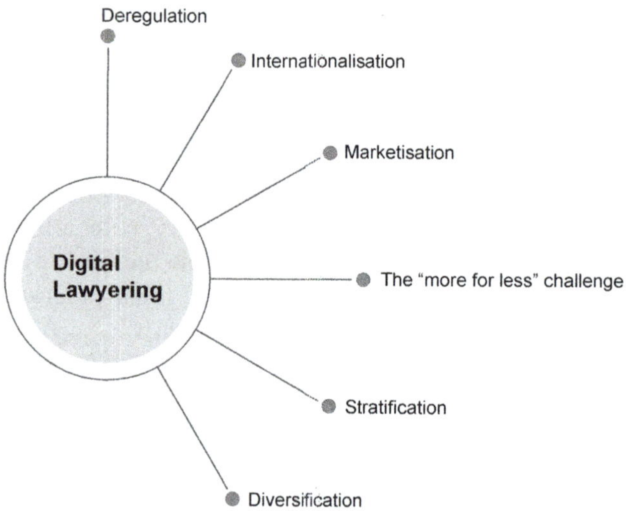

Figure 2.1 Key changes in the legal profession

- *Marketisation.* A majority of lawyers work in private practice, obtaining their work from individuals or businesses who require legal services. This could range from a person seeking to increase their contact with their children to an international company looking to acquire a potential competitor. Such clients can instruct legal professionals directly (e.g. when someone goes to see a chartered legal executive or solicitor) or indirectly (e.g. when a solicitor instructs a barrister on behalf of a client).

  Being in private practice means that lawyers are operating in a commercial environment where they need to compete to obtain and retain clients and generate profits in order for their firm to survive. In other words, law becomes a type of business. This is in contrast to traditional ideas of lawyers as working for the public good rather than for profits.

  Another word often used to describe parts of this process is commodification. This reflects the idea that law and legal advice have become a commodity, used for economic gain, rather than being viewed as having wider societal functions, such as maintaining the rule of law and promoting democracy.

- *The "more for less" challenge.* This is a phrase coined by the author Richard Susskind[1] which has links to the marketisation of the legal profession. It refers to the way in which wider economic pressures lead to businesses seeking to spend less money on legal services. However, at the same time they increasingly need specialist legal advice to assist them in their work. Individuals too are facing cuts in the public funding of legal services (such as legal aid) despite the massive impact legal issues can have on their lives (e.g. in relation to housing, employment and family issues). Therefore, the difficulty for the legal profession is how to provide more legal assistance at a time where there is less funding and fewer resources available to do so.

  In addition, businesses and individuals may have expectations that their disputes will be resolved faster and more effectively through the use of modern technology, but this may not always be the case. For example, despite the increasing use of online court hearings (see Chapter 9), there can still be significant delays in procedures.
- *Diversification.* The profession has shifted (at least in part) from being largely male, white and middle class. For example, the Law Society of England and Wales has identified that more women than men now hold practising certificates (enabling them to work as solicitors).[2] Although there are still barriers to progression within the legal profession, there is increasing recognition of these issues and a number of schemes have been developed to promote equality, diversity and inclusivity. For example, in the United States, the American Bar Association Commission on Sexual Orientation and Gender Identity and the National LGBT Bar Association are both working to ensure that lesbian, gay, bisexual and transgender persons participate fully in the profession.
- *Stratification.* Traditionally, the legal profession consisted of a (relatively small) number of professionals and law firms that would deal with a wide range of disputes. However, over time different groups of professionals and firms have emerged, often specialising in particular areas.

1 Richard Susskind, *Tomorrow's Lawyers: An Introduction to Your Future* (Oxford, Oxford University Press, 2017), 4.

2 The Law Society of England and Wales, 'Annual Statistics Report 2018' <https://www.lawsociety.org.uk/support-services/research-trends/annual-statistics-report-2018/> accessed 7 October 2019.

As a result, today's legal profession includes a wide range of different roles, types of firms and businesses, and categories of clients spread across many geographical locations. For example, solicitors' firms range from a sole practitioner in a small town who largely does conveyancing work (buying and selling houses) to a global chain of law offices that works with international organisations on corporate deals. Many large businesses will also have in-house legal departments, and there is an increasing number of entrepreneurial lawyers creating new ways of practising law.

Such a broad and diverse spread means that it is difficult to refer to the legal profession as a single, homogenous group. Even within one particular sector, or firm, individuals now often specialise in a particular area of law, such as housing or shipping law, making it even more fragmented.

- *Internationalisation.* The legal profession has reflected the broader globalisation of society in often working across borders on international disputes. Many law firms also offer legal services in a range of countries.
- *Deregulation.* Traditionally, legal services have only been offered by a relatively small group of people. To protect the public and to retain the status of the legal profession, the way in which these services have been offered has been tightly regulated. For example, the type of business structure used to provide a specific legal service would be tightly prescribed.

In England and Wales, the Legal Services Act 2007 has resulted in the removal of a range of restrictions that previously governed where, how and by whom different legal services are offered. In particular, it allowed the use of alternative business structures (ABSs).

ABSs: Doing business differently

ABSs were created to generate competition in the legal services market. They do this by making it easier for non-lawyers to own and invest in law firms. This means that a wide range of organisations, including charities, trade unions, insurance companies, estate agents and many more, now offer legal services. This has made a significant contribution to the stratification of the legal profession referred to previously.

In England and Wales, a number of bodies, including the Solicitors Regulation Authority (SRA) and the Bar Standards Board (BSB) have the power to grant licences to ABSs. In October 2019, the SRA's records showed that 1,025 ABSs had been licenced in total. The first to become an ABS was The Co-operative Legal Services, part of the Co-op Group, who are a large food retailer, and also offer funeral and insurance services.

Different jurisdictions have different rules governing ABSs. For example, in Scotland an ABS must still be majority owned by solicitors and other regulated professionals.

It is not only England and Wales which allow these structures. The first common-law jurisdiction to do so was New South Wales in Australia in 2001, with other Australian states following its example. However, despite discussions on the issue, ABSs are not currently permitted in the United States.

Although the introduction of ABSs opened up the market for legal services, it would be wrong to think that this meant regulation of the sector has been abolished entirely. The Legal Services Act 2007 also created a new regulator to oversee the whole of the legal services market (the Legal Services Board) and introduced the Office for Legal Complaints, which in turn set up the Legal Ombudsman for England and Wales to deal with consumer complaints against lawyers.

Sync 1: The legal profession today

You should allow around 20 minutes for this activity.

Choose one of the key changes discussed in this section and think about:

1. Whether this change has been influenced by the growing use of technology in the legal profession.
2. Whether this change could influence the future use of technology within the legal profession.

Using an Internet search engine, find at least one example to support your answer.

Depending on which change you selected, you may have come up with a variety of answers. If you chose to consider deregulation and ABSs, you probably found a range of articles indicating that these are promoting technological innovation within the legal sector. A recent Legal Services Board survey of 1,502 organisations offering legal services in England and Wales found that SRA-regulated providers were two times more likely to use the ten technologies referred to in the questions as other providers. ABSs were three times more likely than other types of providers to use these types of technology.[3] It could also be argued that the growth in technology was one of many factors which prompted the change in regulation. The Clementi Review of the Regulatory Framework for Legal Services in England and Wales (which preceded the Legal Services Act 2007) referred to individuals such as information technology (IT) professionals who were involved in the management of law firms but were not at that time able to be the principal (the individual with executive authority) of the firm.[4]

THE IMPACT OF TECHNOLOGY ON DAY-TO-DAY PRACTICE

This section will consider what impact modern technology is having upon contemporary legal practice. This is a very broad question and, to some extent at least, the answer will vary depending on jurisdiction, type of legal service and many other factors. The next activity is designed to assist you in breaking down some of the key issues to think about.

Sync 2: How to explore the impact of technology

You should allow around 10 minutes for this activity.

You are a trainee in a law firm and have been asked to write a report assessing "what is the impact of technology upon the legal profession". Identify the key issues to look at, or further questions to ask, to help you write this report.

3 Legal Services Board, 'Technology and Innovation in Legal Services—Main Report' (November 2018) <https://research.legalservicesboard.org.uk/wp-content/media/Innovation-survey-2018-report-FINAL-2.pdf> accessed 7 October 2019.

4 David Clementi, 'Review of the Regulatory Framework for Legal Services in England and Wales' (December 2004) <http://www.avocatsparis.org/Presence_Internationale/Droit_homme/PDF/Rapport_Clementi.pdf> accessed 10 October 2019.

When considering this question, you may have identified a range of issues, ranging from questioning how you define terms such as "technology" and "legal profession" to pinpointing large topics such as artificial intelligence or the impact of technology on legal ethics. When asking herself this question, the author of this chapter realised that one way to consider this was to divide it into two as follows:

- What is the impact of technology on the day-to-day work of legal professionals?
- What is the impact on the legal profession as a whole?

For the purposes of this chapter, she decided to focus on the former question (the other question will be discussed in subsequent chapters). This led her to the following further questions:

- What impact does technology have on the day-to-day tasks which legal professionals perform?
- What impact does technology have on the ways in which legal professionals interact with their clients?
- What impact does technology have on the ways in which legal professionals interact with other colleagues?
- What impact does technology have on the ways in which legal professionals interact with the courts?

To think about the questions just raised, it is useful to compare a lawyers' office from the 1980s with a lawyers' office today. So, let's start with a look at the firm of Glossop, Charlesworth & Co Solicitors in around 1985. Figure 2.2 is a reminder of some of the technology available at that time!

Figure 2.2 Lawtech in the 1980s!

The firm is based in a large town and has eight partners, ten assistant solicitors, two trainee solicitors and 13 legal secretaries. They deal with a wide range of work, from transactions between businesses to conveyancing and family disputes. Each partner has their own office. Assistant and trainee solicitors share offices in pairs. The working hours are 9 am to 5.30 pm with a break for lunch, but most solicitors will be in the office from around 8.30 am to 6.30 pm.

The firm conducts most of its correspondence with individual clients through the postal system. Letters to clients are typed out on typewriters by the legal secretaries. Where possible, they send post second class to save on expense (meaning it takes around three days before it is received by the client). The firm will also ring clients on their home or work telephone lines if there is an urgent matter to discuss. None of their clients has a mobile telephone, but a number do have an answering machines on their landlines.

For business clients, the firm will also send facsimiles (known as faxes). This involves an original document being scanned through an optical scanner and then transmitted to another fax machine, where a copy appears. The firm has a dedicated fax number to avoid their landline being tied up. Other law firms are communicated with via fax or the direct exchange system, which is a form of internal postal system within the legal profession for the sending of hard copy letters.

The firm has a file for each client, stored on shelves and in filing cabinets. There is a sheet on the front of each file on which employees record their time whenever they work on the file. Inside the file are copies of all correspondence and other documents relating to the case.

Court documents are either typed on a typewriter or completed by hand by the legal secretaries; documents are taken to the nearest court in large bundles by the trainee solicitor three times a week. A significant number of matters involve litigation, although often they are settled via negotiation between legal representatives.

Most legal research is undertaken by the trainee and assistant solicitors using the volumes of *Halsbury's Laws of England* and other large law books which are kept in the partners' offices. Occasionally they will need to travel to the larger law library in the nearest city. No one in the firm has an Internet connection.

The firm has recently invested in a new word processor, but only one legal secretary is confident in using it. The aim in the next couple of years is to create a number of precedent documents to use and store on floppy disks.

The firm markets its services through a double-page advertisement in the weekly local newspaper and on two billboards which are located on the major roads in and out of the town.

Now, let's move on to the present day, when the original Glossop, Charlesworth & Co Solicitors has evolved into Glossop Law. Figure 2.3 provides some clues to the changes that have occurred.

Figure 2.3 Contemporary digital lawyering

The firm is still based in the same large town and now has eight partners, six assistant solicitors, one trainee solicitor, four paralegals, seven legal secretaries, an office manager and an IT and finance manager.

They continue to deal with a wide range of work, from transactions between businesses to conveyancing and family disputes. However, in recent years they have received fewer instructions on straightforward conveyancing issues. Several of its partners are trained mediators and their services are advertised on the firm's web page.

Each member of staff has a computer in their office. The office arrangements remain the same, but several solicitors also have firm laptops and work from home one or two days a week. Some of the partners, assistant solicitors and paralegals use voice-to-text software. Client correspondence is usually emailed, unless a client has specified a preference for postal copies. Phone calls are still made to clients on urgent matters, often to their mobile phones. A couple of the solicitors use WhatsApp to communicate with regular clients too. Other solicitors are commonly contacted using email, and the fax machine has recently been removed.

The firm uses an online case management system licenced from an international software company. It enables employees to record their time, make notes of conversations with clients and set reminders for key deadlines (e.g. for the return of court documents). Most client documents and correspondence are also now stored on computer, freeing up space for an additional office.

Court correspondence is regularly dealt with via email, and for some claims documents are submitted via the Money Claims Online system. Hard copies are still taken to the court by the trainee solicitor once each week. However, overall significantly fewer cases result in litigation, and the firm now advises on methods of alternative dispute resolution.

The majority of legal research is undertaken by the trainee and assistant solicitors and paralegals. It is all now conducted online and the firm subscribes to several major online legal databases. It also subscribes to an online database of forms and precedents which the secretaries use to generate documents as needed.

In addition to a bespoke website, the firm also has a Twitter account and is considering expanding its social media presence. Several solicitors regularly write short articles on recent developments in the law, which are then posted on the firm's website.

Sync 3: Looking back

You should allow around 45 minutes for this activity.

1 Comparing the snapshots of Glossop, Charlesworth & Co Solicitors and Glossop Law, what do you think are the key differences in terms of the day-to-day work of the firm's employees?

2 Write a similar pair of scenarios for either (a) a sole practitioner, (b) the London office of a large law firm with offices globally or (c) a barrister in private practice.

3 Thinking about the new pair of scenarios you have written, to what extent do you think the impact of technology differs between different parts of the legal profession?

Your answers to Sync 3 have probably demonstrated that different types of legal professionals and firms will have been impacted in different ways, but it is clear that all parts of the legal profession have significantly evolved in technological terms.

Some of the key differences between the two eras are explored under the following sub-headings.

THE TYPES OF SERVICES BEING OFFERED

The example of Glossop, Charlesworth & Co Solicitors stated that the firm dealt with a wide range of work. The example of Glossop Law mentioned that the firm was dealing with less routine conveyancing matters. This is likely to be because of the rise in online conveyancing firms offering such services, often at a reduced rate. Other types of services may well be affected by competition from online alternatives, such as complaining about a consumer product or applying for a patent. The increased amount of legal information available online may also encourage some clients to research and deal with minor issues without involving a third party.

It is also likely that new areas of work have emerged, or become more significant, as the law develops to regulate the use of technology itself; for example, a marketing company may find it requires advice on whether its use of a third-party service to manage its client database and mailing list is compliant with data protection legislation.

The Legal Services Consumer Panel's 2019 Tracker Report on consumers' use of legal services found that the number of legal services users accessing online legal services (via the Internet or email) rose from 21% in 2011 to 33% in 2019 with a particular emphasis on conveyancing and consumer issues. It also found that the use of the telephone was most common in accident and injury cases. Its findings show that conducting legal services by post is in decline, falling to 8% in 2019 from 16% in 2012, although face-to-face delivery has remained fairly static in recent years at around 45%.[5]

The use of technology has also encouraged the "unbundling" of legal services. Previously a client would instruct a solicitor (or other legal professional) on a legal matter and their retainer would cover all issues arising from that matter. Nowadays a client may instead retain

5 Legal Services Consumer Panel, 'Tracker Survey 2019. Briefing Note: How Consumers are using Legal Services' <https://www.legalservicesconsumerpanel.org.uk/wp-content/uploads/2019/07/2019-07-25-How-consumers-are-using-2019-FINAL.pdf> accessed 18 October 2019.

control over the matter and instead buy-in advice or assistance only as needed.[6] For example, an individual with a small claim against a builder for faulty workmanship may pay for a legal professional to draft a claim form but then conduct the rest of the litigation themselves. A landlord may purchase a template lease online and seek to adapt it to their own needs. A company may pay for assistance to draft a defence to a supplier's claim against them but then focus on negotiating a solution themselves.

THE GROWTH OF ELECTRONIC METHODS OF COMMUNICATION

The example of Glossop, Charlesworth & Co Solicitors noted that most correspondence was through the postal system, supplemented by calls to landlines. The example of Glossop Law noted that emails and telephone calls to clients (including to mobile telephones) are now a routine part of their work. Further examples of the use of these communications within legal practice generally are also given in Chapter 3. The shift from paper communications to electronic communications has a range of consequences. A number of these can be beneficial, for example, in saving on paper waste and ensuring that answers and information are provided promptly without letters getting lost or delayed.

However, there can also be some potentially negative impacts. Some of these are technology focused, as electronic communications do not always reach their destination. They can still get accidentally deleted or misdirected. There is the risk of viruses and malware being passed on, with ransomware becoming an increasing problem.[7] Firms and their clients can also be the victims of phishing, where emails appear to be sent from a trusted body in an attempt to obtain financial and other information. For example, in 2014 the Law Society of England and Wales reported that solicitors' firms were receiving emails fraudulently using its @lawsociety.org.uk domain.[8] There may also

6 The Law Society of England and Wales, 'Unbundling Civil Legal Services' (4 April 2016) <https://www.lawsociety.org.uk/support-services/advice/practice-notes/unbundling-civil-legal-services/> accessed 18 October 2019.

7 Lawyers Defence Group, 'The Impact of Ransomware on Law Firms' (28 November 2017) <http://www.lawyersdefencegroup.org.uk/ransomware/> accessed 15 October 2019.

8 Law Society of England and Wales, 'Phishing Email Scam' (24 April 2014) <https://www.ft.com/content/4da1117e-756c-11e9-be7d-6d84653 7acab> accessed 18 October 2019 <https://www.lawsociety.org.uk/support-services/advice/articles/phishing-email-scam/> accessed 15 October 2019.

be issues around confidentiality if apps such as WhatsApp are used. An extreme example of this is demonstrated by a recent news story in which a UK human rights lawyer was allegedly targeted via WhatsApp with spyware developed by an Israeli company.[9]

The use of electronic communications can also have other, human consequences. Lawyers may feel under pressure to be available 24/7 and to provide immediate responses to emails and other electronic communications. As solicitors usually draft and send their own emails rather than dictating them to be typed, sometimes they may send them before taking the time to reflect on the content. This may be particularly problematic when dealing with another party's lawyer, as demonstrated by a case before the Solicitors Disciplinary Tribunal, where a solicitor was reprimanded for calling his opponent's solicitor a "plonker" and making other abusive comments in emails sent during afternoons when (it was argued) a medical condition made him angrier.[10]

In addition, there may be an impact on the relationship between a lawyer and clients. If lawyers are communicating more electronically, it may result in less face-to-face client meetings. This may mean it is harder to build a rapport and establish an effective professional relationship in some situations. Without being able to read the body language of the person in front of you or see their facial expressions, it may be more challenging to interpret what they are saying and gauge their reactions to situations.

Such electronic communications can also lead to issues with record-keeping. If you are sat at your desk speaking to a client, whether by the telephone or in person, it is relatively easy to make notes of the discussion. If you take a quick call from your client on your mobile phone when travelling in between meetings, it can be harder to remember to record the details.

THE CHANGING ROLE OF LEGAL SUPPORT STAFF

The example of Glossop, Charlesworth & Co Solicitors stated that the firm has 13 legal secretaries. The example of Glossop Law noted

9 Mehul Srivastava, 'WhatsApp Voice Calls Used to Inject Israeli Spyware on Phones' (*Financial Times*, 13 May 2019) <https://www.ft.com/content/4da1117e-756c-11e9-be7d-6d846537acab> accessed 30 April 2021.

10 Chloe James, 'Solicitor Reprimanded for Email Calling Opponent a Plonker' (18 August 2015) <https://www.lawgazette.co.uk/practice/solicitor-reprimanded-for-email-calling-opponent-a-plonker/5050611.article> accessed 18 October 2019.

that the number of legal secretaries has been reduced to seven but that there was now an office manager and an IT and finance manager as well.

The increasing use of technology has impacted on the type of support which lawyers now require. While the focus may previously have been on clerical and administrative tasks, support staff now are more likely to be involved in aspects of work such implementing and managing online systems for recording chargeable hours and billing clients. Even within a particular role, such as that of a legal secretary, there are likely to be significant changes in the type of work being carried out. For example, as legal research becomes easier to conduct online, a lawyer may ask a secretary to log on to a legal database and find a particular case or article rather than going to the law books themselves.

Although in our example the firm has had an IT and finance manager for around ten years, their role has changed significantly too. The IT side of their work has expanded significantly, as they now not only need to support the hardware and software needs in the office and maintain firm-issued equipment, but they must also have the skills to manage and interact with a wide range of cloud-based services. They must understand the nuances of managing data and communications, particularly relating to the different devices that solicitors now use when on the move or working from home.

The types of technology being used will also have changed significantly; for example, it is probable that lawyers' diaries will now be managed online, with a secretary having access to all calendars to manage appointments. This is likely to require new skills, which may in turn require additional training to upskill employees. It may also require a review of the firm's standard contracts of employment to ensure they reflect the new ways of working for legal support staff.

THE DIGITALISATION OF KNOWLEDGE MANAGEMENT

Knowledge management is about handling documents and information in the most effective manner possible. The example of Glossop, Charlesworth & Co Solicitors stated that the firm had large files stored on shelves and in filing cabinets. The example of Glossop Law noted that a large number of documents were now stored online instead. One academic article has termed such a digitalisation of documents the "digital advantage" because it enables information to be "instantaneously stored, copied, organised, tagged, searched, transmitted, modified, quantified, annotated, linked, etc."[11]

One simple example of the way technology can be utilised in knowledge management during the routine work of lawyers is note-taking. Traditionally, notes would be written by hand during a client interview, conference (meeting) with counsel or any other significant discussion or meeting. They would then be stored in hard copy in the client's file afterwards. However, it is now possible for notes to be typed up and stored online or even (with appropriate permissions) for the interview or meeting to be recorded.

In their 2018 survey of the use of technology and innovation among legal service providers, the Legal Services Board found that over half of the 1,502 participants used the cloud or similar types of data storage. The term "cloud" refers to data being stored in a separate online location, hosted by a third-party provider, which is accessed online. This made it the most frequently used form of technology. An example of drafting a document using the cloud is given in Chapter 3.

Using forms of electronic data storage not only reduces the need for physical storage space but also potentially makes retrieving and managing information easier and simpler, and also ensures it can be accessed remotely. At the same time, it opens firms up to a range of security risks, from deliberate hacking with malicious intent to accidental downloads by employees.[12]

Problems with storing data on third-party systems

The cloud document storage service Dropbox is one third-party system used by a number of lawyers and law firms. Eliu Mendez, writing in 2013, uses Dropbox's operating procedures at that time to highlight potential issues with confidentiality. He refers to the common use of encryption, which involves data being secured by a "key". Without the encryption key, the data is unreadable. Mendez suggests that a cybercriminal will attempt to obtain such a key to enable them to read the data. He argues that Dropbox at that time maintained the keys longer than required and also stored unencrypted

11 Conrad A. Johnson and Brian Donnelly, 'If Only We Knew What We Know' (2013) 88 *Chicago-Kent Law Review* 729, 735.

12 Cheryl B. Preston, 'Lawyers' Abuse of Technology' (2018) 118 *Cornell Law Review* 881, 923.

versions of documents because of its system of file synchronisation. As a result, he suggests that legal documents may be more vulnerable to inappropriate disclosure.[13]

It is also important for lawyers to be aware of the rights and responsibilities of the third-party providers of such storage, something which requires careful study of their privacy and data protection policies.[14] These issues will be discussed further in Chapters 3, 6 and 7.

Another aspect to knowledge management is the way that legal documents are created and drafted. The Legal Services Board's survey also found that one in five participants used Automated Document Assembly.[15] This could include using electronic precedents (as in the case of Glossop Law) or by using other electronic systems, such as decision trees, to create documents such as contracts or wills (for further discussion, see Chapter 3).

Using such systems can make the process faster and more effective for everyone involved. However, there are arguments that such automation will eventually make it unprofitable for law firms to offer drafting services for documents that clients may increasingly be able to assemble themselves utilising technology, once again impacting on the types of services offered by law firms and possibly their financial survival.[16] It could also potentially lead to fewer opportunities for lawyers working in some areas and impact on the type and level of support staff involvement required. Despite this, at present the limitations of such systems mean that less routine, more complex or nuanced forms of contract will still require a lawyer's involvement.

13 Eliu Mendez, 'Dropping Dropbox in Your Law Practice to Maintain Your Duty of Confidentiality' (2013) 36 *Campbell Law Review* 175.

14 Eliu Mendez, 'Dropping Dropbox in Your Law Practice to Maintain Your Duty of Confidentiality' (2013) 36 *Campbell Law Review* 175, 190–2.

15 Legal Services Board, 'Technology and Innovation in Legal Services Main Report. An Analysis of a Survey of Legal Service Providers' (November 2018) <https://research.legalservicesboard.org.uk/wp-content/media/Innovation-survey-2018-report-FINAL-2.pdf> accessed 21 October 2019.

16 Eduardo Reyes, 'Who's Afraid of Computer Generation?' (28 October 2010) <https://www.lawgazette.co.uk/analysis/whos-afraid-of-computer-generation-/57836.article> accessed 12 November 2019.

A GREATER FOCUS ON ONLINE LEGAL RESEARCH

In the example of Glossop, Charlesworth & Co Solicitors, the junior members of the firm spent much time and effort researching points of law using hard copies of legal books and journals. Law firms would commonly have shelves of books or (in the larger firms) libraries devoted to printed material, and these would form the basis of all the legal research conducted. Some hard copies would come in binder-style covers so that updates could be posted out by the publishers and inserted into these volumes as the law developed and changed.

In contrast, at Glossop Law the legal research required is now conducted online. If you are studying law, you are probably already familiar with online databases such as Lexis Library, Westlaw and Lawtel, which allow quick access to primary (and some secondary) sources of law. There are also online databases of journal articles (e.g. Heinonline), and e-book versions of law books are now commonplace. Other examples of the impact of digital technology on legal research are given in Chapter 3.

Legal professionals are still required to have the more traditional skills of legal research, such as identifying key legal principles within a court judgment or being able to interpret and summarise the wording of a piece of law accurately. However, in order to effectively carry out research online they also need various digital skills, including being able to formulate key words for searches, identifying appropriate sources, organising and filtering search results digitally and storing the results.

INCREASES IN SOCIAL MEDIA USE AND DIGITAL MARKETING STRATEGIES

The example of Glossop, Charlesworth & Co Solicitors states that their advertising is done via the local newspaper and billboard advertisements. The example of Glossop Law mentions the firm has a bespoke website and a Twitter account and is considering expanding its social media presence. This change in marketing methods mirrors the rapid expansion of digital advertising and social media in recent years. The Internet (via the World Wide Web) only became publicly available in 1991, and popular social media platform Facebook was only founded in 2004, with Twitter beginning in 2006 and Instagram following in 2010. In contrast, sales of local newspapers and the use of billboard advertising have both been steadily declining in recent years. It appears businesses, including law firms, view digital advertising and social media as potentially cheaper and more interactive ways to market themselves to a wider audience.

The use of different marketing methods does require people with relevant expertise to ensure they are used effectively. Glossop Law uses a local marketing agency to run twice-yearly online marketing campaigns for them. Larger firms may have one or more individuals to focus on marketing.

The use of social media by individual lawyers and law firms also raises new ethical questions and dilemmas; for example, should an individual lawyer accept a client's offer to connect on a platform such as Facebook? Should a law firm take into account an individual's social media presence when deciding whether or not to hire them for a particular job? These are questions that will be considered further in Chapter 5.

THE GROWTH OF FLEXIBLE WORKING PATTERNS

The example of Glossop, Charlesworth & Co Solicitors states that the solicitors work long hours in their offices. The example of Glossop Law noted that some solicitors now have laptops and regularly work from home. The use of email and a variety of online systems and resources means that there are increasing opportunities to work remotely, although it is likely most clients will require some face-to-face contact. Lawyers can also manage their time using software and project management tools (see Chapter 3).

Many law firms now have arrangements in place to allow individuals to work from home at least some of the time. There are many advantages in homeworking for individuals, including:

- Greater flexibility in managing your work and time.
- Better work-life balance (e.g. spending more time with family).
- Avoiding the time and money involved in commuting.
- Avoiding the environmental costs involved in commuting.

At the same time, there can be disadvantages for individuals, including:

- Finding it hard to separate out work from other areas of their lives.
- Feeling lonely and/or isolated from colleagues.
- Dealing with domestic interruptions and distractions.

For employers, the advantages to individuals working from home include having staff who are well-motivated, work independently and are committed to the firm. On the other hand, it may make it harder to foster a sense of collegiality, coordinate teamwork and manage individuals. It may also involve firms having to undertake health and safety assessments to ensure their employees are working in safe and appropriate environments.

Many of these advantages and disadvantages have been demonstrated by the increase in flexible working patterns, homeworking and virtual meetings that have been necessitated by the COVID-19 pandemic. Although the long-term impacts of this are unclear, there have been suggestions that it could result in wider changes to the culture of law firms.

In terms of technology, allowing staff to work from home requires employers to invest in the equipment and software required for successfully working at a distance. This will include providing individuals with the right equipment, such as laptops, chargers and perhaps even mobile telephones. It could also involve purchasing and setting up new software and ways to manage the transfer of information. For example, it may be necessary to establish a virtual private network (VPN), an encrypted Internet connection that individuals connect to remote in order to assist in the safe transfer of data.

Another way in which technology allows lawyers to work flexibly is through allowing forms of communication that can take place at different times in different ways; for example, it would not be possible to telephone a client at midnight, but it is possible for someone to send an email at any time of the day or night. Some of the issues that arise with working remotely are discussed further in Chapter 3.

CHANGING FORMS OF COLLABORATION

Changes in terms of collaboration have occurred both within law firms and between law firms and other individuals/organisations. Traditionally, it might have been assumed that the large majority of employees working within a law firm had a legal background and training (as is the case in Glossop, Charlesworth & Co Solicitors). As such, they were more likely to share a common understanding on various issues. Changes in the skills required from employees mean that in many law firms there is now likely to be more individuals from non-legal backgrounds (e.g. the office and IT and finance managers who work for Glossop Law). This can be challenging, as such individuals may not be used to legal terminology or legal processes and procedures. However, it can also lead to positive forms of collaboration, with new insights and ideas being generated. For example, the IT and finance manager may be able to suggest a new way of recording billable hours and invoicing clients which would make timekeeping more efficient.

Internal forms of collaboration are also likely to change as a result in the growth of flexible working patterns discussed earlier. For example, face-to-face team meetings and discussions may be replaced by virtual meetings and chats via email or instant messaging.

External forms of collaboration are also likely to now rely more heavily on digital means, from emails to virtual meetings. Documents may be shared via online links rather than in hard copy. For example, contract amendments could be carried out via a shared storage area such as OneDrive or Google Drive.

These shifts may mean that collaborations can progress more quickly and efficiently. However, they may also mean that it is harder to build up a rapport and shared understanding with the other parties involved when there is less opportunity to read body language and have more casual conversations in person.

CHANGING APPROACHES TO DISPUTE RESOLUTION

The example of Glossop Law states that several of its partners are now trained mediators. Alternative dispute resolution, including mediation, conciliation, arbitration and adjudication, is increasingly a part of contemporary legal practice (and encouraged by the courts in civil cases). Technological changes have contributed to shifts in dispute resolution, with an increasing focus on online dispute resolution both within and outside the court system. This will be explored in more detail in Chapter 9.

CHANGES IN FINANCES AND BUSINESS STRATEGY

This section has identified a number of key changes which have taken place in law firms as a result of technological developments. However, it is also important to appreciate that any one of these changes cannot be viewed in isolation. The different changes are often linked; for example, developments in the forms of technology used will require either additional training for existing employees or potentially the creation of new roles, which will in turn require investment and possibly impact on individuals' working patterns. It may also mean physical changes (e.g. in terms of office layout) and changes in recruitment, employment and training.

Ultimately, such changes will have an impact on the overall finances and strategy of a law firm. In terms of finances, any form of new technology will require investment in software and/or hardware and training for users. It is also likely to require some form of ongoing maintenance and updating. In terms of strategy, when considering making such financial investments, law firms will have to consider how they want to position their firm in the legal services market and what their plans are for the future. A recent global survey of general counsels (who run corporate legal departments within organisations) found that there was a growing interest in and use of technical solutions, but that some common technologies were not being utilised:

> This paradox suggests many legal departments may be investing piecemeal in a variety of disparate point solutions. This disjointed approach creates functional gaps and knowledge silos while trapping data in multiple, stand-alone applications. As a result, information and activities are not integrated, information is not easily shared, data cannot be effectively analysed, and efficiency wanes.[17]

In other words, without a strategic approach to digital lawyering which takes an overview of its different uses, there is a danger that a range of individual solutions will be implemented for various issues which do not join up or connect with each other, generating further problems.

Sometimes these financial and strategic considerations will be driven by external factors. For example, as technology means some legal services can be outsourced more cheaply to others or done in-house by clients, there will inevitably be changes in the type of work potential clients require. New areas of law, such as fintech and cybercrime, will also require new forms of legal expertise. Sometimes such decisions will also be influenced by internal factors; for example, the way in which senior managers view technology and the level of resources and skills they have to adapt to changing circumstances.

17 Thomson Reuters, 'Digital General Counsel Are Transforming the Corporate Legal Department' (2020), 3 <https://legalsolutions.thomsonreuters.co.uk/content/dam/ewp-m/documents/legal-uk/en/pdf/reports/tr1135788-transforming-the-corporate.pdf> accessed 18 February 2021.

Daniel Acosta has referred to the question of whether or not law firms embrace digital lawyering as the "lawyer's dilemma".[18] In other words, law firms have to make a choice whether to continue with their existing (and often profitable) model of business or whether to risk innovating and seeking to transform their business model. Retaining a well tried-and-tested business model may be attractive as it does not require significant change or investment. However, it could result in the firm being overtaken by more innovative competitors. Seeking to transform their business model offers the potential for greater profits and success, but also holds greater risks in terms of the amount of investment and training required and the need to make more significant changes.

THE IMPACT OF TECHNOLOGY

Sync 4: Analysing the impact of technology

You should allow around one hour for this activity.

The discussion following Sync 3 identified four questions to explore:

- What impact does technology have on the day-to-day tasks which legal professionals perform?
- What impact does technology have on the ways in which legal professionals interact with their clients?
- What impact does technology have on the ways in which legal professionals interact with other colleagues?
- What impact does technology have on the ways in which legal professionals interact with the courts?

Based on the preceding discussion, select one of these questions. You should also undertake some further independent reading and research. Write a blog post of 800–1000 words, aimed at an audience of law students or lawyers, answering your selected question.

18 Daniel Acosta, 'The Lawyer's Dilemma: Challenges for Law Firms Adopting Legal Tech' (2 October 2020) <https://www.legaltechnologist.co.uk/the-lawyers-dilemma-challenges-for-law-firms-adopting-legal-tech/> accessed 19 February 2021.

Regardless of which question you chose to answer, your answer to Sync 4 has probably identified that technology has had a significant impact.

In terms of day-to-day tasks, technology has impacted in myriad ways ranging from how legal research is conducted to the make-up of the staff within law firms. With regard to interactions between lawyers and clients, the format of these has shifted from letters and faxes to electronic communications. This can ensure quicker and more effective contact; however, it may potentially impact on the human aspects of the relationship by removing elements of personal contact. In terms of interactions between legal professionals, more flexible working patterns may once again lead to less face-to-face contact and more emphasis on communicating by other means, although it could also aid new forms of collaboration (e.g. via online meetings). The ways in which disputes are resolved is also evolving, with online dispute resolution and the digitalisation of the courts, and this will be considered further in subsequent chapters. It is likely that the moves towards greater use of digital technology in the workplace generated through COVID-19 will require law firms to make difficult financial and strategic decisions around whether and to what extent to embrace digital lawyering.

Digital lawyering skills: Traditional skills and legal research

Despite the transformative nature of digital technologies within law, digital lawyers still need to apply a number of more traditional legal skills in their work. These are often skills that law students are encouraged to develop during their time at law school, including:

- Reading documents for different purposes (e.g. skimming and close reading).
- Taking notes of information or discussions.
- Undertaking legal research.

Conducting legal research itself involves a variety of skills, including being able to take a research topic or question, analyse the key issues and break it down into manageable parts.

As discussed previously, there have already been significant changes in the way law students and lawyers undertake their research, with online databases of cases, legislation and journal articles becoming commonplace. Issues around law and technology tend to be fast-moving, meaning sources that are rarely used in academic law, such as web pages, blogs, and social media, can all be useful sources of information.

As a law student, getting into the habit of evaluating your sources as you conduct your research is very important. You need to check that the information is:

- Up to date
- Accurate
- Trustworthy; and
- Uses appropriate evidence and/or research methodology.

Becoming competent in such evaluation at an early stage will assist you in conducting research effectively and accurately within legal practice.

TECHNOLOGY AND THE LARGE LAW FIRM

So far, this chapter has largely focused upon a type of typical high street law firm (a small- or medium-sized firm based in a town). The changes within legal practice at such firms has been significant (as the example of Glossop Law demonstrates). However, the changes at many larger firms have been even more far-reaching. The online legal magazine *Legal Cheek* runs annual awards, which include an award for the most technologically advanced firm in the UK. Responses to their 2020 survey (which shortlisted 13 firms) referred to paying for coffees by Bitcoin, using Skype rather than telephones and having virtual desktops with gadget bars.[19]

A number of firms offer trainee solicitors a seat (period of training) focused upon law and technology. For example, the firm Addleshaw Goddard offers a six-month lawtech seat in its innovation and legal technology group. During this seat, trainees work alongside lawyers and technologists to develop products for use in other parts of the firm; for example, building a system for a major property transaction to produce automated documents and encode aspects of the process.[20]

19 Legal Cheek, 'Revealed: The Best Law Firms for Tech 2020' (6 March 2020) <https://www.legalcheek.com/2020/03/revealed-the-best-law-firms-for-tech-2020/> accessed 18 February 2021.

20 Tom Hinton, 'What is a Lawyer?' (25 June 2019) <https://www.addleshawgoddard.com/en/insights/insights-briefings/tech-talks/what-is-a-lawyer/> accessed 19 February 2021.

The international law firm Allen & Overy has a learning lab called Fuse, where legal professionals, technical providers and clients work together to devise innovative technological solutions to legal and commercial issues.[21]

THE RISE OF DISTRIBUTED AND VIRTUAL LAW FIRMS

A number of organisations have made a more radical shift to become distributed or virtual law firms. These types of firms are sometimes referred to as NewLaw. A distributed law firm is more likely to have a number of physical office locations but also have employees or consultants working remotely. The first such distributed law firm, FisherBroyles, was founded in the United States in 2002. It currently has 23 international offices and hundreds of partners. Its website argues that its model allows it to avoid expensive investment in offices and ensure that it can hire the best lawyers, regardless of their physical location.[22]

Are all virtual lawyers happy and healthy?

Champions of distributed and virtual law firms often refer to the flexibility involved—the idea lawyers can work when and where they want. This can be seen as a significant benefit; for example, if you have children or other caring responsibilities, you can fit your work in around your caring routines. However, it is important not to assume such flexibility is wholly positive.

Such flexibility can make it harder for lawyers to establish healthy work-life boundaries; for example, they may end up answering client calls and emails during mealtimes or late at night. It could also lead to clients expecting you to be available 24/7, increasing the pressures upon you. Anecdotally, a number of legal professionals have noted experiencing these issues when working at home during COVID-19.

21 Allen & Overy, 'Tech Innovation' (2020) <https://www.allenovery.com/en-gb/global/expertise/advanced_delivery/tech_innovation> accessed 19 February 2021.

22 FisherBroyles, 'Distributed Disruption' (2021) <https://www.fisherbroyles.com/distributed-disruption> accessed 19 February 2021.

A virtual law firm is likely to have no physical premises and to work entirely online. For example, the US firm My Virtual Lawyer has no dedicated premises. They sell themselves to potential clients on the basis that clients' fees are spent upon communicating and carrying out legal work, with very little spent on administrative tasks and none spent on "fancy offices".[23] They encourage lawyers to join them by referring to the benefits of being able to work flexibly, reduce costs, be more easily available to clients, improve wellbeing and be more eco-friendly by reducing office waste.[24]

BENEFITS OF, AND BARRIERS TO, THE USE OF TECHNOLOGY

When considering the impact of technology, you may have begun to think about a range of advantages and disadvantages arising from its application in legal practice. Often there are both benefits and challenges which arise.

A good example of this is the issue of accessibility. On the one hand, technology can improve accessibility for clients. For example, a client in a remote location may be able to access advice online or communicate with their lawyer electronically rather than having to spend time and costs on travel.

On the other hand, it cannot be assumed that all clients are comfortable and experienced with technology. Globally, over four billion people do not have Internet access.[25] In the UK, the Office for National Statistics has identified that, in 2018, 10% of the adult population had either never used the Internet or not used it in the last three

23 My Virtual Lawyer, 'About Our Team' (2021) <https://myvirtual.lawyer/our-team/> accessed 19 February 2021.

24 My Virtual Lawyer, 'You Should Become a Virtual Lawyer: Here's Why and How to Begin Your Law Firm' (2021) <https://myvirtual.lawyer/why-and-how-to-become-a-virtual-lawyer/> accessed 19 February 2021.

25 Department for International Development, 'Digital Strategy 2018–2020 Doing Development in a Digital World' (2018) <https://assets.publishing.service.gov.uk/government/uploads/system/uploads/attachment_data/file/701443/DFID-Digital-Strategy-23-01-18a.pdf> accessed 12 November 2019.

months.[26] For lawyers to meet their ethical obligations and provide an appropriate quality of service, they must keep clients properly informed and ensure they understand the advice and guidance they are given. Therefore, it is vital for them to be aware of their clients' capabilities.

Another example is that of data protection. Using a cloud-based system to store documents can prevent important information from being lost if files are accidentally deleted from a law firm's computer system or if it is attacked by a virus or hacked into. It may mean documents can be accessed quickly and more efficiently, even if a member of the team is on leave or ill. At the same time, to move to using such a system, a firm will need to check the terms and conditions of the service provider it chooses to use for data storage. It will also need to ensure it is complying with the law on data protection in its jurisdiction. It will have to carefully review its regulatory body's rules and/or guidelines on data protection. It is likely that it will also have to review, or even rewrite, its internal policies on data protection. Staff will then need to be trained to use the relevant system in accordance with these rules, policies and guidelines.

Therefore, it can be seen that making what may seem like a simple change can involve a number of benefits and barriers and have a range of wider impacts and effects which will need to be anticipated in advance.

Sync 5: Analysing the benefits and barriers

You should allow around 30 minutes for this activity.

Read sections 6, 7 and 8 of the Legal Service Board's *Technology and Innovation in Legal Services 2018* main report (available at <https://www.legalservicesboard.org.uk> under "Research"). If this is unavailable, or to expand on your answers, you may wish to search for other reports and articles around the use of technology in the legal profession.

Based on your reading, think about the potential benefits and barriers to the following proposals:

- You are a junior lawyer in a law firm. The partners in the firm have proposed removing individual offices and replacing them with an open plan

26 Office for National Statistics, 'Exploring the UK's Digital Divide' (March 2019) <https://www.ons.gov.uk/peoplepopulationandcommunity/householdcharacteristics/homeinternetandsocialmediausage/articles/exploringtheuksdigitaldivide/2019-03-04> accessed 12 November 2019.

area with lots of communal desks. They will issue everyone with laptops so they can work at whichever desk they choose.

- You are a partner in a law firm. The team who you manage has presented you with a plan in which they all work from their homes at least three days per week and keep in touch using email and virtual meetings.
- You are a self-employed lawyer and you want to advertise the legal services you offer in your local community. You are thinking about setting up accounts on social media to help you obtain more clients.

You may wish to make some notes on the key benefits and barriers you identify, to refer back to them or add to them as you work through other chapters in this textbook.

In Sync 5 you probably identified a wide range of benefits and barriers. You may have also noted that some of these would depend upon specific details, including the size of the firm, its current specialisms and client base, its financial position and its style of management.

In the first scenario, there would potentially be benefits to people being able to work whenever and wherever they wanted, possibly making them more productive. However, individuals may be resistant to the idea of losing their own personal space or to feeling less of a sense of belonging. In the second scenario, flexible working may be very useful for members of the team with caring and other responsibilities. It could also make people more productive, as they no longer have to spend time commuting to work. However, it could make it harder to communicate quickly and effectively with each other (e.g. what if someone does not answer their email?). It could also make it harder to access any files and other information that is in paper form rather than online. In both scenarios, there could be issues which arise in relation to identifying the most suitable systems to use to communicate and store data in a safe but accessible manner.

The third scenario raises issues that will be returned to in Chapter 5 of this textbook around the use of social media. It would be necessary to check what rules or guidance your regulatory body had on the use of social media as a starting point. Benefits could include having a free and quick way to connect with members of the local community and market your services. Barriers could include the need to be familiar with how to use the social media platform in question, the time required to keep it updated and the need to avoid inadvertently breaching client confidentiality when adding news stories.

TECHNOLOGY AND ETHICS IN THE LEGAL PROFESSION

> Lawyers are highly educated and, allegedly, of higher than average intelligence, but sometimes individual lawyers demonstrate colossal errors in judgment, especially when insufficiently trained in the new and emerging risks involved with the technological age.[27]

The example of social media discussed earlier raises potential ethical issues. What can and should be shared on social media? What is the distinction between writing in a business and private capacity online? Such ethical issues are not restricted to social media but arise in relation to all aspects of digital lawyering. This can include seemingly minor everyday issues which lawyers may fail to recognise as potential ethical issues. Examples include stepping away from your computer screen for a few minutes leaving a confidential document open, sending an email to the wrong address, using a weak and easily guessable password to protect important information, or inadvertently signing up to the terms and conditions of a website or social media platform which enables it to access private data. The very human issues involved in communicating by email or online can also have consequences, from informality and unprofessional writing styles to misinterpreting responses and reacting inappropriately.

The contemporary digital lawyer has to be aware of these issues and proactive in thinking of ways to avoid such potential ethical pitfalls. Similar issues may also arise for law students; for example, if they share lecture and seminar notes provided by the university more widely online or use so-called essay mills which provide ready-written answers to assignments. The importance of such ethical issues is a theme that will be returned to throughout this textbook given its importance at all stages of a legal career.

27 Cheryl B. Preston, 'Lawyers' Abuse of Technology' (2018) 118 *Cornell Law Review* 879, 881.

Conclusion: the 21st-century lawyer

This chapter has demonstrated that the 21st-century lawyer is working in a very different environment than the 20th-century lawyer. Although the law itself evolves relatively slowly in many areas, the processes and procedures surrounding it have been changing rapidly in recent years. The results of this on individual legal professionals can be significant. Technological changes affect much more than the technology itself: From different career paths to different types of colleagues; from new skills and training to new ways of researching, resolving disputes and collaborating with others; and from challenging ethical issues to challenging client demands. The impacts of all these changes will not just stay within the legal workplace. They will also have consequences for the personal lives of lawyers, from the benefits of flexible working to the challenges of managing client expectations and being pushed out of your comfort zone through the introduction of new technologies.

Although this chapter has largely focused upon lawyers working in what could be termed a "traditional" legal workplace, it is also important to acknowledge that digital technologies are making wider changes within the legal profession so that such "traditional" career pathways and environments may eventually become obsolete. NewLaw is one example of this, and others will be discussed in Chapter 12.

For aspiring lawyers, it is important to reflect upon what digital lawyering will mean for their career, their personal life and their professional identity. Some of these issues will be discussed further in subsequent chapters, in particular Chapter 13. As you read through this textbook, it is worth spending some time beginning this process of reflection and asking yourself, what does it really mean to be a 21st-century lawyer?

Additional resources

For more information on ABSs, see McMorrow JA, "UK Alternative Business Structures for Legal Practice: Emerging Models and Lessons for the US" (2016) 47 (2) *Georgetown Journal of International Law* 665–711.

For a timeline on the development of email, see <https://www.theguardian.com/technology/2002/mar/13/internetnews>

For a discussion of social media and professional conduct, see <https://www.ibanet.org/Committees/Divisions/Legal_Practice/Impact_of_OSN_on_LegalPractice/Impact_of_OSN_Home.aspx>

For a discussion of virtual law firms, see <https://www.americanbar.org/groups/law_practice/publications/law_practice_magazine/2019/MJ2019/MJ19Wasserman/>

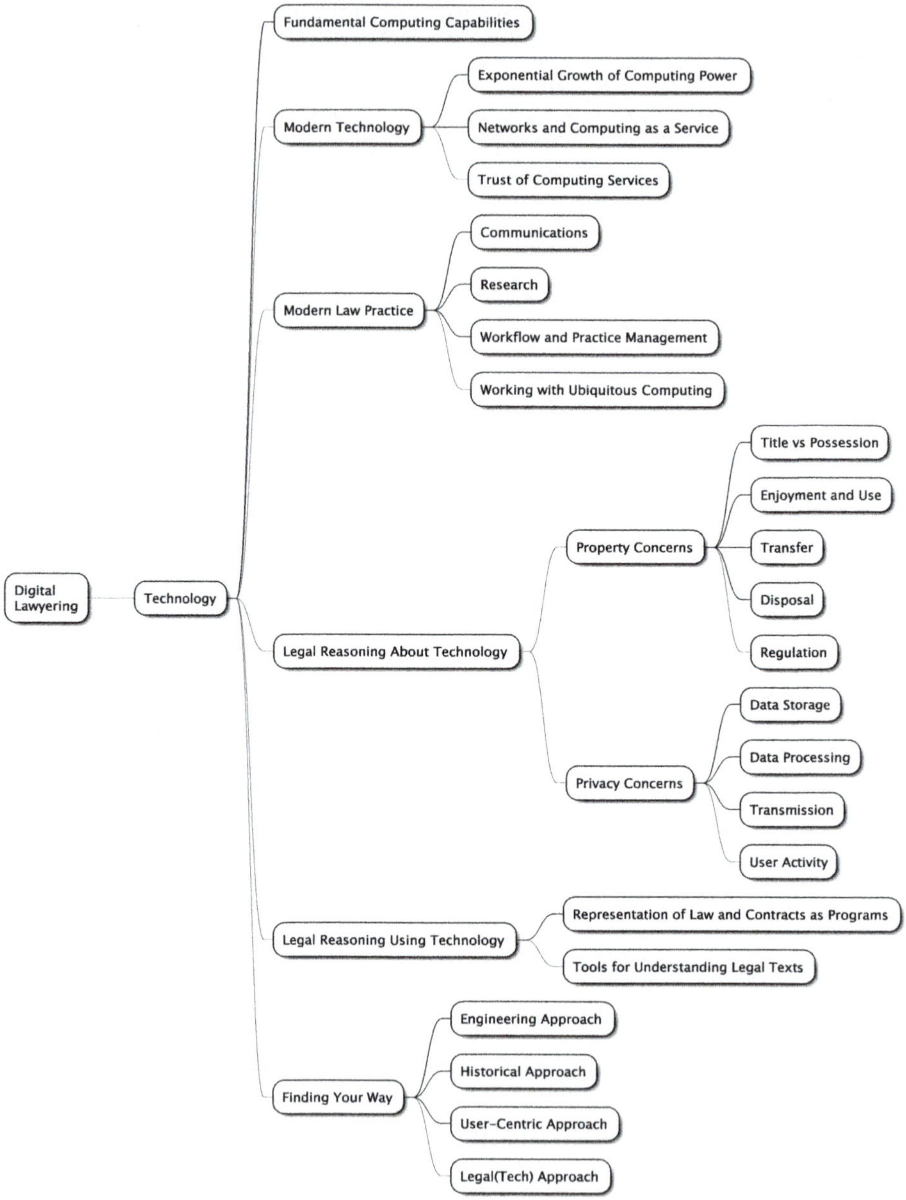

Mind Map 3.1 Chapter topics

3 A GUIDE TO TECHNOLOGY

Terry Wong

INTRODUCTION

This chapter is an introduction to several central concepts underpinning modern computing and communications technologies. An active lawyer must be aware of a widening range of relevant technologies and their use, not only in the practice of law but in the ways these technologies impact the rights, obligations and options open to their clients. We take the opportunity to explore the background and implications of those technologies for lawyers, to suggest ways to learn more about specific areas and to outline ways to remain knowledgeable in a space characterised by continuous, accelerating change.

Chapter hot spots

When reading this chapter, questions to think about include:

- How does the interconnected, dynamic nature of computing and communications technologies affect their use when employing such technologies in the daily practice of law?
- Trust is a concept with many facets and is central to the rule of law, legal practice (critically with respect to lawyer-client privilege) and the smooth conduct of commerce. How do the complexities of digital technology, with its many interacting layers, affect the various spheres of trust one might expect in certain legal and commercial contexts?
- In what ways might a lawyer stay current with the rapid evolution of digital technology in order to employ technologies effectively in the

DOI: 10.4324/9780429298219-3

practice of law, and to advise clients using new technologies to work in their day-to-day business?

Having read the title and introduction, you can add any other questions you want to explore here:

ILLUSTRATION: A RIDESHARING APP

Consider a ridesharing application ("app"), such as Uber, Lyft, or Grab. These are three examples of a widely used class of applications that has seen rapid development and adoption, quickly moving beyond being a novel convenience to become a viable, even relied-upon alternative form of transportation, challenging long entrenched models of mobility in urban and suburban areas. Interaction with a smartphone to reserve a ride involves many of the capabilities of modern computing and communications technology:

1. Selecting the app (by tapping on the app icon on the home screen of the smartphone) and entering the destination (by tapping on the input fields and typing on the on-screen keyboard) are two *input* actions supported by the device.
2. Automatic suggestions (or auto-complete) of the destination as you type involve *processing* of your inputs and *communications* with location services (GPS) and the ridesharing service to determine known addresses.
3. The lists of possible location matches being displayed as the user types are an example of real-time *output*.
4. Later, when the ride is completed and payment is taken, securely stored payment credentials are retrieved from *storage*, unlocked through the *input* of a password or a facial image via a camera input and used to enable that payment to be completed.

Figure 3.1 shows these capabilities in action, together with the various interactions and infrastructure needed to deliver the service through the application.

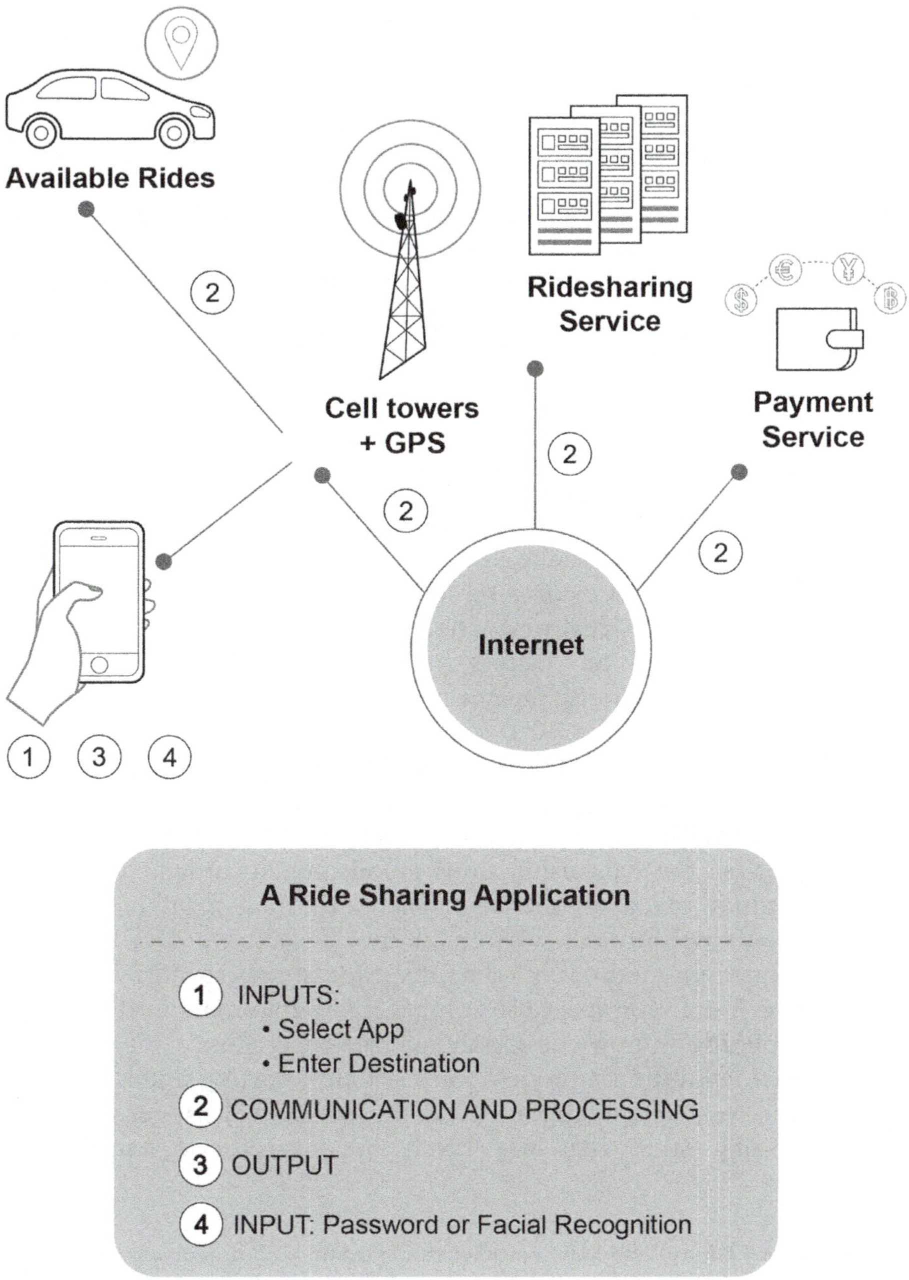

Figure 3.1 Ridesharing application example

In the following section, we will go on to define the terms we have highlighted in this illustration to clarify their meaning and application.

UNDERSTANDING MODERN TECHNOLOGY

We experience most of our digital life through a small number of personal electronic devices—three to four, on average.[1] There is, most often, a smartphone and then a portable laptop or desktop computer both at home and in the workplace. In addition, there may be a tablet device, an electronic book reader and perhaps a connected smart watch. Each of these devices contains a few crucial capabilities that all modern computing devices share:

- *Input*. A way to enter information or direct the device's activity, through a physical or on-screen keyboard or through clicking a mouse, tapping a screen, gestures such as pinching or rotating with multiple figures on a screen or touch pad, or physical movement of the device or an attached accessory such as a mouse. Inputs can also be readers for media such as a magnetic or optical disk, magnetic tape, a memory card or an array of sensors in a factory.
- *Processing*. A device will take information supplied to it and reorganise it for better comprehension or to support itself or the user in the accomplishment of a given task, or perform calculations or summarise the data using understood and documented methods, sometimes called algorithms, which take real form in machine-readable specifications written in specific languages or encoding. One or more modules of computer code are packaged by advanced "power" users or specialist computer programmers into programs or applications, now commonly referred to as apps.
- *Output*. Inputting a request for a search, selecting a link to a page on the web or opening a file on the device will trigger a series of processing steps that will result in the retrieval and possible

1 A study by GlobalWebIndex, a market research firm with headquarters in the UK, found that the global average for connected devices per person in 2017 was 3.23 devices <https://blog.globalwebindex.com/chart-of-the-day/digital-consumers-own-3-point-2-connected-devices/>

transformation of some information that can then be delivered to the user, usually on the screen, or in the case of other forms of media, through an audio output such as speakers or a printer.

- *Storage.* Computing devices must have a way to store information in varying levels of permanence, depending on the need. Memory, in temporary (RAM, or random-access memory) or permanent (ROM, or read-only memory) forms, is found in hardware components that supply the working areas (think of scratch pads when working mathematical figures by hand) and permanent programs required by the computer to supply basic functions. Data, files and media are held in semi-permanent storage, either optical (e.g. DVDs or CDs), magnetic (hard disks) or chips.
- *Communications.* The ability to send data over interconnected links (or networks) to other devices is vital to modern computing, since it is impossible to store all the data that one would normally need to access locally (e.g. for practical physical reasons like limited space on devices), or in central locations (in the cloud). Communications networks that are interconnected allow instant access to remote information, dramatically increasing the power and information a person has at their command at a given instant, wherever they are in the world, so long as they have a device capable of interacting with a network. The largest and most powerful network, the one we all know and use today, is the Internet.

Together, these capabilities allow modern digital devices to deliver the information-rich, interactive and productive experiences to which our society has grown accustomed and reliant. In Chapter 8 you will go on to think about the role such digital devices can also play in providing digital evidence through digital forensics.

Sync 1: Thinking about digital devices

You should allow around 10 minutes for this activity.

Take a look at a digital device you currently own (if you do not have any, think about a common device such as a smartphone). Using the aforementioned list of capabilities, identify the capabilities of your chosen device: For example, how do you input information? What are the outputs? What form of storage does it use? How does it communicate?

Depending upon the device you chose, you may have identified a range of different capabilities. For example, a smartphone involves inputting information via a touchscreen keypad and by swiping left or right. There are audio outputs (when speaking to others or listening to music) but also visual outputs (when using the Internet or watching a video). Information is stored in a microchip known as an SD (Secure Digital memory) card and there is a range of methods of communication, from text messages to an Internet connection.

BEGINNINGS: THE AFFORDABLE COMPUTER

Histories of computing describe early digital computers that filled large rooms and drew great quantities of electricity during their operation. They were very expensive, scarce resources, with every attempt made on the part of their owners and operators—typically military, government, or well-funded corporate entities—to ensure that they were operated with maximum possible usage for a given period. To ensure that the machines were as idle for as little time as possible, programmers or users were required to submit their programs or requested computations as jobs, to be run in batches by operators, with the results returned in printouts.

Timesharing, together with interactive input and output capable devices called terminals, were innovations introduced to allow a programmer or user to interact with a computer directly, while others could also use the same machine in a similar manner. The insight designers had was that interactive users would not be taxing a machine with heavy loads when they were reading results and thinking about the next action. This allowed a certain degree of (what appeared to users to be) the simultaneous interactive use of a large computer (Figure 3.2).

As microcomputers emerged in the 1970s and early 1980s, their pricing[2] meant that a single person could be the exclusive user of a

2 Just a few months after its introduction in August, 1981, a review in BYTE, a widely read computer magazine, listed the price of the IBM PC (Model 5150), with one floppy disk drive, adapter card, and DOS operating system software, at $2575. This amount was substantial, but within the reach of small business and office users with budgets for automation.

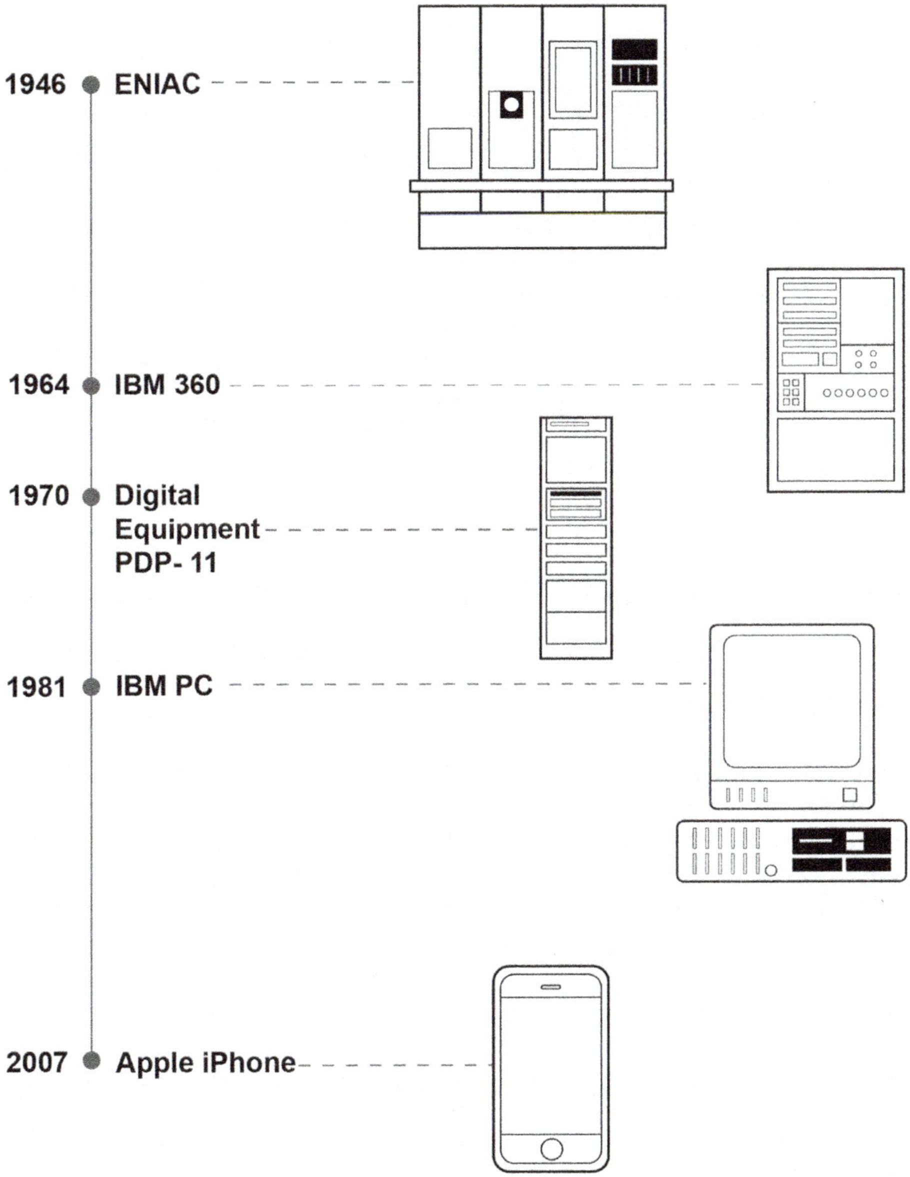

Figure 3.2 Timeline of technology evolution and miniaturisation

computer with access to all the resources built into it. Given the early stage in the development of hardware technologies, especially microchip fabrication, early microcomputers were neither high in processing speed nor storage,[3] but their easy accessibility paved the way for an explosion in individual learning about computer programming and the creative application of that learning in the development of applications for the early microcomputing platforms.

The downward direction of prices that made computers affordable and accessible was driven in part by improvements in research and development that enabled the doubling of transistor component density on microchips and the halving of computer prices every two years, described by an observation known as Moore's law.[4] The continued exponential rise of computing power and its accompanying exponential fall in prices now allows a consumer to carry a smartphone in his or her pocket that is 120 million times more powerful than the computer that guided the Apollo Lunar Modules in their landings on the surface of the Earth's moon.[5]

Computing and communication: the importance of the network and Metcalfe's law

Since the mid-1980s, the period that saw the growing mainstream adoption of affordable personal computers, emphasis has been placed on the word "personal" in the term "personal computer" or "PC". First-person physical ownership of devices and data has been the dominant relationship between individual users and their computing resources. Perhaps reflecting the nature of their human users, economic observers note that the value of connected computer networks increases as the square of the number of members in each network. This observation, formulated as Metcalfe's law by George Gilder, described and promoted the advantage of computer networking with Ethernet,

3 An IBM PC (Model 5150) for sale in 1981 had a single Intel 8088 processor core with a clock speed of 4.77 MHz, with a maximum of 640 kilobytes of memory. By way of comparison, an iPhone 11 available in 2020 featured six processor cores, including two running at 2.65 GHz and four running at 1.8 GHz, in addition to 4 gigabytes of memory.

4 G. E. Moore, 'The Future of Integrated Electronics' (1965) 38 *Electronics* 4.

5 'Smartphone Is Millions of Times Faster than NASA's 1960s Computers' <http://www.zmescience.com/science/news-science/smartphone-power-compared-to-apollo-432/>

the dominant form of hardware technology for local area networks (LANs).[6]

To understand the importance of networks as described by Metcalfe's law, consider that a network with two computers or devices can make at most one connection between them, while four devices could make six connections and eight devices could make up to 28 connections. As the number of devices on the network increases, the total number of connections c for a network of n devices is described by the mathematical equation $c = n(n - 1)/2$. This property of network growth and connectivity is illustrated in Figure 3.3.

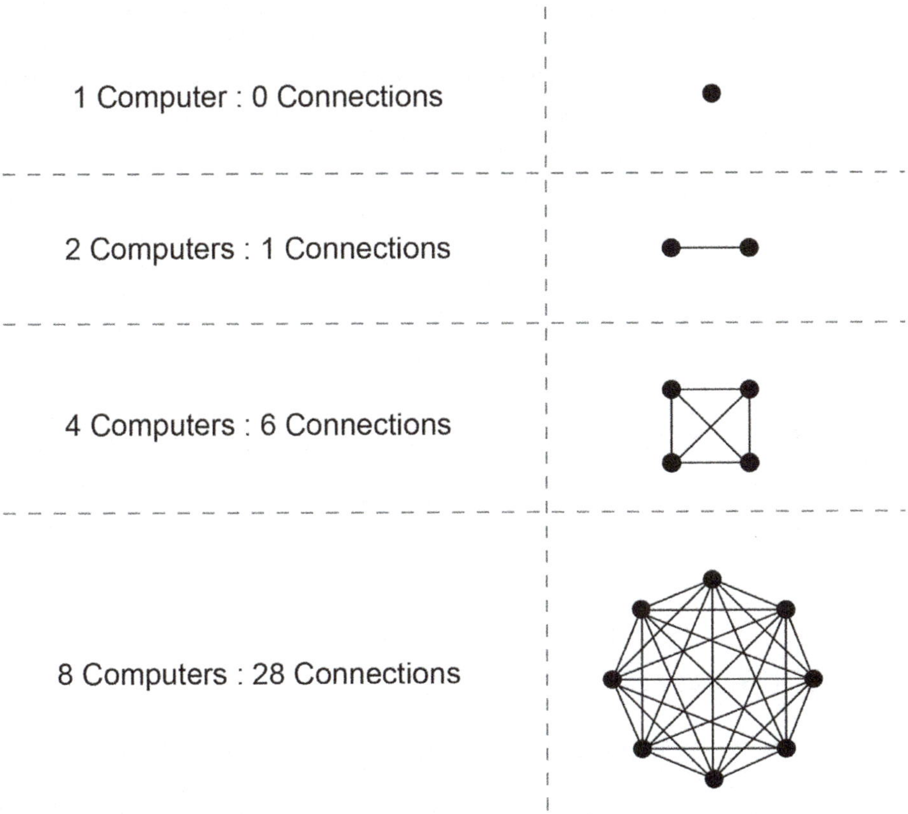

Figure 3.3 Increase of connections and growth of network

6 A local area network (LAN) is a computer network installed in offices and homes for the purpose of connecting the devices on that network to each other, and possibly for the purpose of sharing an Internet connection.

As each connection would support the transfer of a file containing a document or the data necessary to deliver a specific app, one can see that the value of the network increases dramatically as the number of devices connected to it increases, and data flows freely between an ever-increasing number of nodes on the network.

Local networks, whether in separate offices on different floors of the same building, across the street or on the other side of the globe, and belonging to the same or different organisations, can be connected using wide area network technologies (WANs) in interconnected networks, or internets. Multiple internets, connected to each other through enough layers of intermediate networks, eventually developed the ability to route and deliver data traffic in ways that were reliable and resilient, and speedy enough to support interactive use of applications running on a digital device directly in front of a user, accessing data and supporting computing resources over very large distances in a seamless manner. The Internet (spelled with a capital "I")[7] is the current largest example of an internet, serving as the indispensable infrastructure of most modern connected applications we use today.

The age of ubiquitous computing

As both networks and connected computing devices became more capable and more economical to own and operate, the use of connected computing devices became a fact of daily working life, no longer a novelty but rather an expectation. This is referred to as "ubiquitous computing".

Computing as a service

Shortly after the beginning of the 21st century, Amazon Web Services began offering infrastructure as a service (IaaS). No longer were businesses required to manage physical infrastructure to support the development and operation of online computing services. With technical personnel now mostly freed from the need to devote resources

7 Always spell "Internet" with an upper-case "I"; it is incorrect usage to refer to it with a lower-case "i".

to the fundamental aspects of technology installation and operations, more efforts could be deployed to the design and implementation of new and innovative services. Google Workplace, Microsoft Office 365, Dropbox, Slack, and a host of other well-known services that we now consider indispensable parts of daily working life online appeared and gained adoption as users became more comfortable with the safety, reliability and ease of online services in the cloud. In Chapter 2 it was explained that the term "cloud" refers to data being stored in a separate online location, hosted by a third-party provider, which is accessed online.

Illustration: drafting a document

Consider using a cloud office suite, such as Office 365 or Google Workplace to draft a document. This process can be used to illustrate how computing services are now delivered to support the task at hand:

1 Entering the URL of the cloud service or using your mouse or trackpad to click on the bookmark in your browser is an *input*.

2 The browser looking up the address of, and requesting the page from, the cloud service is a *communication* activity.

3 The cloud service verifies your access to the service through *processing* passwords and cryptographic credentials, and sets up resources to allow your creation and editing of documents through further *processing* (on its network-connected server computers), *input* (from its storage facilities in the data centre), *output* (formatting and preparing the web pages) and further *communication* as the web page and the web application components are sent to the browser on your computer.

4 Your computer, receiving the resources over the network, *processes* them and draws the web page and application components (the document, editing toolbar, buttons, etc.) in your browser as *output*.

5 As you edit the document, typing at the keyboard, and selecting and clicking text and buttons on the screen are *input* that will be *processed* by your computer. Occasional updates will be sent to the cloud service as it *communicates* and coordinates the state of the document and the web application with the services in the cloud that support it.

6 As the document is input and updates arrive at the cloud service's data centre, the state of the document is *processed* and saved as *output*, enabling you to close the application and browser and resume working in exactly the same place when you return to the document by repeating step 1. It should be noted that, with many cloud services, resuming work on a document in a different location and on a separate computer is entirely possible, with only the need to validate identity and authorised use by logging in on the device at the other location. Thus, one can start drafting a document on a desktop computer in a firm's office and complete the document at one's home office on a laptop computer.

7 When you have finished drafting the document, the formatted results from further *processing* can be downloaded (a *communication* activity) and printed (as *output*), or sent in a *communication* via your email program to your client or another party for further review.

It can be seen from this illustration that a cloud-based application provides users with several key benefits:

- *Location independence.* A person using a cloud-based service usually has access to the service on all devices on which the service is available, subject to having a valid login and possible limits on the number of simultaneous logins imposed by the operators of the service.
- *Timeliness.* Location independence and a good range of device support ensures that needs for the service are satisfied sooner and closer to the point of identified need, allowing more immediate fulfilment and possibly resulting in a greater speed of doing business.
- *Backup, recovery and security.* Cloud services tend to save their data using storage facilities in data centres, generally providing mechanisms for preventing data loss from physical failure, accident or from malicious intent resulting in physical theft of devices or physical media such as disks or flash drives. A range of issues related to custody of data, including its location, the means of storage and its stored state (e.g. encrypted or not encrypted at rest) arise through the use of cloud services, which we will explore further in Chapters 5 and 6.

MODERN TECHNOLOGY AND EVERYDAY LAW PRACTICE

Applying the concepts discussed in the previous sections, we can now examine the applications of modern networked computing technologies to three critical areas of the practice of law; namely, communications, research and drafting. The impact on workflow and practice management will also be considered.

COMMUNICATIONS

One may say that a lawyer is the communicator of the first and last resort. A lawyer is often the one sent by a client to explore ways to initiate dialogue with another party, or the lawyer is the one who is sent to attempt to save a negotiation or to begin to mitigate the harms in an unresolved dispute. Through informed dialogue with all the parties involved, a lawyer can help understand the particulars of a matter, the goals and constraints for the client, and the concerns and requirements of possible other parties in transactions or opponents in a dispute. In all cases, effective communication leading to greater understanding is a prerequisite to achieving good outcomes.

Technology mediated communication today takes many forms:

- *Voice.* Once limited to traditional fixed telephone lines in the home, office or pay telephone locations, voice communications can now be found on mobile handsets, and with the growth of Internet penetration and bandwidth, any device with an Internet connection may be a point for voice communications, at a cost that was once unthinkable. One notable fact of Internet telephony (voice communications supplied using telephone network numbers but transmitted over the Internet) has been the location independence of numbers using VOIP (voice over Internet Protocol) technologies. It is now possible for a telephone number originally allocated for a telephone exchange in one city to ring in a city on the opposite side of the planet. For example, a number originally allocated to the City of London may now ring in the central business district of Christchurch, New Zealand, if a firm supplying services in London but based in Christchurch had a need and had purchased and set up such service. It should be noted that the costs for basic implementation of such service can be had for under £10 per month at the time this textbook was written.

- *Video.* Video conferencing was once the province of well-funded large companies with dedicated facilities and possibly additional staff to support the sophisticated audio-visual equipment needed to support even rudimentary video conferencing activity. Today, the average mobile handset is capable of video conferencing, even with large numbers of simultaneous participants. During the COVID-19 pandemic, video conferencing took on a new central role in not only facilitating meetings between remote participants but serving as a key enabler of continuity and cohesion for business meetings, classroom instruction and social gatherings as lockdown measures and social distancing rules were put in force to contain the spread of the virus.
- *Email.* More formal online communications are now done via email, almost entirely replacing the paper memorandum and letter. In many jurisdictions, email is considered an acceptable form of notice for certain contracts and even government notices from different departments and levels of agencies, from local town councils to national departments and bureaus. Email has long operated with varying forms of validation and security. In some cases, email users may be vulnerable to attack from abusers sending spam (unsolicited, irrelevant messages often selling or trying to bait recipients into illicit activities or attempting to defraud them) and from malicious operators leading to phishing attacks, identity theft and even extortion.
- *Short messages.* Short messages sent on mobile handsets and using text messaging applications fill a wide-ranging set of roles, from casual streams of communication between friends and family to formal notification of important events such as deliveries or bank transfers. Once limited to standard messaging protocols provided by telecommunications carriers, there now exist a range of messaging applications, including WhatsApp, WeChat, Facebook Messenger, LINE, and others. In practice, lawyers will often use short messages to coordinate meetings, exchange documents and conduct workflow.
- *Multimedia messages.* Extensions to short messaging applications allow the sending of attachments and embedded images, videos and other multimedia content. Drafts or sections of text are often sent as attachments for immediate review and feedback using multimedia messaging (e.g. attaching a PDF draft to a WhatsApp message to a counter party for rapid, informal review).
- *Forums and social media.* Online forums and social media platforms allow participants to communicate with others in various

communities using postings of text and other media, in settings of varying formality. Twitter, a popular social network based on the message size of a short message (280 characters), has grown into a leading social network, with participants ranging from casual groups of friends, to online influencers, to global politicians. The use of forums and social media for legal communication is limited but not unknown, and will be discussed further in Chapter 5.

Each of these forms of communication depends on access to connectivity and resources available on traditional telecommunications networks or, more likely, the Internet.

RESEARCH

The lawyer in a law firm burning the midnight oil in the library remains a central image of the legal profession. While many texts are still only available in traditional paper, microfilm, or microfiche form (sheets or reels to store highly miniaturised images of texts for reading on magnification devices), many important texts, including recent statutes, regulations, and court proceedings can now be found in electronic form, indexed and searchable using modern search engine technology. The tools can resemble popular Internet search engines such as Google or Bing, but often incorporate more advanced tools to refine searches. Depending on the area of legal practice, various resources now exist to make the research process more efficient and comprehensive. Some examples include:

- *Intellectual property.* Many governments now make patent, service mark, and trademark applications and grants searchable, significantly reducing the time and risks associated with searches for the purpose of ascertaining existing protections and potential liabilities, making the preparation of applications or actions to assert rights more efficient, safe and complete.
- *Regulatory compliance.* Businesses contemplating investment in areas that are heavily regulated (e.g. exploration for oil and gas, heavy manufacturing) will need to ensure that the particulars of the given investment are compliant with relevant, current regulations and those to come into force in the relevant investment period—or if not, that the range and severity of exposure can be understood and managed before approaching regulators for approval. Similarly,

when a business is found to have breached a regulation, it may look for ways in the regulatory texts to argue for more favourable terms, whether citing precedents, emerging regulatory regimes, or approved practice in similar situations.
- *Civil litigation.* When bringing civil actions, relevant statutes and codes vary depending on jurisdiction and also the complexity of the matter. The relevant contracts and supporting documentation are also likely to be relevant for building a case. Complex matters may see rooms full of documentation, mostly irrelevant to a particular point in question. Search engines applied to documents scanned and converted to electronic form make easy work of sifting through large volumes of text.

In the context of a global law firm with many offices spread around the globe, internal search engines linked with client management systems not only support more integrated service across geographies and jurisdictions, but they also allow the firm's relationship managers and partners to recognise and seize opportunities to offer more advantageous advice in potentially strategic, cross-border, company-wide matters, delivering greater value and promoting more client loyalty. In some cases, client management systems linked to and monitored by advanced analytics systems can warn partners of potential conflicts in interest or regulatory impediments to taking on specific items of client work.

DRAFTING

The core activity of document drafting changed dramatically with the spread of word processing software such as WordPerfect and Microsoft Word in the 1980s and 1990s, allowing significantly more flexibility in editing and formatting as well as incorporating tools such as spell checking, grammar suggestions and reference management, both internal and external to a document.

Cloud-based office productivity suites such as Microsoft Office 365 have increased the flexibility for lawyers to work on drafting not only in their offices but also while at client sites or in their home offices, on a number of devices including their office computer, their tablet device and, when the need arises, even on a mobile handset with the same word processor software, with current changes synchronised and made available for work on any registered device. All this is done safely with secure logins and sharing controls so that only the authoring lawyer and the right collaborators and counterparties will have access at the right time in the process.

In recent years, legal technology entrepreneurs have developed online services that specialise in the delivery of document drafting capabilities, offering standardised libraries of high-quality document templates that not only lawyers but in some cases clients themselves use to draft documents for routine matters and transactions.

WORKFLOW AND PRACTICE MANAGEMENT

Even in a small legal practice, as workloads increase, the complexity of managing work between different clients and matters for each client can easily get overwhelming. Legal practice requires a level of organisation and punctuality that can best be termed as exacting, indeed challenging and distracting for a lawyer needing to focus on billable work. Lawyers often resort to to-do lists in paper or electronic planners, while others turn to task managers in office suite software, and more sophisticated practices have turned to project management tools like Microsoft Project or online process coordination and collaboration tools like Basecamp, Smartsheet, or Monday.com.

Practice management software purpose-built for legal practice combines communications, process, drafting and filing, often in tandem with familiar office software tools like word processing and email software.

WORKING WITH UBIQUITOUS COMPUTING

During the COVID-19 pandemic, the legal profession faced significant challenges in settings where presence in an office was considered a necessary condition for work. Many partners and principals (individuals with executive authority) in firms had previously invested heavily in prestigious offices in central business district locations, both to project an image of success and to make it easier to arrange meetings with clients. In the early months of 2020, as the scope and gravity of the pandemic became clear and governments began to impose lockdown and social distancing measures, firms scrambled to articulate policies for personnel to work from their homes, aided by the full range of online tools we have discussed in this chapter.

It is not our purpose here to examine or advance opinions on the effectiveness of remote working arrangements in legal practice, but rather to highlight three important issues that arise when ubiquitous computing technologies are used in legal practice. All of these issues were thrown into sharp relief when firms had to adapt, often reluctantly, to work enabled and mediated with these technologies. In brief, they are:

- *Trust.* How can legal practitioners ensure client confidentiality when working with a wide range of technologies and tools that rely on the Internet, inherently open and (in some people's perception) insecure by nature?
- *Ownership of property.* When it is not only possible but even expected that personnel will use both firm-owned and personal devices to interact with online resources belonging either to the firm or to clients, how can the control of the information on the various devices that make up a given user's digital footprint be ensured, such that firm or client rights to intellectual property and information are not compromised, and indeed are handled in a context of trust? The issues that arise when an individual is working for a firm using their personal devices are sometimes referred to as bring your own device (BYOD) issues.
- *Ownership of time.* Ubiquitous computing now makes it possible for personnel to complete substantive, valuable work outside of the traditional office on schedules that more suit their individual needs and situations. Communications technologies can also be abused, and there are many stories of employers encroaching on time outside of normal business hours, to the extent that some employees feel that they must be available around the clock, even during appointed personal time, weekends and holidays.

An issue often raised in the age of always-connected digital work is the fluidity of the online environment, with devices that encourage multitasking and constant consumption of often unrelated, disjointed content that arrives and demands attention, often through notifications that interrupt the flow of work or intrude on personal activities. As the current time-billing model continues in the legal profession, the management and accounting for billable time will remain paramount to one's practice of law. The potential impact of this upon wellbeing was raised in Chapter 2. It also raises further questions, including:

- How can a lawyer manage their technology tools in such a way that they can maximise the effectiveness of the time spent using those tools?

- What concrete steps might they take to minimise interruptions in the flow of work, while also ensuring that they are responsible to the legitimate demands of their clients or colleagues in the firm for time and support?

Unexpected events and ubiquitous computing

During the COVID-19 pandemic, several jurisdictions, including Hong Kong, experienced at least two working days when severe weather necessitated the declaration and hoisting of tropical cyclone warning signals. Under such conditions, employees are not expected to report for work at their offices. With lockdown and social distancing measures driving work from home arrangements, many knowledge workers, including lawyers, found themselves in a grey zone with respect to the application of this regulation. It is perhaps instructive to consider what points about the realities of always-connected work you would raise if asked by an employer for advice in this scenario, bearing in mind that they may already struggling with productivity and cash flow under the serious restrictions and economic conditions imposed by the pandemic response. For a lawyer, it is possible that tensions may arise between their personal needs and those of their clients in such scenarios.

Sync 2: BYOD issues in the workplace

You should allow around 20 minutes for this activity.

Consider a lawyer who is a specialist in an area of practice working as a consultant to a small firm. Her arrangement is such that she is not issued a computer belonging to the firm but instead is allocated an account in the firm's online office services, which includes email and productivity software as well as practice management and workflow tools. The consultant will log into those services and use them to complete and deliver her work using her own laptop computer, and use her smartphone to access the firm's email and calendar services. Consider the following questions relevant to this and many other BYOD scenarios:

- What are some of the issues with client confidentiality that arise in this situation?

- What would be a consultant's express or implied duties to the firm and the client with regard to the safeguarding of data and information related to any client- and firm-related matters?
- What rights does the firm the consultant is doing work for have with respect to the information on the consultant's devices, and the devices themselves?
- How might policies be framed and enforced, such that the property and privacy rights of all parties concerned in a BYOD scenario would be protected, and what might be an equitable and/or legal basis for prioritising such rights?
- While some firms and clients may not traditionally have provisions in their policies for remote or work-from-home (WFH) scenarios, unexpected contingencies such as COVID-19 made the immediate adoption of such scenarios not only a precondition of productivity but a strict necessity for the sheer survival of many organisations. In such cases, even when the principals of a firm were normally not receptive to such arrangements, they found themselves acquiescing, and scrambling (sometimes failing) to put in place robust policies. What steps could you take, while advising a client or the managing partner of your firm, to ensure that you could frame a set of working criteria with which to evaluate such measures, and to protect your clients and balance the rights of your employees to privacy and control of their devices?
- Clients in many cases prefer to communicate using bursts of text or chat application messages. These exchanges often take place on personally owned smartphone devices. Given such preferences and the advantages realised, what steps can a lawyer take to ensure that such messages are protected, especially in the event of theft or accidental loss of the device? How might a lawyer recover from such a loss, assuming the use of a major messaging service that provides seamless backup and recovery procedures? Are such services in fact always desirable in legal work?

When answering Sync 2, you needed to be mindful of the fact that this is an emerging area in business and employment law, with wide variations among jurisdictions. Awareness of the range of controls that online software products provide, the already established precedents in a particular jurisdiction, and existing individual company policies will be instrumental in your formulation of guidelines and advice for clients in the future.

LEGAL REASONING AND TECHNOLOGY

With a firm grasp of technological concepts, we can now turn to the ways in which we can think critically about it with two related, equally important, though in practice quite different views of technology as lawyers:

1 How do we reason about technology, not only about its use but also its creation and management as it affects the legal positions and options open to clients?
2 How do we think about using technology in the practice of law? What concepts can we apply in order to evaluate new tools? How does one stay abreast of and apply new technologies at the right time in the technology evolution cycle to balance the benefits against possible risks and costs?

LEGAL REASONING ABOUT TECHNOLOGY

As we have seen, ubiquitous computing has transformed the nature of media and its consumption, not just limited to print, video, and music forms but also the software that enables these experiences. The next part of this chapter will demonstrate the importance of legal reasoning about technology by discussing property concerns and privacy concerns.

PROPERTY CONCERNS

Legal frameworks of thinking about property are relevant, as they are seeing varying levels of application and transformation as case law develops and technology trends continue their ongoing rapid evolution. When thinking about technology in a legal context, it is often helpful to consider a few aspects of the law of property:

1 *Title.* As with physical property, digital property (of which video, music, or software are but a few representative examples) has

relationships with individuals or entities defined by law. It is important to understand who has title to (owns and controls) the digital property in question.

2 *Possession.* Having physical possession of a piece of digital property, on physical media such as an optical disk or in the memory of an electronic device, does not necessarily mean having control of that piece of digital property. Digital rights management, licensing and service entitlements are important aspects to consider.
3 *Enjoyment and Use.* The extent to which a person may use a piece of digital property may be limited by certain licencing or service agreements.
4 *Transfer.* Delivering a piece of digital property may be done with physical media, although it might just as easily be done over the Internet, using a range of schemes for conveying the location and procedure for delivery.
5 *Disposal.* In some contexts, particularly in work involving intellectual property, most of the assets in questions are now in digital form. This means that obligations to safeguard and (when possession is no longer necessary or permitted by agreement) to dispose of such digital property are incurred.
6 *Regulation.* While many regulations apply to the people, property, and activities within the borders of a legal jurisdiction, the global reach of the Internet has made enforcement of such regulations and even relevant law difficult to interpret, let alone enforce in relation to digital property.

Let us explore each of these aspects of reasoning, informed by our recent reading about the fundamentals of technology in earlier parts of this chapter. For the remainder of this section, we will use the term "digital property" to refer to consumable media (texts, images, and audio and video recordings) as well as software.

Title versus possession

The distinction between title to digital property and physical possession of a copy of the digital representation of that property is extremely important in reasoning about technology. For digital media and for software, it is understood that the creator of the software, or the employer or commissioning entity in the case of work for hire, has ownership of that property. This means that copies that are distributed on media or via download, either as complete files or streamed and managed by specialised apps (such as music or movie players on modern devices), are merely licenced for limited uses, limited audiences, or limited sets of users (a certain number of users at a specified location, or certain named individuals in some cases).

Possession of the digital asset, therefore, does not necessarily entitle one to unlimited use, but instead obligates the holder of the physical media containing the asset to comply with the terms of the licence. To enforce compliance with licence terms, creators of digital assets have long relied on encryption, wherein a mathematical equation takes a digital file and scrambles the contents according to a well-known algorithm. The complexity of the bits of information contained in the digital file, together with large random numbers known as keys, is used by a program implementing encryption algorithms to scramble the contents of the file such that they are not readable unless decoded. The decoding operation is the reverse operation of the same algorithm, enabled through the possession of an appropriate key, sometimes combined with a process to check the validity of an applicable licence, a paid-up subscription, or some other indicator of a valid entitlement. Such validations can be done on the device, but more often now, they require at least intermittent network connectivity so that the access to the digital asset may be controlled by the owner of the digital asset from a central location.[8]

This method of using digital rights management (DRM) systems, wherein a person who pays for a digital access does not receive possession of it but rather limited access increasingly mediated through the use of network-based verification, is a subject of intense, sometimes impassioned cultural and political debate. It goes beyond the content of the law, with deep implications for culture and the preservation of what is becoming a digital heritage. The fact that companies who distribute these assets are also in sole possession of the legally sanctioned means to access those assets, even beyond the period of what would be considered the normal term for copyright, has profound yet untested implications. One might ask what would occur if the business owning the rights to a significant work protected by DRM goes out of business, and enough time passes during which not only the creators of the work, but also the distributors and the software vendors for the DRM all cease to exist, and in many cases do not have successors or heirs.

8 A glimpse at some of the complexity in digital rights management can be found here: <https://ottverse.com/eme-cenc-cdm-aes-keys-drm-digital-rights-management/>

Publicly available, but not public domain

In 2002, Marcel Proust's famous novel series *In Search of Lost Time* was published in a translation by Penguin UK. However, because of the copyright regulations in the United States under the Sonny Bono Copyright Act of 1998, only the first four of the six volumes could be published in the United States.[9] Readers who wanted to read the books in other earlier translations could find them online at public domain book sites like Project Gutenberg,[10] but again could only find the first four volumes, as the Project Gutenberg servers were located in the United States at the University of North Carolina at Chapel Hill. Readers who wanted the last two volumes as electronic books could buy the previous translations from online booksellers such as Amazon.com or could find them available for download from Project Gutenberg Australia,[11] a sister site to Project Gutenberg but not formally affiliated in any way.

This is a good point to pause and take some time to think about the implications of a file being available on the Internet from a jurisdiction in which copyright protection has expired, and whether a person in a jurisdiction in which such protections are still in force would commit an act of copyright infringement or piracy if they were to download and save that file for personal use. What regulations would possibly be applicable if they were then to distribute and share that file?

Consider that in many jurisdictions, online privacy laws do not allow the monitoring of user traffic without investigators meeting a certain standard showing reasonable suspicion of a crime being committed. Law enforcement are much more active in targeting illegal distribution and file sharing than individuals downloading, simply because of the practical considerations and sheer effort in gathering evidence.

So far, we have discussed ownership and licencing of online content and software. Consider the reverse situation for content creation, where users generate content and post it on a social media platform. This sync gives you the opportunity to read and review some facts regarding two popular services that manage and offer a considerable amount of user-generated content.

9 <https://slate.com/culture/2005/03/the-new-proust-translation.html>
10 <https://www.gutenberg.org/ebooks/search/?query=proust>
11 <http://gutenberg.net.au/plusfifty-n-z.html#proust>

Sync 3: Who owns user generated content?

You should allow around 30 minutes for this activity.

Examine Facebook's terms of service, as described and summarised in this FindLaw blog post <https://blogs.findlaw.com/law_and_life/2014/10/who-legally-owns-your-facebook-posts.html>

Also consider the copyright selection features of flickr, a popular photo sharing service, which recognises its users' needs to control the licenses granted for photos shared on the service <https://blog.flickr.net/en/2011/05/13/at-flickr-your-photos-are-always-yours/>

What are the limitations of the service provider's use of that content to promote use of its service?

It may come as a bit of a surprise to see the broad scope of usage rights granted to service providers by service agreements for the purpose of marketing their service offering and in generating engaging feeds of user content. There is a substantial amount of value given to the service provider in exchange for engaging user experiences, not least the ability to see the activities and photos of friends. A good amount of debate has been generated around the fairness of this exchange and whether service providers of social media offerings do enough to protect their users from malicious actors on their service, misinformation, data leaks and a range of other online perils.

Enjoyment and use: open source, creative commons and public domain

As we have seen, in addition to legal, not always practicable means of enforcement, DRM mechanisms allow digital asset owners direct ways to enforce restrictions on the use of those assets. When considering the enjoyment and use of digital property, it is important to consider other models, ones that many technologists and industry observers have identified as critical to the accelerated development of the computing environment we have today.

Another widespread approach for managing the legal ownership and licensing of digital assets entails the use of sharing models, wherein licenses are granted for digital assets that include the right to inspect and change the asset (as in the end user directly modifying the source code of a program or an artist remixing an audio track of music). Some licenses may go further in allowing the redistribution of the original or derivative works, usually with some stipulations on the preservation of copyright notices and attribution, whether fees for distributions may be charged and whether subsequent recipients also enjoy rights to modify and redistribute the original and intermediate derivative works.

Sync 4: What does free software really mean?

You should allow around 60 minutes for this activity.

Download and read the three most commonly used licences for open source software:

1 The GNU General Public License v3.0 (GPLv3) <https://www.gnu.org/licenses/gpl-3.0.en.html>

2 The MIT License <https://opensource.org/licenses/MIT>

3 The Apache License, Version 2 <https://www.apache.org/licenses/LICENSE-2.0>

These licences grant rights to use and modify the software to which they are attached (usually significant bodies of software used as infrastructure for services delivered over the Internet) and in some cases stipulate requirements for attribution, permissions to modify and redistribute original or derivative versions, and (in the case of the GPLv3) to transfer the same rights in the case of derivative works.

Consider the following questions:

1 What are the differences between these licences and the terms for an actively developed piece of software in the public domain like SQLite? <https://sqlite.org/copyright.html>

2 In the case of the GPLv3, where the protection of user rights is paramount, what possible steps must the developer and operator of an online service using pieces of source code to build a commercial service take to ensure compliance?

You will have seen in Sync 4 that the intention of many open source software licenses is to protect the rights of the user to access and use software. This is in tension with the interests of those who wish to incorporate open source software in proprietary commercial software services. This is an act the GPLv3 license does not discourage per se, but it requires that software incorporating GPLv3 components also be licensed under the same license and that the resulting source code be made available to all users on demand.

Transfer

Because of the limitations of networks in the past, digital assets were originally distributed—and to some extent, for very large assets (e.g. high-definition movie-length videos and large data sets), continue to be distributed—on physical media such as optical disks (e.g. Blu-ray, DVD). Smaller assets, such as music tracks, many electronic books and documents, can all be provided for download using a wide range of proven Internet tools and protocols, the most common of which is of course the World Wide Web.

Improved network infrastructure and availability, even over the air to mobile devices, have enabled many owners of digital assets to provide controlled access to their assets only over the network on demand, optimising delivery by sending small chunks of the asset to the device in near real time as it is being consumed, in what is known as streaming.

Streaming began with music, with implementations of digital radio, and gradually evolved with network infrastructure to streaming of on-demand music and on-demand full length movies in popular global services such as Spotify and Netflix. Streaming access also applies to software in situations where the physical copies of even the user interface are operated in a remote infrastructure. A remote-control view of the interface is provided to the user, much like fly-by-wire controls in a large airplane, where the electronic control signals in a cockpit are conveyed by wire to computers that do the work of mechanically controlling flight, embedded deep in the body of the plane or in the wings. Banks, health care organisations, research and development organisations and even some law firms requiring ways to assure clients of strong controls over copies of legal documents and other digital assets will resort to using streaming access to software as another layer of protection in desktop-as-a-service configurations, made possible with networks and ubiquitous computing resources.[12]

12 A good example of streaming application services in use at the time of this writing is Amazon Workspaces: <https://aws.amazon.com/workspaces/>

Disposal

Licenses for digital assets are now often enforced with DRM schemes, which prevent access after the expiration of a subscription or rental term. The problem of disposal becomes one of deleting the encrypted bytes (units of digital information), a generally safe and reliable experience. In the workplace, however, data files and other digital assets are exchanged between parties or disseminated to employees in the course of doing everyday business. Some of these files may contain information of a confidential or proprietary nature, and in government may even include matters of state security. It is imperative, depending on the sensitivity of the information contained in those files, that individuals, and especially lawyers advising them, understand and can state clearly the obligations for disposal that are attached to physical possession of those files, whether in a non-disclosure agreement, provisions in an employment contract or service agreement, or other applicable documents.

Regulation

The regulation of online technologies and digital assets can be understood from two perspectives:

1 The sale, distribution and use of digital assets within a given jurisdiction.
2 The use of digital assets and services, based on the location of the computing infrastructure elements providing those assets and services over the network and the location in which they are used.

It is our purpose here to introduce the key concepts to consider when reviewing regulations and legislation in consideration of a given matter.

In many cases, with or without DRM, digital assets are licensed for use in a single jurisdiction. The use of those assets by residents of that jurisdiction while travelling outside the jurisdiction is of course an area of ambiguity, unless there are applicable treaties in place. Physical enforcement of such regulations is usually in the form of checking the location of a user using his network location[13] and then permitting access based on certain rules.

13 A practice known as reverse IP address lookup.

In addition to user access, regulations may affect the required practices of service providers and publishers. The country in which a service provider is domiciled may affect the practices it must adopt with regard to user identity and data privacy as well as the nature of the services it may provide to those users. We will consider identity and privacy concerns in a subsequent section. First, let us consider aspects of regulation with regard to the provision of services.

Certain services, such as electronic marketplaces (including those that deal in the sale of goods and commodities such as drugs, pornography, and food sourced from rare or endangered plants and animals) or services for online gambling, have fallen under the scope of legislation and regulations in many jurisdictions seeking to extend policies and norms in those societies to the online activities of their citizens.

While certain activities such the sale and delivery of physical goods can still be controlled and taxed within and between jurisdictions through existing trade and customs laws, the sale and delivery of digital goods is not so easily controlled, even when the exchange is legitimate and permitted, in part due to the varying levels of political will to enforce existing laws, and in some cases because of the magnitude of the resources required for enforcement.

The practice of place-shifting[14] allows a user in one jurisdiction that prohibits certain activities online to engage in those activities in another jurisdiction, provided they have access via the network to services in jurisdictions where such activities are available or indeed even encouraged. Depending on the jurisdiction in which the services are hosted or offered, there may or may not be agreements to regulate users from other jurisdictions. Two examples of place-shifting are particularly relevant when studying the effects of law and regulation on digital activities and assets:

1 *Online gambling*. Using virtual private networks (VPNs), citizens in countries where gambling is banned may connect to services hosted in countries promoting online gambling, such as Gibraltar or

14 To be compared with time-shifting, enabled with Video Cassette Recorder (VCR) and Digital Video Recorder (DVR) technologies that allow users to record broadcast television programs for viewing at a time convenient to the user, simultaneously supporting the skipping of advertisements and multiple viewings and archiving at the user's discretion: <https://variety.com/2016/biz/news/dish-nbc-autohop-lawsuit-settled-1201797895/>

Denmark. The legal implications of such services and their use are beyond the scope of this discussion, but this example is raised for the purpose of making you aware of just one of the many situations where legislation, regulation and inter-jurisdiction cooperation vary greatly. These can either limit or create opportunities for clients and their lawyers, depending on the context.

2 *Electronic signatures.* Many jurisdictions now consider an electronic signature as valid for many transactions up to certain limits, often stopping at matters involving the conveyance of real property or articles above a certain value to exclude adjudication in a small claims process. Electronic signatures may take the form of hand-drawn signatures on a document using a pen, trackpad or mobile device; pasting an uploaded signature; or a more sophisticated process involving secure signatures that validate the user's identity and the contents of the document being signed.

Sync 5: In what contexts are electronic signatures legally binding?

You should allow around 40 minutes for this activity.

Research and familiarise yourself with the requirements for electronic signatures in your jurisdiction, taking note of the limits for validity and use of such signatures. Are there fixed values for transactions, above which only traditional (so-called wet signatures) are required? Are there specific classes of transactions that require wet signatures, such as probate matters or the conveyance of real property or moving vehicles?

Depending upon where you are based, you may have found a variety of different requirements relating to electronic signatures. Considering the rationale behind these requirements may well demonstrate the wider approach taken within a jurisdiction to technological developments; for example, whether they are embraced or treated with suspicion.

Privacy concerns

When computers were stand-alone devices, physical security measures were sufficient to ensure the safety of the data stored on removable media and hard disks. Computing services delivered via the Internet now require users concerned with safety and legal position to evaluate services and service providers on four critical aspects:

- *Data storage*. How and where data is stored has direct impact on the expectations of privacy a user may rely upon.
- *Data processing*. The manner in which data is processed for various services and for what purpose, whether used for marketing purposes (with or without consent) or for influencing opinions, affects whether a person may be targeted for advertisements or certain communications that, if not desired or even embarrassing, may constitute a breach of privacy.
- *Transmission*. The means and methods by which data is prepared and transmitted from each machine involved in the delivery of a service may affect a user's privacy, especially if networks are compromised and unauthorised access to data is obtained by an untrusted or malicious third party.
- *Identity and user activity*. Users of online services will not necessarily want records of their online activities made available to unknown third parties. Identification of a user in a setting outside the interactions in question may be inappropriate or compromising to the user, who will often expect and demand control over such information.

PRIVACY IN DATA STORAGE

If a service provider follows prescribed best practices for securing access to physical computing assets and networks (physical security), a factor that is often important is the state of the data when it is stored on a medium such as a disk, whether accessible via the network or not. Users of sensitive services such as financial or government services will expect that their data is stored in encrypted form, a condition known as "encrypted at rest", requiring some sort of encrypting software and key to decrypt the data for access and processing. Sophisticated service providers will also employ algorithms requiring user input, such as a password or encryption key generated by a security application, such that only a user can unlock the data stored on the service's infrastructure.

PRIVACY IN DATA PROCESSING

In some cases, data processing produces by-products, such as logs (electronic records), intermediate results and copies of data stored within an app's or device's memory. While data processing professionals should be trusted to apply good practices to the management and disposal of intermediate data and to ensure that data is used only for the purposes under relevant terms of service and privacy policies, it is perhaps incumbent on lawyers advising clients in particularly sensitive situations or those running online businesses to be aware of the specific regulations related to the processing of data and the duties of the service operator with regard to privacy in data processing.

PRIVACY FOR TRANSMISSION

Because networks like the Internet are public networks, safety of data transmission from source to destination is paramount so that third parties may not access data in transit. Encryption technology is employed to ensure safe transmission in ways transparent to the user and (for the most part) to the software developer and system operators, using such technologies as SSL (Secure Sockets Layer) or TLS (Transport Layer Security). As a lawyer, it is important to ensure that the technologies and services one uses for professional work all use some scheme for securing transmission of data.

PRIVACY FOR USER ACTIVITY

The tracking of user activity for various purposes, whether to improve a physical device, online service or app, to profile the user to target content for marketing or influence campaigns, or to ascertain compliance to law and regulations are all matters of concern. Jurisdictions have varying levels of completeness with regard to the treatment of activity tracking and privacy, ranging from no regulations to a presumption that all activity is at least tracked and reported to operators, and perhaps authorities.

This is a developing area of law. Societies are beginning to recognise the importance of user consent for tracking, the need for explicit mandates for opting out of tracking and use of that data, and more comprehensive policies such as ensuring the right to be forgotten, wherein all data pertinent to a person's usage history must be expunged from a system according to law. Of particular concern are regulations requiring the complete expunging of data from systems, and the complexity of compliance when there are multiple backup copies and information technology (IT) organisations, overwhelmed with workloads, limited in their ability to comply fully with the letter of the law.

Sync 6: Where is data stored?

You should allow approximately 15 minutes for this activity.

Consider the modern use of cloud-based services. As you use online services to handle client matters, you may have a copy of a document stored in a cloud storage area or cloud drive, a local copy of that same document synchronised with the copy in the cloud, and one downloaded when you had a few minutes to spare in a taxi travelling between client meetings. What steps must you take to ensure that those copies remain in control and confidential?

The proliferation of forgotten downloads on every device is a common condition in modern digital life. Perhaps you thought that a practice that restricted downloads to a single download directory that is periodically purged, or a strict practice of filing downloads immediately in an appropriate folder for each client or matter, would work well for you. Some might minimise downloads and use a synchronisation function found with some cloud-based services that allows a user to work in offline mode when travelling or for whatever reason. There is no universal solution, but you now have a starting point to develop your own method for managing this critical practice.

Case study: Health care app security leaks

Health care applications on connected mobile devices are indispensable for providing a bridge for exercise and personal body measurement and telemetry data (such as pulse rate) as part of fitness and health improvement regimes. All such devices require the support of online services in the cloud, and thus face the challenges to user privacy we have examined in this section. Three high profile data breach incidents occurred over the two-year period from 2018 to 2019 for three prominent apps:

- MyFitnessPal, owned by Under Armour. Attackers[15] accessed personal data for over 150 million users, taking names, addresses, email addresses, and location information.

15 We use the term "attackers" here, instead of "hackers", more accurately conveying the malicious or felonious intent of the individuals. Mass media will often refer to individuals obtaining illicit access to systems and data as "hackers", ignoring and

- PumpUp, an online fitness community, had the data of over six million users stolen, including contact information, photographs, and health data.
- Strava, an online shared fitness map service, had data openly shared for users who engaged in fitness activities like running and cycling. The community-sourced map and routing information was valued for its richness and currency. It also, however, had the unintended characteristic of being widely used by military personnel, whose open sharing of location data allowed some people examining the openly available data set to deduce the location of secret military installations where those personnel were stationed.

More detail on these three incidents can be found in an article by a design firm exploring ways to prevent such incidents <https://www.ego-cms.com/post/most-expensive-healthcare-app-security-fails-in-2018-2019>

You may want to spend some time reviewing these incidents and identifying the issues that come to mind related to the elements of privacy we have discussed in this section; namely, data storage, data processing, transmission, and user activity.

LEGAL REASONING USING TECHNOLOGY

In this section we examine some ways in which technology can be used to enhance legal reasoning and the practice of law. Legal texts generally pose two problems in which technology can be of service and sometimes of great utility.

First, there is the problem of representation of legal constructs, specifically in the way the substance and intent of a legal construct such as a law or contract is communicated. The analogy of a legal text as a program—more concretely, a declarative program specifying the constraints placed upon actors, whether they be individuals or legal parties under the law, or whether they be parties to an agreement, and whether they must act under pain of some specified penalty or

inaccurately co-opting the long-held positive use of the term in technology and computing culture, celebrating hackers and hacking as the ingenious developers of know-how to solve problems, particularly in software development or in prankster tomfoolery at engineering schools.

liability—is often employed to illustrate the notion of the representation of the law for purposes of explanation or discussion. We examine in this section some techniques in representation and semantic analysis that have emerged as technology has evolved to help the understanding of natural language texts.

The second problem is of surveying and comprehension of legal texts. While lawyers may rightly or not take pride in their drafting and syntactic prowess, the typical non-lawyer is often challenged to understand any legal language. Even trained lawyers with many years of practice will have widely divergent readings of complex texts, a reality that often figures as a condition for eventual litigation to settle the meaning of particular points in laws or contracts. In the need for precision and comprehensive specification, texts can grow, not only resulting in verbose and sometimes tortuous language but also in sheer volume and complexity, such that legal texts rival engineering endeavours for complexity. Just as in software engineering, where a single person will have difficulty understanding the full scope of a complex software system, so a single person may have difficulty understanding fully a body of legal text.

Note that we will omit discussion in this section of applications in which artificial intelligence (AI) or machine learning techniques are applied to simulate or implement machine understanding of law or in which they are used to aid or replace decision-making on the part of a human judge or lawmaker. You will find an introduction to those topics in Chapter 8.

REPRESENTATION OF LAW AND CONTRACTS AS PROGRAMS

Since the late 1950s, researchers have looked for ways to apply rigorous mathematical reasoning, specifically tools such as symbolic logic and logic programming, to the modelling and interpretation of laws and, to a limited extent, to commercial contracts. An academic paper published in 1957, titled "Symbolic Logic: A Razor-Edged Tool for Drafting and Interpreting Legal Documents",[16] is an example of such efforts. By applying a technique of linguistic analysis and decomposition, author Layman E. Allen advanced the concept of "systematic

16 Layman E. Allen, 'Symbolic Logic: A Razor-Edged Tool for Drafting and Interpreting Legal Documents' (May 1957) 66 (6) *Yale Law Journal* <https://digitalcommons.law.yale.edu/fss_papers/4519/>

pulverization", in which language constructs are reduced to concise statements that can be sequenced and represented as logical assertions suitable for evaluation by humans (and, as technology advanced, machines). Thus clauses in a legal texts can be restated in more precise terms, reducing or eliminating ambiguity, while also serving as an aid in the drafting of legal texts.

The use of computing tools to aid in evaluation and understanding of legal texts was largely out of the realm of practicality, until gains in commodity computing power and data handling in the 2000s matched the computing needs that came with theoretical advances in the 1980s and 1990s in methods for the systematic representation of knowledge in text, such as ontologies and rhetorical structure theory,[17] and methods to discern and disambiguate the meaning of words and texts.[18] Growing use of ontologies allowed the identification of discrete concepts (such as actors, objects, requirements and constraints) and the delineation of the relationships between those concepts, while rhetorical structure theory supports, as its name suggests, the identification of conceptual representations in text and the pieces of text that relate to specific representations. Between ontological methods and rhetorical structure theory, concepts in their idealised, abstract forms can be rendered comprehensible with the former, and concepts in their textual representation can be understood and evaluated with the latter.

Investigation into the use of symbolic logic continued, with a notable 1986 paper examining the British Nationality Act 1948 as the specification of an algorithm for determining the eligibility of an individual to be classified as a British national. This was a rich study illustrating, with non-trivial cases of reasoning, the difficulty of various approaches to encoding the application of law as a system of rules in an expert system or as other unspecified AI applications.[19] One can imagine efforts to encode the semantics of a given statute or regulation in an attempt to build an impartial "weighing machine" or "automatic

17 William C. Mann and Sandra A. Thompson, 'Rhetorical Structure Theory: Toward a Functional Theory of Text Organization' (January 1981) 8 (3) *Text & Talk*.

18 Michael Lesk, 'Automatic Sense Disambiguation Using Machine Readable Dictionaries: How to Tell a Pine Cone from an Ice Cream Cone' *SIGDOC 86: Proceedings of the 5th Annual International Conference on Systems Documentation* (June 1986), 24–26 <https://doi.org/10.1145/318723.318728>

19 M. J. Sergot and F. Sadri, et al., 'The British Nationality Act as a Logic Program' (May 1986) 29 (5) *Communications of the ACM* <https://doi.org/10.1145/5689.5920>

judge" to be used in case of a dispute. Such a tool would, in theory, remove the fallibility, imprecision and arbitrary bias of a human interpreting a given legal text and matter.

A class of applications known as expert systems emerged as IT systems analysts took knowledge of certain laws and regulations, derived using the techniques described in this section, and developed specifications—intermediate representations of the legal constructs—that computer software developers could translate into runnable representations as computer programs or, in expert system parlance, "rules". These rules could be evaluated by expert system kernels or rule engines—programs purpose built to take rules as inputs and operational instructions—to answer specific applications of law. Examples of expert systems used in legal applications might include the determination of a person's eligibility to acquire British nationality or whether to recommend to a judge whether an accused criminal should be granted bail while awaiting trial. Note that these applications are representations of law translated by direct human effort, sometimes in multiple steps, from a text in a natural language such as English into a machine-runnable representation as software.

Expert systems applications are distinct from AI or machine learning applications, which will take data representing the range of conditions that may be embodied in or describe the subjects of the law, together with the desired outcomes of applying the law, and train a machine by building a mathematical model mapping such conditions to known correct outcomes. The resulting mathematical model, trained on a set of known inputs, enables the machine to evaluate previously unseen combinations from the same domain of possibilities and render a specific application of that law as a determination or recommendation.

Machine learning systems can be classified as supervised (requiring measurement and human input and tuning after each iterative attempt to improve the model through training) or unsupervised (fully automated, improving using algorithmic techniques such as randomisation, or programmatic limiting of inputs based on specified measurements). A comparison of supervised and unsupervised machine learning systems is seen in Figure 3.4. Both types of systems are in wide use. The choice of one type over the other is highly dependent on the problem to be solved, the available data and the other components of the approach selected by the engineers building and operating the system.

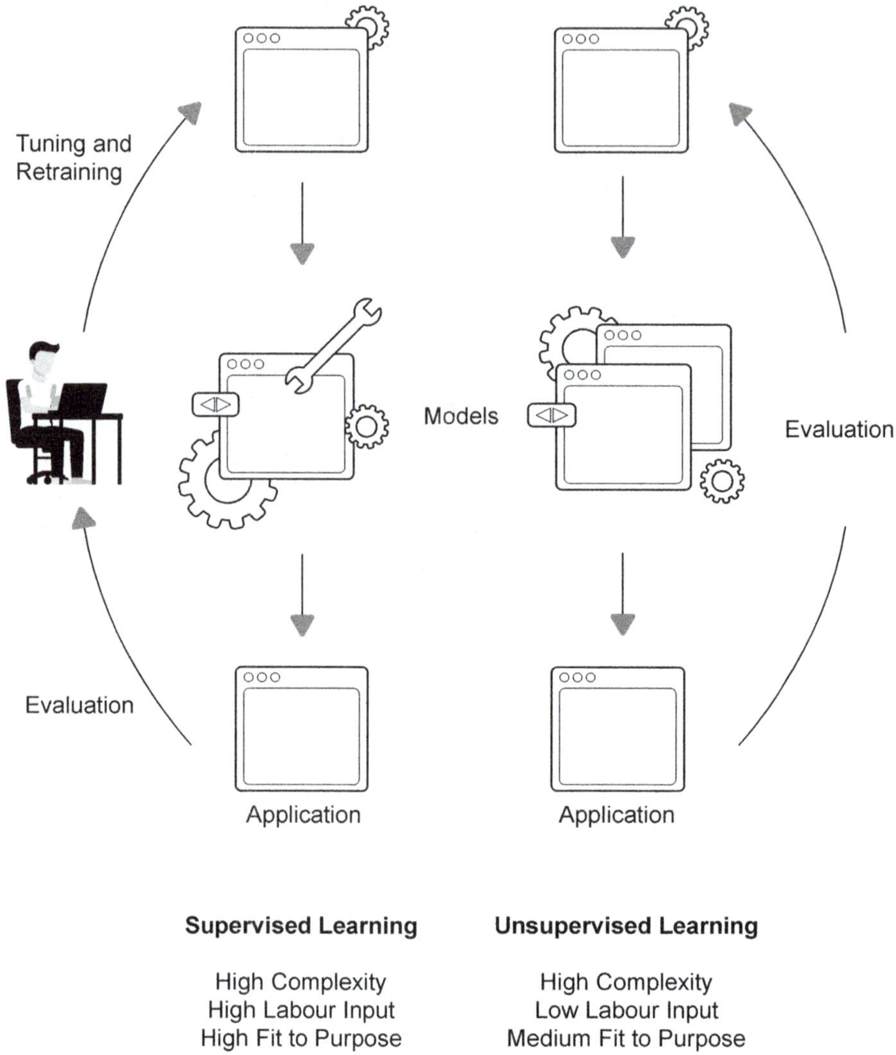

Figure 3.4 Supervised versus unsupervised machine learning

TOOLS FOR UNDERSTANDING LEGAL TEXTS

So far, we have examined ways in which people have begun to use symbolic logic and related forms of systematic modelling and semantic analysis to build machine-readable, "computable" representations of legal constructs. While these techniques do support the development of some levels of understanding of the legal texts they represent, and in some cases can be used to build systems attempting to apply the same texts as law or contracts, they may not contribute to a lawyer's everyday ability to understand a text for the purposes of serving a client, providing an opinion or building a case for action. Tools normally used by software engineers to manage and process large bodies of source code (the components of a computer program) have proven useful to lawyers and legal scholars approaching larger bodies of legal text or complex regulations, by supporting the finding of facts about the text itself, of what is known as the metadata related to the text.

A 2015 study[20] by researchers at the Massachusetts Institute of Technology (MIT) and Harvard University examined ways in which software engineering tools and techniques can be applied to legal text analysis, using multiple major revisions of the US Code as the study subject. The team explored the analogy between legal code and software code, asserting that four key principles and practices from good software design (conciseness, change, coupling and complexity) all matter in the drafting of law for comprehension as much as they do in software engineering. They reasoned that just as software engineers strive to communicate their rationale for future maintainers of their code and to work to make the code comprehensible for others joining the team, so lawyers could benefit from the practices and tools in the application to legal drafting.

- *Conciseness.* Software engineers, as a matter of best practice, strive for compact expression, as less code means less code to understand, debug and maintain over the long term. In a similar way, well-written prose will display compactness and clarity in expression. Software engineers often employ tools to count lines of code, check for correct syntax and use tooling to achieve compact expression. Lawyers have similar tools built into modern word processing tools, as well as online services for grammar correction, word choice, and usage enhancement, but there are few tools currently in mainstream use to assess textual complexity and structure, let alone provide assistance in improvement in clarity or conciseness.
- *Change.* Managing, tracking and controlling the release of changes to a body of code is a critical skill to permit software developers to

20 William Li, Pablo Azar, David Larochelle, Phil Hill and Andrew W. Lo, 'Law Is Code: A Software Engineering Approach to Analyzing the United States Code' (2015) 10 *Journal of Business & Technology Law* 297 <http://digitalcommons.law.umaryland.edu/jbtl/vol10/iss2/6>

have confidence in the changes they are making. While many lawyers may use a change tracking function in their word processing software to manage a single document, doing so across a collection of documents is not a common practice, nor is it supported by generally accessible office productivity tools. Change management tools also allow the assessment of percentage of change, highlighting for lawyers the texts that may need the most attention for review.

- *Coupling*. In software, dependencies between modules directly affect the functions a system can provide. The presence and ordering of those modules in some systems affect the way functions are manifested in the running code. In law, a sufficient understanding of interdependencies between bills and related laws is necessary to ensure that the desired outcomes for legislation are achieved. Software engineering tools build reference tables of significant entities in a code base, as well as relationship maps. The same types of tools can be used to build indexes, summaries and cross-reference tables, as well as text network diagrams, to show relationships between significant portions of a legal text and, in some cases, reveal relationships that may otherwise be overlooked in the absence of such tools.
- *Complexity*. Software engineers use discovery tools that can generate diagrams to provide overviews of bodies of code. Similar tools exist to provide semantic structure analysis and diagrams that provide overviews of significant bodies of text.[21]

In addition to using code management tools, software developers have begun applying natural language processing (NLP) techniques that involve the construction of mathematical models that describe the structure of texts, permitting functions such as search, analytics, discovery and redaction. These are also referred to in Chapter 6, but here we give some examples of how these tools might be used:

- *Search*. Indexing strategies developed through years of investment in search engine technologies now allow easy location of words or phrases of interest and documents containing such fragments. Summarisation algorithms support more efficient overview processing of

21 M. Abdeen, R. El-Sahan, A. Ismaeil, S. El-Harouny and M. Shalaby, 'Automatic Generation of Mind Maps from Text with M2Gen' (2009) *Science and Technology for Humanity (TIC-STH)*, 2009 IEEE Toronto International Conference 2009.

large bodies of documents, such that painstaking examination of boxes of documents can now be done with significantly greater speed and accuracy from a connected device's browser.

- *Analytics.* Lawyers looking to build a case on publicly available records may use analytic tools to confirm assertions of complaint frequency and build quantitative evidence quickly and cost-effectively before approaching a regulator with a claim or request.
- *Discovery.* Computing statistics showing frequently or (as the case may be) infrequently used terms in context in legal documents sometimes reveal unusual conditions, previously unknown persons who may have interest in a specific matter, and other facts that might be overlooked when reading large bodies of text for other purposes.
- *Redaction.* When releasing certain documents to comply with discovery requirements or other lawful requirements for visibility, organisations may be required to redact certain sensitive items of information, such as personally identifiable information (PII) of individuals, trade secrets and so forth. A suitably trained set of tools using NLP techniques can automatically redact sensitive documents prior to final review and release.

The state of tools being developed for understanding and reasoning about the law evolves as rapidly as software techniques and data processing capacity, and is expected to continue to accelerate in the coming years. A digital lawyer will need to keep abreast of developments in technology, looking for ways to experiment and apply such developments that are reasonable in terms of protecting the client and one's firm or practice from risk and that can take advantage of tools and techniques that provide significant advantage in finding solutions for the range of matters a digital lawyer may encounter.

Digital lawyering skills: interdisciplinary working

The need for digital lawyers to follow and understand developments in technology demonstrates the interdisciplinary nature of digital lawyering. Today's legal professional will find themselves working and communicating with specialists in other areas, particularly IT, digital technologies, legal design and project management as they apply such developments and provide advice and guidance to clients.

As a law student, it is easy to become immersed in legal terminology and jargon. However, as a digital lawyer you may well find yourself having to use technical terms which fall outside the usual language of law. You may also find yourself having to explain complex legal concepts and issues in a way which is accessible to colleagues working in other disciplines. Conversely, you may need to explain unfamiliar technical concepts to clients when identifying solutions to problems.

There are some simple ways that students can begin to develop the skills required for interdisciplinary working, including:

- Reading books, articles, blogs and websites from different disciplines to acquaint yourself with frequently used terminology and key issues.
- Looking at whether your law school offers any non-legal optional modules or any voluntary opportunities to work with students from other disciplines.
- Attending events and conferences which have an interdisciplinary focus (such as those run by Legal Geek).
- Seeking out opportunities for work experience or internships in different industries and sectors to gain valuable transferable skills.

All of these are methods of familiarising yourself with different disciplines in a way that will help you to work and communicate with others clearly and effectively.

FINDING YOUR WAY

In this section, we offer some general pointers for you to learn more about the intersection of technologies and the law, to build on the foundations that we have laid down in this chapter.

ENGINEERING APPROACH

In this chapter, we have attempted to avoid extensive detail behind the technologies that underpin devices, networks and services that are now indispensable for the digital lawyer. Those so inclined may benefit from learning some fundamentals of technology implementation, for instance, by learning to write software code in a modern programming language. A hands-on understanding of the process and techniques, even at a beginning level, would help a lawyer to appreciate the issues and complexity faced by software developers behind the tools and services in everyday use.

HISTORICAL APPROACH

In parts of this chapter, we have taken the historical approach to give a sense of the evolution of technology from its simpler roots to the complex, multilayered networks we have in use today. The historical approach to learning about technology will become more important as we continue using computing and communications technology in everyday life, if just to set technologies in context when we encounter them. The historical approach is certainly useful in order to understand how copying and pasting entered conceptually into user interaction design, or, perhaps more concretely, to know that some organisations use magnetic tapes as their primary backup and archiving medium and will continue to do so because of the sheer volume of data to be handled. Such knowledge will help a lawyer advising clients in the transfer of certain digital assets to specify the transfer of all backup media as well and possibly to require means to ensure the ability to read potentially discontinued recording formats.

USER-CENTRIC APPROACH

A user-centric approach to learning about technology considers a user's goals while examining only those technologies that are needed to serve those goals. User centricity frequently incorporates aspects of design thinking and user experience design, ensuring that the elements that directly affect the user—in this case a client or a fellow lawyer, counterparty or even oneself—are understood. This means that the focus is on whatever technologies are needed for the user goals, and only those technologies are considered.

LEGAL(TECH) APPROACH

Learning about technology from a legislative and regulatory perspective is perhaps the more traditional way for lawyers to encounter technologies in everyday practice, and then conceptually rather than in practice. The legal approach is of course useful to stay abreast of one's peers and colleagues and to ensure a common vocabulary for discourse with peers and other parties.

As more technology-minded lawyers and technologist-lawyers have been building legal technology (legaltech) businesses that become going concerns, general awareness of technology and technology-related issues in the profession has grown, leading to events, community organisations, media outlets and conferences. In addition, there are legaltech-focused funding programs with hackathons and incubation schemes to support and advance innovation.

STAYING CURRENT

As with any field, staying current with technology involves keeping abreast of developments through reliable mainstream media, but more importantly, profession-oriented news sources and media. For lawyers interested in technology, the legaltech sections of popular professional sites such as Law.com's LegalTech News[22] and Stanford University's CodeX Techindex[23] are good places to start, as are the legaltech groups at local law society or bar association organisations.

ADDITIONAL RESOURCES

Ford P, "What Is Code? If You Don't Know, You Need to Read This" (*Bloomberg.com*) <https://www.bloomberg.com/graphics/2015-paul-ford-what-is-code/>

Kernighan BW, *Understanding the Digital World: What You Need to Know about Computers, the Internet, Privacy, and Security* (Princeton, NJ, Princeton University Press, 2017).

Lessig L, "Code Is Law" (*Harvard Magazine*, 1 January 2000) <https://harvardmagazine.com/2000/01/code-is-law-html>

22 <https://www.law.com/legaltechnews/>

23 <https://techindex.law.stanford.edu/>

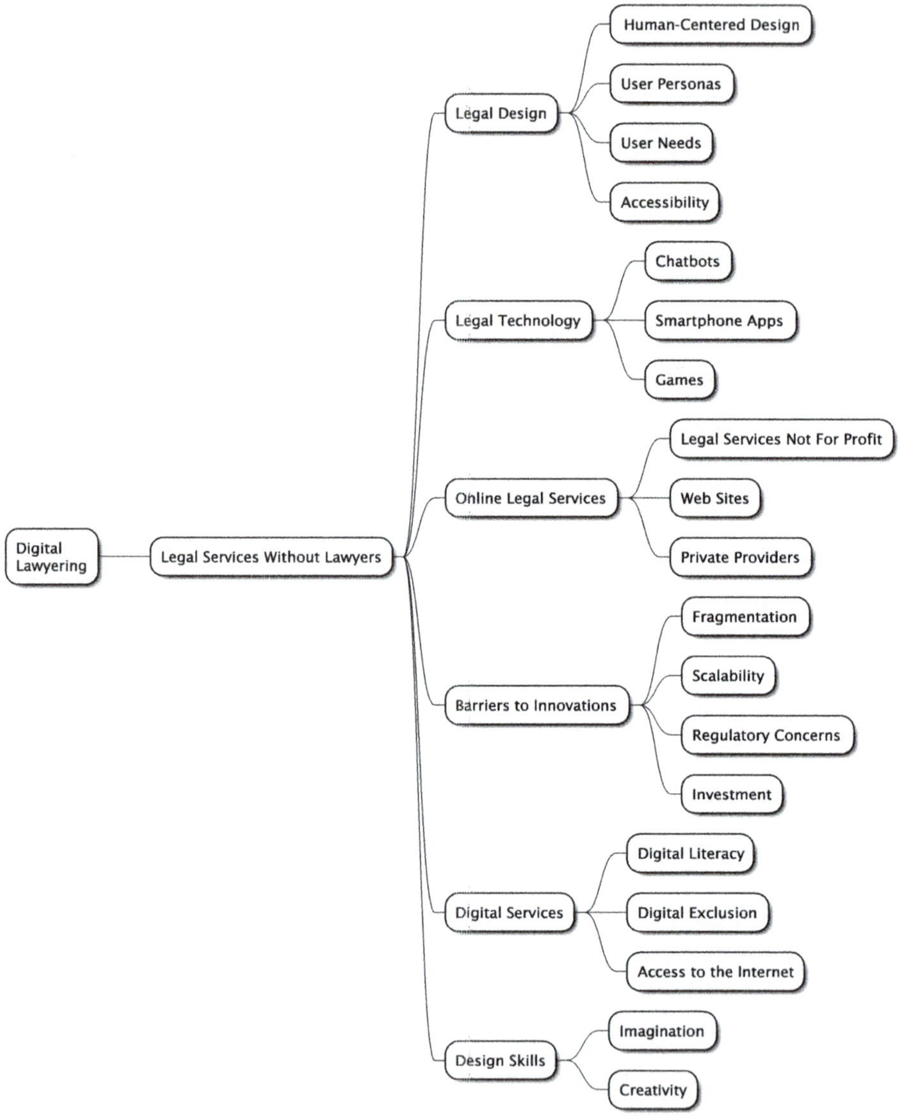

Mind Map 4.1 Chapter topics

4 DELIVERING LEGAL SERVICES WITHOUT LAWYERS

Francine Ryan

INTRODUCTION

This chapter will consider the delivery of legal services without the use of lawyers. It will examine this issue through an exploration of how we can improve access to justice using digital technologies. You will be encouraged to think about how technology can be used to support individuals to resolve disputes without the need for lawyers. It will consider ways in which technology is developing to provide innovative solutions; for example, chatbots like DoNotPay (see Chapter 3), digital platforms to store and archive legal documents, and legal docs companies that allow individuals to create personalised contracts online. It will analyse the emerging legaltech market and discuss the potential and concerns of using technology to transform access to justice.

Chapter hot spots

When reading this chapter, questions to think about include:

- What types of online service exist?
- How is technology being developed to widen legal access?
- What is design thinking?
- Why is understanding users' needs important?
- What are the risks associated with the proliferation of technological tools?

Having read the title and introduction, you can add any other questions you want to explore here:

DOI: 10.4324/9780429298219-4

Technology is having a profound impact on business and the provision of legal services. The cloud, cybersecurity, the Internet of Things, mobile technology and legal design are all important aspects of digital transformation. The pace of change is rapid, and it can feel overwhelming trying to keep abreast of and understand the emerging technology trends. This chapter attempts to demystify how technology is impacting on the delivery of legal services. This is an exciting time to study law. Technology is changing the legal landscape, but there are lots of opportunities to think creatively about how we use technology to democratise the public understanding of law and improve access to justice. Understanding the intersection between law and technology will ensure you are able to thrive in the new digital age.

Writing in *Tomorrow's Lawyers*[1] in 2013, Richard Susskind argued that technology was going to radically change the provision of legal services and the legal profession. Susskind has long been an advocate for technology and, although the pace of change has perhaps not been as radical as he has predicted, it is clear that new technologies are affecting the legal landscape. The COVID-19 pandemic has had a significant impact on the delivery of legal services and digital innovation may increase to help mitigate some of the issues that have arisen as a result of this. In Chapter 2 you began to explore how technological innovation impacts upon those who provide legal services. You will return to this theme in subsequent chapters. However, the focus of this chapter is upon how technological innovation is relevant to the ways in which we deliver legal services.

WHY IS THERE A NEED TO DESIGN LEGAL SERVICES WITHOUT LAWYERS?

Why are so many people turning to the Internet to help them resolve their legal problems? The problem is that most people cannot afford to pay for legal advice and the availability of legal aid has been restricted. In the UK in 2013, the Legal Aid, Sentencing and Punishment of Offenders Act 2012 (LASPO 2012) came into force. This legislation introduced significant funding cuts to legal aid, meaning that fewer people had access to legal advice in the areas of family, immigration, employment and welfare benefits law. In other jurisdictions legal aid is also restricted from the very poorest in our society.

1 Richard Susskind, *Tomorrow's Lawyers* (Oxford, Oxford University Press, 2013).

There are some types of cases such as personal injury claims where, if the case is successful, the legal costs are recovered from the opposing party. Under a conditional fee agreement (sometimes referred to as a "no win, no fee agreement") the law firm agrees with the client that they only have to pay the legal costs if their case is won, and they receive compensation. If the claim is not successful, the client does not have to pay have legal costs to their solicitors, but they are likely to be ordered to pay the other side's costs under the costs rules. There are insurance policies that can be purchased to cover these risks. The law firm can charge a success fee for this type of arrangement, and this is deducted from the compensation the client receives if their case is successful. Another way of funding a case is through a damages-based agreement where the law firm takes a percentage of any compensation awarded as payment for their services.

However, in many instances clients want advice on legal issues where there will be no recovery of damages (e.g. in the case of a divorce). In those cases, unless a client qualifies for legal aid they will have to pay for the legal advice. Instructing a lawyer can be very expensive, and many people cannot afford to pay privately. They therefore turn to other sources of help to assist them with their legal issue.

WHAT IS LEGALTECH?

Lawtech and legaltech are interchangeable ways of describing "technologies that aim to support, supplement or replace traditional methods for delivering legal services, or that improve the way the justice system operates".[2] Lawtech refers to a range of different technological tools including chatbots, legal document drafting automation, and knowledge and research tools, some of which were described in Chapter 3. Technology is being leveraged to provide resources to enhance the public understanding of law and to provide legal advice through chatbots and triage tools. There are now examples of technological tools that are being used by the free advice sector to help support those who cannot afford to pay for legal advice. Throughout this chapter we will explore some of the different ways technology is being used to improve access to justice.

2 The Law Society, 'Introduction to LawTech 2019' <https://tlsprdsitecore.azureedge.net/-/media/files/campaigns/lawtech/introduction-to-lawtech-october-2019.pdf?rev=fc0013791e0c474198daaabd648a304d&hash=F030B90541BF66B22233A9702F4B22A5>

The increasing range of online help has been fuelled by the growth of lawtech start-ups. The organisation Legal Geek publishes a start-up map each year, and in 2021 there were over 250 lawtech start-ups featured on the map. The start-ups focus on different areas of law and different types of services; some are more business orientated, providing ways to support the legal profession to become more efficient. One example is Made In Law,[3] which is an online service for incorporating a business in Europe. Other start-ups are around Law for Good, designing solutions to support access to justice.

Sync 1: Legaltech start-ups

You should allow around 15 minutes for this activity.

1 Access the Legal Geek start-up map <https://www.legalgeek.co/startup-map/>

2 Click on the link to three start-ups to find out more about what they do.

As you will have seen from the map, it is divided it into sections including managing the business, managing and/or performing, performing work and consumer services.

TYPES OF ONLINE LEGAL SERVICES

Digital legal tools are being developed in the form of websites and applications that can be downloaded onto a smartphone to provide legal information and services to support non-lawyers in resolving legal problems. In 2019, Sandefur[4] carried out the Survey of US Legal Technologies to find out what kind of digital technologies exist to support non-lawyers in resolving their legal problems. The main findings of the survey were:

- Over 320 digital tools exist in the United States to assist non-lawyers on areas of law including civil, criminal and employment.
- Fifty-two percent of the tools facilitated the user being able to take some form of action (e.g. diagnosing a legal issue, creating a form).

3 <https://madeinlaw.com/en/>

4 Rebecca L. Sandefur, 'Legal Tech for Non-Lawyers: Report on the Survey of US Legal Technologies' (2019).

- The legal design of many of the tools was out of date; often there was too much reliance on text; and many were a collection of information about the law.
- Often there wasn't a correlation between the digital tools created and the types of problems non-lawyers required help with.
- As yet, there is no single tool that offers a complete solution to a legal problem.
- Some of the tools were free but quite a number charged the user.

In the UK, there are an increasing number of Internet sites offering free legal information and services to the public. The market is changing, with new providers emerging offering paid legal services that in the past would have been provided by legal professionals. Hagan[5] classifies the different types of online help as shown in the following sections.

Government help

These are online sites where the law and legal procedure are explained. For example, the UK government website has a section on crime, justice and the law. It provides information on a wide range of issues including prisons and probation, reporting crimes and getting compensation, young people and the law, and your rights and the law. It provides sources of information and provides links to other organisations.

Non-profit referrals/information

These are online sites where individuals can find out information about their legal issue and use the information to help them to try to resolve their legal problem. For example, AdviceNow[6] has a selection of legal information on a range of legal issues and links to other trusted sources of help. They also provide a help directory to signpost users to other organisations that may be able to offer legal assistance. Citizens Advice[7] provides extensive legal information on a range of topics including benefits, work, housing, immigration and much more.

5 M. Hagan, 'The User Experience of the Internet as a Legal Help Service' (2016) 20 (2) *Virginia Journal of Law & Technology* 394–465.

6 <https://www.advicenow.org.uk/categories>

7 <https://www.citizensadvice.org.uk/>

Legal services/not for profit

These are online sites that provide a mix of legal information and paid-for legal assistance. For example, Which Legal[8] is owned by the Consumer Association, which is a registered charity. Which Legal provides legal advice on consumer issues, employment law and small claims. The guidance is provided by email and telephone. There is a joining fee and then a monthly charge.

Private legal information sites

These are online sites where individuals can access personalised legal information for free; for example, Ask A Lawyer[9] and Free Legal Advice.[10] These sites offer to answer legal questions for free on a range of topics, but they don't guarantee they will answer every question. They also provide legal information and post answers to questions that have been asked by other users. Although it is not completely apparent, these sites are often linked to law firms and probably serve as a way of generating new business to the firm.

Private legal self-help tools

These sites share similarities with the private legal information sites, but they charge for their services. For example, Just Answer[11] and Expert Answers[12] offer services where they charge for answering legal questions. Legal Zoom[13] is an online legal service provider that offers legal advice on conveyancing, wills and supporting small businesses. Rocket Lawyer[14] provides a range of services, offering free legal guides and paid-for services including legal advice and legal documents.

One of the issues to consider with the development of these types of sites is reliability and trustworthiness. These sites are often not subject to the same regulation as lawyers, but people accessing these sites might be unaware of this. An increase in the provision of legal services delivered online raises questions about how we protect users of these

8 <https://legalservice.which.co.uk/>
9 <https://www.askalawyer.co.uk/>
10 <https://www.free-legal-advice.co.uk/>
11 <https://www.justanswer.co.uk/>
12 <https://www.expertanswers.co.uk/>
13 <https://www.legalzoom.com/uk/>
14 <https://www.rocketlawyer.com/gb/en>

sites. Although there has been growth in the number of digital tools available to help non-lawyers, there are regulatory challenges in the adoption of such technology.

UNDERSTANDING USER NEEDS

Both Sandefur and Hagan agree that many of the digital tools developed do not meet the need of the users. Defining what is a "legal need" has been problematic and what constitutes the definition of legal need is subject to much debate.

> "Legal need" arises when citizens (or businesses) require support from legal services (broadly defined) in order to resolve problems, which have a legal definition.[15]

Research[16] has found that many people struggle to recognise their problem as a legal issue. Over many years, legal needs surveys have been conducted which have demonstrated that many UK citizens have been denied access to justice because they do not have sufficient legal knowledge or capability to navigate their legal problems.[17] However, many of the digital tools that have been created assume that a person already knows they have a legal problem for which there is a legal remedy. Let's take an example of a tenant who has a problem with their hot water. Do they fix it themselves or recognise the situation as legally actionable because their landlord has failed to repair the property under the tenancy agreement? Although many websites provide legal information on tenancy issues, without some form of diagnosis tool a non-lawyer may struggle to recognise the legal aspects of their problem.

15 Pascoe Pleasance, '"Legal Need" and Legal Needs Surveys: A Background Paper' (Open Society Foundations, 2016) <https://namati.org/wp-content/uploads/2016/11/OSJI-Legal-Needs-Surveys-Background-Materials-1-An-Introduction-to-Legal-Needs-Surveys-1-v3.6-2016-06-22-web_Pascoe.pdf> accessed 2 October 2019.

16 Rebecca Sandefur, *Accessing Justice in the Contemporary USA: Findings from the Community Needs and Services Study* (Chicago, IL: American Bar Foundation, 2014).

17 The Civil and Social Justice Panel Survey (CSJPS) 2010, 2012 see also <https://www.lawforlife.org.uk/wp-content/uploads/LASPO-Implementation-Review-Consultation-Law-for-Life-Advicenow-response-Final-Sept-2018.pdf>

Although the Internet offers the potential to help people resolve their legal issues, the current provision is not always effective because it is not user-friendly and often it is designed in ways that replicate how lawyers think and operate.[18] Therefore, to understand how to use technology to support individuals dealing with legal problems, it is important to think about the design of legal information to ensure that it is user-friendly.

Hagan[19] conducted a study in the United States to better understand how people use online services. She found that:

- Google search was used first when people wanted to better understand their legal issue, and the highest-ranking search engines were where the information was drawn from.
- The Internet searches and sites visited gave users basic information on how to resolve their problem.
- Users wanted free help that was clear, had interactive navigation, and included case studies and some form of marker to demonstrate that the information provided was authoritative and legitimate.

Hagan then looked at the features users wanted from online services. She found that these included:

- The site must be easy to use and navigate, with information presented in small segments so that it does not overwhelm the user.
- A site that is authoritative and legitimate, so ideally affiliated or linked in some way to an official organisation.
- When in the initial stages of finding out information about their legal problem, users do not want advertising, marketing or paywalls.
- Ideally users prefer all the information in one place or on one site.
- The site needs to be designed well with interactive features, search facilities and menu choices.
- The visual look of the site has to meet modern design standards.
- There was a preference for case studies, narratives and stories that reflected similar situations to the user's experience.

18 Queensland Association of Independent Legal Services Inc., 'Queensland Community Legal Centres Use of Technology Literature Review and Discussion Paper' (2014) 18.

19 Supra n. 5, p. 413.

- The ideal site would take the user through each step of the legal process to navigate their legal problem. It would include assistance in helping the user identify their legal problem, develop a strategy to tackle the issue, and allow them to complete any forms/documents to resolve the problem.

HOW IS THIS ACHIEVED?

To help non-lawyers use online sites, developers need think about their design and navigation and ensure that search tools are easy to use. There should be menus, headings and icons to orientate the user to easily find the information that is relevant to them. In designing content, it should be framed around how a non-lawyer experiences a problem rather than framing the information around legal topics. Sites should include text, video and images to engage different types of users. Interactive tools that allow users to customise the information to the specifics of their case should also be included. Online sites should be as comprehensive as possible to avoid the user having to visit multiple sites. It is helpful to provide links to other sites to guide the user through their legal journey. For example, if the online site provides legal information, it should provide a clear link to a court site to complete court forms and file them electronically if possible. Overall, the site needs to have an interactive design that supports non-lawyers to navigate their legal journey efficiently and effectively.

There are several different ways that technology is being used to support access to justice. One way is through the improvement of processes to make the operation of the service more efficient and more accessible; this is highlighted through the examples of Justice Connect and Access to Justice Author.

Justice Connect

In most jurisdictions, significant levels of unmet legal help exist. There is the potential to revolutionise access to justice by leveraging technology to build systems and digital tools that deliver legal assistance directly to people in need. One example is the Gateway project in Australia. There are three elements to the project, an online intake and triage tool, a referral tool and a pro bono portal. In 2017, the project received seed corn funding of $250,000 from Google. The project was designed in conjunction with 22 community legal centres, 49 help seekers testing the tool in person, 80 intake tool users involved in research, and 14 law firms participating in the pilot.

The online intake tool

There are two elements to the tool: A program sorter and program-specific questions. The program specific questions enable the individual to be linked to the correct Justice Connect service. Each Justice Connect service has its own specific pathway by answering a series of questions the user is matched directly into the relevant service. The intake tool was designed in conjunction with users over a two-year period.

The referrer tool

The referrer tool allows a person or an organisation to refer someone to Justice Connect. The tool allows a referral directly to a service within Justice Connect or asks a series of questions to refer someone who needs legal assistance to the right pathway.

Pro bono portal

This is a technology-driven system that matches people with legal problems and lawyers who will take their case for free. At the time of writing, 49 law firms in Australia use the portal. To find out more about Justice Connect[20] and the Gateway project, visit their website.

Access to Justice Author (A2J Author)

In the United States, A2J Author software has been developed to support self-represented litigants to complete court paperwork and documents. It facilitates this process through the development of guided interviews which allow end users to create web-based documents. The software is available free to organisations such as courts, law schools and legal aid providers. There is also a portal that matches law schools and legal aid organisations so they can work together on a project. Many law schools in the United States use the tool as part of classes in legal technology and access to justice.

20 <https://justiceconnect.org.au/>

Both of these projects use design thinking in conjunction with user testing to develop the digital tools and build the systems to deliver legal assistance. This will be explored in more detail later in the chapter.

DEVELOPING LEGALTECH TOOLS

Another way in which technology is being used to support access to justice is through the development of chatbots.

WHAT IS A CHATBOT?

A chatbot is a piece of software that allows you to perform an automated task. There are different definitions of a chatbot, but the most capable form of chatbot is one that can have a conversation with a human. If you ask the chatbot questions it can respond with an answer.

There are three different types of chatbots: scripted, intelligent and application.

- *Scripted*: The interactions within a scripted chatbots are determined by a set path. The user will pick from various options to move on to the next step. The bot can be programmed to respond to text, voice or touch.
- *Intelligent*: These chatbots use artificial intelligence (AI) to allow the user to put in a free-form response, and with AI, the more they are used the better they perform. It is important to note that bots struggle to recognise ambiguity or context; it is not like conversing with a "real" human.
- *Application*: These chatbots allow for interaction via a graphical user interface (a visual way of interaction, for example, via menus and icons). This can form part of an intelligent and scripted chatbot.

Current technology does not allow a chatbot to converse as a human does. There is considerable potential, but it is important not to overestimate its capabilities and have unrealistic expectations of what can currently be achieved. You will find chatbots in platforms like Facebook Messenger, Slack and SMS. Alexa, Siri and Google Home. If you like coffee and have downloaded the My Barista app from Starbucks, then you are using a chatbot to pre-order your latte or americano.

THE LEGAL ACCESS CHALLENGE

The UK's Legal Access Challenge[21] is run in collaboration with the Solicitors Regulation Authority (SRA) and the innovation foundation Nesta.[22] The £500,000 challenge is to encourage and support innovation to help individuals and small businesses access legal information and advice. In April 2020, the two winners were CourtNav and FLOWS by RCJ Advice and Rights of Women and Mencap and Access to Social Care.

The Mencap and Access to Social Care project is a legal chatbot developed using IBM Watson and hosted on the IBM Cloud.[23] It provides free legal information to help people with a learning disability to understand their social care rights and explains how to challenge an unlawful decision. The chatbot is already being used by the charity and the plan is to make it available to other free legal advice organisations as an advice portal.

Sync 2: Flows

You should allow around 15 minutes for this activity.

1 Access the FLOWS website <https://www.flows.org.uk>

2 Have a look around the website to see what help it provides.

3 Click on "Browse safely" and reflect on why this is an important element of the design of this website.

The FLOWS website offers a variety of different sources of help for anyone who is experiencing domestic violence. One of the most interesting features of the website is the ability to apply for a court order

21 <https://www.legalaccesschallenge.org>
22 <https://www.nesta.org.uk/>
23 <https://www.ibm.com/watson>

online. CourtNav is an online decision tree tool which helps the users to automatically create an application for a court order, which is then checked by a legal advisor.[24] These projects are examples where technology is being leveraged to support access to justice and demonstrate the potential of digital technologies to help meet unmet legal need. You can read more about the finalists of the Legal Access Challenge and some of the barriers to innovation in their report.[25]

In addition to innovation in the not-for-profit sector, there are developments in the commercial sector to develop legaltech to support non-lawyers accessing legal services.

Case study: DoNotPay

Joshua Browder was born in London in 1997 and graduated from Stanford University in America. He taught himself to code at 12, and at 18 he created a chatbot called DoNotPay. DoNotPay allows users to challenge disputed parking tickets. Joshua Browder used technology to disrupt the traditional way in which legal services are delivered. When he came up with this idea, many lawyers were dismissive of the idea that technology could be used to resolve legal issues.

DoNotPay originally used Browder's own natural language processing (NLP) algorithms, but in 2016 he teamed up with IBM and starting building bots on IBM Watson. DoNotPay first launched in London, and within 6 months it was reported that it had been successful in 160,000 cases.[26] The bot works by asking a series of questions to determine whether you are entitled to appeal your parking fine. If it determines you qualify, it generates an appeal letter.

DoNotPay expanded in 2017, launching new bots across the UK and United States that addressed other legal issues including data breaches, late package deliveries and unfair bank charges. The new bots work in a similar way to the original chatbot. They ask a series of questions about the legal problem; using those answers, it works out what the legal issue is and produces the necessary documentation to make a claim.

24 <https://www.courtnav.org.uk>

25 <https://legalaccesschallenge.org/wp-content/uploads/2020/06/Legal-Access-Challenge-Report-FINAL.pdf>

26 Cheyenne Macdonald and Stacey Liberatore, 'The Robot that Could Get You Off a Parking Ticket: DoNotPay System Has Won 160,000 Disputes in London and New York' (*Daily Mail*, 28 June 2016) <https://www.dailymail.co.uk/sciencetech/article-3664413/The-Robot-parking-ticket-DoNotPay-created-student-won-160-000-disputes-London-New-York.html> accessed 26 April 2021.

From an outside perspective it is hard to determine how successful Browder's bots have been, and there has been some criticism of the effectiveness of the bots. But what cannot be disputed is that Browder is an innovator and has challenged the traditional ways of doing things. As a result of his work there are now a plethora of new bots emerging. There is a lot of excitement about the potential of legal technology to develop new solutions to challenge current ways of working. Browder refers to the bots as robot lawyers, so perhaps one question to consider is whether bots will ever replace lawyers.

BARRIERS TO IMPROVING ACCESS TO JUSTICE THROUGH TECHNOLOGY

The not-for-profit sector does face barriers to technological innovation. It is more challenging to secure investment and harder to encourage start-ups to develop legaltech for non-profit than for commercial ventures. More work is being done in collaboration between free legal advice and the commercial sector, but there are issues of resourcing, fragmentation and scalability that must be overcome. The development of legaltech also raises regulatory concerns. The legislation governing data protection can be a barrier to innovation, and this issue is explored further in relation to Big Data in Chapter 6. Digital solutions that collect any form of data must be compliant with data protection regulations. If the solution provides legal advice, then in some circumstances the advice given may also be subject to professional indemnity rules. In the UK, the SRA recognise that the development of new technologies can widen access to legal services, and they state they are committed to simplifying regulatory rules to enable growth and innovation. SRA Innovate is a space that has been created to support innovation in legal services.[27] The regulatory framework is an important consideration for the development of technological tools and will differ depending on the jurisdiction.

Although there is potential to explore how technology can help non-lawyers with their legal problems, it is also important to recognise

27 <https://www.sra.org.uk/resources/innovate/sra-innovate>

that some people struggle to access or use technology. There needs to be careful consideration of the implications of using technology to widen access to legal advice and information. There is a lot of work happening within the free advice sector to consider how technology can be leveraged to support access to justice. Citizens Advice's Future of Advice: Strategic Framework 2019–22 sets out its vision for using technology to test out new ideas around machine learning and automation.[28] One of the key points in the strategy is around the risks of digital exclusion.

DIGITAL EXCLUSION

Technology may offer innovative ways to address access to justice, but it is not without its challenges. One of the other major problems with the proliferation of technological tools is digital exclusion. There is a risk that sections of society who do not have access to technology and/or do not have the required digital skills to engage with technology will be excluded. Chapter 9 discusses the digitalisation of the court system. There are concerns that many parts of our society may become further excluded from the justice system with greater use of technology because they will be required to use technology to communicate with the courts and to enforce their legal rights. As more and more services move online, it is essential that everyone has the required digital skills to access and use these platforms.

This is a useful opportunity to consider the essential digital skills that people require to successfully navigate and use online sites. We need to be clear about the skills and level of skills we are expecting people to have. We need to consider whether people require only basic skills such as how to use email, access the Internet, navigate websites and complete documents online, or whether there is a requirement for more advanced skills. Many of us probably feel reasonably confident about our own digital skills; we might not recognise that other people might struggle, and we may underestimate the scale of digital exclusion. Can you recall a time when your Wi-Fi or mobile data didn't

28 Citizens Advice, 'Future of Advice: Our Strategic Framework 2019–22' <https://www.citizensadvice.org.uk/about-us/future-of-advice-our-strategic-framework-2019-22/> accessed 26 April 2021.

work? How did that make you feel? You might have felt frustrated or a bit panicky that you were suddenly cut off from the digital world; if you are digitally excluded you might feel that a lot of the time, especially as more services move online.

Sync 3: How do you rate your digital skills?

You should allow around 30 minutes for this activity.

1 What digital skills do you think are important to effectively engage online?

2 Complete the following table.

Skill	**Essential skill**	**Desirable skill**	**Rate your confidence 0–10**
Creating and editing events in calendars (Outlook, Google, etc.)			
Sending an email			
Filling in an online form			
Creating a spreadsheet			
Setting up and using online banking			
Creating a strong password			
Setting up an email account and an email address			
Understanding the difference between mobile data and Wi-Fi			
Creating a digital signature			
Creating a witness statement in Word			

Skill	Essential skill	Desirable skill	Rate your confidence 0–10
Using WordPress to create a blog or a website			
Using webchat			
Taking and editing photos on a mobile device			
Making a Gantt chart in Excel			
Knowing the risks of using public Wi-Fi			
Inserting a digital signature into a form or a document			
Attaching a document to an email			
Creating a letter in Word			
Searching and accessing websites			
Converting a Word document to PDF format			

3 Thinking about your own skills, how confident would you feel about using technology to resolve a legal problem?

4 What are the consequences for the rule of law if parts of our society feel digitally excluded?

Hopefully you feel confident that you have the skills to confidently engage online. Access to justice and the rule of law are connected, and it is essential that lack of digital skills do not preclude people from exercising their legal rights. You will go on to consider the type of skills which a digital lawyer requires in Chapter 11 and have further opportunities to reflect upon your own skills in Chapter 13.

Digital skills: digital literacy and digital competence

Sync 3 demonstrates the importance of digital literacy to enable you to carry out relatively routine and everyday tasks. For students who are aspiring digital lawyers, it is important to focus upon developing your digital literacy and also your digital competence (in other words, your abilities to use your digital skills) within legal practice in appropriate and effective ways to meet the needs of clients.

As a student there are a range of ways you can develop your digital literacy and digital competence. These range from doing your own research online (e.g. watching a YouTube video on how to use a different application or piece of software) to looking out for courses at your university (e.g. many university libraries offer helpful courses on using legal search engines). You may want to use any spare time you have to experiment with using technologies in different ways, from creating a website or podcast to developing a programme or application. These can be great ways to have fun while developing your digital skills.

THE SCALE OF THE DIGITAL DIVIDE

The Lloyds Bank Consumer Digital Index report in 2020 identified 2.7 million people can access the Internet but lack the basic digital skills to use it effectively. In addition, 33% (16.9 million) of the UK population scored in the lowest category for digital interaction only ever using their mobile phone, but not using it for services such as email or online banking.[29]

A framework was created to measure and assess digital skills. The following are the essential digital skills for life, and across these categories are 29 digital tasks.

- *Handling information and content*: Use a search engine to look for information online; find a website that they have visited before; download and save a photo found online.

29 Lloyds Bank UK Customer Digital Index 2020, <https://www.lloydsbank.com/assets/media/pdfs/banking_with_us/whats-happening/lb-consumer-digital-index-2020-report.pdf> accessed 22 April 2021.

- *Communicating*: Send a personal message via email or online messaging service; carefully make comments and share information online.
- *Transacting*: Buy items or services from a website; buy apps and install on a device.
- *Problem-solving*: Verify sources of information found online; solve a problem with a device/digital service using online help.
- *Being safe and legal online*: Be careful about sharing information online and how to keep online content secure, recognise suspicious links and understand about not sharing other people's data or intellectual property without consent.

In 2020, 78% of the UK population could do at least one of the tasks within the five essential digital skills, which means that 11.7 million people did not have the essential digital skills for life. There is a digital divide between older and younger people: The research shows that there are now no 15- to 34-year-olds with no (0) basic digital skills. Geographical disparities also exist across the UK: The East Midlands and Yorkshire and Humber have the highest proportion of people who can only do one task per life skill. Women are still more likely to be digitally excluded. The data suggests that there is a relationship between education and level of skill. Digital exclusion is also linked to social and financial exclusion. In 2017, a UK Government Strategy stated:

> Financial exclusion and digital exclusion often go hand in hand. People who are the least online are often the heavier users of public services, highlighting the need to design services to include them. . . . A significant proportion of the adult population may never attain the digital skills to use online services without support, because of disabilities or lack of basic literacy skills.[30]

There are also particularly vulnerable groups, such as the homeless or detainees, who struggle to access the Internet and risk being excluded from essential online services. The world is now digital, and research from Lloyds Bank found that people thought that the COVID-19 pandemic had increased the need for digital skills.[31] Digital exclusion is an

30 Cabinet Office and Government Digital Service, 'Government Transformation Strategy: Background Published 9 February 2017' <https://www.gov.uk/government/publications/government-transformation-strategy-2017-to-2020>

31 Lloyds Bank UK Consumer Digital Index 2020 at p. 28.

issue for many groups in society, but certain people and groups are disproportionally affected. The ability to resolve legal problems without the need for lawyers is only possible if people have more than basic digital skills. There is a risk of a deepening social justice crisis if digital exclusion is not addressed. It is important to ensure that everyone has the same opportunities to benefit from technological transformation, and part of that challenge is to think about how we design legal services to be digital inclusive. This is an issue for everyone connected to the administration of justice and the delivery of legal services. It is essential that law students understand and recognise these issues because as future digital lawyers they have a key role in helping to ensure that legal technology and design meets the needs of all users.

One important way to tackle these issues is through innovation and design. In the next section we will explore design thinking and the importance of human-centred design in helping to develop technological solutions to support the delivery of legal services without lawyers.

DESIGN THINKING

Design thinking is an iterative process that provides a framework to help solve complex problems. It involves seeking to understand the user, challenging any existing ideas and beliefs to generate innovative solutions to problems. There are many different versions of design thinking; the one outlined here was developed by the Hasso-Plattner Institute of Design at Stanford, which is also known as the d.school.[32] According to the d.school there are five phases of design thinking (Figure 4.1):

- *Empathise* with your users.
- *Define* your user's needs, their issues and your thoughts.
- *Ideate*: challenge any pre-existing ideas and think about innovative solutions.
- *Prototype*: start the process of creating the solutions.
- *Test* the solution created.

The steps in the process are not necessarily sequential. They do not have to be followed in a specific order, they can occur together, and

32 <https://dschool.stanford.edu/>

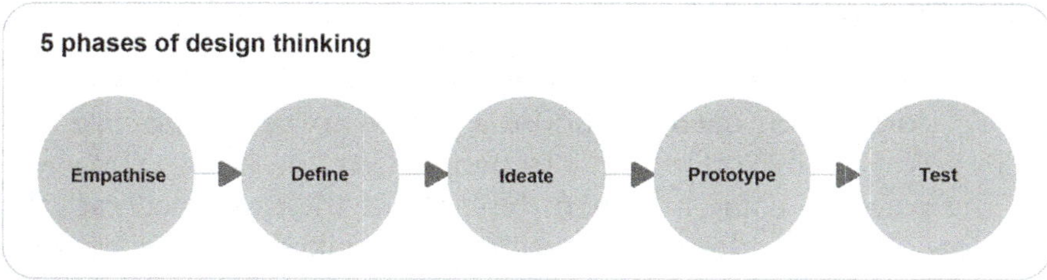

Figure 4.1 Five phases of design thinking

they can be repeated. It is important to involve the user at each stage of the process to understand their needs. This is an iterative process which means you may need to go back to refine and retest your ideas. Through the testing process you learn more about users which might lead to you redefining the problem.

The next part explains the process you might adopt to apply design thinking in the creation of a digital tool.

INITIAL PROCESS MAPPING

The first stage in designing any digital tool is to create a process map that identifies how a person will use the tool. Using a series of sticky notes is a helpful way of doing this, because they can easily be moved around to reflect changes in the design process. It is important to map out each stage of the user journey and clearly understand how the user will navigate through each part of the tool.

UNDERSTANDING THE USERS

The next stage involves understanding the experiences of the user. In this process it is essential to think about how they identify their problem, how they look for help and how would they use the tool. This could involve journey mapping, storytelling, reflecting on their experiences of using other services, and testing the tool. It is important to engage with a range of different users because they will have a variety of experiences and may use the tool in different ways. A digital tool will only be successful if it reflects the needs of the users, and the user must be at the heart of the design process. It is therefore essential to have a clear understanding of what users want before finalising the design of the prototype tool.

USER PERSONAS

To really understand your users, it is a good idea to create user personas. To do this you need to choose a person to be the persona. This can be a real-life person or a mix of people that you know. You should give the person a name and then think about their experiences, values and ideas. As you create your solution, you think about how your user would respond to the tool and put the user's needs at the forefront of the design. It is recommended that you create several different personas to inform your design and solution. The types of information you might want to capture are detailed in Figure 4.2.

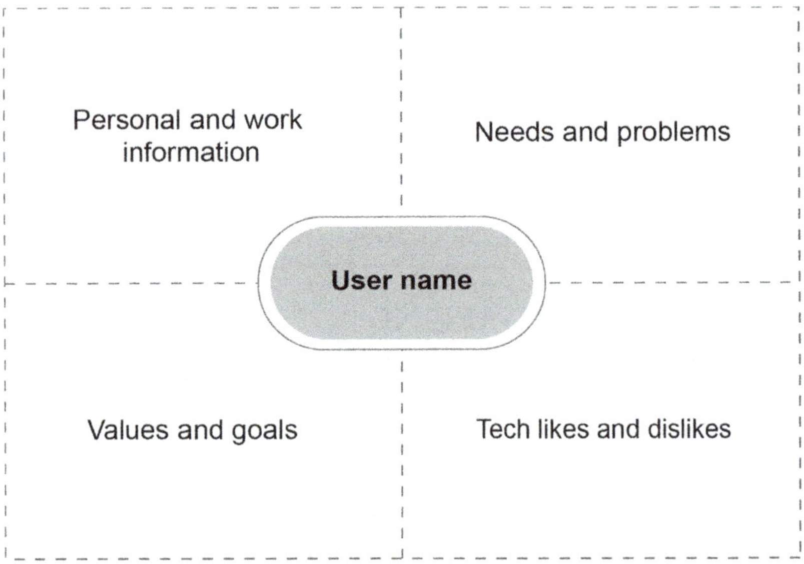

Figure 4.2 User persona

Figure 4.3 provides a completed user persona.

Sync 4: Creating a user persona

You should allow around 20 minutes for this activity.

1 You are designing a smartphone application to provide information and support to people who have suffered domestic violence.

2 Using the matrix above, create a user persona for someone who you think might use the smartphone application.

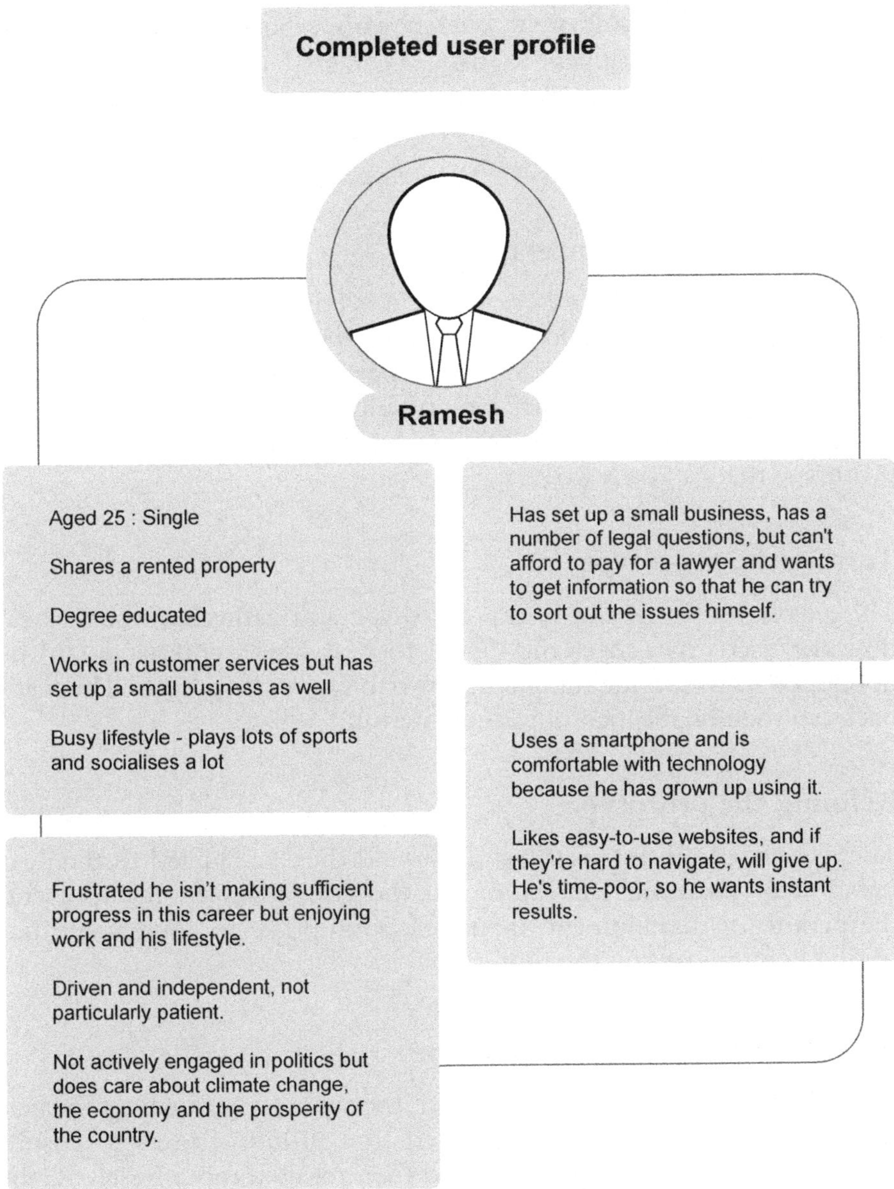

Figure 4.3 Completed user persona

If you were designing a smartphone application to support survivors of domestic violence, you would create several user personas to incorporate the different categories of people who are likely to use the application; for example, you might create male and female personas.

Although it is predominately women who experience domestic violence, it does also happen to men. Women and men may use the application differently, so it is important to capture the differences in the user personas to ensure that the tool will be effective if you are designing it to be used more widely.

Initial design and prototypes

The tool should be mapped out before it is built. It is essential to create an initial design that supports the development of the prototype tool. Once the mapping process has been done and there is an initial design, then the prototype is built. It is important to remember that the initial design does not need to be perfect; what is important is to have a prototype that can be tested.

Testing the prototype

This involves user testing of the prototype and gathering feedback on how the user experiences the digital tool. A list of criteria should be developed to determine the minimum viability of the project. The feedback can then be mapped onto the criterion.

Refining the prototype

The feedback from the user testing should then be applied to the next iteration of the tool. Depending on the complexity of the tool and the period for development, it may be appropriate to conduct further testing before finalising the tool.

Finalising the design and content

Once user testing has been completed, the tool can be finalised for first release. First release may be restricted to a group of users to ensure that the tool works appropriately, and then released more widely. Consideration needs to be given to how the tool will be marketed and promoted.

Evaluation

Once the tool has been released and used for a set period of time, an evaluation should take place. It could comprise:

- *Data collection and analysis*: Usage data, Google Analytics, data within the tool.
- *User testing and user surveys*: Focus groups, interviews, surveys to collect feedback from the users on their experience of using the tool.

The evaluation should inform further iterations of the tool. In designing and developing legaltech it is important to accept that the perfect version of the tool will not be created straight away. The purpose of the design process is to refine the tool several times. It is not uncommon to want to spend too much time trying to perfect ideas in the initial design stage. Often there is a reluctance to move on to the creation of the prototype before perfecting the initial design. Creating a digital tool is a fluid process, so it is important to embrace the uncertainty and messiness of the project. It is also not a linear process, and there is no requirement to proceed through each stage sequentially. The testing of the prototype is critical because the collection of data provides more information on how the digital tool performs, a greater understanding of the user and how much refinement will be required to move on to the next stage.

The process of developing legaltech requires being able to work iteratively, embracing an experimental approach and becoming comfortable with uncertainty. The process can be frustrating when what might appear to be a well-designed tool may not work effectively with users. Several bugs and glitches may be found in the testing process that need to be addressed. Each part of the process is a learning opportunity and provides a deeper understanding of how the tool might work with larger groups of users.

To find out more about evaluation of a digital technology, read the evaluation report from Justice Connect[33] on their Gateway project. Points to think about include:

- How will users respond to the tool?
- Is the tool easy to navigate?
- Is the tool visually appealing?
- Is legal terminology explained clearly?

33 <https://justiceconnect.org.au/about/our-approach/digital-innovation/gateway-project/our-intake-tool/>

Design principles

Understanding legal language is complex and can be baffling to non-lawyers.

If you have studied law, it is easy to forget that non-lawyers might struggle to understand words such as estoppel, liability or breach. A digital tool should use plain English to ensure the information is accessible by a non-lawyer. For example, if you were thinking about designing a digital tool that provides information on contract law, the first question might be: Is there a contract in place? This seems a reasonable question to ask, but how many non-lawyers will be familiar with the elements that make up a valid contract? The phrasing of the questions is important to prevent errors and misunderstandings. An alternative approach might be to ask whether the parties have an agreement and then follow up with questions to establish whether there is a legally binding contract. Failing to understand legal language puts non-lawyers at a disadvantage; therefore it is essential in the design of a digital tool that we do not inadvertently build in that disadvantage.

Margaret Hagan argues that "design, put shortly is the practice of making things that are useful, usable, and engaging. It is domain agnostic—it is about methods and outcomes, not about a particular subject matter".[34] A human-centred approach to design and innovation is about understanding user needs to creatively think about how technology can be used to solve a problem. Designing a digital tool that helps a non-lawyer with their legal problem is only effective if it connects with and meets the needs of its users. Technology by itself is not going to support non-lawyers to resolve their legal problems, but if technology is designed in such a way that it addresses the needs of its users, then there is a stronger possibility it will be "useful, usable, and engaging".[35]

Organisations are now encouraging designers to think about putting people at the centre of the design process. Earlier in this chapter we discussed user personas; these are important when thinking about a human-centred design and innovation approach. The Design Justice Network has an agreed set of principles to help support collaborative and creative practices. The principles include putting at the centre the voices of those who are directly impacted by the outcomes of

34 M. Hagan, 'Design Thinking About Law: A Perfect Match' (January 2014) *Legal Practice Today*.

35 <https://www.lawbydesign.co/en/home/>

the design process. The principles link to the human-centred approach and emphasise the importance of the collaborative process in design. You can find out more about the principles by visiting their website <https://designjustice.org/read-the-principles>

DESIGNING TECHNOLOGY WITH ACCESSIBILITY IN MIND

Haben Girma[36] became the first deaf-blind graduate of Harvard Law School; she works as a disability rights advocate and is passionate about the power of technology to improve inclusivity. She argues that when technology is being designed, inclusion and accessibility should be considered from the start. She also advocates for engaging users from the initial design stage through to when the technology is updated. There are universal benefits to designing with accessibility in mind from the outset. Technology has enormous potential to help all users to understand and access their legal rights, but as part of the development of digital tools designers need to ensure they have considered inclusion and accessibility.

Apple produces human interface guidelines that explain the accessibility features that can be incorporated into an accessible app; these include VoiceOver and increased text size.[37] Google also has a platform which helps developers build more accessible apps for Android devices.[38] Universal design is not about designing for users with disabilities but about designing for everyone irrespective of their ability, experience or capability. Designers need to think about a number of elements, but particularly simplicity and perceivability.

- *Simplicity*: making tasks simple and easy to perform.
- *Perceivability*: to ensure that the content can be perceived regardless of whether users are using sight, hearing or touch.

There are a range of resources and tools to help design and build digital tools that are accessible. According to Google there are one billion digital

36 <https://habengirma.com/>

37 <https://developer.apple.com/design/human-interface-guidelines/accessibility/overview/introduction/>

38 <https://developer.android.com/guide/topics/ui/accessibility/index.html>

users in the world with some form of disability; therefore when we think about designing technology tools it is imperative to prioritise accessibility and inclusion.[39] There are many factors to consider when creating digital solutions to help non-lawyers resolve their legal problems, and it is not a straightforward process. There needs to be more research done to understand how we improve the ways in which we communicate legal information. The next activity gives you an opportunity to reflect on some of these issues and consider how you might design a digital tool.

Sync 5: Designing a digital tool

You should allow around 90 minutes for this activity.

You have just signed up for a law and tech module, and part of the course involves the creation of a smartphone application. One aspect of the smartphone application is the creation of smart answers (sometimes called decision trees) which allow you to present complex information in a quick and accessible way. Smart answers work by taking the user through a series of questions until they reach the answer to a legal question. The information is tailored to their specific circumstances.

1. Go to <https://www.gov.uk/pay-leave-for-parents>
2. Use the calculator to see an example of how smart answers work.
3. Then look at the Guides to Statutory Maternity Pay and Maternity Allowance on the Government website. You can compare how the information is presented through smart answers and then in the guide. Make a list of the benefits to users of each approach.
4. Then think of a legal question; for example, who is a worker? Map out (using sticky notes) a series of questions to allow someone to arrive at the answer to the question.
5. You might want to show what you have done to a friend to see if they understand the questions you are asking.

Distilling complex legal information is not easy. Designing digital tools requires you to work hard to simplify the law to help a non-lawyer

39 Channing Ritter, 'Reach More Users: 4 Tips for Designing Accessible Apps and Websites' (2018) <https://www.thinkwithgoogle.com/marketing-strategies/app-and-mobile/website-app-accessibility-guidelines/> accessed 28 April 2021.

understand how it applies to them. Developing digital tools requires creative and innovative solutions to help people understand their legal rights and responsibilities. It requires imagination to think how technology can be used to develop new solutions, meaning you need to be creative and innovative to design digital tools. These are essential skills for a digital lawyer and highly valued by law firms. If you move into legal practice and have the opportunity to work with developers to create more complex legaltech tools, your experiences of designing even a very simple tool will help you think about the opportunities and risks that should be addressed when designing technological solutions.

SKILLS FOR THE FUTURE LAWYER

In 2011 the Institute for the Future identified skills[40] that will be required by all future workers, and the Law Society endorsed them in their report Horizon Scanning: Future Skills for Law.[41] These skills include:

- Novel and adaptive thinking
- Virtual collaboration
- Design mindset
- New media literacy.

The Law Society also suggest that in addition to those skills, future lawyers require three further attributes:

1 Agility and adaptability
2 Curiosity and imagination
3 Initiative and entrepreneurship.[42]

These are skills that may become even more significant in the future and are likely to feature in the recruitment of legal professionals.

40 Institute for the Future (IFF), 'Future Work Skills 2020' (University of Phoenix Research Institute, 2011). We have included the ones that relate to technology to find out more: visit <https://www.iftf.org/futureworkskills>

41 The Law Society, 'Horizon Scanning: Future Skills for Law' (2018) <https://www.lawsociety.org.uk/support-services/research-trends/horizon-scanning/future-skills-for-law/>

42 Supra n. 41, p. 10. The Law Society identify initiative, proactivity, agility and adaptability, enterprise, communication, connectivity and collaboration, curiosity, resilience and lifelong working as the attributes of the future law graduate.

IMAGINATIVE LAWYERS

The Law Society argues that legal practice now requires lawyers to be able to work in teams with both an understanding of technology and creativity. Designing digital tools provides an opportunity to experiment and to come up with imaginative solutions that use technology to disrupt how things have traditionally been done. Looking into the future, blockchain, AI and machine learning will impact on legal design and legal technological solutions. We face complex challenges, and there are benefits and risks of using technology to address legal issues. Having the opportunity to engage with digital tools and understand the process of legal design allows you to explore your creative side and offers insights into the relationship between law and technology.

Historically, successful lawyers required deep knowledge of the law and legal skills such as drafting, communication and advocacy. This is changing, however: Legal knowledge and legal skills are still required, but non-legal skills such as teamwork, collaboration, creativity and an understanding of technology are now highly prized. In 2014, R. Amani Smathers introduced the idea of a T-shaped lawyer.[43] The top of the T represented the multidisciplinary skills lawyers required as a result of the impact of technology, and the changing market for legal services. The model was then developed further by Natalie Runyon, Alyson Carrel and Shellie Reid, who created the Delta Model. You will find out more about these models and the changing nature of skills in Chapter 11. What these models highlight is how the profession is changing, and that lawyers now require a much broader skill set. If you are prepared to develop these skills, then you will be in a good position as you start your career.

HOW TO KICK-START CREATIVITY

Sync 6: The daily drawing

You should allow around 1 minute for this activity.

Ozenc and Hagan[44] suggest that you can use daily rituals to encourage a creative mindset. One exercise they suggest is a daily drawing task. You

43 <https://www.americanbar.org/publications/law_practice_magazine/2014/july-august/the-21st-century-t-shaped-lawyer/>

44 K. Ozenc and M. Hagan, *Rituals for Work* (John Wiley & Sons, 2019).

spend one minute doodling anything, but it must be a drawing and must take exactly one minute! It doesn't have to be good: There is no requirement for you to be Picasso or Banksy! They suggest that you should do this activity at the start of each day, as it helps to encourage creativity.

Try it for a week and see if you feel a little more creative.

The previous section discussed the skills that lawyers will require to practice in a changing legal market, and we have focused on the importance of innovation, imagination and creativity. Lawyers in the future will need to take ideas and methods from other fields and apply them in a legal context. It is important to remember that creativity is a mindset: It is a way of thinking about new solutions to existing problems. It is about being open to ideas and challenging yourself to be curious.

LEGAL GAMES

One of the ways to make the law more accessible and engaging is through the creation of legal games. Legal games offer an innovative and creative solution to educating people on their legal rights and responsibilities.

Sync 7: Let's play a game

You should allow around 15 minutes for this activity.

1 Go to <https://lawdojo.co/> and select one of the games to play.

2 Rate the game from 1 to 10 on how useful you think the legal game is to educate people on their legal rights and responsibilities.

You might want to engage your imagination and creativity to devise your own legal game. The earlier example of Joshua Browder illustrates how a pre-existing problem can be tackled in an innovative way using technology.

Where do we go from here?

This chapter has explored how technology is impacting on the delivery of legal services. Currently there are no fully enabled technology solutions that support non-lawyers in addressing legal issues, but we are seeing pockets of innovation that are making a difference. We have seen from examples such as DoNotPay how members of the public can use technology to navigate legal systems to resolve their legal problems. DoNotPay is expanding and developing new bots to provide greater assistance to users. It is likely that we will see more of these types of tools being developed over the next ten years. There has been recognition that technology can be leveraged to assist non-lawyers, but as this chapter has identified, there are challenges in designing legal services for non-lawyers. There are barriers to overcome, and there are valid concerns around the reliability and trustworthiness of online sites and the implications for the regulation of these services.

Technology alone will not solve access to justice or facilitate the delivery of legal services without lawyers. In fact it is legal design, not technology, that is critical. Legal design focuses on the needs of users and empowers people to understand and resolve their legal problem. Developers must think carefully about the importance of legal design and accessibility. We must also be aware of the digital divide and think carefully how we develop solutions that do not further exclude the most vulnerable parts of our society. It is important to understand the potential of legaltech but also to be aware of how we ensure trust and confidence in the tools that are designed. Throughout this textbook you also need to consider the broader relationship between law and technology. The future digital lawyer needs to be creative, open to new ideas and able to recognise the potential of and challenges of technology.

Conclusion

This chapter has considered the delivery of legal services without the use of lawyers. It has examined this issue through an exploration of how we can improve access to justice using digital technologies. You have been encouraged to think about how technology can be used to support individuals to resolve disputes without the need for lawyers. The chapter has considered ways in which technology is developing to provide innovative solutions to support non-lawyers resolve their legal problems. The problems associated with digital exclusion have been discussed, and also how the lack of digital skills impacts on the way in which technology can transform access to justice.

ADDITIONAL RESOURCES

If you want to improve your digital skills, there are lots of free courses available. You may want to visit <https://makeitclick.learnmyway.com/directory/search>

Law by Design (Margaret Hagan) <https://www.lawbydesign.co>

The Legal Design Lab (Stanford University) <https://law.stanford.edu/organizations/pages/legal-design-lab/>

The Legal Design Alliance <https://www.legaldesignalliance.org>

Haben Girma—Designing Technology with Accessibility in Mind: <https://www.youtube.com/watch?v=44VEwsBfux0>

A2J Access to Justice Author system <https://www.a2jauthor.org>

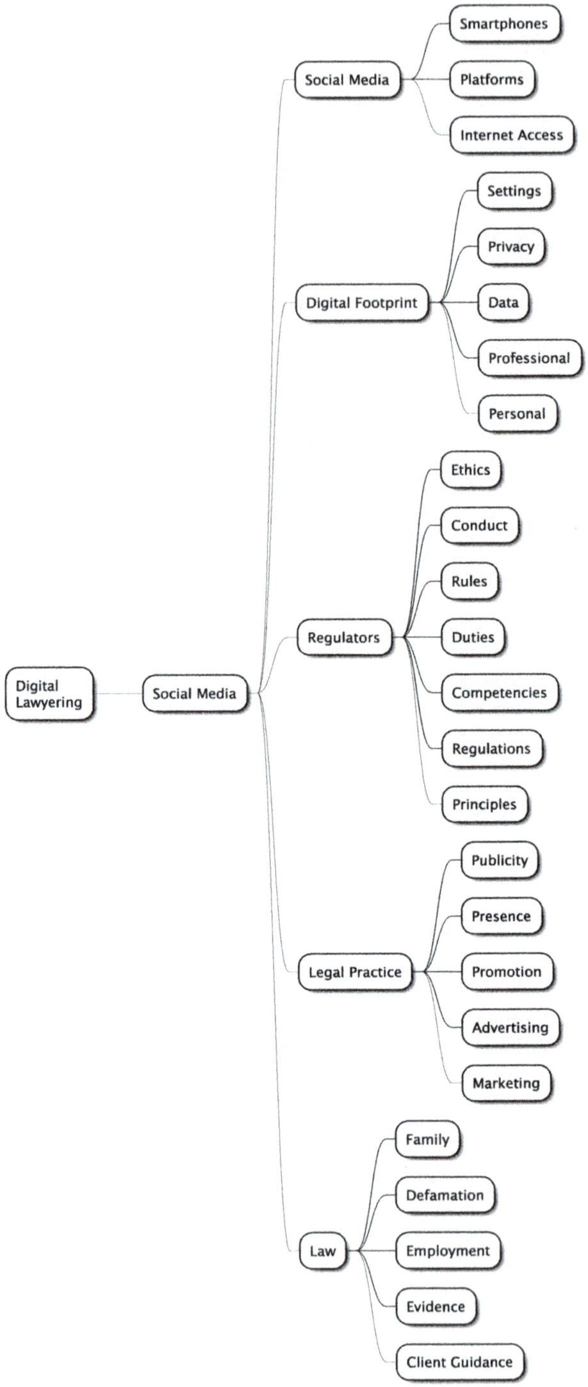

Mind Map 5.1 Chapter topics

5 THE USE AND PRACTICE OF SOCIAL MEDIA

Francine Ryan

INTRODUCTION

This chapter will apply the principles of digital lawyering within the practical context of social media. It will begin by asking you to reflect upon your own existing digital footprint and think about the implications of your online presence for you. It moves on to consider the wider use of social media within law and the legal profession. The chapter explores some of the relevant professional conduct rules and considers some examples where lawyers have been in breach of those rules. It refers to the topic of privacy and confidentiality, which is also discussed in Chapter 6, in the context of the marketing and promotion of legal practices. It then allows you to consider how changes in law and practice associated with technology have become an essential element of a lawyer's role and to think about the skills you need to be a digital lawyer. Following on from this, there are several case studies on the ethical implications of using online social networking both as individual practitioners and within digital lawyering practices. It is important for future lawyers to understand the risks and benefits of social media use.

Chapter hot spots

When reading this chapter, questions to think about include:

- What does my digital footprint say about me?
- How can I manage my social media channels to ensure I have a positive online presence?
- What are the professional rules on the use of social media?

DOI: 10.4324/9780429298219-5

- How is social media impacting on the practice of law?
- What are the ethical implications of using online social networking both as individual practitioners and within digital lawyering practices?

Having read the title and introduction, you can add any other questions you want to explore here:

WHAT IS SOCIAL MEDIA?

Social media refers to the collective term for online communication channels that facilitate the interaction and sharing of information. Social media is defined broadly. It comprises a variety of different communication tools, with social media channels sharing some common features including profile pages, newsfeeds, friends, followers, like buttons, notifications and rating features. Social media allows users to connect and share information. There is no legal definition of social media, but the first time it was referred to in an English court was in 2011 by the Lord Chief Justice dealing with the case involving Facebook and the riots that took place in London.[1] Although it may appear that social networking platforms have been around forever, Facebook only launched in 2004. Mobile technology has fundamentally changed social networking, and the capabilities of the smartphone have facilitated the experiential growth of social media platforms. There are 5.22 billion people in the world who use a mobile phone.[2] The COVID-19 pandemic saw an increased use in social media platforms. The amount of interaction with different social media platforms shapes our online presence, and people are becoming increasingly aware of how much data they share.

1 *R v Blackshaw and others* [2011] EWCA Crim 2312.

2 Simon Kemp, Digital 2021: 'Global Overview Report' (*Datareportal*, 27 January 2021) <https://datareportal.com/reports/digital-2021-global-overview-report> accessed 14 April 2021.

Sync 1: Social media platforms

You should allow around 5 minutes for this activity.

1 Make a list of all the social media sites you are familiar with.

2 Circle the ones you use regularly.

In 2020 in the UK, 96% of households had access to the Internet; 89% of adults used the Internet daily, and 100% of 16- to 24-year-olds used it daily or nearly every day.[3] Internet penetration has allowed social networking sites to create online communities connecting all aspects of our lives and offering new opportunities in both the personal and professional space. There are a variety of different types of social media platforms such as Instagram, Pinterest, TikTok and VKontakte. We have categorised some of the current social media platforms in Figure 5.1.

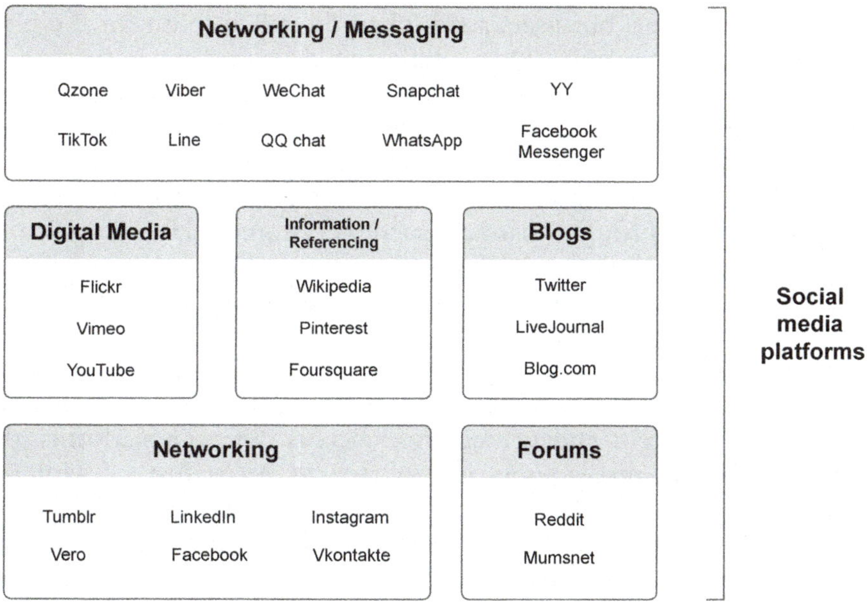

Figure 5.1 Social media platforms

3 Office for National Statistics, 'Internet Access, Households and Individuals, Great Britain: 2020' (*ONS.Gov*, 7 August 2020) <https://www.ons.gov.uk/peoplepopulationandcommunity/householdcharacteristics/homeinternetandsocialmediausage/bulletins/internetaccesshouseholdsandindividuals/2020> accessed 14 April 2021.

The increasing popularity of social media means that new platforms launch regularly, and you may be aware of other sites which are not listed here. It is worth exploring the popularity of different platforms by examining the statistics for certain demographics, locations and markets.

The rise of mobile technology has increased the popularity of social networking. The Datareportal Global Overview report states that there are now 4.20 billion social media users in the world; in the past year that figure has increased by 490 million.[4] This number equates to 53% of the world's population. Typical social media users spend around 2 hours and 25 minutes per day on social media. There are differences around the world in the frequency of social media use, with the most active users in the Philippines and the least activity users in Japan.[5]

In terms of the most used social media platform, Facebook remained the most popular in the last year, followed by YouTube and WhatsApp. It is reported that typical users have eight different social media channels and use different platforms for different reasons. When you look at the social media data, there are some interesting age-related trends. The number of over 65s using Facebook increased by around 25% in the last year, but users aged 25 to 34 still account for the platform's largest age group.[6] One interesting development is the rise in growth of TikTok, particularly as there are concerns over how it collects and uses data.[7] Facebook also owns three other social media platforms: WhatsApp, Facebook Messenger and Instagram.

Organisations are also using social media tools to engage with their employees through channels such as Yammer, Huddle, Chatter and Facebook's Workplace. These platforms facilitate the formation of groups, offer useful ways for communications and promote engagement within the workplace.

Social media platforms have had a significant impact on our lives, allowing people to connect across borders. Although we will continue to see different engagement rates across different platforms, the number of social media users is expected to grow further with the increased availability of mobile devices. Although social media has brought many benefits, there are concerns around some of the harmful aspects of increased use of social media. There are growing calls for

4 Supra n. 2.
5 Supra n. 2.
6 Supra n. 2.
7 BBC News, 'TikTok Sued for Billions Over Use of Children's Data' (21 April 2021) <https://www.bbc.com/news/technology-56815480> accessed 29 April 2021.

governments to regulate social media platforms to address some of the issues around the policies for the collection and use of personal data. Users are starting to recognise how powerful their data is, and younger people are now much more aware of the need to protect their personal information and security.

Digital footprint

A data trail is formed from our interactions with the Internet and social networking sites, creating a body of data that represents our online presence. It comprises a range of actions such as identifying visited websites, Facebook posts, emails sent, or photographs uploaded. There are two types of digital footprints: Active and passive. A passive digital footprint occurs when data is collected from the user without their knowledge. An active digital footprint happens when the user chooses to share information via the Internet and social media sites.

Sync 2: Digital footprint

You should allow around 15 minutes for this activity.

'Google' yourself. Search using Google.co.uk or Google.com. Start with just your name and then your name and where you went to school or university. Then choose another search engine and make the same searches. Did you get different results? What did you find out about yourself? Were there any surprises?

A person's digital footprint is not just what they have posted online, but also what others have published about them, which might include information shared with or without their knowledge. It might be important to curate a separate public and private online presence and actively manage how that presence is shaped.

Privacy and data

Technology governs so many aspects of our lives and we no longer remain in control of how our data is used, distributed and stored. A tension exists between our increasing reliance on technology and retaining control of our data self. Several incidents have happened involving large breaches of data, causing individuals to be hacked or exploited. When thinking about data privacy and protection, it is important to recognise our vulnerability. Social media platforms are a permanent and public reminder of everything we do. Even if you can remove a post, it could still be screenshotted and reshared. It is quite an involved process if you want to delete a social media account. If you are using social media sites, you should review the privacy settings so you understand how they work. We all have a personal responsibility to manage the privacy settings of the platforms we use.

Sync 3: Whose data is it?

You should allow around 10 minutes for this activity.

Go to YouTube and watch "Who owns your data? (Hint it's not you)" <https://www.youtube.com/watch?v=y1txYjoSQQc> Then reflect on the implications for you in your professional life from the data trail you have created.

Juan Enriquez suggests we should think of our online life as a digital tattoo.[8] Therefore, an awareness of how we use social media platforms and the creation of our digital footprint is important. Our online presence represents our personal brand: It says a lot about who we are, and our values. A brand is a very powerful asset, so it's important to protect it. In 2013, the youth and crime commissioner, Paris Brown, resigned because of tweets that she had sent between the ages of 14 to 16.[9]

Social media spaces are used for different purposes, and the audience and the message will not be the same for Facebook and LinkedIn. However, we cannot ignore the unintended audience—someone who likes, shares, retweets or finds us online. Therefore, regardless of what site we are using, we must be confident the posts, pictures and comments reflect who we are.

8 Juan Enriquez, 'Your Online Life, Permanent as a Tattoo' (*Ted2013*, February 2013) <https://www.ted.com/talks/juan_enriquez_how_to_think_about_digital_tattoos#t-338590> accessed 3 February 2021.

9 BBC, 'Paris Brown: Kent Youth PCC Resigns after Twitter Row' (*BBC News*, 9 April 2013) <https://www.bbc.co.uk/news/uk-england-22083032> accessed 14 April 2021.

Think about these two examples and reflect on the implications of them from a personal and professional viewpoint.

Instagram or Facebook

Posting pictures of you on holiday are looking a little worse for wear. Would you be happy and/or would it be acceptable for your employer to see your photographs and your posts?

LinkedIn "specialties" and "skills"

Exaggerating your skills and experiences on your LinkedIn profile, or getting your friends to endorse you for a skill that you do not have. Is LinkedIn an equivalent of an online CV? Do you need to ensure that what you write about yourself is not misleading or untrue?

USING SOCIAL MEDIA IN A PERSONAL CAPACITY

It is now commonplace for recruitment companies and prospective employers to check candidates' social media profiles. You might have an impressive curriculum vitae or résumé, but if your Twitter feed contains comments that don't meet with an employer's values, you may find yourself struggling to find a position. Having a positive profile may improve your prospects of being offered an interview or getting a job. Having a profile that does not reflect the image you want to portray may have a negative impact on your prospects. Understanding how privacy settings work is important to ensure you protect your online appearance. Turning on your privacy settings to make your profile entirely private may appear an attractive option. However, if your social media site portrays a positive image, allowing some restricted access may be beneficial. It is important to prioritise active management of your social media platforms and check your digital footprint regularly to ensure that you control how you appear in your online life. A key skill is knowing how to curate and manage an effective online presence so that you achieve the most from how you present yourself online. The boundaries between professional and personal are blurring, so it is essential you consider your online presence from both perspectives.

USING SOCIAL MEDIA IN A PROFESSIONAL CAPACITY

In England and Wales, solicitors are regulated by the Solicitors Regulation Authority[10] and barristers by the Bar Standards Board.[11] It is important you familiarise yourself with the relevant professional regulations that apply in your jurisdiction. The Australian Solicitors' conduct rules include similar duties to those that govern solicitors in England and Wales.[12] Lawyers have special responsibilities to ensure that they do not act in a way that damages the reputation of the profession and are held to be very high standards of honesty and integrity. The Bar Standards Board Handbook has published guidance for barristers on how they should conduct themselves when using social media and some of the issues that can arise.[13] The Solicitors Regulation Authority have set out the requirements for how solicitors must act when using social media.[14]

The boundaries between our private and professional lives are increasingly blurring, especially in our use of social media platforms. Therefore it is important to be aware that, when lawyers interact with social media networks, professional conduct rules apply. This means that any inappropriate social media posts, regardless of whether they are in a personal or professional capacity, are subject to professional conduct rules. The profession expects high standards of behaviour from its lawyers, and inappropriate conduct may result in disciplinary action from the relevant professional body. The rules apply to posting material online, sharing content, networking and liking or commenting on posts. This applies in both a personal and professional capacity, as something posted on a social media site in a personal capacity may still be considered to diminish the trust and confidence of the public and

10 <https://www.sra.org.uk>

11 <https://www.barstandardsboard.org.uk>

12 <https://www.lawcouncil.asn.au/policy-agenda/regulation-of-the-profession-and-ethics/australian-solicitors-conduct-rules>

13 The Bar Standards Board Handbook, 'Social Media Guidance' (2019) <https://www.barstandardsboard.org.uk/resources/resource-library/social-media-pdf.html> accessed 29 April 2021.

14 Solicitors Regulation Authority, 'Use of Social Media and Offensive Communications' (25 November 2019) <https://www.sra.org.uk/sra/corporate-strategy/sra-enforcement-strategy/enforcement-practice/social-media-offensive-communications/> accessed 29 April 2021.

would be subject to the rules. The rules remind of us of the need to be careful when we are posting in both public and in private and to think through the implications of our actions.

BREACHING PROFESSIONAL CONDUCT RULES

The following case studies illustrate breaches of the professional conduct rules, all of which relate to different aspects of social media.

Case study 1[15]

Social media posts

A solicitor working as a sole practitioner was rebuked, fined £1500 and ordered to pay £600 in costs for a series of social media posts where he had posted inappropriate comments or emoji icons following visits to the police station, prison or court, including:

- "From Attempted Murder at Smethwick", followed by two emoji icons to show crying with laughter.
- "DV (Domestic violence) . . . Christmas Coming Up. . . . What you Expect".
- "Drugs". When another person responded "What kind? Lol x" He responded "Not From the Pharmacy That's For Sure pms", with emoji icons to showing crying with laughter.
- "Sexual Assault", with two emoji icons showing a sad face and a tear.
- In two social media posts he disclosed specific confidential information about a client matter.

The SRA found he was in breach of Principle 6 of the SRA Principles 2011 and failed to achieve Outcome 4.1 of the SRA Code of Conduct 2011. (The SRA Code has been updated since this decision).

15 You can read the full decision in this case: Solicitors Regulation Authority, 'Decision: Harmal Singh Paul' (*SRA.org*, 13 August 2009) <https://www.sra.org.uk/consumers/solicitor-check/339008/> accessed 14 April 2021.

Case study 2[16]

LinkedIn

A barrister was suspended from practice in relation to three charges. It involved him broadcasting serious allegations made by a third-party (A) against a barrister (M) in the robing room of a Crown Court. The third charge involved the barrister contacting M's partner (L) via a professional networking site and making references to issues relating to M. M invited L to connect with him via LinkedIn (there had been no previous contact between the two prior to this) and then sent a message to L when L started work at a new firm of solicitors:

> M: "Congratulations. Glad to see you are doing well considering everything".
> L replied, asking the barrister to explain what he meant.
> M's response was "Oops, I have heard your husband has a personal difficulty. I hope I am in error".
> L replied: "I don't know what you mean".

The BSB found he was in breach of: Core Duty 3 and 5 of the Bar Standards Handbook.

Case study 3[17]

Blogging

The complaint involved a lawyer in the US state of Illinois who published a blog relating to her legal work. The blog contained confidential information about her cases and derogatory comments about judges. In her blog, the lawyer had attempted to protect client confidentiality by anonymising the clients, but from the facts provided it was possible using public records to identify the clients and judges the lawyer was referring to.

The lawyer received a 60-day suspension from the two state bars she was admitted to.

16 *Forz Khan v Bar Standards Board* [2018] EWHC 2184 (Admin).
17 *Office of Lawyer Regulation Complainant v Kristine A Peshek* [2011] WI 47 <https://www.wicourts.gov/sc/opinion/DisplayDocument.pdf?content=pdf&seqNo=66464>

Case study 4[18]

A solicitor was fined for a series of tweets made over an 18-month period. The Solicitors Disciplinary Tribunal (SDT) fined him £2500 because "he used his Twitter account which publicly identified him as a solicitor to publicly post offensive and profane communications". The solicitor had been subject to a series of offensive tweets, but the fact he had responded meant that "he had not behaved in a way that maintained the trust that the public placed in him and in the provision of legal services".

Are you surprised by the conduct and behaviour of the lawyers? These cases demonstrate the risks lawyers face when using social media. There can be significant consequences for a lawyer's career if their social media activity breaches professional regulations. The lawyers all received immediate sanctions from their professional bodies, but there are also implications for their future practice of law. The examples highlight the need to think before you act when using social media platforms, otherwise there are risks of breaching professional standards.

Digital lawyering skills: understanding ethics and values

The preceding case studies demonstrate the importance of ethical issues when using social media as a legal professional. However, this is broader than simply complying with a particular code of conduct. Ethics is also about acting in a manner which accords with your own personal values and beliefs. As a digital lawyer, you may need to navigate complex ethical issues which are not covered in codes of conduct but which will impact on your actions (and potentially have consequences for other people). For example, to what extent would it be appropriate to explain a legal rule around divorce to people seeking help via a wholly anonymous online forum on parenting? How should you deal with a request to connect on social media from your colleague or line manager?

Of course, as a student you are already developing ideas around ethics and values. For example, most students choose not to use so-called essay

18 Neil Rose, 'Lewis Case: "Wishing Death on Neo-Nazis" Went Too Far' (*Legal Futures*, 17 December 2018) <https://www.legalfutures.co.uk/latest-news/lewis-case-wishing-death-on-neo-nazis-went-too-far> accessed 29 April 2021.

mills (websites selling essays to students) because they feel it would be an unethical way in which to approach their assignments. As you work through topics within your studies, you may also find yourself formulating opinions upon ethically controversial subjects which are informed by your personal ethical perspective and values.

For aspiring digital lawyers, it is important to have an awareness of your ethics and values, how these inform your actions and how these may apply when you move into the legal workplace. Sometimes this can involve questioning any assumptions or unconscious bias that lies behind them. Sometimes it can involve working out your boundaries and how you will apply them. This is a challenging and ongoing process but one that will inform your professional development going forward.

SOCIAL MEDIA TIPS

Even though social media has been a feature of our lives for a long period of time, the preceding examples illustrate the risks of a lack of self-awareness and the implications for lawyers if they make mistakes. The consequences of making inappropriate posts could end or significantly impact on your career. It is easy to think we are immune from doing something stupid, but the spontaneity and reach of social media does pose a risk. Saying something inappropriate in a tweet or posting something late at night to a few friends can be shared and read by many other people and have far-reaching consequences.

Here are some tips that you might find helpful to reflect on when managing your online presence:

1. Think before you post! Social media platforms can be a permanent and public reminder of everything we do.
2. Understand and check your privacy settings. Decide on how much access you want to give and carefully monitor who has access. Check your privacy settings on a regular basis because the terms and conditions are continually updated.
3. Social media changes all the time, so it is critical to keep up to date with the development of the platforms and optimise your use of the tools.
4. Keep your personal and professional online lives separate. If you integrate your Twitter, Facebook or LinkedIn accounts with other apps, this will allow other apps to see your connections. If, for

example, you have connected with a client on LinkedIn through an application that integrates different accounts, you may have revealed that connection without the client's permission.

5 Never comment or discuss clients, cases, other lawyers, law firms, chambers or judges on social media.
6 Never send confidential information via social media.
7 Think very carefully about whether to discuss politics or religion on social media if you want to engage in debate. This article has some useful tips on how to argue more effectively on social media <https://www.theguardian.com/media/2017/jan/28/how-to-stop-arguing-and-actually-change-someones-mind-on-social-media?CMP=oth_b-aplnews_d-1>
8 It is important to consider not just what you post but also the tone of your post. You might post something that you think is reasonable but other people might not consider to be in good taste. Always think carefully about whether your regulatory body would consider your comments to undermine the profession in any way.
9 Do not use location services when you meet clients, attend chambers or court hearings because your location could risk unintentionally revealing that you are acting for a client.
10 Think about who you follow on social media, what you share and what you like because all those activities are associated with approving of the person, organisation and content.
11 Employers are concerned about the reputational risks from social media. Make sure you read and abide by your workplace social media policy and ensure your online behaviour is in line with the requirements of the organisation.

Lawyers are required to understand how social media platforms operate to be able to identify potential issues that may arise for themselves and their clients. Having an awareness and an understanding of social media platforms can prevent you making any mistakes when using social media. Understanding your ethical obligations and the professional conduct rules that apply will ensure that you engage with social media appropriately and maximise the opportunities social media provides to develop both your personal and professional profile.

The first part of this chapter has considered individual use of social media. It will now explore how social media can be used in the context of the marketing and promotion of legal practices.

MARKETING AND PROMOTION OF LEGAL PRACTICES

Chapter 2 introduces the ways in which social media has changed the way law firms communicate with their clients and potential clients. An online presence offers law firms the opportunity to market their practice, raise their profile and create awareness of the law firm. A social media strategy provides a way for a law firm to build and curate its brand. Through different social media channels it can manage its reputation, demonstrate its values, recruit new staff and develop and maintain client relationships. Although content must be developed to be placed on different platforms, it is an efficient way of marketing a law firm that has a wide reach. Law firms now make use of websites like YouTube to create their own channels and post video content. YouTube offers a powerful medium to develop a visual relationship with clients. In the United States, the American Bar Association's 2018 report stated that LinkedIn was the most popular social media platform for lawyers.[19] A company profile can be created on LinkedIn which then offers a platform for law firms to discuss legal issues and promote the firm.

A firm's social media presence and messaging needs to be actively managed in terms of content and frequency. Social media accounts need to be active to attract and maintain followers, they must have a wide range of legal and professional content that will interest readers and they need to engage with influencers by retweeting and tagging them in other posts. A law firm can only use social media effectively if it forms part of its overall communication strategy that includes marketing, and business development. FTI Consulting report that the top 30 law firms have one million followers across Twitter and LinkedIn.[20] Social media platforms offer opportunities for law firms to showcase their work, add a voice to a high-profile topic or debate and help them win new clients.

19 Trevor Molag, 'The Complete Guide to Social Media for Lawyers' (*Clio.com*, 23 February 2021) <https://www.clio.com/resources/digital-marketing-lawyers/social-media-lawyers/> accessed 12 April 2021.

20 Kathryn Bowditch and Andrew Williams, 'The Verdict: Social Media in the Legal Sector' (*FTI Consulting*, 2016) <https://www.fticonsulting-emea.com/~/media/Files/emea--files/insights/reports/legal-sector-social-media.pdf> accessed 14 April 2021.

ADVERTISING AND PUBLICITY

Social media is categorised as a form of publicity, and therefore both the individual lawyer and the law firm in England and Wales must adhere to the SRA Code of Conduct. There are similar rules across other jurisdictions.

Social media content must be accurate and not misleading in accordance with outcome 8.8 of the SRA Code of Conduct.[21]

A law firm must ensure that it keeps clients' affairs confidential. This means it must avoid developing content such as case studies which potentially risk breaching client confidentiality. Outcome 6.6 of the SRA Code of Conduct sets out the duties on confidentiality and disclosure.[22]

A law firm should ensure it has systems and controls in place to manage its online presence and its social media engagement. Outcome 2.1 of the SRA Code of Conduct sets out responsibilities for compliance that law firms must have in place.[23] These duties include having the appropriate governance processes in place.

Law firms also need to be aware of the risk of creating lawyer-client relationships through their use of social media. For example, if a law firm answers a legal question via a social media platform, it could be inadvertently creating a retainer by implication. The SRA recommends that law firms avoid any discussion on a potential matter with a client via a social media channel and ensure this is done at the first meeting.

SOCIAL MEDIA IN LAW FIRMS

In 2014, the Law Society of England and Wales asked for information from law firms about their use of social media.[24] Data was gathered around:

- The social media platforms used.
- The perceived risks and benefits of social media.
- Who within the firm was responsible for social media.
- The social media policies or procedures that were in place.

21 <https://www.sra.org.uk/solicitors/standards-regulations/code-conduct-solicitors/>
22 <https://www.sra.org.uk/solicitors/standards-regulations/code-conduct-solicitors/>
23 <https://www.sra.org.uk/solicitors/standards-regulations/code-conduct-firms/>
24 The Law Society, 'Social Media: Practice Note' (*lawsociety.org.uk*, 5 December 2019) <https://www.lawsociety.org.uk/topics/business-management/social-media> accessed 14 April 2021.

Although law firms used social media platforms as part of their communication strategy and were positive about the benefits of doing so, one area of concern noted was the issue of clients or third parties using social media to raise grievances or comment negatively on the firm or individual solicitors. But, most law firms recognise the importance and value of having a strong social media presence and will have a strategy in place for optimising their use of social media.

Sync 4: Researching social media presence

You should allow 30 minutes for this activity.

Go to the websites of Clifford Chance <http://www.cliffordchance.com/home.html> and Tuckers Solicitors <http://www.tuckerssolicitors.com>

1 Identify how many and which social media platforms each firm uses.

2 Choose one of the platforms and review the content. You might want to consider who is the target audience; what is the engagement rate; how many comments, likes and followers the firm has; and how you would rate the social media presence of the firm.

3 What similarities and differences did you identify in relation to their social media presence?

If you are in a different jurisdiction, you may want to choose other law firms to review.

When a law firm is reviewing its social media strategy, there are a number of factors it might consider to ensure it is building an effective presence:

- Who is the target audience?
- Which social media platforms are currently being used, and which ones should be considered?
- What content should be created and shared?
- What are the goals of the strategy and how will they be measured?
- What policies are in place to respond to negative comments?

Firms are now investing significantly in digital marketing because they recognise the importance of developing their brand and it is an essential part of their business strategy. You may be asked to comment on a law firm's social media presence at an interview; therefore it is essential that you understand how social media is being used within the profession.

DIGITAL LAWYERING AND SOCIAL MEDIA

Lawyers need to understand how social media platforms work and how information is shared to be able to effectively practice in the digital age. In the United States, the American Bar Association (ABA) has updated their professional conduct rules to require a new duty of competence regarding technology. ABA Rule 1.1 Competence, comment 8 states that a "lawyer should keep abreast of changes in the law and its practice, including the benefits and risks associated with relevant technology".[25] At the time of writing, 39 US states have adopted the duty of technology competence.[26] The rule has been discussed in case law:

Womack v. Yeoman, 2011 WL 9330606 (Cir. Ct. Va. 2011).

A case in Virginia discusses the danger for lawyers of not being conversant in technology.

James v. Natl. Fin. LLC, No. 8931-VCL 2014 WL 6845560 (Del. Ch., Dec. 5, 2014)

Counsel: "I have to confess to this Court, I am not computer literate. I have not found presence in the cybernetic revolution. I need a secretary to help me turn on the computer. This was out of my bailiwick".

The Delaware court stated: "Professed technological incompetence is not an excuse for discovery misconduct".

25 American Bar Association, 'Model Rules of Professional Conduct, Rule 1.1. Competence' <https://www.americanbar.org/groups/professional_responsibility/publications/model_rules_of_professional_conduct/rule_1_1_competence/comment_on_rule_1_1/>

26 Robert J. Ambrogi, '39 States Have Adopted the Duty of Technology Competence' (*Law Sites*) <https://www.lawsitesblog.com/tech-competence> accessed 29 April 2021.

Lawyers are required to effectively represent their clients, and to do that they must understand social networking sites and be aware of the changes in law and practice associated with technology. Technology impacts on every aspect of legal practice, and being proficient in technology does not just extend to an area of practice, but also to how law firms develop their services. Ethics opinions from the US states of New York, Pennsylvania, North Carolina, Florida and West Virginia and from the District of Columbia have said that to properly advise clients, lawyers must understand social media. Technology competence is not a requirement for all lawyers.

Earlier parts of the chapter have already identified some of the potential pitfalls of social media, but lawyers also require an awareness of ethical issues that may occur when dealing with social media, including:

- Unethical information gathering.
- Failing to assert client control.
- Evidence preservation and spoliation.

UNETHICAL INFORMATION GATHERING

Lawyers need to advise clients on their use of social media prior to, during and after legal proceedings. In a social media world, it is important to advise clients not to discuss their case on social media and the requirements to preserve evidence.

Case example: family law

Using evidence from social networking sites in a family law case is becoming increasingly common. Social media posts can provide evidence of a new job, an affair or the purchase of new items such as a car.

What might you advise your client?

- What social media evidence to gather.
- How to gather social media evidence to ensure they are not contravening the law.
- How social media can be used in their case.
- What social media evidence is likely to be admissible.
- How to address negative social media evidence in their case.

What practical matters might you advise your client on?

- To deactivate their social media accounts, but that they are not allowed to delete posts in anticipation of proceedings.
- Reset their profile settings so that mutual friends cannot share posts with their spouse.
- Public posts can be used as evidence, but they can't hack into another account and use those posts as evidence.

A study from Australia showed that social media evidence was adduced in 136 first-instance decisions in family law cases between 2009 and 2014.[27] The examples included evidence of the financial circumstances of the parties, the suitability of one party's ability to be an effective parent and evidence supporting or denying another relationship. The study found that in 36% of cases the social media evidence was weighted heavily in the proceedings and Facebook private messages had probative value. The study shows the importance of the lawyer knowing about their client's social media activity. The fact that so many people are active users of social media means that what a client uploads or posts can have an impact on their case.

FAILING TO ASSERT CLIENT CONTROL

The rapper 50 Cent

The rapper 50 Cent was ordered by a bankruptcy court judge to explain why he was posting photos on Instagram during the bankruptcy proceedings—pictures of him surrounded by money. One post spelt out "I'm Broke" in piles of hundred dollar bills.

Advising a client on how they engage with social media also applies after the case has concluded.

27 Victoria Blakeley, Patricia Easteal, Emma Fitch and Jessica Kennedy, 'Social Media Evidence in Family Law: What Can Be Used and Its Probative Value' (2015) 5 *Family Law Review* 81–101.

Gulliver Schools, Inc. v. Snay (Fla. Dist. Ct. App. 2014)

The daughter of the winning plaintiff posted on Facebook:

> Mama and Papa Snay won the case against Gulliver. Gulliver is now officially paying for my vacation to Europe this summer. SUCK IT.

The Facebook post breached the confidential agreement and the settlement was successfully appealed.

The cases of Snay and 50 Cent demonstrate why it is important that lawyers understand social media and manage their clients' usage.

Social media is being used in many different types of cases. The following examples show how social media can be used to challenge the credibility of a claimant in a personal injury case.

Saunderson and Others v Sonae Industria (UK) Ltd [2015] EWHC QB

One of the claimant's was cross-examined over a Twitter conversation which could have suggested that his claims may be fraudulent.

Cirencester Friendly Society v Parkin [2015] EWHC 1750 QB

Judge Seymour said:

> Nemesis overtook from Mr Parkin most dramatically because like so many people nowadays, in particular those who seem minded to perpetrate frauds, he seemed incapable of keeping off the Internet and sharing the true nature of his activities through social media.

Mr. Parkin made a serious of representations to say he was incapacitated from working. There was a video on YouTube showing him refurbishing and racing a sports car.

EVIDENCE PRESERVATION AND SPOLIATION

A lawyer has a responsibility to advise their client about the implications of their social media activity. This includes advising a client on the consequences of altering or destroying social media posts, pages or messages, known as spoliation. The advice needs to be clear and unambiguous because there are serious consequences for both lawyers and clients if social media evidence is compromised. Lawyers may use social media to gather evidence, but they also are required to have effective protocols in place to ensure the preservation of evidence. The increase in digital evidence is having significant consequences in criminal trials. In 2018 the *Guardian* reported comments from Alison Saunders, formerly the Head of the Crown Prosecution Service (CPS), following a review of 3,637 rape and sexual offences cases:

> Social media presented huge challenges, Saunders said, and the CPS had been too slow to respond. It was a challenge dealing with pages and pages of social media downloads.[28]

The review found that 47 cases were discontinued due to a failure to disclose digital evidence. One of the issues was the volume of digital content from mobile phones and social media that had overwhelmed prosecutors.

It is important to understand the data collection process, such as screenshots, web capture tools and social discovery tools, to ensure the evidence from social media platforms is collected properly and can be authenticated. Facebook allows you to download your data. You can download a copy of your Facebook information over specified date ranges and by type, including posts, photos, comments, likes, friends, stories, following and followers, messages, groups, events, profile information, pages and places. You can also retrieve a history of your searches, location, and security and login information, which includes periods of time you have been active on Facebook. It is available in HTML or JSON format and allows data to be preserved electronically. Issues around digital evidence will be discussed further in Chapter 8.

Social media platforms have tabs and expandable comment sections that may not be immediately visible. Locating those will allow the full archived conversation to be revealed. To ensure the authenticity of the data, it is important to collect key metadata such as IP addresses, timestamps and URLs. If web content is collected as part of any litigation, it has to be saved in a format that is exactly how it appears online.

28 Caroline Davies and Vikran Dodd, 'CPS Chief Apologises Over Disclosure Failings in Rape Cases' (*theguardian.com*, 5 June 2018) <https://www.theguardian.com/law/2018/jun/05/scores-of-uk-sexual-offence-cases-stopped-over-evidence-failings> accessed 14 April 2021.

Understanding how to capture and preserve social media data is essential to ensure that evidence is collected appropriately. Lawyers also need to address with their clients any inconsistencies between the client's social media presence and their legal claim and be vigilant about their client's social media activity. Ultimately, lawyers have a duty to uphold the law and the administration of justice.

SOCIAL MEDIA RISKS: LEGAL PERSPECTIVE

Having an awareness and understanding of social media is now a key part of being a lawyer. The pervasiveness of social media means it is relevant for a number of different areas of legal practice. Lawyers are required to advise on issues relating to social media in different areas of legal practice, and it is likely that future issues will emerge. The purpose of this textbook is to raise your awareness of how law and technology intersect so you can apply your skills of critical thinking and analysis to the emerging legal issues. By understanding some of the issues connected to social media, you can think about how you can learn more about these areas of law if you are planning to go into legal practice.

EMPLOYMENT LAW

The cases of *Weeks* and *Creighton* illustrate the employment law consequences for inappropriate postings on social media. *Creighton* demonstrates how actions on social media can have long lasting implications.

Weeks v Everything Everywhere Ltd [2012] ET/2503016/2012

Mr. Weeks posted on social media that his work was like "Dante's inferno". His employer had a social media policy that applied to postings in their own time and a requirement not to criticise the employer. He was dismissed for gross misconduct and the decision was upheld by the Employment Tribunal.

Creighton v Together Housing Association Ltd [2016] ET/2400978/2016

Mr. Creighton was a long-standing employee who had three years earlier made some derogatory comments about his colleagues and his employer on

Twitter. The comments only came to light following an investigation into another employee for bullying.

He argued that he thought his tweets were private, that he had posted them two or three years ago and that he "deserved to be treated sympathetically" after nearly 30 years' service.

He was dismissed and the decision was upheld by the Employment Tribunal.

DEFAMATION

The cases of *Davies*[29] and *Hopkins* demonstrate how comments on Twitter can be defamatory and the consequences from tweeting or retweeting.

Lord McAlpine v Alan Davies **[2013]**

In 2013, comedian Alan Davies paid £15,000 in damages to Lord McAlpine in a libel action. Alan Davies had tweeted "Any clues as to who the Tory paedophile is?" and then retweeted a message that named Lord McAlpine. The action was resolved in a settlement agreement.

Jack Monroe v Katie Hopkins **[2017] EWHC 433 (QB)**

Jack Monroe was awarded damages of £24,000 and costs in a defamation claim against Katie Hopkins. In 2015 Hopkins published two tweets accusing Monroe of vandalising a war memorial and implying that Monroe would support such behaviour.

Hopkins had intended to publish the tweets to another columnist and tweeted them to Monroe by mistake. Monroe offered to settle the case at an early stage but was ignored by Hopkins, so subsequently legal proceedings were issued and the matter went to trial.

Annexed to the judgment is a note on how Twitter works.

These cases highlight some of the social media risks that lawyers will be required to advise on. There are also similar examples in other

29 Mark Sweeney, 'Lord McAlpine Settles Libel Action with Alan Davies Over Twitter comment' (*Guardian*, 24 October 2013) <https://www.theguardian.com/media/2013/oct/24/lord-mcalpine-libel-alan-davies> accessed 14 April 2021.

jurisdictions. In the next sync you will research an area of law to explore the impact of social media.

Sync 5: Social media and the law

You should allow around 15 minutes for this activity.

Choose an area of law and consider some of the issues that might arise in relation to social media. You can choose from:

- Employment law
- Defamation
- Data protection and confidentiality
- Online advertising and marketing communications
- Third-party intellectual property (IP) rights
- Criminal law.

This list does not represent all the areas of law that social media might be relevant to, but it does demonstrate how the use of social media crosses many areas of legal practice. If you considered third-party IP rights, you may have thought about issues relating to counterfeiting or how you would advise a client if their IP rights had been infringed on Facebook.

There are a number of issues you could have considered relating to employment law. You may have thought about how you would advise a client on its social media policy or what clauses should be contained in an employment contract that relate to social media. Social media is a high-risk area for defamation and, as we have seen from examples in this chapter, people do not always consider the consequences of their actions when posting online.

Online advertising includes social media advertising. To find out more about how it is governed, you can look at the UK Code of Non-broadcast Advertising and Direct and Promotional Marketing (CAP Code). The UK's Financial Conduct Authority has rules on advertising when it is capable of being a financial promotion on social media. There are numerous examples of criminal offences relating to social media including cyberbullying, sexting, revenge porn, trolling and virtual mobbing. The UK's Crown Prosecution Service have produced guidelines on prosecuting cases involving communications sent via social media; the guidelines are available on the CPS website.

Governments around the world are increasingly concerned about how social media platforms protect their users. In the UK, the Department for Digital, Culture, Media and Sport (DCMS) and the Home Office published an online white paper which puts forward plans for a new regulatory framework.[30] The framework is a way of tackling the prevalence of online harms to protect users and for the UK to be the place to start and develop a digital business. It is important to be aware of future trends in social media law and regulation and to consider how that may impact on lawyers and the delivery of legal services.

Although social media is not yet an area of law in its own right, it is essential that you have knowledge of how social media works and its impact on your area of practice. Gaining an understanding of the relationship between law and social media will ensure you are better placed to take advantage of the opportunities that present themselves.

SOCIAL MEDIA RISKS: BRINGING IT TOGETHER

This chapter has discussed the implications of our social media use in personal and professional capacities, explained the relevant professional conduct rules and considered some examples where lawyers have breached the codes. The impact of social media is profound: It affects the law and is relevant to legal proceedings. To practise in a digital age, lawyers are required to understand how social media works and keep up to date with changes to social media platforms.

To bring this all together, these case studies give you the opportunity to apply what you have learned and to think about the practical implications of social media.

Sync 6: Social media case studies

You should allow around 60 minutes for this activity.

Read each case study and consider the related question before reading the comment. These comments draw upon the law and the professional regulation of solicitors in England and Wales. If you are based in another jurisdiction or are interested in a different legal role, you might like to consider whether similar laws and regulations would apply.

30 HM Government, 'Online Harms White Paper' (*Gov.uk*, April 2019) <https://assets.publishing.service.gov.uk/government/uploads/system/uploads/attachment_data/file/973939/Online_Harms_White_Paper_V2.pdf> accessed 14 April 2021.

Case study 1

Law firm A has a Twitter feed and a Facebook page with lots of content and regular postings, but the firm doesn't have an overall social media strategy and messaging from their online presence is confused. The firm has a social media policy but it is vague and poorly drafted, and it appears that anyone with access to the Twitter account can tweet. Some of the firm's lawyers have sent tweets showing them attending conference dinners and events.

What are the implications for law firm A?

A law firm should have a social media policy which is clear, unambiguous and easily accessible. The policy should set out the firm's expectations on social media use, what obligations are placed on lawyers, and what lawyers can and cannot do in their personal and professional capacities. The policy should restrict who is authorised to post on behalf of the firm. There should be procedures in place to make sure those with access to social media accounts are properly trained. Training explaining the social media policy should be provided to new starters, and regular refresher training should be offered.

In this case study, the law firm should consider how their social media posts may appear to the outside world, and what message they convey about the law firm. If there are tweets and photographs of lawyers attending conferences, it is important to think about how that may be perceived by clients. It is important to consider any reputational damage that might result from what might appear to be quite an innocuous post. This is also relevant to your own individual social media accounts; always think about why you are posting and what could be the potential impact of your posts.

Case study 2

Law student B has just completed his law degree, and he is starting to apply for training contracts. At university he was a regular user of social media; he enjoyed an active and fulfilling university experience, a lot of which he documented on social media.

What issues do you think law student B may have when applying for a training contract?

It is important to be aware of the risks of putting public posts on social media. We should all consider what information an employer might find if they conduct an online search and to what extent that could convey a negative impression. This example illustrates the problem of habitually sharing information. It is incumbent on all of us to regularly check privacy settings, to review our data trail and critically reflect on our online presence to ensure it does not impact on any future jobs and careers. Self-awareness is imperative: We have the tools to control and actively manage our online presence. It is also important to remember that social media can be helpful in developing your networks and securing opportunities. LinkedIn is a good example of how social media can be used to help build your profile and connect with people who may assist you in your career. Eve Cornwell, a law graduate from Bristol University with 371,000 YouTube subscribes (at the time of writing) and a training contract with a Magic Circle law firm, has demonstrated how social media can be used positively to enhance career progression.[31]

Case study 3

Lawyer C is searching the Internet one day and comes across a chat room for families and victims of a recent fire at a chemical plant. The chat room home page states that the purpose of the chat room is to provide emotional and practical support for the victims and their families. Lawyer C enters the chat room and posts a message to say that she is really sorry to hear about the disaster, that she is a lawyer and that she is happy to answer any legal questions. The family of one of the victims posts a message back with a series of questions on their legal right to compensation, and Lawyer C answers the questions.

What issues do you think arise from lawyer C's conduct?

The SRA Principles state a lawyer must behave in a way that maintains the trust the public places in them and in the provision of legal services. There is a risk that entering a chat room that has been created

31 Aishah Hussain, 'Two Months into Her Training Contract and Eve Cornwell Reveals What Magic Circle Trainee Life is Like' (*Legal Cheek*, 19 November 2019) <https://www.legalcheek.com/2019/11/two-months-into-her-training-contract-and-eve-cornwell-reveals-what-magic-circle-trainee-life-is-like/> accessed 29 April 2021.

to provide emotional and practical support for the victims and their families risks exploiting vulnerable people and may damage the trust that the public places in the profession. A lawyer must act with integrity, as these interactions may be considered a breach of integrity. There is also potential here for the inadvertent creation of a lawyer-client relationship which contravenes requirements of the SRA Code in terms of confidentiality, conflict of interests and publicity.

Case study 4

Lawyer D has recently joined a new law firm as a partner. The marketing team are keen to raise the profile of lawyer D and want her to do some public engagement and provide some hypothetical examples of her recent cases to share her knowledge, opinions and experiences. The firm have asked her to write a blog post about a recent case she has been involved in: the blog post will feature on the firm's website; they will also share it via Twitter and Facebook. She is concerned to make sure that she doesn't breach any of the rules on confidentiality, but she hopes she will be fine if she makes it all hypothetical.

What advice would you give lawyer D?

Social media is an effective tool to engage new audiences, but lawyers need to be aware of the risks and understand the professional conduct rules that apply to their conduct online. The SRA Code covers confidentiality, conflict of interests and publicity; a lawyer must ensure they act with integrity and ensure the public trust and confidence in the legal profession. Lawyers also have duties of confidentiality, and even hypothetical examples may still risk breaching those duties if there is a reasonable likelihood that a third party could identify the client or legal situation.

Case study 5

Lawyer E is meeting his client about her personal injury case. He asks about her social media activity. She explains that she is a prolific user of Facebook; laughingly she tells him there are lot of pictures from her holidays "a little worse for wear!", but she tells him not to worry because she has deleted a lot of her pictures and posts recently. Lawyer E asks her about her privacy settings and she explains she has no idea. He recommends that she check and ensure that her account is private.

What advice do you think lawyer E should give to his client?

Lawyer E should advise his client about the implications of her social media activity, including advising her on the consequences of altering or destroying social media posts, pages or messages if they are likely to be relevant to the personal injury claim. Deleting her pictures and posts could constitute spoliation if they are related to her legal claim. Relevance is a prerequisite for spoliation, but what is deemed relevant is not always easy to determine. The advice needs to be clear and unambiguous because there could be serious consequences for both lawyer E and the client if social media evidence is compromised. It is not enough to advise the client on her privacy settings; Lawyer E would also need to consider the relevance of social media posts to her personal injury claim to ensure upholding the rule of law and the proper administration of justice, and that they are acting with integrity and not allowing their independence to be compromised or breached. These same obligations apply in other jurisdictions. The ABA advises lawyers in the United States that they must advise clients on the content of their social media sites, including their responsibility to preserve information and the restrictions on not removing or destroying information.[32]

Case study 6

Lawyer F is representing Miss Mahmood, a former employee of ABC Industries, in an unfair dismissal claim. Miss Mahmood provides him with a list of employees who are unhappy with the company. The lawyer sends Facebook friend requests to two of the employees in the list in the hope that he can find out some information on the employer to help him with his case. He goes into a local café, logs on to his computer using the public access Wi-Fi and sends a tweet from his firm's Twitter account: "In a café outside ABC

32 Daniel J. Siegel, 'Ethics Corner: 12 Rules for Ethically Dealing with Social Media' (*ABA*, 16 February 2017) <https://www.americanbar.org/groups/business_law/publications/blt/2017/02/ethics_corner/> accessed 11 April 2021.

Industries if anyone can provide any help to Miss M, please tweet me back". He is waiting for his client to arrive, so he decides to update his LinkedIn profile. He adds some information on the areas of law he has expertise in; he thinks he might have slightly exaggerated his experience, but he is confident that everyone does this, so he figures it will be fine.

What potential breaches of the professional conduct rules can you identify?

In this case study there are several potential breaches of professional conduct rules. Have a look at the rules that govern lawyers in your jurisdiction.

- Was it appropriate to send the Facebook requests?
- What are the implications of using public access Wi-Fi?
- Does the tweet breach client confidentiality?
- Have there been any breaches of the firm's social media policy?
- Is it appropriate to exaggerate your experience on LinkedIn?

These cases illustrate some of the issues that need to be considered in practice and the importance of understanding your ethical obligations when using social media platforms.

CONCLUSION

This chapter has applied the principles of digital lawyering within the practical context of social media. It began by asking you to reflect upon your own existing digital footprint and think about the implications for you of your online presence. It then considered the wider use of social media within law and the legal profession, exploring the relevant professional conduct rules and considering some examples of where lawyers have been in breach of those rules. Aspiring lawyers need to have a rounded skill set that is more than just knowledge of the law. Firms expect lawyers to understand the legal ramifications of social media use. The ability to use and understand the potential of social media is an important aspect of legal practice, particularly in the context of the marketing and promotion of legal practices. In this chapter we have considered how changes in law and practice associated with technology are now an essential element of a lawyer's role, and you had the opportunity to think about the skills you need as a digital lawyer. Finally, you considered a number of case studies on the ethical implications of using online social networking both as individual practitioners and within digital lawyering practices.

ADDITIONAL RESOURCES

Digital skills: social media <https://www.futurelearn.com/courses/digital-skills-social-media>

Social media risk and law <https://www.routledge.com/Social-Media-Risk-and-the-Law-A-Guide-for-Global-Communicators/Grantham-Pearson/p/book/9781032017990>

Tims B, "Unguided: Social Media Usage in the Legal Profession and the Need for Practical Guidance" (24 January 2021) <https://ssrn.com/abstract=3772116>

Mind Map 6.1 Chapter topics

6 Big Data and Analytics

Terry Wong

Introduction

This chapter will introduce the concepts and applications of Big Data, with illustrations in both legally oriented and general contexts. It will go on to highlight important considerations for data protection in light of legislation, revealing risks that lawyers will need to bear in mind, whether as users or when advising clients in legal practice.

Chapter hot spots

When reading this chapter, questions to think about include:

- What are the opportunities and benefits that large data sets and analytic techniques present to clients, lawyers, governments and society?
- What are the risks in trusting analytic models, and how might lawyers mitigate those risks in the course of daily practice?
- How might a lawyer maintain a balanced perspective of openness and scepticism when examining the opportunities and risks presented by Big Data, especially when advising clients in everyday legal practice?
- What challenges and opportunities does the legal profession face as it encounters Big Data, a technology that requires ways of thinking and decision-making that are fundamentally different to critical aspects of its traditional culture?

Having read the title and introduction, you can add any other questions you want to explore here:

DOI: 10.4324/9780429298219-6

ILLUSTRATION: FRAUD DETECTION

Every day, as a shopper makes an online purchase with a credit card, the authorisation process for the transaction initiates a number of checks that occur automatically, unobtrusively, on the systems of the credit card processor. The purchase is compared to previously known patterns of spending from the shopper, derived from data on previous transactions. These data may include the spending amounts, types of products purchased and the locations of retailers, among other items. If activity identified by algorithms trained to detect anomalous spending appears, the shopper will receive a communication from the credit card issuer asking for verification of the transaction, in some cases refusing further transactions until such verification takes place. This process of fraud detection is shown in Figure 6.1.

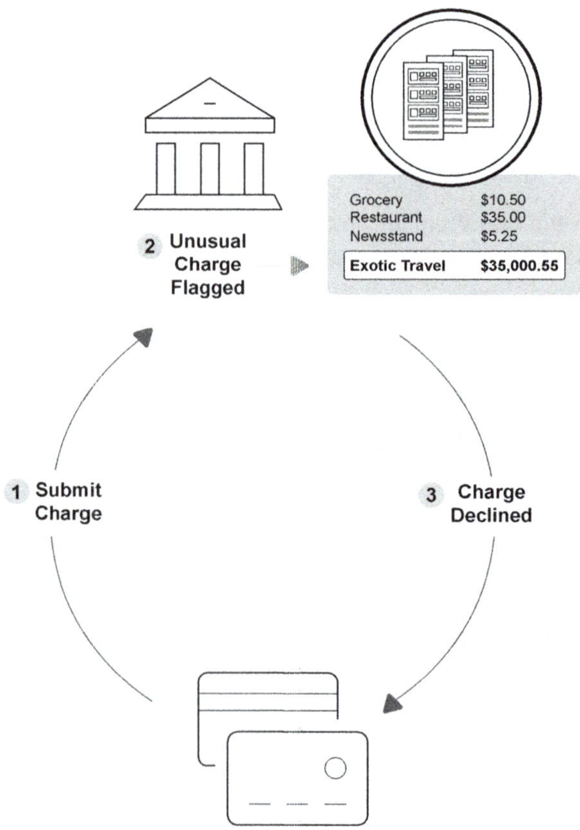

Figure 6.1 Credit card fraud detection

Credit card transactions occur every day in significant volumes, with 39.2 million payments occurring per day in the UK in 2016, projected to rise to 60 million payments per day in 2026, according to one report published in early 2021.[1] Fraud detection systems are a classic example of a mature Big Data application, having evolved from early applications of data warehousing and analytics.

WHAT IS BIG DATA?

Big Data can initially be understood to involve collections of data sufficiently large as to be difficult, if not impossible, to store in files or databases and to process using traditional computing systems. The data may be what is termed "effluent" from processing, meaning data that results as a by-product from the processing of everyday activities and transactions at a large scale—for example, as might be recorded in conducting and servicing individual electronic transactions, web browsing activity and telephone call records. Other examples of Big Data sources include, but certainly are not limited to, security cameras, sensors in factories, utility meters in homes, connected household appliances and assistants and any number of other devices in an emerging network of devices sometimes termed the "Internet of Things" (IoT).

Organisations providing goods and services, from governments to multinational companies to small entrepreneurial ventures, amass significant volumes of data which, when processed and analysed, can enable a wide array of innovative applications of high utility. A frequently cited example of large-scale Big Data investment is that of Walmart, one of the largest retailers in the world, which generates 40 petabytes[2] of data per day in its over 20,000 stores worldwide. According to a report published in 2017, the company at that time was processing at least 2.5 petabytes of that data per day.[3] Two well-known and often cited examples of government Big Data applications include the email metadata mining conducted by the US National Security Agency (NSA) with

1 'Card Payments per Day UK' (n.d.) Statista <https://www.statista.com/statistics/719708/card-payments-per-day-forecast-united-kingdom/> accessed 7 February 2021.

2 For a sense of scale, consider that a petabyte is one billion megabytes.

3 'Big Data at Walmart Is All About Big Numbers; 40 Petabytes a Day!' (n.d.) Datafloq <https://datafloq.com/read/big-data-walmart-big-numbers-40-petabytes/1175> accessed 2 January 2021.

data sourced from telecommunications providers, and China's Social Credit system, in which the activities of citizens across a wide range of domains are recorded and mixed with law enforcement and financial data in a state-built application to establish a score for the trustworthiness of an individual. Later in this chapter we will highlight some points to consider when looking at issues of government data and citizen privacy.

WHAT ARE ANALYTICS?

No matter the volume of data available, it does not become useful information until it is organised, processed and interpreted in light of a specific goal. The process involves using tools and techniques requiring a level of mathematical transformation and calculations with some level of systematic process formalisation, known in a general sense as *analytics*.

Analytics can be more concretely broken down into several types, rising in complexity and in the risks involved in their implementation and application (Figure 6.2):

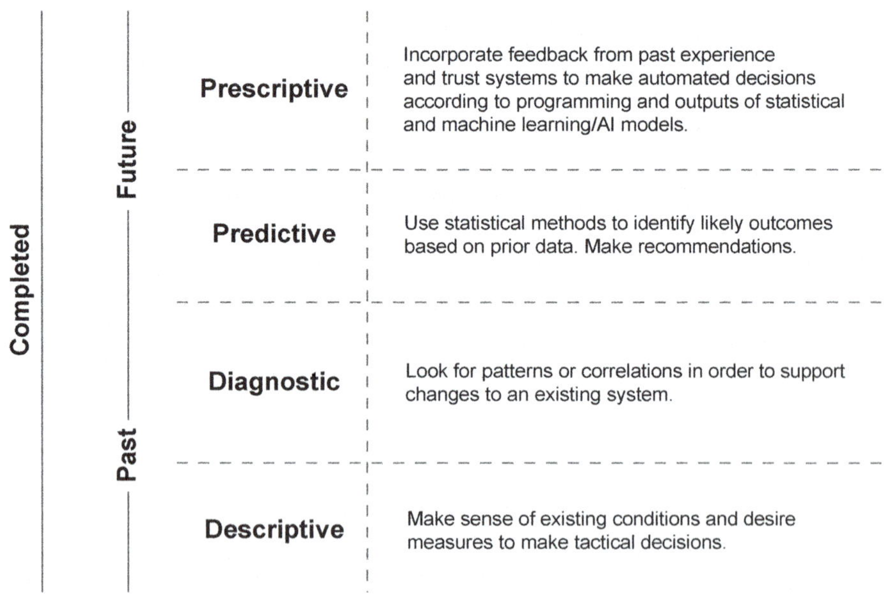

Figure 6.2 The types of analytics

- *Descriptive analytics.* These are what have been traditionally thought of as analytics in business contexts, providing measurements, descriptive statistics (such as averages) and visualisations of activity in the form of graphs and dashboards. The term "dashboard" refers to an application that collects frequently viewed information around a specific activity, such as the key performance metrics of a business. The power of such analytics to inform is sometimes strained or even impeded by overlaying an inappropriate automobile dashboard-like concept with many gauges and dials, as a business dashboard merely presents information and does not offer switches or levers to control the underlying machine.
- *Diagnostic analytics.* These are tools that support inquiry and exploration of data sets, allowing an analyst to look for patterns and discover paths of inquiry to apply in solving a given problem. They also support analysts in efforts to uncover as yet unrealised opportunity in user activity data. Developers of online software products rely upon "click stream data" (logs showing how people navigate through a website) and diagnostic analytic tools (investigating why something happened) in efforts to understand user behaviour and uncover opportunities to optimise existing functions or develop new ones.
- *Predictive analytics.* These analytics take data and apply certain statistical techniques such as linear or logistic regression, and attempt to construct models that enable an analyst to develop options for a decision maker. Predictive analytics drive recommendations that are presented in online electronic stores and commerce platforms as well as marketing campaigns and promotions.
- *Prescriptive analytics.* These advance the work done with predictive analytics, feeding experience data from applying certain options and training a system to recommend courses of action on new incident data based on results from previous data-driven decisions with known outcomes. Examples include material requirements planning (MRP) applications in manufacturing and routing applications for logistics or ridesharing driver applications.

Król and Zdonek[4] examined a number of maturity models, which measure an organisation's capacity for improvement, that are used in industry and academia to describe analytics practices. They saw in common among those maturity models a continuum starting from

4 Karol Król and Dariusz Zdonek, 'Analytics Maturity Models: An Overview' (March 2020) 11 *Information* 142 <https://doi.org/10.3390/info11030142>

descriptive analytics building up to prescriptive analytics, continuing through to the introduction of artificial intelligence (AI) applications in what are termed "cognitive analytics".

Experts also view the evolution of analytics in three waves:

- *Analytics 1.0.* Data was stored using traditional databases and analysis was possible using snapshots of daily operational data.
- *Analytics 2.0.* Large data sets required advanced storage and processing techniques as well as flexibility in the definition of structures to hold data. Technologies such as cloud storage and large processing clusters as well as NoSQL databases marked the arrival of Big Data as we now know it.
- *Analytics 3.0.* The introduction of advanced, optimised processing techniques as well as machine learning and AI techniques defines Analytics 3.0 as a stage of rapid evolution and innovation, with potential to revolutionise operations and practice in the business domains where applied.

Sync 1: Everyday Big Data

You should allow around 20 minutes for this activity.

List some recent interactions you may have had with an online buying experience or after clicking on an advertisement while browsing a website.

Recall how the specific items you clicked on informed the advertisements or product recommendations you were shown on websites you browsed later that day or for several days afterwards. What related items were shown to you?

You probably identified that the advertisements and recommendations you were shown were closely linked to your initial purchase. These effects which occur based on browsing behaviour are well known but perhaps are no longer noted in everyday experience as novel. They are, however, ubiquitous and a feature of Analytics 2.0 and the predictive analytics applications behind modern digital marketing.

Technology enabling Analytics 3.0

A few key developments that have enabled the rise of Analytics 3.0 include:

1 *Increasingly bigger data.* Sensor data from home devices and other IoT devices like voice-driven assistants, and rich, real-time location data are but a few examples of rising technologies that contribute to burgeoning volumes of raw data as Big Data sources.
2 *Mature statistical techniques and pattern recognition.* These allow the data itself to embody what is normal and also to classify new examples as normal or not according to the definition derived from "experience" (i.e. large volumes of samples from Big Data sets or the data itself).
3 *Computer vision.* This term refers to the way computers understand and interpret the visual world (such as pictures and videos). Growing mainstream knowledge and application of AI techniques in computer vision have supported the derivation of data from photos and video streamed from continuous live feeds, as well as in more complex text recognition and visual conversion applications,[5] increasing the size of available data in Big Data sets by orders of magnitude and with greater speed of data acquisition.
4 *Natural language processing and text mining.* Natural language processing (NLP) techniques have allowed technologists to build useful tools from simple foundations like word frequency counts, word groupings and significant word identification. NLP techniques also allow spelling and grammar correction, concept mapping and the creation of fast search techniques. NLP works best when there are large bodies of text data to use in the building and training of models. Because of the text-intensive nature of law and legal texts, NLP becomes the keystone of technologies applied to the practice of law with Big Data.

BIG DATA IN ACTION

In this section we examine several examples of mainstream applications built with analytics and Big Data, with emphasis on applications that may have implications for lawyers advising or representing clients.

VISIBILITY OF WORKER ACTIVITY AND PRODUCTIVITY

Workplaces with time cards provided a scalable means for employers to gather attendance data for payroll functions. A tamper-resistant time

5 Examples include invoice and expense receipt conversion to data and high-volume scanned document ingestion and conversion to text (i.e. automated transcription).

clock and a policy requiring workers to clock in and out during paid work periods enabled accurate time reporting, fostered a sense of trust that employers were paying for work actually done, and ensured that workers would get paid for the time put in.

Updated time and attendance systems work in similar ways with key code systems and biometric inputs such as fingerprint or facial recognition scanners. Beyond the entrance to the business, technology has enabled measurement of activity inside the workplace to be significantly more detailed, with a wide range of counting tools and monitors to measure individual worker productivity and time spent on specific tasks and breaks, and even monitoring the content of the websites and other resources accessed from employees' computer workstations. The online retailer Amazon received significant amounts of mixed coverage in the press for its technology measuring every aspect of their warehouse employees' productivity and efficiency. In recent years, the company has turned that technology into a packaged product available for other business to buy and implement in their workplaces, with the data streamed to subscription cloud services hosted by Amazon.[6]

SURVEILLANCE AND SECURITY SYSTEMS

Security systems and surveillance systems for law enforcement generate large volumes of streaming video data, which is often fed into recognition systems for subject identification and tracking, and for counting in aggregate to assess security in venues with specific requirements (e.g. during events, protests or visits by high-profile individuals). Figure 6.3 shows an application of a surveillance system used in a public space, identifying possible persons of interest using automated facial recognition techniques applied at scale.

The US Federal Bureau of Investigation (FBI), in cooperation with participating states, maintains a national mugshot repository for use in developing leads upon request from state and local law enforcement agencies. Probe images are submitted to the national database for comparison and facial recognition, not to generate a positive identification—a recognition of the limitations of facial recognition models—but to generate a lead for local law enforcement to follow, possibly leading

6 See, for example, Jack Morse, 'Amazon Announces New Employee Tracking Tech, and Customers Are Lining up, Mashable UK' (2 December 2020) <https://mashable.com/article/amazon-aws-panorama-worker-customer-tracking-technology-smart-cameras/?europe=true>

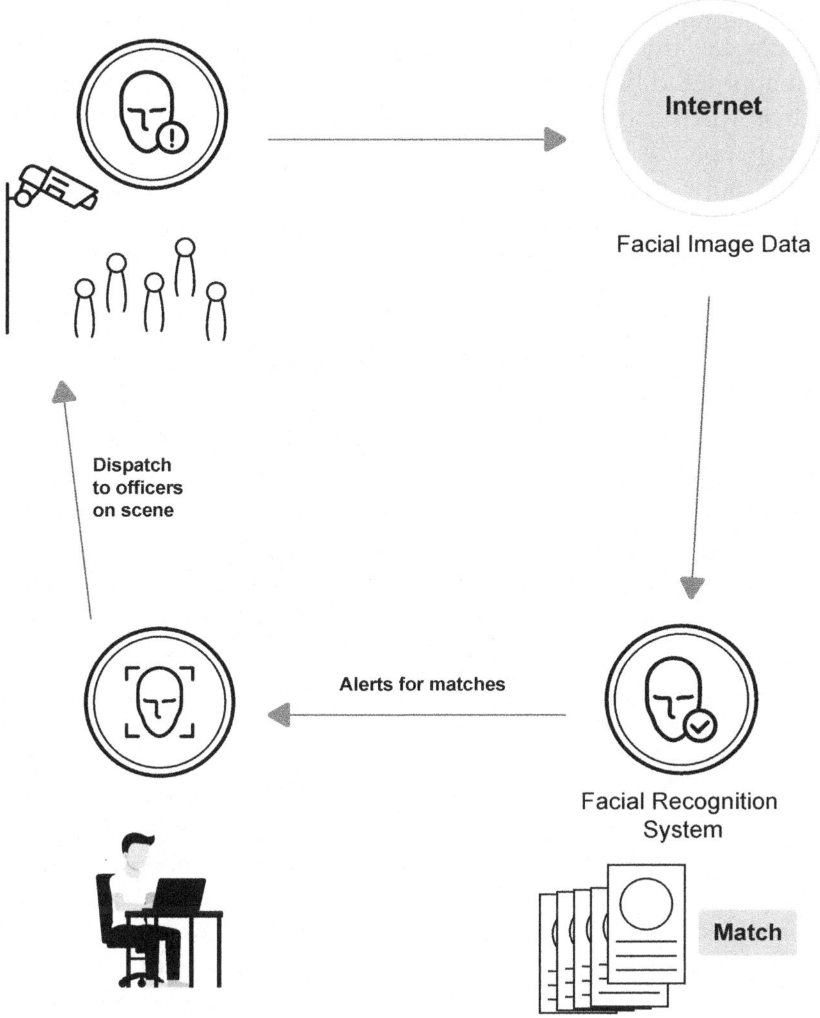

Figure 6.3 Illustration of camera surveillance apps and data

to a subsequent positive identification through additional means. The FBI operates the database and analytic tools for facial recognition under congressional oversight[7] and makes explicit policy on the handling of the requests and disposal of the request images and materials, detailed in Privacy Impact Assessments. Similar programs in the UK also have

7 See a 2017 statement to the House Committee on Oversight and Government Reform: <https://www.fbi.gov/news/testimony/law-enforcements-use-of-facial-recognition-technology>

publicly appointed oversight. In England and Wales, for instance, the programs fall under the oversight of a Surveillance Camera Commissioner appointed by the Secretary of State.

It is worth noting that facial recognition, gait recognition (identifying people by how they walk) and other technologies are in an evolving zone in the law, where gains in effective investigation must be balanced, sometimes in conflict with the rights guaranteed in a civil society under the rule of law.

Sync 2: Public surveillance

You should allow around 30 minutes for this activity.

Undertake some independent research to explore the use of mass surveillance in China and the UK, noting especially its use in China for its Social Credit System. You should also note the comprehensive scope of the data gathered by the Chinese government. While avoiding political judgement, contrast the approach of China with that of the UK regarding access to justice for suspected offenders, individual freedoms, the role of government, and the possible benefits and dangers involved in the continuum of trust in complex organisational and technological systems.

You may find after this sync that the stated goals of mass surveillance in public spaces in both jurisdictions are the same; that is, to preserve public safety and support law enforcement. You may generally find that the outcomes for law-abiding citizens do not differ, at least not in the short run. The methods in both systems use cameras and video record processing technology. In the case of suspected wrongdoing, where facial recognition is applied, the technologies and methods are in fact the same. The differences in law enforcement methods when infractions are detected and the processes for redress afforded to offenders may seem to be different, prima facie, but are they? Did you find yourself asking whether having points deducted from a social credit score differs from being issued a speeding ticket or traffic fine from an automated video record processing system, which we accept without question, or at least as a matter of settled law?

PREDICTIVE ANALYTICS IN POLICING

Crime incident data has been used to build predictive models for the times and conditions under which crimes have been known to occur.

The Los Angeles Police Department in the US state of California and the Police Department of Kent in the UK ran trials of such a model, implementing epidemic-type aftershock sequence forecasting originally used to predict the spatial distribution and timings of earthquake aftershocks. The models allowed dynamic adjustment of parameters using various methods, including randomising inputs, to support the generation of predictions for crime occurrence. The predictions enabled the police departments involved to achieve up to a 7.4% reduction in crime volume as a function of patrol time.[8] Such results enabled more effective deployment of limited personnel, held as an indication of the promise of predictive analytics in improving law enforcement effectiveness.

OPEN DATA

The availability of large data sets for the public to access, develop applications, and re-publish is commonly known as Open Data. While a single data set may be a small silo of data, complex applications involving the mixing and cross-referencing of multiple data sets rise to a level of complexity to be called Big Data applications.

Big Data as Open Data

One example of a successful Big Data initiative, referred to in Chapter 4, is DoNotPay, a company started by Stanford University law student Joshua Browder. Originally more of an expert system type of AI application, DoNotPay expanded into travel fare optimisation, in which subscribers could register for real-time monitoring of price fluctuations for already booked tickets, and have the option to be notified and instantly accept an automatic rebooking to a lower-priced ticket with a refund of the difference if available and if booking rules permit. DoNotPay's technology monitoring real-time feeds, applying a set of relatively complex rules and regulations, and then passing on savings to the customer[9] is held up as a case study of using Open Data to deliver value to consumers in an area with complex laws and regulations.

8 G. O. Mohler, M. B. Short, Sean Malinowski, Mark Johnson, G. E. Tita, Andrea L. Bertozzi and P. J. Brantingham, 'Randomized Controlled Field Trials of Predictive Policing' [2016] *Journal of the American Statistical Association* <https://amstat.tandfonline.com/doi/full/10.1080/01621459.2015.1077710>

9 'When Big Data Meets Big Law' (*Legal Insights Europe*, 20 September 2019) <https://blogs.thomsonreuters.com/legal-uk/2019/09/20/when-big-data-meets-big-law/>

Open Data is also concerned with the availability of legal texts to the public, in particular codes, statutes, regulations, edicts and judicial rulings. Article 2(4) of the Bern Convention for the Protection of Literary and Artistic Works[10] places the status of such texts at the discretion of the signatories to the Convention. Most have placed them in the public domain, while the UK has them under Crown Copyright, and some Commonwealth countries have similar regimes in place, with latitude for use while respecting the copyrights.

Attempts have been made in certain jurisdictions to make it illegal for texts to be republished by individuals as a means of ensuring access to those texts and equal access to justice, conflicting sometimes with the interests of legal publishers. If you are interested in this topic you might want to read the ruling by the US Supreme Court in *Georgia v. Public.Resource.Org, Inc.*[11]

There are ongoing initiatives in many jurisdictions by citizens and non-profits, in cooperation with government, to digitise legislation and the proceedings of legislative bodies (known as Hansard in Commonwealth jurisdictions) that are not already in electronic form. While apparently a simple task, only the texts from recent decades are available, often converted from word processing formats and Adobe Portable Document Format (PDF). These formats, while optimised for the purpose of printing on paper, are poor starting places in practice for making those texts accessible in Big Data and NLP contexts, as they are not created with the structure of the text as the primary objective but rather the appearance of the text. Workers must often spend significant time manually cleaning such texts or must rely on the help of programmers to write text filtering software that will not inadvertently destroy content in the course of conversion.

Sync 3: Law as Open Data

You should allow around 30 minutes for this activity.

Briefly examine the online Hansard systems of the UK Parliament at Westminster, and then of a Commonwealth or former Commonwealth jurisdiction like Singapore or Hong Kong. Note the available downloadable text

10 Berne Convention Texts at the World Intellectual Property Organization <https://www.wipo.int/treaties/en/ip/berne/>

11 *Georgia v. Public.Resource.Org, Inc.* <https://www.supremecourt.gov/opinions/19pdf/18-1150_7m58.pdf>

formats, search facilities, and the presence or absence of tools like an API (application programming interface) for software developers to use in building automated interactions and applications to interact with the Hansard system.

You will be able to recognise an API where there is documentation in a section possibly titled "For Developers", with terms such as REST and references to toolkits compatible with common programming languages such as JavaScript, Java, Python and PHP.

Consider the following:

- How far back in time do the Hansard texts online reach?
- Do the downloads or searches yield formats suitable for computer systems and software developers to work with in developing new applications, for instance XML, JSON and plain text formats, or do they exclusively provide word processing files like Word or formatted print formats like PDF?
- What challenges can you see with limited availability of texts when attempting to build certain applications?

Your answers to this sync will vary depending upon which jurisdictions you have researched. In terms of the challenges faced, it may help you to draw an analogy with the situation of physically working in a legal library when most of the texts are not available.

LAWYERS AND CLIENTS

Tools in legal practice for tracking work and time can vary from a collection of spreadsheets and isolated pockets of automation to integrated practice management suites with linkages to office automation tools, specialised time reporting and client portal software. More sophisticated, cloud-enabled offerings allow clients to access specific project details and documents and see time spent, offering the client control in managing the expense in collaboration with the lawyer(s) working with them on specific matters.

In larger firms, tools to automate and collect practice data can support a number of objectives related to law firm competitiveness; for example, ensuring teams meet their targets for billable hours or ensuring the firm is achieving the right mix of client work in designated practice areas. More sophisticated tools help law firm partners manage their contacts; for example, to build wider relationships across different parts of the same client organisation, and to deliver higher value service when practice management tools highlight cross-region client relationships and work being done in other locales. The same tools also support knowledge exchange and access to expertise in larger and/or national and international law firms beyond the one department or office, when practice management data is processed with the right analytic tools. For example, a partner in a law firm may receive instructions on a new matter from the marketing department of a large international manufacturing firm. They may then be able to use analytical tools to identify that another partner is working with a different part of the firm based in a different jurisdiction on an issue where there is the opportunity to share relevant information.

USE OF ANALYTICS IN DISCOVERY AND COMPLIANCE

Large bodies of documentation can be instrumental in determining the path a lawyer may take when handling a matter. If the documentation is in a machine-readable form and formatted in such a way as to allow human annotation and possibly enrichment with additional data sources, NLP and machine learning techniques can be applied using analytic tools that are now becoming more available and accessible to smaller firms and individual practitioners.

Language-based analytic tools consuming text as Big Data can, for instance, identify parties of interest or those affected by specific events. Visualisation tools showing connections or common occurrence of certain parties, concepts or items across a large body of documents can cut down discovery time drastically, sometimes limited only by the amount of computing resources available.

For organisations with an obligation to protect their consumers from certain harms, analytic tools monitoring news and court claims may alert them to a possible issue with their products or services and prevent possibly costly liability claims that could result. An illustrative case can be found in a case concerning Fosamax, by the pharmaceutical company Merck. There were, according to the case history, a substantial number of reports of adverse drug interactions, such that the company had an obligation to issue a warning. The ruling against Merck was based on testimony from a data scientist noting the presence of the reports, and the ability to have known of those reports had

Merck used certain Big Data sources and descriptive analytic tools to process and deliver reports on those interactions.[12]

BIG DATA AND ANALYTICS TO INCREASE ACCESS TO JUSTICE

In a society that espouses the rule of law, access to means by which to settle disputes, whether through litigation or arbitration or other procedures mandated under the law, is of primary importance for the functioning of the system. This problem of access to justice is characterised by three conditions:

1. *Complex processes involving significant paperwork* to file for even the simplest of complaints at the lowest levels of the justice system, making necessary the services of legal professionals and increasing the expense for small claims. It can be clearly seen that in some cases, the expense to take action may exceed the value of the possible remedy, effectively subordinating justice to a purely economic calculation for the parties. The aggrieved party must decide whether it is worth it to pursue the matter. The defendant in some cases will not be deterred from acting badly or contrary to the law.
2. *The process of adjudication is complex*, designed to ensure correctness and adherence to the letter of the law, if not the spirit. The process involves in many cases several steps from beginning a claim through perhaps multiple hearings before a trial or mandatory mediation. Again, the economic costs associated with the time come into the calculus applied by the parties.
3. *The reality in the justice system is one of increasing caseloads*, such that the complex process as discussed in point 2 are drawn out, in some cases creating additional hardship for those seeking justice.

A proposal for the use of predictive analytics as one possible way to address this problem has been made, described in popular media[13] and the writings of Richard Susskind,[14] a leading thinker on the digital

12 <https://e27.co/how-big-data-is-impacting-the-legal-world-20190408/>
13 <https://www.forbes.com/sites/bernardmarr/2020/01/17/the-future-of-lawyers-legal-tech-ai-big-data-and-online-courts/>
14 Richard Susskind, *Online Courts and the Future of Justice* (Oxford, Oxford University Press, 2019).

transformation of law. In the proposal, complaints may be filed using online tools, which will take the facts of the complaint as a set of data that may be assessed using predictive analytics. The analytics will have access to a set of judgments and settlements data from similar cases, making a prediction as to the likely outcome if the complaint were to proceed as usual through the judicial system to its conclusion. The parties, if they accept the recommended result, agree to be bound by the predicted outcome as the terms of the settlement, and the matter is thus closed.

It can be argued that such a system, if implemented, would speed claims through the system, reducing or eliminating the economic burden that the existing process imposes in terms of required funds, advice and time, making access to justice more equal for all under the law.

The risks of Big Data

As with many technology developments, Big Data offers attractive benefits when supporting advanced analytics as we have described. We can also look forward to further innovations as applications built on the foundations of Big Data sets gain sophistication and reliability. However, Big Data also entails risks, as we will explore in this section.

DATA COLLECTION

It is now possible for anyone with the inclination and some basic investment to collect significant volumes of data rapidly. There are increasingly diminishing, already low barriers to entry in getting started with the necessary tools. Indiscriminate data collection is indeed possible, creating volumes of data that can easily exceed any organisation's aspirations to manage with intention and care. While some may argue that such an approach may lead to serendipitous opportunities, it can also lead to exceeding the boundaries of granted authority or permission, especially when gathering data from persons giving explicit consent in terms of service agreements and other legal contracts, or when granting authority to the entity collecting data under regulations or statute.

Lawyers working with organisations collecting Big Data can serve their clients well by offering guidelines and assisting in reviewing data collection agreements to check they comply with relevant laws, ensuring that clients are aware of the limits and consequences of non-compliance in the relevant jurisdictions.

DATA CUSTODY, CLOUD COMPUTING RESOURCES AND REGULATORY RISK

Big Data necessarily is large in volume, can grow rapidly and may in some cases be exploited for a range of unspecified purposes different from those originally intended during collection. It is imperative, therefore, that data containing confidential facts and personally identifiable information (PII) be handled with adequate care from the moment of acquisition, with clear procedures and safeguards for its lifetime in the organisation's care, from transport, storage, retrieval, processing, delivery and use to disposal.

Aspects of network and physical computing infrastructure security that apply to computing environments also apply to those hosting Big Data operations. Given the favourable economics of cloud computing, much Big Data is stored in online, on-demand infrastructure, prompting concerns over agreements with cloud computing providers to ensure compliance with regulations, adequate security, and safe handling of data in those environments.

Major cloud computing providers such as Amazon Web Service, Google Cloud Platform and Microsoft Azure have developed detailed understandings of the requirements for effective, safe computing operations in cloud environments. Each provider, as a competitive act, fields a range of features and tools to ensure compliance by default for regulatory standards such as the US Health Insurance Portability and Accountability Act (HIPAA), the UK Data Protection Act 2018 and the EU General Data Privacy Regulation (GDPR). We will examine some of these regulations in a later section in this chapter.

Smaller providers, chosen for specific advantages of service level, features or price, are building similar programs as the hosting space matures. Their stated policies and practices for protections may require more detailed review and advice from lawyers depending on client goals, risk profiles, and jurisdictional requirements.

Sync 4: Cloud provider data privacy and compliance

You should allow around 30 minutes for this activity.

Perform an Internet search for the data privacy and compliance pages for the major cloud hosting providers. Familiarise yourself with the policies and technical support offerings of each provider, noting similarities and differences. Consider the following questions:

- What are the positions each provider takes with respect to ownership of data stored in the respective cloud environments?
- What responsibilities are outlined for the cloud provider with regard to security of data stored in the cloud, and what are those of the customer?
- What items would you take as starting points for discussing data privacy compliance with a client who approaches you for advice in looking to manage the risk for a cloud-hosted online service offering?

You should have found a nearly uniform set of statements in various forms respecting customer ownership of data and the undertaking of the hosting providers not to disclose or expose customer data in any circumstances unless compelled to do so to comply with applicable law or investigations by law enforcement. Certain cloud providers go on to state the general compliance and support in their infrastructure offerings for customers needing to run applications in certain domains such as financial services or healthcare, having to comply with additional regulations such as PCI (Payment Card Industry Data Security Standard) or HIPAA. It is important that you note that these offerings are merely tools, and they require active selection, setup and review by competent technologists and reviewers in real-world applications.

DATA PROCESSING AND SECURITY

The analytic tools that are developed to process Big Data sets, together with the policies and procedures used to manage operation of those tools, are clear areas of concern for security during processing. Both internal and third-party suppliers of tools and services should be required to define, together with the client, a set of actionable, auditable processes to ensure not only the satisfaction of business objectives but also that those processes do not violate regulatory requirements or ethical standards in the relevant jurisdictions.

Another concern in data processing is the safeguards put in place around intermediate forms of data as they are transformed from raw input into working forms that may involve enriching the original data with lookups from reference sources like databases of names or addresses or product catalogue data. To understand this concept of intermediate forms, consider a website that tracks its visitors with a website cookie or similar mechanism, where a code unique to that web browser is generated and stored on the browser at a website provider's request, to be made accessible to that same website's provider in the user's future interactions using that web browser. With anonymous visitors, repeat visitors consenting to cookie use will be known and tracked but not identifiable using this mechanism, nevertheless forming the basis for digital marketing and targeted online advertisements as well as product recommendations. Because of the website cookies, these capabilities are available even in the absence of a user account on a given website.

When a visitor finally registers or logs into that website with specific credentials and consents to creating and completing a user record, the activity information prior to that registration or login already collected on the web server platform is now available to the provider together with the PII provided during registration, significantly enhancing the ability of the website provider to analyse the behaviour of the individual and to tailor interaction with the site and its services. The cookie data can be linked using simple data processing tools to the PII provided by the user, and is typically held in that intermediate form in memory on a running system. Meant to be purged once a specific processing activity is completed, it is safe as long as it is protected against unauthorised outside access and is not stored in unencrypted form on a disk or other storage medium.

Some of these operations are computationally expensive and may involve large amounts of intermediate data that needs to be retrieved and held in working storage. Although most of these operations are detailed procedures in the IT and data management domain of expertise, a lawyer may serve a client engaging in such activities by ensuring awareness of these issues. They may also need to offer guidance to ensure that the organisation is taking sufficient actions to ensure compliance with privacy and data protection regulations even during complex processing protocols.

CONTENT PUBLISHING, PRIVACY AND SECURITY

Cloud computing services with a heavy content delivery component in their offerings, notably websites and social media networks, are often reliant on a large body of user-contributed, user-owned content (e.g. blog posts, videos, comments on online forums). As these services have grown and matured, privacy and content ownership considerations have come to the fore, with users demanding significant control and accountability from providers for content visibility, sharing policies, and the permitted uses of the content.

Following the 2016 US presidential election, with the growing debate over truth in media and the posts of elected public officials, came calls on one side to regulate the social media posts of figures like the US president, who was notorious for posts that could be deemed inflammatory and misleading. When the president disputed the 2020 elections, this raised arguments over the merits of his efforts and those of his legal team and his supporters on social media with those with more extreme views choosing alternative platforms. A riot at the US Capitol on January 6, 2021, and the subsequent activities of the president and his supporters led to the deactivation of his primary social media accounts on the social media service Twitter,[15] and the social media network Parler being taken offline by Amazon Web Services, Parler's hosting provider.[16]

News accounts and blog posts in the days after the takedown of Parler showed that technically skilled individuals were able to exploit a fundamental security flaw in Parler's login system to save a large portion of the user content posted to the service. Included in this body of content were videos and images posted by the insurrectionists who entered the US Capitol illegally, boasting of their exploits and attempting to rally others in the attempt to overturn the results of the 2020 presidential election.[17]

The incident illustrates several key points regarding privacy and data in these contexts:

- *Service providers have obligations to protect user data.* Operators of such services must take care to ensure that their system implementations are fit for purpose and tested for safety. Although the individuals who compromised protected data and engaged in

15 N. Tiku, T. Romm and C. Timberg, 'Twitter Bans Trump's Account, Citing Risk of Further Violence' (*Washington Post*, 9 January 2021) <https://www.washingtonpost.com/technology/2021/01/08/twitter-trump-dorsey/>

16 T. Romm and R. Lerman, 'Amazon Suspends Parler, Taking pro-Trump Site Offline Indefinitely' (*Washington Post*, 2021) <https://www.washingtonpost.com/technology/2021/01/09/amazon-parler-suspension/>

17 WIRED, 'This Site Posted Every Face from Parler's Capitol Hill Insurrection Videos' (*Ars Technica*, 23 January 2021) <https://arstechnica.com/tech-policy/2021/01/this-site-posted-every-face-from-parlers-capitol-hill-insurrection-videos/>

downloading it may have been violating terms of service and possibly copyright regulations, there was also an apparent failure on the part of the service provider to put in place basic protections.

- *Hosting providers exercise wide discretion when service providers and end users engage in activities violating service terms.* Hosting providers have terms of service that often provide them with a wide latitude in deciding whether to continue or terminate services in matters involving law enforcement. There is limited recourse for the individuals using those hosting services in the case of a dispute.
- *Media posted on content services and social networks may be used for unintended purposes if safety controls fail.* Concerned individuals who downloaded the Parler data applied Big Data analytic techniques to isolate images of the rioters' faces and subsequently posted them to websites in efforts to support investigators' efforts to identify and charge those who participated in the riot. Other individuals who came into possession of the data applied NLP techniques to identify topics of concern and possible targets for further violence in the discussion data.

Sync 5: Conflicting concerns in online breaches of Big Data

You should allow around 30 minutes for this activity.

Consider the case of Parler and its role as an online service and unintended source of data for concerned citizens and law enforcement attempting to bring rioters to justice following the US Capitol riot and insurrection of January 6, 2021. Consider the following questions:

- What possible liabilities with misuse of customer data might Parler have faced, assuming its terms of service (no longer online as of the writing of this text) maintained ownership of user content with its users?
- What possible actions for violations of user data regulations did the concerned citizens potentially face because of their possible use of the data set from Parler?
- What are the ethical considerations when there is data that is unwittingly made publicly available for download, distributed through third-party hosts, of disputable provenance, when there are legitimate law enforcement aims, concerned citizens technically capable and willing to help, and content owners and service providers who exercise varying degrees of

discretion, interpretations of personal responsibility and physical control of the data in question?

- What considerations might you need to take into account if you were advising investigators or prosecution teams gathering evidence to prosecute the Capitol insurrectionists, given the means by which some of these items of evidence were obtained?

Given the politically and culturally charged nature of this incident, you may have found yourself in the first moments of the exercise applying your personal reaction to the questions. Perhaps you reacted positively to the ingenuity and application of skills on the part of the concerned citizens to exploit the data for a subjectively judged positive outcome. Perhaps you jumped straight to the question about the ethics and legality of downloading a publicly accessible but not licensed data set. These are all questions you may encounter as a digital lawyer. Always challenge yourself to clarify your reasoning as you examine the facts surrounding every question, seeing especially the many grey areas where technology makes things possible, but not always absolutely right or ethical.

UNANTICIPATED OUTCOMES APPLYING ANALYTICS TO BIG DATA

One of the benefits of Big Data with the analytic tools and practices that have developed is the uncovering of unforeseen facts, often reverently termed "insights" in popular parlance. Insights gained and applied, in the right context, are the precursors for good decisions and the resulting activities that convey advantage to the individuals and organisations that acquire them.

An unanticipated arrival

At the intersection of online and offline commerce, combining online browsing records with in-store buying behaviours revealed through loyalty and rewards card incentive programs, retailers have built some of the largest data collection, management and analysis programs, starting with data warehouses in the 1990s. Those systems have evolved in complexity from descriptive analytics built on large (for the time) data snapshots to prescriptive analytics built on Big Data today. We have already remarked on the scale of the data operations at the retailer Walmart. It should be understood as a matter of course that competitors engage in similar efforts, with similar goals, challenges and risks.

An incident that received substantial media attention involved Target, a major global retailer headquartered in the United States. As described in detailed accounts published in the *New York Times*[18] and *Forbes*,[19] the marketing group at Target, working with in-house analytics teams, developed a predictive analytic model that identified customers who had a high probably of having entered the second trimester of pregnancy, based solely on their recent purchasing behaviour in Target stores and online at Target.com, their e-commerce website. The model was robust enough in its predictions that the marketing organisation incorporated it into a program to send coupons to such customers to establish and reinforce a habit of buying. According to the account, the buying of certain items in the second trimester of pregnancy also predicted continued purchasing following delivery of the child and beyond.

Although Target took steps to prevent what would appear to the customer to be an invasion of privacy by sending coupons for other, unrelated items and never using messages revealing its purpose, a father made a complaint in person to a manager in a Target store when his teenage daughter was sent coupons for maternity wear and nursery accoutrements. The news accounts concluded by reporting that following a string of apologetic communications from the father, it came to light that the daughter was, in fact, pregnant.

Together with frequently occurring news accounts of online tracking by technology and advertising firms, and calls for the regulation of tracking, data custody, and the permitted applications of such data with powerful analytic tools, it is easy to see the wide range of legal and ethical concerns around customer privacy that follow.

This is an evolving area of law where technology innovation, commercial opportunity and user appetite far outpace collective understanding in society. To appeal to societal norms that either do not exist

18 Charles Duhigg, 'How Companies Learn Your Secrets' (*New York Times*, 16 February 2012), sec. Magazine <https://www.nytimes.com/2012/02/19/magazine/shopping-habits.html>

19 Kashmir Hill, 'How Target Figured Out a Teen Girl Was Pregnant Before Her Father Did' (Forbes. n.d.) <https://www.forbes.com/sites/kashmirhill/2012/02/16/how-target-figured-out-a-teen-girl-was-pregnant-before-her-father-did/> accessed 1 January 2021.

or which are being shattered by the continued evolution of technology would be premature and certainly an exercise in futility. A lawyer fielding calls for advice in this area would certainly be well-served to read widely regarding emerging privacy issues and legislation and to cultivate working relationships with technical experts who may be consulted for understanding in this fluid area.

BIAS IN ANALYTIC MODELS

Facial recognition systems are often used to identify possible suspects in law enforcement incidents. These systems use algorithms trained on Big Data sets consisting of faces that allow the algorithm to develop its model for identifying a person and expressing a level of probability that the identification is correct. Researchers at the Massachusetts Institute of Technology and Microsoft Research showed that the under-representation of black and Asian faces in training sets caused systems trained with those data to be less capable of correctly identifying persons or indicating their genders. A report by the US National Institute of Standards and Technology (NIST) also indicated that algorithms by vendors submitted for testing had significant difficulty identifying individuals of Asian and African descent, and least difficulty with faces from individuals of Eastern European descent.[20]

In June 2020, the *New York Times* reported the first documented and publicised case in which a person was arrested for a crime he did not commit, due to a false positive identification made by a facial recognition system.[21] According to the account from Wayne County, Michigan (US), despite the fact that photos taken from surveillance footage at the scene of a theft did not appear to match the face of the suspect, a decision was by law enforcement officers to arrest the suspect, who was a black man. Observers noted that a possible escalation in the situation, compounded by distrust of law enforcement[22]

20 P. Grother, et al. 2019. "'Face Recognition Vendor Test (FRVT) Part 3: Demographic Effects' *NISTIR 8280* (Washington, DC, National Institute of Standards and Technology, 2019) <https://doi.org/10.6028/NIST.IR.8280>

21 K. Hill, 'Wrongfully Accused by an Algorithm' (*New York Times*, 24 June 2020) <https://www.nytimes.com/2020/06/24/technology/facial-recognition-arrest.html>

22 The incident in Wayne County occurred just weeks after the death of George Floyd, an incident which triggered massive, sometimes violent protests alleging systemic racism in law enforcement around the United States that lasted for weeks, making racial inequality and justice under the law a critical issue in the 2020 national election in that country.

and mistaken identity, could have resulted in highly undesirable (if not fatal) outcomes had the suspect not yielded and cooperated.

Sync 6: Tools in criminal justice

You should allow around 15 minutes for this activity.

Some jurisdictions currently use tools to assist judges in assessing the eligibility of alleged criminals for bail based on several criteria, including an assessment of flight risk (how likely the individual is to attempt to leave the country before their hearing). These tools provide judges struggling with increasingly large caseloads with consistent guidelines for evaluating bail eligibility, which are intended to remove bias and support impartiality. While such tools might be programmed with a reasonable freedom from bias, the data used to train an algorithm implementing such an evaluation might reflect the fact that minority groups are more likely to be arrested, leaving those groups at a disadvantage when requesting bail.[23]

- What are the possible sources of bias that could be found in data sets used to train systems recommending decisions for bail granted to alleged criminals?
- What precautions must be taken by legislatures and courts to ensure that the effects of bias in such automated tools can be recognised, and what guidelines must be issued to give judges necessary latitude when deciding courses of action prior to trial?

You may have found yourself laying the onus of ensuring freedom from bias in training data squarely on the technology provider. While technologists have methods and tools for ensuring that their tools and models are checked and reasonably guard against certain forms of bias, those tools and models are only as good as the information and knowledge (especially of bias) available to their creators. A fruitful dialogue between technologists and jurists evaluating or designing such tools would also seek actively for and incorporate knowledge from a wider range of experts and expertise, incorporating and going beyond crime and criminal court statistics to take in and give weight to the findings of social scientists, specialists in corrections and advocates for access to justice.

23 <https://www.justia.com/criminal/bail-bonds/bail-algorithms/>

Digital lawyering skills: problem-finding and problem-solving

In this chapter you have considered a range of scenarios and issues, including those discussed in Sync 5. All of these require a digital lawyer to be able to both problem-find and problem-solve. The term "problem-finding" refers to having the vision and insight to be able to anticipate and identify potential problems before going on to frame them in a way which enables you to seek appropriate and workable solutions.

Law students usually spend a considerable amount of time preparing answers to problem-style questions, replicating the types of scenarios that may arise when advising a client in practice. These are very helpful in assisting you to think about and apply the content of the law. However, they are often very focused on a specific topic and do not factor in the many variables that arise in reality.

Other ways to develop your abilities to problem-find and problem-solve could include looking for voluntary opportunities with law clinics or similar organisations, becoming involved in events such as hackathons and even playing board games and puzzles.

REGULATION AND COMPLIANCE FOR BIG DATA

Having examined in brief a few of the possibilities of Big Data in application and the risks that its use and misuse with modern analytics technology may raise, we now turn to an introduction of the characteristics of regulatory regimes for data, data processing and privacy.

GDPR

Regulation (EU) 2016/679 of the European Parliament, known commonly as the General Data Protection Regulation (GDPR), provides for the protection of rights related to the data concerning individuals. We provide here only a brief summary of the regulatory points sufficient to further our discussion of Big Data. You are, of course, warmly invited to download and read the regulation for deeper understanding.[24]

24 The text of the GDPR can be found at <https://eur-lex.europa.eu/eli/reg/2016/679/oj>

Rights of the individual

The GDPR first defines and mandates protection of specific rights of the data subject; that is, of the person identifiable from the data or to whom the data pertains. These rights include:

- *Right of information.* Individuals must be informed about data collection activities, the purposes for which the data are collected and processed, and the ways and duration of time the data will be kept and shared with other parties.
- *Right of access.* A person must be given access to their personal data and information regarding how that data is processed, including how it is obtained, the purpose of the processing and to whom the data is shared.
- *Right of rectification.* Individuals have the right to have inaccurate personal data rectified, or completed if it is incomplete.
- *Right of erasure.* Individuals can request that organisations erase data pertaining to them, on any number of grounds defined in the GDPR. This was originally more broadly defined in a "Right to be Forgotten", but that provision was changed to the Right of Erasure in the version of the GDPR adopted by the EU Parliament in 2016.
- *Right of portability.* In order to comply, data controllers (e.g. online services) must provide data to individuals when requested in structured, commonly used electronic formats. It would not, therefore, be acceptable to comply with a request for personal information by sending a bulky set of paper printouts, thereby placing a burden on the individual requester to have to input the information into a computer, whether for further personal use or to audit the activities of the online service provider.
- *Right to restrict processing.* The GDPR provides that individuals must be able to restrict the ways in which data controllers process their personal information, whether for sales, marketing or non-service-related activities. Exceptions include situations where the processing is necessary in order to provide the service in question, legal compliance or activities required in the public interest.
- *Right to object.* Individuals must be informed of processing activities undertaken with their data and to be given methods to object with reasonable timeliness and practicability.

Obligations of the data controller and processor

The GDPR also defines specific responsibilities for the content provider, hosting provider or other entity providing services with custody of data pertaining to individuals. This individual or organisation is known as the data controller or, in the case of someone providing processing services (in-house or outsourced), the processor.

- *Pseudonymisation.* Data that is to be on a disk, tape or other storage medium (i.e. stored "at rest") must have PII modified so that it is not readable without a separate piece of data that is not stored together with the data in question, such as an encryption key. This is to ensure that records are not readily able to be connected to individuals. Instead of scrambling records with encryption, some implementations of this measure will issue a string of letters and numbers, known as a token, with a secure lookup facility to provide the corresponding, de-tokenised data from another system that stores the PII in a securely encrypted form.
- *Records of processing.* Data processors are required to document the procedures for processing personal data, as well as the identifying information for all those involved in processing and delivering processed information. Depending on the EU country implementing the GDPR, other items, such as the effective and end dates of the documented procedures and safeguards and security measures to be taken, must also be documented.
- *Personal data security.* Controllers and processors of personal information must notify the individuals or controllers, respectively, within 72 hours after detecting a security breach in which readable personally identifying data is leaked.
- *Data protection officer.* Every organisation involved in controlling or processing data must appoint a member of staff or a qualified contractor who can assist the controller or processor in their compliance with the regulation.

It can be seen from the foregoing description of the GDPR stipulations (also summarised in Figure 6.4) that a comprehensive effort to understand the scope of data under the control and processing of an organisation is necessary to be fully compliant with the regulation.

Other jurisdictions have varying levels of data privacy regulation, sometimes very limited in scope. As students and new lawyers advance in training, they should take care to familiarise themselves with the relevant privacy regulations and existing enforcement practices in the jurisdictions where they practice. Some, like certain US states, do not

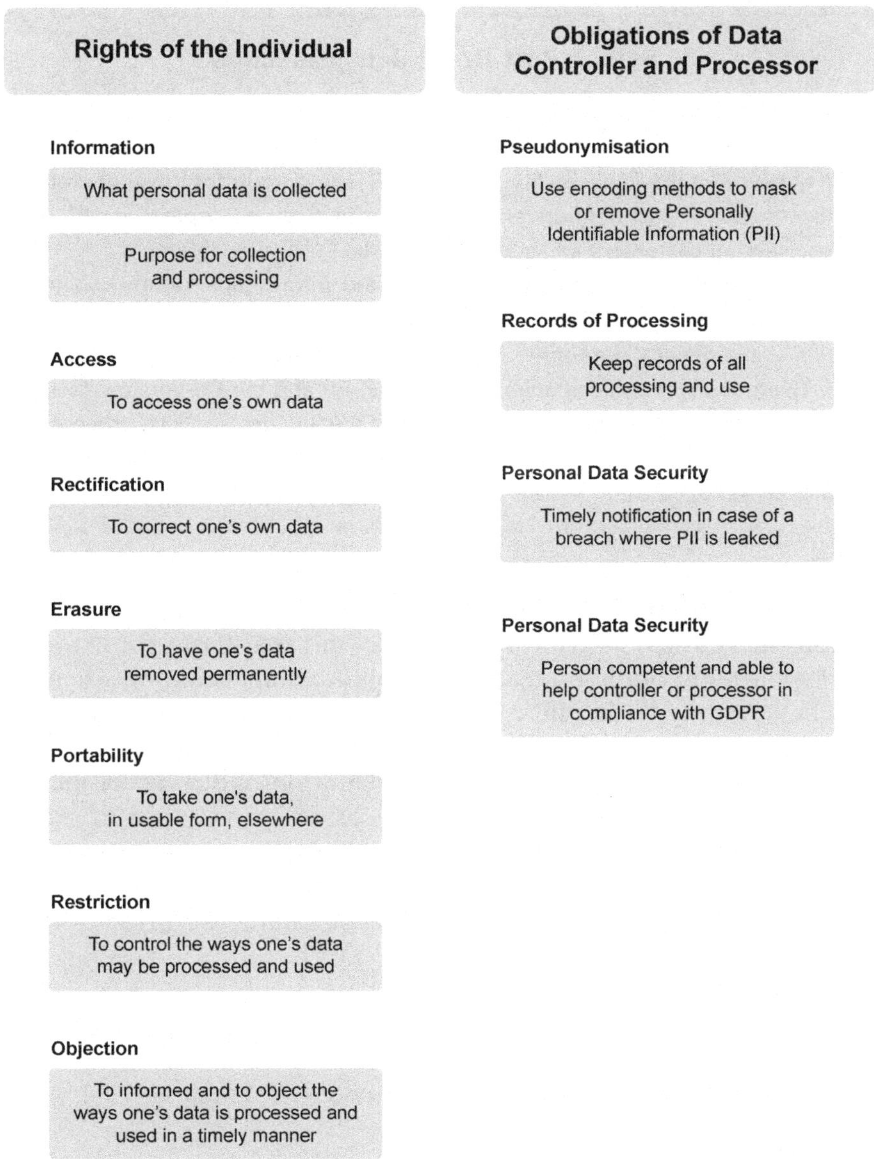

Figure 6.4 Diagram of individual rights under GDPR

necessarily have the same level of protections. California has regulations based on opting out of practices, as opposed to the mandated regulation of the GDPR. At a national level, only health-related records are protected under HIPAA.

Sync 7: Post-Brexit data protection

You should allow around 45 minutes for this activity.

With the completion of the UK's withdrawal from the European Union, the question of the applicability of the GDPR is important for those operating online services and data-driven businesses in the now-separated UK and those serving customers and subscribers in the European Union.

Review the UK GDPR guidelines at the Information Commissioner's Office website <https://ico.org.uk/for-organisations/guide-to-data-protection/guide-to-the-general-data-protection-regulation-gdpr/>

Note the similarities between the UK GDPR and the EU version, including the differences for law enforcement and intelligence services processing in the UK, as well as the considerations for data flowing over networks in either direction between the UK and EU.

You will likely find that the similarities between the two GDPR versions make them in principle the same, but that terms for extraterritorial application of the regulation complicate understanding when they do differ. Another area where you may have some difficulty is with personal data inextricably linked or embedded in other application data. There are yet to be cases to settle the definition under law of inextricable data in processing. Processors and custodians may not in practice remove or obfuscate personal data in cases where it is not economically feasible, or simply impossible in some physical way; for example, when doing so will corrupt or destroy the files containing the PII and data in question.

Big Data driving changes in law practice

Law practice has been traditionally been slow to adopt digital technology beyond local office and network productivity tools, such as an electronic system for organising information about clients. In an article titled "Why Is Law So Slow to Use Data?", Mark Cohen, a lawyer and leader of a global non-profit exploring and promoting digital lawyering, discussed the prevalence of an attitude of exceptionalism in the legal profession which leaves the legal profession, in his words, "a data wasteland in the digital era".[25] Professional exceptionalism in law asserts that the accumulated experience of a single legal mind transcends mere mechanical actions by technology, leaning on vaguely defined notions of the "superiority" of the human mind, dismissing the need to embrace the change that technology brings. Contrary to its normal practice of demanding evidence, perhaps best exemplified in other disciplines like the sciences or entrepreneurship, some members of the legal profession have taken such positions without a basis in evidence and data.

As we have seen, Big Data, using well-chosen, well-implemented and well-fitted[26] models, allow many sectors and even certain aspects of the legal system to realise and deliver benefits to individuals and to society as a whole. The notion that data is the oil of the digital era, first introduced in an influential article in the *Economist*,[27] has even been borne out in the legal profession. Cloud computing, as we have seen in Chapter 3, has started to change the way lawyers can collaborate with colleagues and counterparties. Firms are now looking at ways to adopt and exploit Big Data management and analytic practices as they begin to see the possibilities and look to exploit them as competitive tools. It is not our purpose to judge whether such adoption is voluntary and advantage-seeking or, as the case may be, a shrewd act of self-preservation. A lawyer leading a practice certainly faces such a choice if they are not already an adopter.

In this section we will examine a few of the ways that Big Data is having significant impact on the practice of law.

DIGITISATION

As discussed in Chapter 2, the traditional image of a lawyer hard at work finds her at a desk amid stacked boxes of documents, poring over

25 M. A. Cohen, 'Why Is Law So Slow to Use Data?' (*Forbes*) <https://www.forbes.com/sites/markcohen1/2019/06/24/why-is-law-so-slow-to-use-data/>

26 Machine learning techniques operate on computations that generate a function that when applied to inputs, matches, as close as possible, the data points that make up the example data in a training set. In these applications, there is allowance for a level of variance from the model, which still define examples that are correct and accomplish the goals for the model. When models are too specific, and become inaccurate because of extreme conditions in the data, the model is said to be over-fitted.

27 The Economist, 'The World's Most Valuable Resource is No Longer Oil, But Data' (*The Economist*, 6 May 2017) <https://www.economist.com/leaders/2017/05/06/the-worlds-most-valuable-resource-is-no-longer-oil-but-data>

casebooks, searching for precedents to use in forming an argument. The ability of larger firms, with the sheer size and wherewithal to keep deep benches of junior staff and associates, conferred on those organisations great practical advantages when competing for client business, conducting discovery or assessing the risk at various stages of litigation. Digitisation of documents, through scanning, optical character recognition (OCR) and automated transcription, makes large bodies of documents available as data for NLP tools built with models suited for specific purposes, commonly employed in tools for technology assisted review (TAR), with functions including but not limited to search, classification, semantic analysis and ontology construction.

ANALYTICS IN THE MODERN LAW FIRM PRACTICE

As firms collect data internally from past records, combining them with external sources both publicly and privately sourced, opportunities arise to ensure better outcomes through the judicious use of Big Data sets and analytics.

Big Data practices and maturing analytics offered as products now give lawyers access to case history data compiled from public sources. This data is sometimes enriched with the vendor's proprietary data offerings, together with a firm's own performance data, to assess the probability of success in taking action on a matter; for example, whether a specific course of action in litigation based on the presiding judge or opposing counsel's track records in similar cases would indicate a threshold probability of success. Naturally, such indicators could highlight unacceptable risks in litigation and thus would inform the firm to counsel the client to accept a negotiated settlement that would, in this data-driven assessment, be the best result.

Internally, firms may choose specific lawyers to handle certain types of cases based on recommendations or scoring based on past performance in similar matters. Other firms may combine risk assessments with the need to train junior lawyers to handle certain matters, ensuring that opportunities to develop experience can be taken and ensuring better outcomes for the client and the firm.

REPUTATION MANAGEMENT

With access to large bodies of case data aggregated and processed by legal data providers, firms can develop analyses of their performance in their specialty areas of practice, in some cases creating opportunities to highlight the firm's superior performance in marketing efforts, giving prospective clients greater confidence in their choice of representation. Reputation data and surveys are also useful for highlighting areas of improvement for a firm, whether in practice, client prospecting or recruiting new talent for a firm's practice.

PRACTICE DEVELOPMENT

In the past, leaders in law firms developed new business based on relationships and what their immediate networks showed for "market signal" (pieces of information indicating which way the market is heading). This practice was based on anecdotal information—arguably far from data-driven in the systematic sense. The same data sources that can be used for reputation management can also give indications of emerging new areas of business or areas in which a firm may invest more to support the needs of clients, anticipated with data.

FEE OPTIMISATION

Applications of Big Data and analytics in the modern law firm provide numerous opportunities to optimise the value delivered to clients in the practice of fee optimisation:

- *Lower costs and efficiency.* Machine learning tools supported with Big Data can dramatically reduce the personnel and time required to conduct discovery, search and other traditionally labour-intensive tasks done by junior staff, associates and paralegal personnel. Firms with large databases of practice metrics also have the opportunity to highlight the efficiencies in the execution of tasks together with the cost savings realised.
- *Focus on higher-value service.* Far from reducing billing, the efficiencies realised with Big Data and analytic tools support the application of fees to higher-value service, elevating the practice overall and enhancing experience, reputation and future ability to win and service higher-value client business.
- *Visibility into billings and demonstrated value.* Modern practice management systems support a client portal with visibility into lawyer billings, updated at least daily, if not more frequently. When combined with reports tailored to the concerns of individual clients showing the increases in value realised with the firm through

judicious application of technology, firms not only can service higher-value business but can also demonstrate concretely to cost-conscious clients their effectiveness in doing so. This means they can address multiple concerns of cost, value of time billed, overall legal position and business outcomes.

PREREQUISITES FOR SUCCESS

In this chapter we have introduced the concepts of Big Data and its interrelationship with analytics. We have examined general applications and more specialised applications in the legal profession and justice systems as well as the risks, regulatory and ethical considerations that follow. It is important that we conclude with some points that a new digital lawyer should bear in mind in encountering and navigating the opportunities and challenges of Big Data.

Andrew McAffee and Erik Brynjolfsson, researchers from the Initiative on the Digital Economy at the Massachusetts Institute of Technology Sloan School of Management, discussed the challenges to effective use of Big Data and analytics in their Harvard Business Review piece "Big Data: The Management Revolution". They found that while technical challenges that come with the increasing volume, variety and velocity of data were non-trivial, the way organisations made decisions, starting with the senior executive team, needed critical examination as a prerequisite in the transformation to data-driven practice. While not discounting the value of experience and intuition, they stressed the need for leaders to develop an ability to look at data with objectivity—the same objectivity that a lawyer would bring to evidence—and to develop a willingness to subordinate their experience and intuition to possible conclusions revealed in data. The willingness is best put into practice in a removal of what they termed the primacy of the HiPPO: the highest paid person's opinion.[28]

Most legal firms believe that data-driven understanding and methods for managing legal issues are valuable, though the culture in the profession, education and training have not matched that belief. Instead, prevalent attitudes and mindsets dividing the world into

28 Andrew McAffee and Erik Brynjolfsson, 'Big Data: The Management Revolution' (*Harvard Business Review*, 1 October 2012) <https://hbr.org/2012/10/big-data-the-management-revolution>

"lawyers" and "non-lawyers", with clear distinctions in hierarchy and influence on firm policy and practices, have had profound effects on the profession's understanding and pursuit of data-driven practice.

McAffee and Brynjolfsson identify five key challenges for organisations seeking to transform themselves and benefit from data-driven practices.

- *Leadership*. For a data-driven practice to take root, leaders in a firm must not only have a vision for how to develop and grow their firm, a way to blend creative thought with action, but also a clear commitment to decision-making with data that takes best advantage of the new combination of objective results from data, experience, and intuition. For the legal profession, this type of organisational transformation at the level of the individual firm may well be the most difficult, testing leaders and their structures of governance.
- *Talent management*. Firms seeking to gain a competitive advantage with data will compete with not only with peers in the legal profession for competent and talented professionals skilled in data science but with the entire business sector, as the adoption of the Big Data application accelerates.[29]
- *Technology*. The volume, variety and velocity of Big Data that we have highlighted several times as the defining characteristic of Big Data poses unique challenges to IT departments. Law firms have not treated IT investments as strategic investments. Leaders in these firms must recognise the enablement that comes with strategic IT investment and will benefit from study and consultation with professionals in other sectors who have gone through the process of digital transformation and developed frameworks, and more important, cultures for strategic IT investment and stewardship.
- *Decision-making*. Successful leaders effecting change will locate decision-making closest to problems in the organisation while supplying the broadest range of resources possible. They encourage their colleagues to be problem-solvers with an openness to the information and experience across the organisation, especially those with scale and wide geographic reach. A data-driven culture of decision-making will enhance such efforts, considering evidence that can be evaluated objectively, alleviating scepticism and

29 Thomas H. Davenport and D. J. Patil, 'Data Scientist: The Sexiest Job of the 21st Century' (*Harvard Business Review*, 1 October 2012) <https://hbr.org/2012/10/data-scientist-the-sexiest-job-of-the-21st-century>

"not invented here" behaviours (which do not value external ideas and influences) when confronted with approaches from far-flung colleagues in the firm who are effective strangers.
- *Company culture.* Asking the right questions and letting the data offer possibilities before asking for opinions may produce superior results to starting with advancing opinions or a HiPPO and then sending colleagues forth to gather supporting evidence.

The digital lawyer who has a clear understanding of the range of issues and concerns surrounding Big Data and its applications will be well-positioned to advise clients and to lead in data-driven legal practice. Operation based on information revealed in data is in direct line with the legal profession's tradition of objectivity and considered action based on interpretation of facts under the rule of law.

ADDITIONAL RESOURCES

Davenport TH, "Analytics 3.0" (*Harvard Business Review*, 2013) <https://hbr.org/2013/12/analytics-30> accessed 1 December 2013.

"The Dictatorship of Data." (*MIT Technology Review*, n.d.) <https://www.technologyreview.com/2013/05/31/178263/the-dictatorship-of-data/> accessed 31 January 2021.

Duhigg C, "How Companies Learn Your Secrets". (*New York Times*, 2012), sec. Magazine <https://www.nytimes.com/2012/02/19/magazine/shopping-habits.html> accessed 16 February 2012.

Economist, "The World's Most Valuable Resource is no Longer Oil, but Data" (*Economist*, 6 May 2017) <https://www.economist.com/leaders/2017/05/06/the-worlds-most-valuable-resource-is-no-longer-oil-but-data>.

Gurin J, *Open Data Now* (McGraw-Hill Education, 2014).

Król K and Zdonek D, "Analytics Maturity Models: An Overview" (2020) 11 (3) *Information* 142 <https://doi.org/10.3390/info11030142>

Manyika J and others, *Big Data: The next Frontier for Innovation, Competition, and Productivity* (McKinsey Global Institute, 2011).

Marr B, "Really Big Data at Walmart: Real-Time Insights from Their 40+ Petabyte Data Cloud" (*Forbes*, n.d.) <https://www.forbes.com/sites/bernardmarr/2017/01/23/really-big-data-at-

walmart-real-time-insights-from-their-40-petabyte-data-cloud/> accessed 2 January 2021.

Mohler GO and others, "Randomized Controlled Field Trials of Predictive Policing" (January 2016) *Journal of the American Statistical Association* <https://amstat.tandfonline.com/doi/full/10.1080/01621459.2015.1077710>

Staff CACM, "Big Data" (2017) 60 (6) *Commun. ACM* 24–25 <https://doi.org/10.1145/3079064>

Susskind R, *Online Courts and the Future of Justice* (OUP, 2019).

'What is China's Social Credit System and Why Is It Controversial?' (*South China Morning Post*, 2020) <https://www.scmp.com/economy/china-economy/article/3096090/what-chinas-social-credit-system-and-why-it-controversial> accessed 9 August 2020.

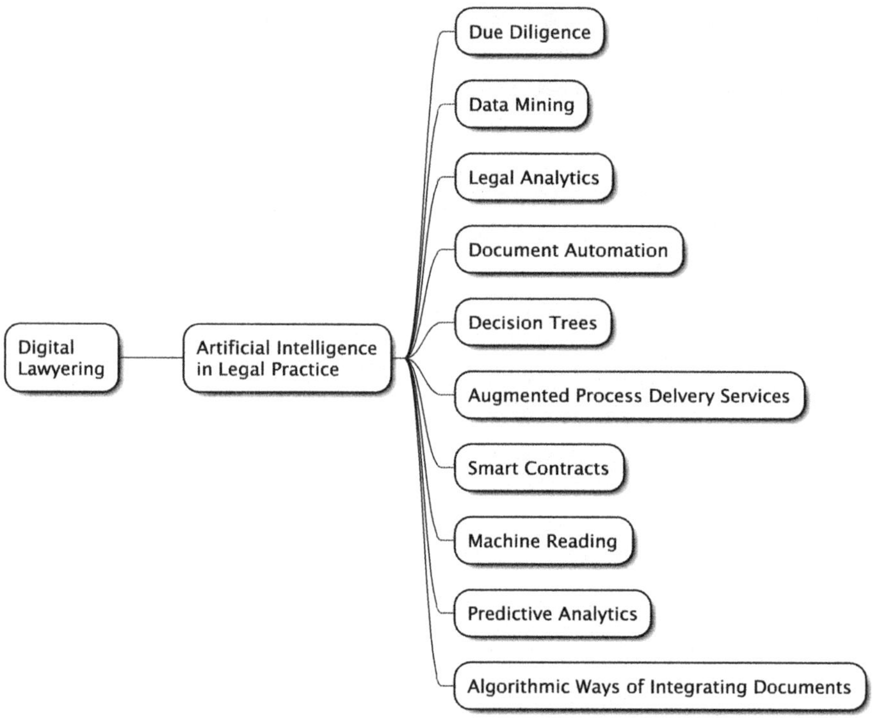

Mind Map 7.1 Chapter topics

7

Using Artificial Intelligence to Enhance and Augment the Delivery of Legal Services

Ann Thanaraj

Introduction

Artificial intelligence (AI) will redefine the legal profession. This redefinition can be seen as an evolution of the role lawyers already perform, creating new ways of working and new roles and responsibilities relating to how we execute legal work. New types of work will be available, including symbiotic new specialisms using a perfect blend of human expertise focusing on complex high-level advisory work supported by technology and its affordances. Whilst efficiency is a benefit of AI, and it is in fact used most commonly for this purpose, AI will also help legal professionals to provide more transparency and value to the delivery of legal services, putting the client in the heart of the service. This chapter will explore how AI is already supporting the profession and what the future holds for our further collaboration.

Chapter hot spots

When reading this chapter, questions to think about include:

- How is AI currently being used in the legal profession, and to what extent is it capable of advancing, enhancing and changing the nature of the way legal services are delivered?
- To what extent can AI foster disruptive innovation, and how is AI starting to change the future of work across occupations, particularly in the legal

DOI: 10.4324/9780429298219-7

profession? Here, you will need to understand the requisite set of skills, tools and assets needed to thrive in the changing legal world.

- To what extent can AI decision-making impact our professional responsibilities and legal ethics?
- How is AI likely to affect how the law is litigated and enforced as AI continues to reshape many aspects of our lives?

Having read the title and introduction, you can add any other questions you want to explore here:

WHAT IS ARTIFICIAL INTELLIGENCE?

This chapter seeks to raise awareness and equip you with the knowledge to understand how AI is being used currently in the legal sector, helping you develop a critical and solid foundation of what AI is and how it can contribute to this perfect blend of collaborating with human lawyers.

In the world of computer science, AI has been around for quite some time. Some of the original concepts can be found as far back as 1950, when Alan Turing posed the question "Can machines think?" in his paper "Computing Machinery and Intelligence". This question helps define what AI is. In its most basic form, AI can refer to any human-like intelligence demonstrated by any robot, computer, program or tool.[1] We will need to dig a little further than this, however, to get a better definition and understanding of what AI is and how it functions. AI operates in a number of different formats, which you will find out as you progress through this chapter.

The tasks which AI can carry out include (but are not limited to) making decisions, responding to problems, understanding human language and requests, and object and image recognition—all of which

1 IBM Cloud Education, 'What is AI' (*IBM*, 3 June 2020) <https://www.ibm.com/cloud/learn/what-is-artificial-intelligence> accessed 25 April 2021.

you would expect a human to be able to do on a day-to-day basis. Further applications of AI which may be more recognisable to you include the following; you possibly use these every day without even realising:

- *Virtual assistants*: These can be most commonly seen in the likes of Alexa and Siri, which will recognise your spoken voice and assist you in a specific manner.
- *Image recognition*: There are numerous programs that assist in the recognition of objects and help make decisions based on this recognition. Fingerprint technology and facial recognition are being used to help protect items like your mobile phone.
- *Recommendations*: You will often see adverts which have been carefully curated to your preferences when browsing the Internet and social media. This is done by processing your personal data and browsing habits into adverts which are tailored to what the program believes you will be interested in.
- *Automation*: There are numerous programs that help make things smoother for the user. These work by automating sequences; for example, Alexa automating a sequence of activities when you arrive home. The lights will turn on, blinds will close and the kettle will boil.

In this chapter, you will read about examples of AI used to improve services to clients, generating efficiencies through legal retrieval and research tools, and improving customer service using automated and conversational interfaces such as chatbots and self-help tools. The impact of AI can be seen in Chapters 2 and 4, where we discuss how the digital transformation is affecting the work of the legal profession and the approach taken in the delivery of legal services, including the use of alternative business structures, the unbundling of services, the digitalisation of services through legal platforms and the automation of procedural work.

Through the sync activities in this chapter, you will be equipped with the critical and comprehensive legal knowledge and thinking to apply to a wide spectrum of real-life situations, including the interdisciplinary knowledge of both technology and law. These activities and questions are designed to help you critically think about the subject matter presented. You will develop your interdisciplinary knowledge of technology and law which will help you critically assess the use of AI in legal practice.

Digital lawyering skills: systematic thinking

Many legal topics, such as employment law, the law of torts and contract law, lend themselves to illustrating principles of the law in a flowchart algorithm to solve a client's problem. The development of the algorithm requires students to think systematically about the processes for solving legal problems, by breaking down each legal issue into components and applying a legal theory and available admissible evidence to help create a formula to solve the issue. This attempts to mimic the systematic and methodological flow of how algorithms are used by AIs in decision-making through logic and reasoning, which are key attributes in designing algorithms. The development of algorithms and learning about its complexities are important parts of the digital literacy required for students to undertake the future role of a lawyer, which requires a strong understanding of technological functions alongside its legalities and ethics.[2] When studying the methodologies of AI, students are encouraged to consider the methodological processes of legal reasoning in a legal matter, to help understand how an AI might be used to answer legal questions and explain its answers.

Although it is unlikely that the online delivery of legal services will require lawyers to code technical and computational designs of software, algorithms and AI, lawyers will require more knowledge around the functions and capabilities of these technologies and will need the ability to identify suitable and efficient technology to meet a client's needs. Raising awareness of current and emerging practices, the affordances, limitations, design and development, and the comparisons between human cognition and the working practices of the AI is part of equipping law students with the knowledge and skills necessary for participating in a technologically advanced, multidisciplinary and complex professional environment.

Sync 1: Understanding AI

You should allow around 15 minutes for this activity.

Read the following article "What Is AI? We Drew You a Flowchart to Work It Out" by Karen Hao in the *MIT Technology Review* <https://www-technology

2 W. Hall and J. Pesenti, 'Growing the Artificial Intelligence Industry in the UK' (*Department for Digital, Culture, Media and Sport' Department for Business, Energy*, 2017) <https://www.gov.uk/government/publications/growing-the-artificial-intelligence-industry-in-the-uk>

review-com.cdn.ampproject.org/c/s/www.technologyreview.com/2018/11/10/139137/is-this-ai-we-drew-you-a-flowchart-to-work-it-out/amp/>

Based on your reading, write a paragraph summary of AI addressed to a client with no previous knowledge of the topic. You should ensure you keep a copy of this summary to refer back to in Sync 3.

Hopefully your paragraph identified that the term "AI" refers to the ways in which machines are increasingly able to learn, reason and act independently, adapting to new circumstances that arise.

THE NEED FOR LAWYERS

Extending our capabilities, predictive technology AI has also been used to identify the best chances of succeeding in a case and determine how the lawyer spends their time supporting clients and undertaking work that involves human interaction. Such work involves building relationships and handling complex interdisciplinary problems which AI does not have the capacity to do. AI is designed on the premise that the law is simply a set of rules that can be applied in a linear way to a problem. Critical reasoning, analysis and interpretive freedom are values that underpin the art of lawyering; as such, the law is more than mere rules and needs to be applied to reflect the changing social and cultural environment. Again, AI is not capable of adapting to that change. Furthermore, lawyers are needed for their ability to understand and adapt with resilience towards changes in regulations and new developments within various sectors in which their clients operate. The flexibility, uncertainty and ambiguity of sectors and industries require in-depth understanding that is open to interpretation to capture the nuances of client needs, which a standardised AI operation is not able to fulfil. A good use of AI though is to help lawyers and law students understand the patterns, similarities and differences that result in a legal decision by comparing cases, facts and judgments.

There is various content online with hype around the lack of need for lawyers and legal professionals because of AI. In this chapter, you will work through various sync exercises to develop your awareness around the need for lawyers and what lawyers will be doing as the profession becomes augmented by AI. It is important for you to understand how AI technologies function and their design purpose. This will assist you in developing a well-reasoned and rational perspective of the changing nature of the profession and the need for AI to expedite routine tasks which frees up digital lawyers' time to handle more complex and creative work.

By developing an understanding of how AI is shaping legal practice, you are encouraged throughout this chapter to question the current use, potential and limitations of AI and the sorts of regulatory landscape needed to facilitate better collaboration between lawyers and AI. Lawyers will be required to establish the regulatory and governance framework for AI operations, automated decision-making and the professional responsibilities of lawyers in the context of AI supporting their work. When you consider areas of property law (buying and selling of land) and contract law (certainty of intention between the parties), whilst AI technologies can undertake tasks such as establishing certainties, checking of contracts and even execution of contracts (smart contracts), a lawyer is still required to take on liability for these contracts, meaning advising their client whether to sign their name at the bottom and taking responsibility for any mistakes made. For this reason, it is imperative that lawyers have a clear understanding of how AI and like-minded technologies function.

Sync 2: The impact of AI

You should allow around 60 minutes for this activity.

Read the article by Frey C and Osborne B (September 2013), "The Future of Employment: How Susceptible Are Jobs to Computerisation?" <https://www.oxfordmartin.ox.ac.uk/downloads/academic/The_Future_of_Employment.pdf> In it, the authors suggest that paralegals, trainee solicitors and lawyers will increasingly have different roles and responsibilities as some previous parts of their roles can be undertaken by AI, freeing up time for more complex and high-level work by human experts.

- Can you think of examples of how a trainee lawyer's role can change?
- What sort of additional skill sets would this trainee require to undertake the changed role?
- What does digital literacy mean in the context of the legal profession?
- What sorts of knowledge, in addition to legal knowledge, should the trainee be equipped with to undertake the changed role?

You may have noted that this article was published in 2013. You may also find it interesting to reflect upon what developments have taken place since then, drawing on Chapters 2, 4 and 12.

EXAMPLES OF AI

Typically an AI system is provided with a "training set", consisting of data about the subject, and its algorithms, and instructions on what to do with the data. It then detects patterns in data, and applies these new patterns to automate certain tasks and identify patterns and relationships within the data. The examples in the following table demonstrate the development of AI by highlighting some key systems that have been designed over the years.

Launch	AI	Achievements
1966	Eliza[3]	The first chatbot that had the ability to process human language, including the ability to compose short written responses. A variant of this prototype was developed into a psychologist.
1970	MYCIN[4]	The first to help doctors diagnose certain blood diseases and also in recommending treatments.
1990	Polly[5]	Used as a navigator with the ability to voice and interact with humans, it led visitors through the computer science and AI lab at the Massachusetts Institute of Technology.
1997	Deep Blue[6]	Famously defeated world champion Garry Kasparov at chess. Remarkably it was capable of evaluating 200 million chess position variables in a second and responding with a move accordingly, unlike human capabilities which typically expand towards learning excellent chess playing techniques.

(*Continued*)

3 Michael Wallace, 'Eliza: A Chatbot Therapist' (*Eliza*, 2016), 1 <https://web.njit.edu/~ronkowit/eliza.html>

4 B. J. Copeland, 'MYCIN' (*Britannica*, 21 November 2018) <https://www.britannica.com/technology/MYCIN>

5 Ian Horswill, 'Polly: A Vision-based Artificial Agent' *Proceedings of the National Conference on Artificial Intelligence* (AAAI, 1993).

6 IBM, 'Icons of Progress' (IBM, N/A) <https://www.ibm.com/ibm/history/ibm100/us/en/icons/watson/>

2011	IBM Watson[7]	Famously defeated top quiz-show champions on the game show, *Jeopardy!* Unlike the human technique of learning information through retrieval and research, it was programmed on semantic analysis, the ability to understand human language and to categorise the meaning of the words and sentences.
2011	Uber[8]	The global transportation company which allows people to move from place to place with just a couple of clicks. The app is built on a complex set of AI technologies. • Uses natural language processing (NLP) technology to understand and undertake human conversations and user experience. • Computer vision software that verifies millions of images and documents like driver's licenses. • Sensor-processing algorithms that are capable of predicting estimated time of arrival, location of vehicle and traffic updates. • Sophisticated machine learning algorithms that predict the location and supply and demand needs in particular areas and at particular times, allowing tailored availabilities to meet needs.
2012	Lex Machina[9]	This is an analytics tool used in the legal profession. A notable use case was in an intellectual property (IP) law case to determine patterns and trends in how a particular judge rules in IP cases. Whether there is a direct link between the analysis produced by the AI and the case being settled instead of heading to the courts has not been established.

7 Ibid.

8 Zheng Huaixiu, 'COTA: Improving Uber Customer Care with NLP & Machine Learning' (*Uber Engineering*, 3 January 2018) <https://eng.uber.com/cota/>

9 'Legal Analytics Platform' (*Lex Machina, A LexisNexis Company*, N/A) <https://lexmachina.com/legal-analytics/>

2015	Ravel Law[10]	A prediction technology tool used in the legal profession. It is known for providing lawyers with information on how a judge rules on a case, affording the ability to predict with a percentage of certainty the success of a case based on precedent linked to a specific judge's record of ruling.
2015	Premonition[11]	A prediction technology tool used in the legal profession. The AI technology mines data on the successes of a particular lawyer's success rating and supplements that information with information on the judges who found in their favour. It has just over a 30% accuracy rate.
2016	AlphaGo[12]	Famously defeated Lee Sedol, a world champion player, at the complex ancient Chinese board game, Go. Using algorithms that functioned like the human brain, AlphaGo's success was due to playing millions of games and absorbing the techniques of logic and intuition, learning the typical moves of human players.
2016	CARA[13]	This is a predictive technology tool used in the legal profession. It has been used by lawyers to predict or forecast their opposition's arguments in a particular case by finding opinions that were previously used by lawyers. It is also a helpful tool for identifying precedents and arguments that can be used to support their own case.

(*Continued*)

10 'Products and Technology' (*Ravel, A LexisNexis Company*, N/A) <https://home.ravellaw.com/>

11 'Lawyer Win Rates Arrive in Canada' (*Premonition*, 7 September 2016) <https://premonition.ai/lawyer-win-rates-arrive-canada/>

12 'AlphaGo is the First Computer Program to Defeat a Professional Human Go Player, the First to Defeat a Go World Champion, and is Arguably the Strongest Go Player in History' (*AlphaGo*) <https://deepmind.com/research/case-studies/alphago-the-story-so-far>

13 'Have CARA AI Find You the Most On-point Authorities Program to Defeat a Professional Human Go Player, the First to Defeat a Go World Champion, and Is Arguably the Strongest Go Player in History' (*CaseText*) <https://casetext.com/cara-ai/>

2016	IBM Watson[14]	A remarkable AI tool that was able to identify and diagnose leukaemia in a patient within ten minutes. It was capable of cross-referencing the patient's condition against 20 million oncology records and detecting gene mutations that are unique to a particular type of leukaemia to ascertain the diagnosis, which medical experts could not do.
2016	Intraspexion[15]	This is an AI technology equipped with Natural Language Processing and Machine Learning functionality for use in the legal profession. It is used to alert lawyers to the threat of any litigation by searching for high-risk documents and displaying them according to the level of risk that the AI has determined. It also identifies the risk within the documents.
2016	Kira[16]	This is an e-discovery tool used in the legal profession. The combination of the AI's capabilities, which speeds up the process by at least 40%, and the expert knowledge from lawyers helps to undertake more accurate due diligence contract review by searching, highlighting and extracting relevant content for analysis.
2016	ROSS[17]	This is an AI technology equipped with NLP capabilities for use in the legal profession. Typically used as a legal research tool, it extracts facts and patterns in cases and analyses information from cases at a rate of over a billion documents per second. Its NLP capabilities provide answers to questions which are crafted using human language. Its machine learning feature improves with use.

14 Ibid., p. 5.
15 'Want to Find the Risks in Your Ocean of Data?' (*Intraspexion*) <https://intraspexion.com/mvp>
16 'How KIRA Works' (*Kira*) <https://kirasystems.com/>
17 'Legal Research Software Made for Fast and In-depth Research' (*ROSS*) <https://rossintelligence.com/features>

2017	Carnegie[18]	Famously defeated the world's best poker players using similar capabilities of human experts such as strategic thinking, the ability to assess the situation and the behaviour of others and an appetite for taking risks at the right moment.
2017	COIN	To reduce errors and improve efficiency of time, COIN has been used to extract 150 errors from 12,000 commercial credit agreements and contracts in only a few seconds. This would have taken around 36,000 hours of legal work by its lawyers and loan officers.
2017	HART[19]	This tool[20] was to support custody officers when determining an offender's risk of reoffending within a 24-month period. Those who are assessed by the tool are categorised as either low, moderate or high risk.[21] The rationale for HART is to help promote consistency in decision-making,[22] while the ultimate goal was to prevent future harm in communities.[23]

(Continued)

18 'Carnegie Mellon and Facebook AI Beats Professionals in Six-Player Poker' (*Carnegie Mellon University*, 11 July) <https://www.cmu.edu/news/stories/archives/2019/july/cmu-facebook-ai-beats-poker-pros.html>

19 'Helping Police Make Custody Decisions Using Artificial Intelligence' (*Cambridge University Research*, 26 February) <https://www.cam.ac.uk/research/features/helping-police-make-custody-decisions-using-artificial-intelligence>

20 Marion Oswald, Jamie Grace, Sheena Urwin and Geoffrey C. Barnes, 'Algorithmic Risk Assessment Policing Models: Lessons from the Durham HART Model and "Experimental" Proportionality' (2018) 27 (2) *Information & Communications Technology Law* 223–50, 227–8.

21 Ibid.

22 'Written Evidence Submitted by Durham Constabulary (ALG0041)' (*data.parliament.uk*, April 2017) <http://data.parliament.uk/writtenevidence/committeeevidence.svc/evidencedocument/science-and-technology-committee/algorithms-in-decisionmaking/written/69063.pdf>

23 Ibid.

2017	Judicata[24]	This is an AI technology equipped with NLP used in the legal profession. It is capable of reading and analysing legal briefs, evaluating their strengths and weaknesses. It is also capable of assessing the quality of the briefs based on the construction of arguments and style of drafting, providing a set of feedback for improvements and avoidance of errors.
2017	PredPol[25]	Between December 2012 and March 2018, Kent Police used predictive crime mapping software called PredPol in an attempt to help reduce the crime rate within the county.[26] PredPol has led to a reduction in certain types of crime, most notably in property crime;[27] along with PredPol, predictive mapping software is more effective at predicting crimes compared with traditional methods.[28] PredPol uses three sources of data to create the predictions: date and time of the offence, crime location and crime category.[29]
2017	ThoughtRiver[30]	This is an AI technology equipped with NLP and machine learning functionality for use in the legal profession. Apart from reading contractual clauses, it is capable of interpreting meanings of clauses and flagging risky contracts automatically.

24 Beth Hoover, 'Judicata' (*Introducing Clerk*, 5 October) <https://blog.judicata.com/introducing-clerk-848abbed8fd3>

25 'PredPol Operational Review—Initial Findings' (*Kent Police*, 2013) <https://www.statewatch.org/docbin/uk-2013-11-kent-police-pp-report.pdf>

26 Ibid.

27 Alexander Babuta, 'Big Data and Policing: An Assessment of Law Enforcement Requirements, Expectations and Priorities' (*RUSI*, September 2017) <https://rusi.org/sites/default/files/201709_rusi_big_data_and_policing_babuta_web.pdf>

28 Ibid., p. 19.

29 Ibid., pp. 19–20.

30 The company provides a brief tour of their product in this three-minute video, including a detailed look at the user interface and basic functions of the software <https://vimeo.com/233981953>

2018	LawGeex[31]	This is an AI technology used in the legal profession to evaluate contracts. In a competition, the technology was competing against a human lawyer to review five non-disclosure agreements. They both had four hours to review the non-disclosure agreements and report the risks presented. It was capable of ascertaining with 94% accuracy the risks that were presented, compared to a 85% accuracy for the human lawyer. The AI completed the work in 26 seconds, whilst the lawyers took 92 minutes to complete the task.[32] Where inaccuracies are identified, the AI is capable of providing editing suggestions through its machine learning and analytics functionality.

AI REVOLUTIONISING THE WAY LEGAL WORK IS DONE

From the preceding examples, AI consists of a variety of different applications. In a law firm, this could typically include:[33]

- Document automation, such as the use of digital templates to create filled-out documents based on data input. This is becoming more and more prevalent at the beginning of legal work. Law firms will use automation to obtain client instructions in order to begin to carry out the legal work. The instructions will then form the basis of letters and go into the relevant client file for further use.
- The use of decision trees, a type of flowchart that poses a series of questions, the answers to which determine which branch is followed, until there are no more questions and a conclusion (or decision) has been reached. Law firms are adopting decision trees in order to help ascertain the risks that litigation may pose. The questions are designed to look at all possible outcomes which are attached to litigation and from here work out the possible financial

31 'How the Platform Works' (*LawGeex*) <https://www.lawgeex.com/platform/>

32 'Comparing the Performance of Artificial Intelligence to Human Lawyers in the Review of Standard Business Contracts [2018] LawGeex <https://images.law.com/contrib/content/uploads/documents/397/5408/lawgeex.pdf>

33 'Technology and Legal Services' [2018] *Solicitors Regulatory Authority* 11.

risk attached. Questions include: What will happen if this litigation ends up in court? What happens if this litigation is settled? From there, financial costs are attached to assess risk.

- Automated process-driven services using workflows, document generation, case and document management, document storage, reporting and systems integration. Adopting AI-based workflow models allows law firms to cut costs and save time on carrying out some of the administrative tasks involved in legal practice. Adopting AI practice management allows software to take the initiative in recommending templates for communications and contracts. It also helps file documents and process documents in a manner which are compliant with the firm's policy.
- Smart contracts are becoming more and more prevalent in legal practice, especially in land law and conveyancing. These are contracts which are self-executing and make the process of completing property transactions simpler. The contracts, when completed by both parties, will perform the transaction, allowing it to run more transparent and efficient. These are discussed further in Chapter 10.
- Predictive analysis forecasting case outcomes based on currently available databases of legal cases and judgments. Algorithms have been created in order to review client instructions and ascertain their chance of succeeding in court. This looks at the judgments of the courts and even the specific judges to numerically assess their chances of winning the case at hand.
- Algorithmic means of interrogating documents. Programs have been developed to review all manners of legal documents. The work has been done to assess the risk that each document poses and the accuracy of the information that is in them. This is done primarily with legal contracts and allows the user to ascertain the risks attached to each specific clause included in the contract.
- Data mining of legislation, case opinions and contracts for any consistencies to draw conclusions about judicial opinions, opposing counsel arguments and contractual amendments.
- Due diligence including contract review, legal research and electronic discovery. A lot of time is wasted in legal practice on due diligence. This has been sped up in order to give lawyers more time to focus on their clients. Systems have been put in place which can ascertain risk in legal documents, find specific evidence in a trial bundle and research precedent which will be effective for your client. All of this is done by using the vast databases of legal documents and cases which are already available. Algorithms are created which will match your current client's instruction and documents to a database of others and inform the lawyer involved to make the next decision.

The preceding examples illustrate components of AI and its various uses. It also demonstrates that AI does not have one singular definition; depending upon the context and where the AI is to be used, the definition may vary significantly.

The House of Lords Select Committee Report "AI in the UK: Ready, Willing and Able?" discusses this concept.[34]

Sync 3: AI and legal practice

Figure 7.1 below displays a flowchart illustrating the use of AI in the legal profession. For this activity you will need to refer to this flowchart and also look back at your notes and/or the article referred to in Sync 1.

Having looked at this chart and information, think about the following questions:

- Are there other areas of legal practice which may be impacted by AI?
- Can you list the advantages and the disadvantages of AI's impact on the legal profession?
- Is the legal profession suitably equipped to deal with this impact?

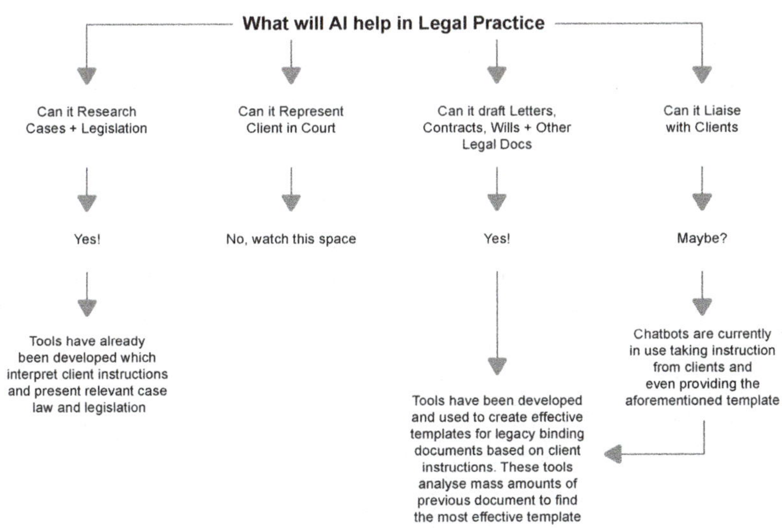

Figure 7.1 AI's role in legal practice

34 Select Committee on Artificial Intelligence, 'AI in the UK: Ready, Willing and Able?' (*HL 2017–19*, 100), paras 10–19.

How AI works

In order to understand AI and its true potential—what it can do and what it cannot do—you will need to understand how the technology works. This section introduces you to four core components of AI: data, machine learning, robotic process automation and natural language processing.

DATA

Data allows AI to come to life. Without data AI is unable to operate. Data allows AI to undertake pattern recognition and provide insights to the match between data sets. AI technology is only as effective as the quantity and quality of data it has access to. Figure 7.2 shows

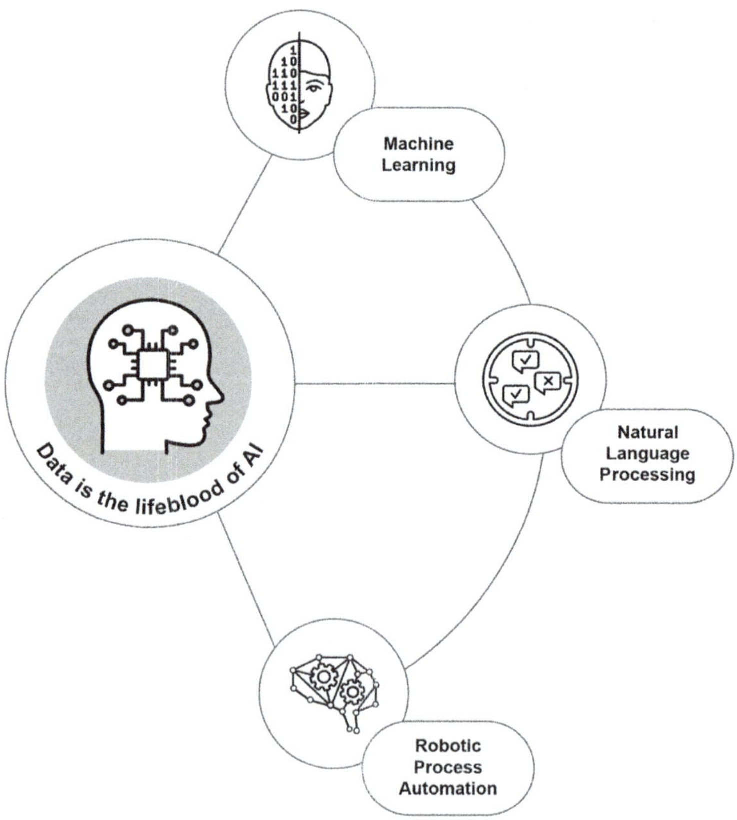

Figure 7.2 AI and data

how data helps AI to produce better patterns and matches and consequently predictions and outputs. The quality of data determines the accuracy of the AI matches, decisions and predictions. Data with inaccuracies and bias will generate matches and decisions which do not reveal the realities of a particular situation. There is a reciprocal relationship between data and AI functionalities, and usefulness with the latter depends heavily on the former for success.

Bias within data sets could be built into AI systems unknowingly. The increase in data being collected, stored and mined has led to today's breakthrough in the usefulness of AI technologies. Therefore, for AI to function as accurately and as efficiently as possible, it will require access to large volumes of data. When seeking to develop or purchase AI technologies, it is important for lawyers and law firms to understand how this data is stored, protected and used by the technology. In Chapter 6 you were introduced to the EU's General Data Protection Regulation (GDPR), which came into effect in May 2018 in the UK and across the European Union and seeks to safeguard data.[35] GDPR and its compatibility with AI has already drawn a lot of discussion about what the future holds. Fundamentally, the GDPR introduces additional protections around the use of data, in particular data on private individuals. This means that how AI goes on to process this data using the methods already discussed will come under greater focus.

MACHINE LEARNING

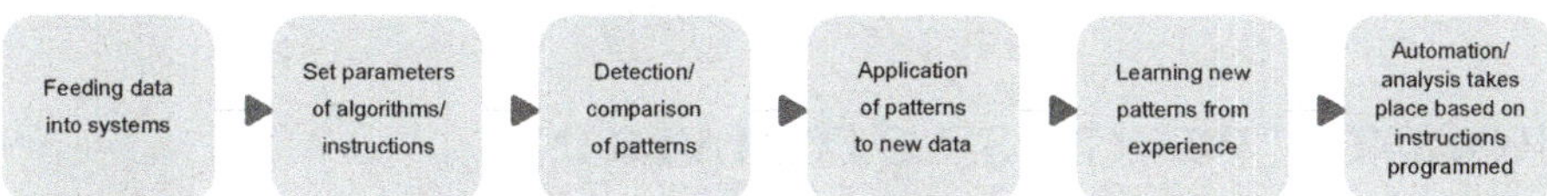

Figure 7.3 Machine learning capabilities

Machine learning involves using AI that can learn from data and continually build on that learning for improvement. It functions when AI is exposed to a data training set (such as documents that have

35 Damon Civin, 'Explainable AI Could Reduce the Impact of Biased Algorithms' (*VentureBeat*, May 2018); European Commission, White Paper on Artificial Intelligence: A European approach to excellence (COM 2020 65).

been reviewed by an experienced lawyer or subject matter expert). It develops a preliminary algorithm based on the expert's decision about the relevance of the documents. This algorithm is then applied to further documents and, through an iterative process where the system's coding decisions are subject to human review, the system is further trained until its results reach a statistically acceptable level of accuracy. The final algorithm is then applied to the entire population of documents to identify or prioritise relevant documents. As such, machine learning can be used on huge volumes of data for analysing, pattern recognition and identification, and making predictions whilst it is continually learning iteratively. Unlike the hype around replacing human experts, machine learning extends and augments the judgements and decision-making of expert lawyers and advisors through problem-solving and efficiency of time.

The examples seen in this chapter demonstrate both simple and complex machine learning functionalities, from identifying errors in documents from a set of pre-trained data to predicting outcomes and decisions. In order to do this, however, the AI needs to be designed in such a way to allow it to learn and act in the way intended, and the training set needs to be unbiased and accurate. As such, a lawyer and an engineer is always required to find a way of encoding the problem that they want the AI to solve in the first place. Decision-making via machine learning can be complex, in that it may be difficult to see how a decision was arrived at, and therefore difficult to verify the accuracy of the decision or its rationale. A lawyer is required in these circumstances to verify the interpretation of the laws and rules and confirm the rationale behind the decision arrived at.

ROBOTIC PROCESS AUTOMATION

Robotic process automation is used to streamline business processes and procedures and to create a more efficient service of delivery for clients and customers. It replaces the cost of human time and expertise used in handling administration and routine and repetitive processes which can be automated via an online workflow system. Figure 7.4 shows the consistency in process and practice in NLP which enables a more professional and auditable service that can be offered throughout the business cycle. Sophisticated systems allow for the initial client contact to be automated before a one-to-one appointment with a lawyer, saving costs for the potential client and time for the lawyer.

What	• Capable of reading and executing instructions. • Capable of undertaking administrative tasks when onboarding clients, completing templates using existing data available, and automatically filing in forms.
How	• Using Natural Language Processing to read and understand instructions, it executes predetermined processes. • With a focus on customer needs, it allows for auto mation and streamlining of business and administrative processes.
Why	• Value add service for clients • Cost saving in the the long term • Staff can work on more complex or more human focused relationships • Opportunity to streamline processes, efficiencies • Consistency in process and operation • Process is logged, providing audit for accountability and tracking • Efficiency in response can be 24/7

Figure 7.4 The role of robotic process automation

NATURAL LANGUAGE PROCESSING

Natural language processing (NLP) was introduced in Chapter 6. It involves using human language to understand spoken or written words. Common examples are Google Assistant, Siri, Alexa and Cortana, which you will find built into digital devices. They are designed to create innovative and effective experiences and interactions between the user and the device. Chatbots are an example of technologies which use NLP and are capable of understanding language, asking questions and deriving meaning from responses. Chatbots further the work of NLP into realms previously thought unimaginable. As Figure 7.5 shows, like with all AI, they are effective based on the instructions designed into them. They become less effective for complex problems, where not only the variables but also the rules change in real time. They also lack the ability to codify intuition and emotional intelligence. The other limitation is that they cannot capture forms of implicit knowledge. For example, in law the interpretation of specific laws is open to social norms and the spirit in which the law was created.

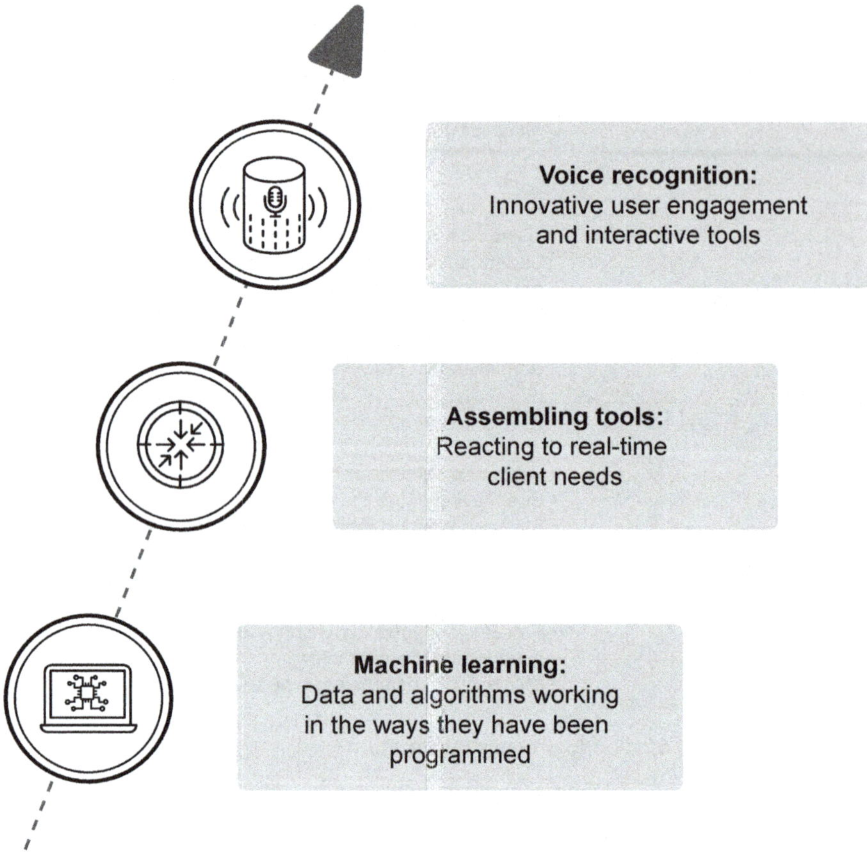

Figure 7.5 Natural language processing

Sync 4: Using chatbots in law

You should allow around 20 minutes for this activity.

Read the following article around an introduction to chatbots by the Law Society of England and Wales <https://www.lawsociety.org.uk/en/campaigns/lawtech/features/chat-show>

Consider the following questions:

- How are chatbots being used in legal practice at the moment?
- What are some of limitations of chatbots which are being used in legal practice at the moment?
- Is the current Solicitors Regulation Authority (SRA) Code of Conduct able to safely regulate the use of chatbots and other NLP tools?

In summary, when working towards understanding how AI functions, we have seen the different components that drive AI with a variety of capabilities. For example:

- AI can be used for pattern recognition drawing from a data training set.
- AI can hear, listen and understand audio or spoken words.
- AI can understand written and spoken human language and styles of expression.
- AI has the ability to reason and create lines of connections between patterns, similarities, differences, facts, people and outcomes.

Sync 5: The limitations of AI

You should allow around 60 minutes for this activity.

Read the article and listen to the conversation on "The Current and Potential Use of AI" <https://www.mckinsey.com/featured-insights/artificial-intelligence/the-real-world-potential-and-limitations-of-artificial-intelligence>

Consider the following questions around limitations:

- What are the key limitations of AI?
- In the conversation, areas such as being able to understand how the AI is functioning, the rules that control its actions, interpreting its decision-making and predictions are deemed as vital when using AI. Why is it important to be able to determine how AI operates?
- Data is the lifeblood of AI. What are the challenges here? How is data obtained, and is there a process for determining if the data is accurate, reliable and credible? Are there conventions on how data is labelled?
- With machine learning automation as a feature of AI, should AI be able to go beyond the instructions set for its function, taking its application of data to new and different contexts and becoming capable of applying them in different problems and contexts? What are your reasons? What sorts of accountability should be put in place to oversee how AI operates in this context?
- AI is already being used in the delivery of legal services. It helps to augment and enhance the work of lawyers rather than replace them. What are the advantages of using AI in legal services?
- Within the practice of law, what are the professional and ethical issues to consider?

ETHICAL CONSIDERATIONS IN USING AI

As part of equipping yourself with digital lawyering skills, knowledge and mindset, you will need to understand how various pieces of technology are used in legal practice and for the delivery of legal services, and also how the technologies operate and the sorts of ethical considerations that you should be aware of when using them. Furthermore, as AI technologies evolve, regular retraining and upskilling in knowledge and skills around the use of AI will become a necessity.

In this chapter, we have covered a range of potential uses of AI and discussed how they have the capability to augment and support the role of lawyers. When lawyers use AI, what are the sorts of key considerations they should be mindful of? AI systems are not without fault. It is inevitable that such systems will make mistakes that may result in incorrect interpretation, the output of information which may only have taken into account data which the AI understands or chooses to use, and consequently inaccuracies and damage. How will liability be determined in such situations? Also, it is not clear whether the existing laws on liability will sufficiently address the damage and harm caused to others should AI inaccurately produce advice and decisions. Will lawyers be subject to negligence or malpractice claims from clients? How do lawyers mitigate these risks and other potential liability issues associated with AI? Asked in another way, as lawyers use AI systems to deliver legal services, make predictions and use outputs from AI, how do they ensure that they still comply with legal ethics and professional conduct rules for the profession?

It is argued that the majority of this work will need to be carried out by the regulatory bodies themselves. For instance, in England and Wales this will be the responsibility of the SRA and the Bar Standards Board. There have already been preliminary reports published by both bodies looking at technology, and in particular AI, and the considerations that the professions will need to have in integrating it into the working lives of lawyers.

What we need to consider is how would we go about regulating AI in legal practice, and how would this align with the ethical considerations of regulatory bodies as they stand today? This area of AI and professional responsibility is still in development. The regulatory bodies in the legal profession have long been discussing the impact of AI and the ethical issues that may arise from more widespread use in professional practice.

We would also suggest that the legal implications of AI decision-making, questioning how liability can be established, including gaps in the current laws, is a necessary part of students' digital lawyering preparation.

Questions students may want to consider include:

1. In the use of AI systems in the legal profession, where do legal ethics and the application of professional codes of conduct lie—whether it is the lawyer or the AI systems themselves who is responsible—especially if an AI is able to learn from its successes and errors and intelligently undertakes tasks and makes decisions on its own initiative.
2. A critical examination of product liability, criminal liability, negligence and contractual liability and how the current laws in this area applies to the design of AIs and establishing their responsibilities. A tricky area here is when an AI is operating after self-learning and self-improving (machine learning) or when it is interacting with other online systems (via blockchains and the Internet of Things), because identifying where the liability lies if something goes wrong is difficult to determine. Due to the current lack of specific laws which are compatible with the functions and operations of AIs, there is a gap in the governance, privacy, fairness, transparency, accountability and determination of responsibility and liability in this area.
3. The need for specific regulations on AIs and algorithm functions. It has been established that there is a need for "careful scrutiny of the ethical, legal and societal dimensions of artificially intelligent systems".[36] The recent 2018 report from the UK House of Lords Select Committee titled "AI in the UK: Ready, Willing and Able?"[37] sought clarification on the current liability laws and their sufficiency towards AI systems. This report suggested the possibility of developing an AI code to help mitigate the risks of AI outstrip-

36 House of Commons, Science and Technology and House of Commons Science and Technology Committee, 'Robotics and Artificial Intelligence Fifth Report of Session 2016–17' (*House of Commons*, 2016) <https://publications.parliament.uk/pa/cm201617/cmselect/cmsctech/145/145.pdf>

37 House of Lords Select Committee on Artificial Intelligence, 'Artificial Intelligence Committee—Publications' (*UK Parliament*, 2018) <https://www.parliament.uk/business/committees/committees-a-z/lords-select/ai-committee/publications/>; Select Committee on Artificial Intelligence, 'Report of Session 2017–19 AI in the UK: Ready, Willing and Able?' (*House of Lords*, 2018) HL Paper 100 <https://publications.parliament.uk/pa/ld201719/ldselect/ldai/100/100.pdf>

ping human intelligence. A consideration of the legal and philosophical possibility and the potential ethical and social implications of "electronic personhood" bestowed upon AIs, similar to that of corporate personhood for companies, is advocated by the EU Parliament's draft report on robotics in 2016.[38]

In 2019, the SRA highlighted, in "Technology and Legal Services", numerous ethical issues that they are aware of with regards to AI. One of prevalent themes highlighted in this report revolved around data. There are many different ethical considerations that need to be made around the data AI will need to use and create. You will find some discussion on these in the following sections.[39]

OPEN DATA

AI depends upon the use of Open Data in order to create and learn from an ever-changing environment. What first needs to be established is what data needs to be made available to creators of legal-based AI. Having looked at some of the examples earlier in the chapter, it is recognised that data on trial judgments and cases will be paramount to developing widespread use of AI in legal practice. It is noted by academics in the field that there would need to be a greater push to have open access to databases containing key case information.

TRANSPARENCY AND BIAS

Transparency will be key to developing widespread use of AI in legal services. With the introduction of GDPR, the use of data has been put at the forefront of protection regulations. Law firms will need to be transparent with clients in how they are planning to use their data. If client data is going to be used in order to help lawyers use AI tools to manage their case, then the lawyers need to be able to explain to the client how they have formulated the advice. The Information

38 Lawyer Monthly, 'Robots and AI: Giving Robots "Personhood" Status' (*Lawyer Monthly: Legal News Magazine*, 3 March 2017) <https://www.lawyer-monthly.com/2017/02/robots-and-ai-giving-robots-personhood-status/>; C. Aveni, 'Alexa, How Private Is My Home?' (2017) 42 (4) *Litigation News* <https://www.cpmlaw.com/wp-content/uploads/2017/08/Aveni-summer17.pdf>; E. De La Garza, 'Charges Dropped in Amazon Echo Murder Case' (*Courthouse News Service*, 29 November 2017) <https://www.courthousenews.com/charges-dropped-in-amazon-echo-murder-case/>

39 'Technology and Legal Services' [2018] Solicitors Regulatory Authority.

Commissioner's Office argues that firms will need to have algorithmic accountability and audibility.[40] This means that firms will need to be able to demonstrate that any tools they have relied upon are complying with GDPR, but one further consideration is that firms will also need to make sure they are adhering to the traditional codes of conduct. This means that they will need to demonstrate that the advice they are giving to clients is competent and fair. This requires a thorough understanding of the tools used to formulate said advice.

GDPR

When it comes to looking at the implementation and development of AI, it is nearly impossible for it not to be talked about in the same sentence as GDPR. The reason being that GDPR is concerned intrinsically with data, how it is used, protected and processed. As we know, AI functions by feeding on data. Therefore, as we are discussing how the legal sector is looking to develop its use of AI in practice, it would be foolish not to have any consideration of how the data it will rely upon will be legally regulated.

As countries across the globe are driving towards a digital economy, the relationship between and GDPR and AI has become very important. It becomes even more paramount as we look at how the entire world is looking at data protection and its regulation, and possibly looking to develop similar systems to that of the GDPR.

It is clear that the progress of AI and its functioning in the legal sector is intertwined with GDPR. Developers, users and clients will need to be fully aware of how data is being stored and how law firms are staying compliant with GDPR in their normal day-to-day practice.

FURTHER ETHICAL CONSIDERATIONS

The relationship between ethics, AI and digital lawyering is still in flux and developing. This provides a good opportunity for current law students and future digital lawyers to gain an appreciation of the professional challenges of the augmentation of AI in the work of lawyers and contribute to the building and development of this area.

40 Information Commissioner's Office, Big Data, artificial intelligence, machine learning and data protection <https://ico.org.uk/media/fororganisations/documents/2013559/big-data-ai-ml-and-data-protection.pdf>

The leading report by the UK's House of Lords Select Committee on Artificial Intelligence, "AI in the UK: Ready, Willing and Able?" (introduced above), focused on ethical principles for the development of AI. The Select Committee recommended that a universal AI code be created which could be used by all AI manufacturers and designers across the world and may allow a standardisation of AI practices.[41]

We will review and analyse the five principles for an AI Code suggested by the Committee:

- The first principle focuses upon developing AI for the "common good and benefit of humanity".

Questions for us to consider here include: Who determines the common good of humanity? In what ways can AI be used for the common good within the legal profession? To develop an understanding of the scope, spirit, and potential uses of the AI system, we can ask questions such as: How is the system intended to work? Who is the system designed to work for? Will it work for everyone equally? How can it harm others?

- The second principle focuses upon how AI will operate and be used, focusing on "fairness".

Questions for us to consider include: What is fairness? How can we ensure fairness within the data sets and in the design and output of AI? Who should be accountable for this fairness? When discussing fairness, it is also important to think about identification of bias in data sets. This involves evaluating where the data came from, understanding how it was organised and testing to ensure it is represented correctly.

This, in turn, raises the question of capabilities of the human operators of AI: Are we sufficiently trained to understand the reliability and validity of the outputs? For example, self-learning systems such as chatbots that have direct interactions with clients, or give basic advice online, are in some ways carrying out the function of a lawyer without a human being directly present. Similarly, a self-executing contract in conveyancing may involve the system carrying out what is known in the UK as a "reserved activity" (which only an authorised member of the legal profession can currently carry out) without requiring human supervision. Is this permitted by the current professional codes for lawyers? To what extent can lawyers rely on such self-learning systems? In determining

41 Technology and Legal Services' [2018] Solicitors Regulatory Authority.

accountability, Microsoft's ethics hub for AI recommends that those who are responsible for the design and deployment of AI systems must be accountable for how the systems operate. It is important that within professional use contexts, the AI system is not the final authority on any decision that impacts people's lives and that humans maintain meaningful control over otherwise highly autonomous AI systems.[42]

- The third principle focuses upon maintaining the "data rights or privacy of individuals, families or communities".

Questions for us to consider include: What is transparency? What role does it play in AI decision-making? To determine this, it is necessary to have an understanding of the sorts of rigorous testing that took place during AI system development and deployment to ensure that systems can respond safely to unanticipated circumstances.

- The fourth principle focuses upon the human capacity for growth and the need to prevent AI stifling the development of human creativity. This requires individuals "to be educated to enable them to flourish mentally, emotionally and economically alongside artificial intelligence".

It is important for curricula in schools, colleges and universities to develop competencies for people to work with AI; for example, an understanding of AI, its affordances and limitations and how to utilise them effectively. Ethics of AI is a relevant part of our education to prepare us for how we work with AI in future. This raises the question: To what extent should topics around data science, statistical reasoning and systems thinking become an integral part of our education system?

An understanding of how AI functions will be useful when evaluating when and how an AI system should seek human input for impactful decisions or during critical situations. This raises the further question: Should humans be ultimately accountable for decisions that leverage AI, especially when AI is used to inform consequential decisions about people?

- The fifth principle draws on the first principle of the "common good", cautioning manufacturers and designers never to afford AI the "the autonomous power to hurt, destroy or deceive human beings".

42 Supra n. 35.

In considering how AI is used and, consequently, the outputs it is capable of delivering, we will need to consider the concepts of bias, fairness and transparency. As we covered earlier, data is the lifeblood of AI. The data is shaped by the manner in which it is obtained or collected. Here the issue could be one of oversampling, where one area or group of people is predominantly featured in the data. The information human operators choose to feed into the AI models, the choice of data and the nature of the data itself, could be contaminated with biases. This was demonstrated in Chapter 6, where the example was given of a report demonstrating the under-representation of black and Asian faces in data sets for facial recognition software, meaning it was less capable of correctly identifying individuals and their genders. This demonstrates that AI models can embed human and societal biases and deploy them at scale, despite the wrongful assumption that the output of a machine is never biased. This is in fact far from true.

Questions to consider here include: To what extent should AI be designed to be capable of making its own decisions? Which areas of our lives and society should these forms of AI be applied to? Is there sufficient trust in data used and the outcomes produced by AI for this to happen? Are there situations in which fully automated decision-making can be permissible at all? How should we codify definitions of fairness?

AI uses processes that are said to be neutral and standardised for the context in which the AI is being used. This may mean there is procedural fairness, but even so, are we certain that a fair procedure will always lead to a fair outcome? Similarly, if the data is diverse, then does it mean that the outcome is fair? AI is not capable of determining and applying procedures in a way which takes account of and adapts to the nuances of social contexts. Therefore, human judgement is still crucial at the right time to ensure that AI outcomes are fair. Human judgement requires knowledge and skill sets beyond one discipline alone; humanities, social sciences, technical understanding, law and science are some of the basics that will need to inform our knowledge sets.

Transparency is a key component of the safe utilisation of AI. When AI systems are used to help inform decisions that have tremendous impacts on people's lives, it is critical that people understand how those decisions were made. The standard operating procedure in the electronics industry is to develop a datasheet for data sets which would help developers understand if a specific data set is appropriate for the use case (the possible specific application of AI being considered) that the datasheet documents. It contains its motivation, composition, collection process, recommended uses, information about training data, training failures that occurred and potential inadequacies with training

As such, it can help with facilitating better communication between data set creators and data set consumers and encourage the machine learning community to prioritise transparency and accountability.[43]

Sync 6: Fairness and AI

You should allow around 30 minutes for this activity.

Watch Professor Sarah Wachter's talk, "Why Fairness Cannot Be Automated: Bridging the Gap between EU Non-discrimination Law and AI":

https://www.oii.ox.ac.uk/videos/why-fairness-cannot-be-automated-bridging-the-gap-between-eu-non-discrimination-law-and-ai/

During the video, consider the following questions:

- Will AI decisions be less biased than human ones?
- Will AI make problems worse?
- To what extent are laws open to interpretive flexibility? Laws and case law are purposefully agile and fluid to offer appropriate legal responses in a constantly changing society.
- What can law learn from computer science around automation of thinking, procedures and rules?
- Some academics say that the GDPR and AI are incompatible. Do you agree with this statement?
- In your opinion, what regulation needs to be put in place in order for AI to develop safely within our society?

Mitigating bias starts with understanding the implications and limitations of AI predictions and recommendations. It is necessary to supplement AI decisions with sound human judgement and be held accountable for consequential decisions that affect others. When designing and building AI systems, developers should understand how bias can be introduced and how it can affect AI-based recommendations. Similarly, when using AI for professional work, lawyers and

43 <https://arxiv.org/pdf/1803.09010.pdf>

others will need to be mindful of potential bias and interrogate data sets to determine the validity of its outcomes.

Conclusion

This chapter should have started to get you thinking about how AI is becoming more and more prevalent in legal practice. Not only does the legal profession need to be able to understand the benefits of AI, but it also needs to be able to understand how it works and the potential drawbacks of the technology.

One of the key themes of this chapter is to highlight what roles AI can play in legal practice now and in the future. There are numerous ways in which AI is making its way into legal practice, whether this is coming through front-end chatbots (which take basic instructions from clients) or complex tools which are scanning previous decisions in order to get an edge in litigation. AI will enable lawyers to think of new ways of providing legal service, thereby increasing productivity and attracting new clients. This in turn will help lawyers to stay competitive in the legal market. However, it must be noted that the implementation of AI into law firms will give rise to the era of a new form of lawyers and law firms (something discussed further in Chapter 12).

However, all of this comes at a cost: The legal profession changing and adapting to meet the demands of 21st-century clients and practice. Governments and regulatory authorities will need to think long and hard about how they adapt their rules and regulations to accommodate this technology. Legal regulatory bodies such as the SRA pride themselves on their ethical approach to regulation. For the SRA, this is based upon principles which they believe are the fundamental tenets of ethical behaviour. These will need to be realigned and readjusted if the legal profession wishes to adopt AI more widely throughout its practice. It has done so in the past with the introduction of alternative business structures, and it can do so again as part of the digital technology age. The groundwork has already been proposed and the stumbling blocks identified. The EU and House of Lords have already started identifying the key areas needed for regulation.

Of course, this leaves a bigger question to answer. What skills and understanding will lawyers need to be equipped with in order to succeed in legal practice? This will be considered further in Chapters 11 and 12. What is certain is that lawyers who are able to understand and apply the same academic and analytical rigour which has served the profession so well, for so many years, to the increasing use of AI will most certainly be at the forefront of how the legal evolves over the next 50 years.

ADDITIONAL RESOURCES

Two key sources of current work in the area of the ethical and professional use of AI:

The European Commission AI Alliance. This organisation has worked in partnership with the experts on its High Level Group on Artificial Intelligence to establish draft guidance on the ethical use of AI <https://ec.europa.eu/digital-single-market/en/news/commission-appoints-expert-group-ai-and-launches-european-ai-alliance>

The works of Professor Sandra Wachter, Research Fellow focusing on law and ethics of AI, Big Data, and robotics as well as Internet regulation at the Oxford Internet Institute at the University of Oxford <https://www.oii.ox.ac.uk/people/sandra-wachter/?profile>

MICROSOFT AI ETHIC HUB

The Microsoft AI Ethic Hub is an area focused on the responsible creation and use of AI. It provides numerous videos and articles looking at different aspects of AI, including <http://www.microsoft.com/en-us/research/publication/responsible-bots/> and <http://www.microsoft.com/en-us/research/publication/guidelines-for-human-ai-interaction/>

THE LAW SOCIETY

The Law Society of England and Wales have a campaign surrounding the introduction of more innovative technology into legal practice. This area publishes useful articles and examples of how this is happening across England and Wales <http://www.lawsociety.org.uk/campaigns/lawtech>

THE EU AND AI

The EU have been at the forefront of pioneering safe and regulated AI principles. Have a look at this website to look at publications by the EU on this topic. The site will provide up-to-date publications from the EU as they develop policy on the use and creation of AI <https://digital-strategy.ec.europa.eu/en/policies/european-approach-artificial-intelligence>

Boucher P, "How Artificial Intelligence Works" (*European Parliamentary Research Service*, March 2019).

Brooks C, Cristian G and Vorley T, "Artificial Intelligence in the Legal Sector: Pressures and Challenges of Transformation" (2020) 13 *Cambridge Journal of Regions, Economy and Society* 135–52.

Gacutan J, "A Statutory Right to Explanation for Decisions Generated Using Artificial Intelligence" (2020) 28 (3) *The International Journal of Law and Information Technology* 193.

Susskind R, *Tomorrow's Lawyers: An Introduction to Your Future*, 2nd ed. (OUP, 2017).

Wachter S and Mittelstadt B, "Why a Right to Explanation of Automated Decision-Making Does Not Exist in the General Data Protection Regulation" (2018) *SSRN Journal* 10.1093.

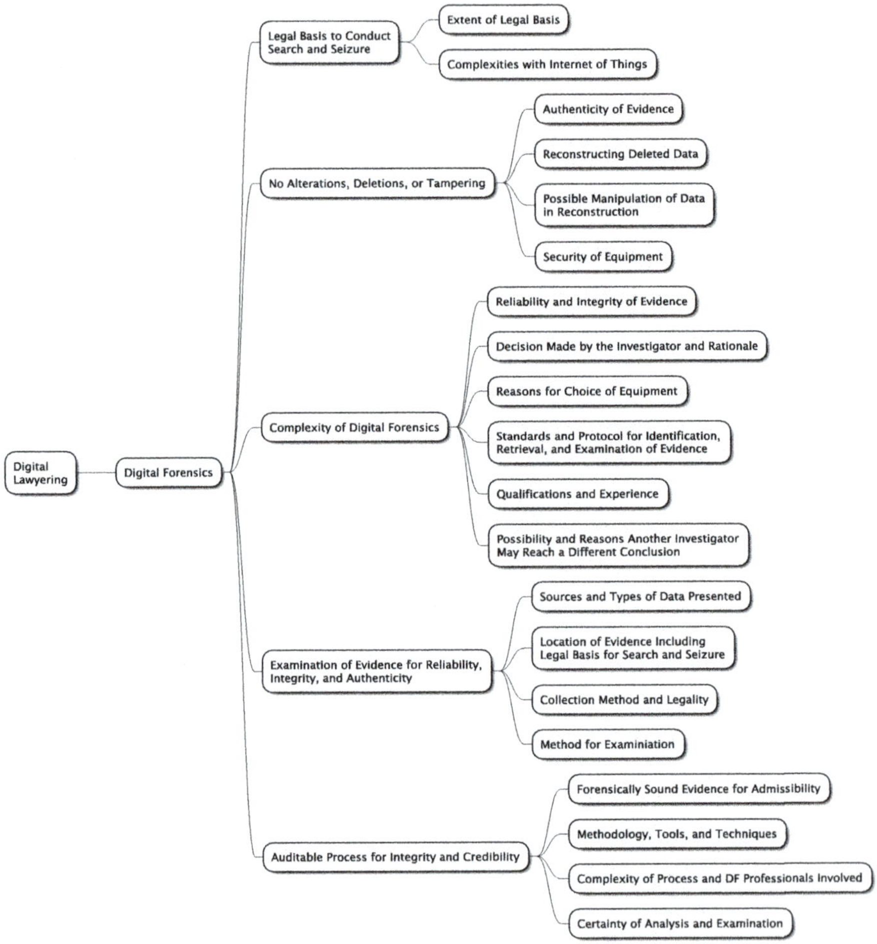

Mind Map 8.1 Chapter topics

8

DIGITAL EVIDENCE AND ITS ADMISSIBILITY IN THE COURTROOM

Ann Thanaraj

INTRODUCTION

Evidence is fundamental to the outcome of establishing the certainty of facts in civil litigation, criminal litigation, corporate matters and settlements outside of court. With the seamless integration of the physical and digital worlds brought on by the rapid developments in technology, digital technologies provide indispensable evidence in the investigation process and where they are admissible in courts. In order to administer justice, the court requires reliable, trustworthy and authentic evidence. The digital forensics practitioner plays a vital role in this: Their qualifications, competencies and integrity along with their duty to present evidence in an objective and factual way supports the court to determine the weight given to digital evidence. Therefore, lawyers and judges require a deep understanding of the important questions they need to ask regarding digital evidence, whether it is to identify digital evidence that is missing in cases or to analyse digital evidence which is presented in court. Lawyers must also be capable of handling digital evidence regardless of its volume and complexity. Whilst digital evidence may be presented to the court by expert witnesses such as professional digital forensic investigators during the court proceedings, a lawyer must be fully equipped to form an opinion of the witness and the evidence itself. This will involve considering its authenticity and integrity, accuracy, facts, acquisition, recovery process and analysis, and the impact of all of this to the case in hand.

By developing an awareness of the digital forensics process and forms of digital evidence, a digitally proficient lawyer will be able to determine for themselves what sorts of evidence they should ask for from a digital forensics investigator and what is discoverable. They should be able to determine its relevance, understand the contents of a forensics report, determine their examination and cross-examination

DOI: 10.4324/9780429298219-8

strategies towards the expert witness, their own client and other witnesses, and be able to explain the evidences to the judge and jury. By developing a solid understanding of the processes and capabilities of modern digital forensics, informed legal professionals can generate a distinct advantage for their clients and cases.

Chapter hot spots

When reading this chapter, questions to think about include:

- What is the relevance of the digital forensics processes and the retrieval of authentic evidence in determining the strengths and weaknesses of a client's case?
- What types of evidence are discoverable from digital sources and devices?
- What digital forensics evidence is admissible in court?
- What sort of framework would be most useful to guide digital forensics professionals to ensure that their processes and evidences are admissible in court?

Having read the title and introduction, you can add any other questions you want to explore here:

AN EXPLORATION OF DEFINITIONS

Digital forensics is a discipline borne out of the need to support law enforcement investigate acts of suspected crime where a digital device may contain relevant data that may describe such events. Digital evidence can provide an insight into the behaviour of an individual via communication records of location information; device interrogation may in some cases be the only source of evidence regarding an event.[1]

1 The Police Foundation, 'Digital Forensics: The Next Steps' (2020) <https://www.police-foundation.org.uk/project/the-next-steps-for-digital-forensics/>

A digitally proficient lawyer must realise that digital evidence is a dominant form of evidence in courts. In addition, they must be able to determine the credibility and integrity of the digital evidence for use in legal proceedings. They should also be able to understand the story that the digital forensics process tells and the impact on this on the case.

Digital evidence is straightforward to define. The Scientific Working Group on Digital Evidence defines digital evidence as being "any information of probative value that is either stored, received or transmitted in digital form".[2] In other words, digital evidence is digital information that can be used to prove a fact or facts within a case. The sources of digital evidence go beyond information that is stored in electronic devices such as computers and mobile phones. It extends to associated networks and cloud technologies including data that can be retrieved from the Internet of Things (referred to in Chapter 6).[3] One's digital footprint across any device or digital platform can be used as digital evidence such as photographs, log files, instant message chats, chats on various digital media platforms, photos, chats, log files and emails. Digital evidence can be fragile and fleeting.

Digital evidence can play both a primary role in the investigation of a suspect or provide supplementary context in other cases. Perhaps one of the most prominent recent cases is that of Mitesh Patel,[4] who murdered his wife. In this case, in addition to traditional physical trace forensic science evidence (which typically includes things like hair or fibres from clothing), a combination of closed-circuit television (CCTV) and mobile phone evidence—particular Apple Health data—provided evidence refuting the defendant's description of events.

Digital forensics is more complex to define. When characterising the forensic investigation of digital technologies, terms such as "digital forensic science" or "digital forensics" best capture the subject discipline, and this goes beyond computer forensics. Figure 8.1 depicts

2 Scientific Working Group on Digital Evidence, 'SWGDE Multimedia and Digital Evidence Glossary' Ver 3.0 (June 2016), 6 <https://swgde.org/documents/Current%20Documents/SWGDE%20Digital%20and%20Multimedia%20Evidence%20Glossary>

3 This is a term used to describe devices connected to the Internet which consequently connect with other devices and sync and talk to each other sharing data. The connections form networks of devices which collect, share and analyse the data to produce context-specific and user-specific solutions to tasks and processes.

4 V. N. Franqueira and G. Horsman, 'Towards Sound Forensic Arguments: Structured Argumentation Applied to Digital Forensics Practice' (2020) 32 *Forensic Science International: Digital Investigation* 300923; Sky News, 'Mitesh Patel: Gay Pharmacist Jailed for Murdering Wife to be with Boyfriend' (*Sky News*, 2018) <https://news.sky.com/story/mitesh-patel-pharmacist-who-murdered-wife-jailed-for-30-years-11572248>

digital forensics as a sub-discipline of forensic science. Contained within digital forensics are a number of specialist areas, typically defined by a technology, service or operating system variant. Each specialist area can contain multiple components due to the number of technology types which exist within it. For example, there are occasions when a mobile phone may be subject to a mobile forensic examination. Mobile forensics is a specialist area of digital forensics, where a practitioner may be a specialist in examining specific device types (e.g. Apple iPhones running iOS).

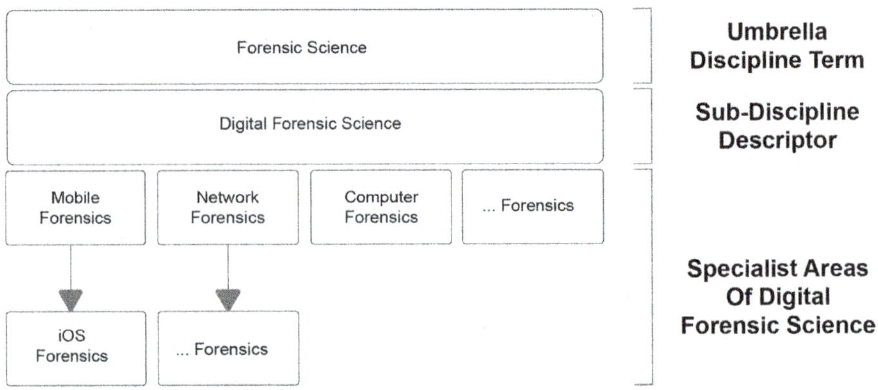

Figure 8.1 Discipline terminology

The Forensics Capabilities Network of England and Wales defines digital forensics as "the examination of digital evidence to support investigations and prosecutions, formally defined as 'the systematic and coherent study of digital traces to address questions of authentication, identification, classification, reconstruction, and evaluation for a legal context'".[5] Another definition is from the Forensic Science Regulator for England and Wales, which defines digital forensics as "the process by which information is extracted from data storage media, rendered into a useable form, processed and interpreted for the purpose of obtaining intelligence for use in investigations, or evidence for use in criminal proceedings".[6]

5 Forensic Capability Network, 'Digital Forensic Science Strategy' (2020), 12 <https://www.fcn.police.uk/sites/default/files/2020-07/Digital%20Forensic%20Science%20Strategy%20EMAIL%20VERSION%20ONLY.pdf>

6 Forensic Science Regulator, 'Newsletter' (2015), 3 <https://assets.publishing.service.gov.uk/government/uploads/system/uploads/attachment_data/file/470526/FSR_Newsletter_26__October_2015.pdf>

In breaking down the definitions that form the components of digital forensics, let's begin with its two fundamental components, "digital" and "forensic science".

- *Digital.* The focus of digital forensics is digital data; binary code utilised by digital technologies in order to function; sometimes colloquially referred to as ones and zeros. Digital technologies process binary code in order to perform functions and store data.[7] Whilst binary content is not easily readable in its native form, software programs translate it into more accessible forms such as the files users commonly see on their device, like word processing documents, pictures or, in some cases, communication data like chat messages. To increase simplicity, the term "digital" encompasses all the contents of a digital device, or in some cases, assessing the capability and function of the device to ensure it is functioning properly. The device itself may give rise to an offence.
- *Forensic science.* Simply put, the *Oxford English Dictionary* defines forensic science as "the application of scientific methods and techniques to matters under investigation by a court of law".[8]

The field of digital forensics is a hybrid of fundamental computer science and investigation, supporting the justice system through the examination of digital devices and the digital data they contain in order to identify and interpret the presence of any digital evidence. In turn, drawing on the Scientific Working Group on Digital Evidence definition of digital evidence as valuable information that is stored "stored or transmitted in digital form"[9] (discussed earlier), the results of the investigation will be used to help indicate whether or not a belief or proposition relating to the case in question is true or valid.[10] As such, the digital forensics examination and process take place on digital artifacts such as computers, mobile phones, hard drives, cloud-hosted applications, software, apps, Internet browsers, servers, or any endpoint networks or infrastructures. The activity also includes collecting information from emails, texts and images, deleted files and much more to determine the digital footprint.

7 TechTerms, 'Binary' (2020) <https://techterms.com/definition/binary>

8 *Oxford English Dictionary*, 'Forensic Science' (2020) <https://languages.oup.com/google-dictionary-en>

9 Supra n. 2.

10 *Oxford English Dictionary*, 'Evidence' (2020b) <https://languages.oup.com/google-dictionary-en>

Digital forensics occurs post-mortem, after an alleged crime or event has taken place which is in need of investigation. As a result, digital forensics is reactive, serving the purpose of attempting to reconstruct behaviours from digital traces and information left on relevant digital devices. In that sense, digital forensics interprets digital information which may be stored upon a device to assess whether it may help an investigation. It tells a story and the origins of the digital evidence. It can explain the conduct of parties and helps to contextualise facts of a case with evidence.[11]

In 2020, the Forensic Capability Network's Digital Forensic Science Strategy noted that "over 90% of all crime is recognized as having a digital element, and society's accelerating use of technology means the critical role Digital Forensic Science plays will only grow".[12] As such, digital forensics is somewhat driven by trends in technology development and use, and the need to investigate these potential evidence sources,[13] leading to it becoming one of the most prominent branches of forensic science in use. The importance of the field of digital forensics cannot be understated, and it is necessary to ensure that the public at large understand what the field of digital forensics is and the role it plays within the justice sphere.[14] Doing so encourages societal trust in digital forensics which in turn shapes best practice, facilitates an understanding of this service and raises an awareness of capability—supporting witnesses and victims to determine when it may be necessary to come forward and engage these services through the reporting of an offence. Doing so not only improves the chance of a positive outcome

11 The Crown Prosecution Service of England and Wales (2020) define the following two categories of cyber crime in which an incidents will fall into: *Cyber-dependent crimes*: Crimes that can be committed only through the use of information and communications technology (ICT) devices, where the devices are both the tool for committing the crime and the target of the crime (e.g. developing and propagating malware for financial gain, hacking to steal, damage, distort or destroy data and/or network or activity). *Cyber-enabled crimes*: Traditional crimes which can be increased in scale or reach by the use of computers, computer networks or other forms of ICT (such as cyber-enabled fraud and data theft).

Crown Prosecution Service, 'Cybercrime—Prosecution Guidance' (2020) <https://www.cps.gov.uk/legal-guidance/cybercrime-prosecution-guidance>; see also C. Wexler, 'The Changing Nature of Crime and Criminal Investigations' (2018) <https://www.policeforum.org/assets/ChangingNatureofCrime.pdf>

12 Supra n. 5, p. 4.

13 G. Horsman, 'Tool Testing and Reliability Issues in the Field of Digital Forensics' (2019) 28 *Digital Investigation* 163–75.

14 Supra n. 5, p. 4.

for those subject to a form of crime where digital evidence may exist, but also for those tasked with investigating such instances.

THE PROCESS OF DIGITAL FORENSICS

Digital forensics can be described as the investigatory process of acquiring and retrieving digital evidence from digital sources and tools. Figure 8.2 sets out the digital forensics process. Here, it describes a process that involves identification, recovery, analysis and presentation in court of relevant information taken from electronic devices. The information or data elucidated from the digital forensics process becomes digital evidence that is presented to court as evidence to establish the causal link between people and events and civil wrongdoings.[15]

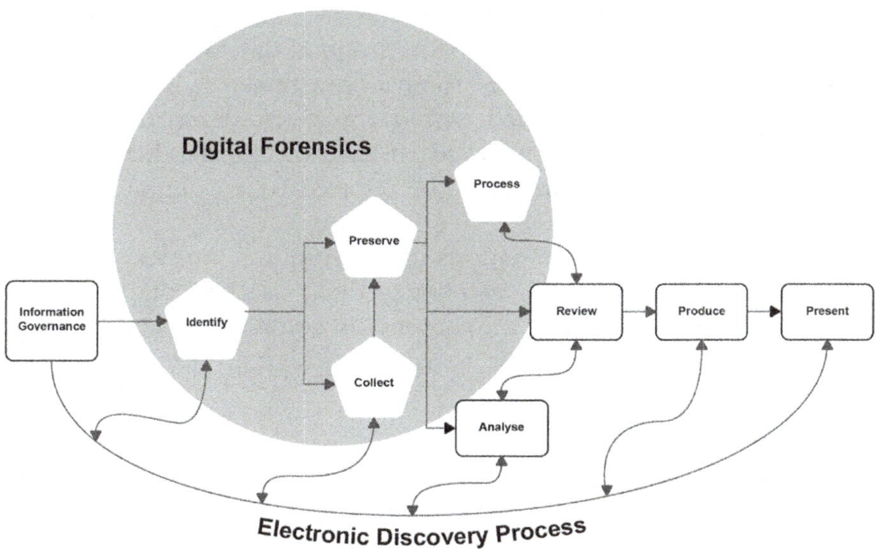

Figure 8.2 The digital discovery process

15 S. E. Goodison, R. C. Davis and B. A. Jackson, *Digital Evidence and the US Criminal Justice System. Identifying Technology and Other Needs to More Effectively Acquire and Utilize Digital Evidence. Priority Criminal Justice Needs Initiative* (Rand Corporation, 2015); D. Lawton, R. Stacey and G. Dodd, 'eDiscovery in Digital Forensic Investigations' (*UK Home Office*, 2014). CAST Publication Number 32/14 <https://assets.publishing.service.gov.uk/government/uploads/system/uploads/attachment_data/file/394779/ediscovery-digital-forensic-investigations-3214.pdf>

In England and Wales, the Criminal Procedure Rules (CPR) specifically address the role of the digital forensics practitioner as a provider of expert evidence in the court process:

1 An expert must help the court to achieve the overriding objective by giving objective, unbiased opinion on matters within his expertise.
2 This duty overrides any obligation to the person from whom he receives instructions or by whom he is paid.
3 This duty includes an obligation to inform all parties and the court if the expert's opinion changes from that contained in a report served as evidence or given in a statement.[16]

The act of searching for digital evidence may imply that such information is deemed to always exist and therefore it is simply a case of finding it, suggesting possible bias. In fact, digital forensic practitioners and those operating in a digital forensics role need to ascertain those events which are depicted by any stored digital data and interpret their meaning. In essence, the digital forensic practitioner's job is to assess whether information contained within any given seized digital device supports or refutes what is believed to have occurred. These pieces of digital information may sometimes be referred to as "digital trace evidence" or digital artefacts.[17]

Digital forensics examinations go through a number of stages before reaching completion, often described as the "digital forensic process".[18] Whilst in reality this process is complex and multifaceted, shaped in part by case-specific variables, a digitally proficient lawyer

16 Crown Prosecution Service, 'The Criminal Procedure Rules 2020, Part 19, Expert Evidence' (updated 10 September 2019) <https:// www.cps.gov.uk/legal-guidance/expert-evidence#:~:text=The%20duty%20of%20an%20expert%20witness%20is%20to%20help%20the,to%20matters%20within%20their%20expertise>; and Civil Procedure Rules, Part 35.

17 G. Horsman, 'Raiders of the Lost Artefacts: Championing the Need for Digital Forensics Research' (2019) 1 *Forensic Science International: Reports* 100003.

18 M. Reith, C. Carr and G. Gunsch, 'An Examination of Digital Forensic Models' (2002) 1 (3) *International Journal of Digital Evidence* 1–12; W. J. Tilstone, K. A. Savage and L. A. Clark, *Forensic Science: An Encyclopedia of History, Methods, and Techniques* (ABC-CLIO, 2006); C. Roux, B. Talbot-Wright, J. Robertson, F. Crispino and O. Ribaux, 'The End of the (Forensic Science) World as We Know It? The Example of Trace Evidence' (2015) 370 (1674) *Philosophical Transactions of the Royal Society B: Biological Sciences* 20140260.

will need to understand a few of the high-level concepts designed to be informative of the general process, but not exhaustive.

- *Identification.* Before any digital forensics device examination can take place, all digital devices and data sources which are of potential relevance to an investigation must be identified and collected appropriately by a first responder (such as a police officer).[19] This activity is often part of any search and seizure process undertaken, which may involve the methodological processing of a particular crime scene to ascertain any "digital presence" and the collection of electronic devices containing the digital evidence. Those conducting these tasks must adhere to any relevant jurisdictional requirements, whilst also considering the impact that such activities may have on those subject to these processes (e.g. intrusion into an individual's privacy).[20]
- *Acquisition.* Acquisition is the process of extracting data from a device in a way which best preserves the device's original state—meaning that where possible, no changes to the device's digital content should have occurred. The result of the acquisition process is the creation of a "forensic image or extraction",[21] which could be thought of as a clone of the data which was present on a device, either in full or part. This will involve a meticulous and diligent review of information available electronically. There are two purposes for device acquisition. The first purpose is to preserve the existing state of any device being examined to maintain its integrity and prevent any contamination of the evidence. This is noted by the UK's Association of Chief Police Officers, who state that "the onus is on the prosecution to show to the court that the evidence produced is no more and no less now than when it was first taken into the possession of law enforcement".[22] The second purpose is that acquiring data from a device allows the examination of it as part of any investigation.

19 G. Horsman, 'The COLLECTORS Ranking Scale for "At-scene" Digital Device Triage' (2021) 66 (1) *Journal of Forensic Sciences* 179–89.

20 G. Horsman, 'Can We Continue to Effectively Police Digital Crime?' (2017) 57 (6) *Science & Justice* 448–54.

21 The Association of Chief Police Officers, 'ACPO Good Practice Guide for Digital Evidence' (2012) <https://www.digital-detective.net/digital-forensics-documents/ACPO_Good_Practice_Guide_for_Digital_Evidence_v5.pdf>

22 Ibid.

- *Examination and interpretation*. Any acquired digital data is then examined by the digital forensics practitioner in order to identify any available information which may be of evidential value. The practitioner will interpret the meaning of this information in line with any case propositions (facts of and issues of particular relevance to the case). Given that many devices maintain large volumes of storage media, in many cases there is the potential for millions of files and pieces of digital data to be sifted and examined. To do this, practitioners will define an appropriate investigative strategy, taking into account the type of device being examined and the suspected type of offence. As part of the examination of data, practitioners will deploy specialist tools to identify, recover and interpret any relevant digital data present whilst also utilising techniques like keyword searching, log parsing and known-file matching.
- *Reporting*. All relevant information identified as part of the examination and interpretation process will be communicated to the digital forensics practitioner's client (e.g. a law enforcement officer), typically in report form. Whilst digital evidence can be complex, all efforts are made to convey its meaning in a way which is accessible to the layperson.

A digital forensics practitioner will need to provide a robust and unimpeachable audit trail so that their digital forensics process, from collection and retrieval to examination, analysis and preservation methods, demonstrates sufficient authenticity, reliability, accuracy and integrity to become admissible in court. All aspects of the digital forensics process should be governed, from oversight and assurances of lawful device search and seizure to lawful device examination and reporting. Practitioners conducting digital forensics should utilise examination techniques which are reliable, ensuring any findings offered are valid. This often includes the use of specialist tools which search, parse and display digital content for their review. Verification techniques should be in place to prevent data from being added or removed maliciously from any examination scenario, which could lead to misinterpretation or an incorrect outcome. In England and Wales, the Forensic Science Regulator helps to define and develop relevant standards.[23]

23 Forensic Science Regulator, 'Newsletter' (2015) <https://assets.publishing.service.gov.uk/government/uploads/system/uploads/attachment_data/file/470526/FSR_Newsletter_26__October_2015.pdf>

THE ROLE OF DIGITAL DEVICES

With widespread technology uptake in society comes an inherent increased risk of technology misuse. However, there is also the potential that these devices themselves may help to describe specific events of interest to any investigating authority; in essence, a device may become a "witness" to an event, recording information about it in digital form.[24] Information found on digital devices now supports the investigation of many traditional physical offences; for example, where recorded footage of incidents has been captured.[25] It is not just those devices seized from a suspect who may be subject to investigation that may be forensically examined, where in some cases victim and/or witness devices may also be required in order to ascertain available relevant information. This may be required where a victim or witness's device possesses the only available records of an event, which are needed in order to further an investigation, for example, victim and/or witness data is required to corroborate the details of an event.

The term "digital devices" may make individuals think of computers and mobile phones, meaning that when digital forensics is discussed, some may gravitate towards defining this field as for use in examining these device types alone. Whilst computing and mobile devices are prolific among society, digital forensics concerns itself with all digital devices which may be of value to a given investigation. Where a device maintains some form of storage capacity (memory in which digital data can be retained by a device), then if its functionality may mean it could offer potential value to an investigation, it may subsequently be submitted for forensic examination.

24 A. Nieto, R. Rios and J. Lopez, 'IoT-forensics Meets Privacy: Towards Cooperative Digital Investigations' (2018) 18 (2) *Sensors* 492; The Open University, 'Digital Forensics' (2020) <https://www.open.edu/openlearn/science-maths-technology/digital-forensics/content-section-4.2#:~:text=Until%20the%20late%201990s%2C%20what,and%20Response%20Team%20(CART)>

25 Home Office, 'Forensic Science Strategy' (2016) <https://assets.publishing.service.gov.uk/government/uploads/system/uploads/attachment_data/file/506683/54493_Cm_9217_Forensic_Science_Strategy_Print_ready.pdf>; Home Office, 'eDiscovery in Digital Forensic Investigations' (2014) <https://assets.publishing.service.gov.uk/government/uploads/system/uploads/attachment_data/file/394779/ediscovery-digital-forensic-investigations-3214.pdf>

Sync 1: Uses and abuses of digital devices

You should allow around 15 minutes for this activity.

A lawyer will require a meticulous eye for detail and clear understanding of what data (digital evidence) is required and an ability to check it has retained its authenticity during the digital forensics process so that it can be relied on in court.

Develop a list of device types which you might expect to be present in a standard dwelling. From this list, identify:

1 The types of digital offences that they could be involved in.

2 The potential types of digital evidence which they may retain.

You may have identified a wide range of digital devices, including some of the following:

- *Computer hard drives.* A digital forensics process will be able to tell the story of how a file was located in a particular place, when the file was last viewed or opened, who has had control over the file and the activities which took place within the file. Files can be encrypted to prevent unauthorised access to contents. Microsoft applications such as Word and Excel or Adobe Acrobat have options to password-protect their files. However, it is still possible to access a version of the file or decode the password as part of the digital forensics process.
- *Smartphones.* Mobile phones, especially those with Internet access built into them, provide an extensive amount of information about an individual, their preferences, behaviours and conduct and can help to form a timeline of events. They are capable of providing a detailed account of one's location and activities at a given moment in time because they have become indispensable to our daily lives, going along with us to almost every place and situation. They contain a wealth of information and metadata about the individual and their social network and frequency of engagement with the social network though Internet browsers, apps which store frequency and exchange of information, calls, emails, texts and other forms of data. Smartphones have become one of the most powerful devices in digital forensics investigations. For example, forensics from mobile phones can provide crucial information about the

conduct of a motorist at the time of an accident. Social media sites and Internet browser histories can provide a timeline of activities and behaviour of others.

- *Ephemeral applications on mobile devices or desktops.* These are messaging applications that cause the sent message or video to disappear in the recipient's device a short while after viewing. Snapchat introduced the concept, and Instagram later added that feature. These apps are built around the premise of privacy and freedom to communicate without leaving a permanent trace of information. However, this is not a foolproof system. There is the possibility to screenshot a message as soon as it is viewed and therefore hold on to a copy of the message before its automatic deletion. There is also the ability to track and retrieve these messages through tools and techniques used in digital forensics. Information in texts, emails and messaging services can provide valuable evidence to support the construction of a case. A number of prominent examples of retrieving information from Snapchat are available online in the UK and abroad, where they have been used in court as evidence of a person's involvement in a crime. An exception to ephemeral applications is messaging applications that offer end-to-end encryption for text, video and voice messaging, which means the information exchange cannot be decoded.
- *Internet of Things* (IoT). This was referred to in Chapter 6. It is a terminology used to describe devices connected to the Internet that subsequently connect with other devices, sync and talk to each other, sharing data. The connections form networks of devices. Each network then collects data, shares data and analyses data to produce context-specific and user-specific solutions to tasks and processes. For example, a smartphone and a TV can be synced, showing viewers' preferences of programmes, a timestamp of what programmes were watched and when. The same smartphone can be linked to one's Amazon or Google home assistant and/or smartwatch, collecting information around movement, characteristics of one's voice or eye movements, location, temperature and so forth.[26] All of these are items of digital evidence that provide a considerable amount of invaluable information about our daily lives. Moving beyond investigating individual devices, a digitally proficient lawyer should enquire about smart technologies and the networks in which

26 'The Amazon Echo: Expert Witness in a Murder Trial?' <https://www.expertinstitute.com/resources/insights/amazon-echo-expert-witness-murder-trial/>

they function. Wearable technologies are another example of IoT, where data gathered from wearable devices can sync with mobile phones and other applications, leaving traces of information that can be linked to persons and locations. An issue with the IoT, when being used as a source of evidence, is data diffusion (the merging together of a range of data from different sources). The nature of IoT technology is the variety of networks which talk to each other and share information. Networks can be shared, and determining whose data it is can be challenging.

TYPES OF DIGITAL EVIDENCE

Legal professionals must possess a working knowledge of specific digital files and information and their potential relevance to an investigation in order to assess when to interrogate this information and in what contexts it may provide investigative support.

Sync 2: Exploring digital evidence

You should allow around 45 minutes for this activity.

1 Consider JPEG picture files. These can often contain additional information called EXIF, which describe additional metadata about the picture including the make and model of the device which took the photo, timestamp information and potentially coordinate information relating to the place which the image was taken. This also allows investigation of possible manipulation (digital forgery) of pictures, video and audio content.

- In what types of crime might JPEG picture files be relevant to examine?
- In what contexts may embedded EXIF data be of value to an investigation?
- What are the sorts of questions a digital lawyer may want to ask a digital forensics practitioner to establish the reliability and authenticity of the evidence being presented in court?

2 Consider the sorts of evidence gathered from electronic storage devices such as desktops, laptops, servers, hard drives and hard disks.

- What sorts of information are you likely to find on electronic storage devices?

- What are the scenarios in which metadata from Internet browsers become useful?
- What sorts of digital evidence may be helpful in creating a description of someone's digital behaviour?
- How would a digital lawyer establish that the authenticity of the information presented in court?

3 When an investigation of a digital device takes place, those examining this content must consider relevant content which may exist as a result of any third-party applications which a user has downloaded. They will also need to consider any data retained by the operating system installed upon that device (for example, Microsoft Windows 10, iOS). Often operating systems contain a range of functions designed to provide the user with a "good user experience". Achieving this experience usually means making the use of the device as easy as possible. This includes ensuring many functions remember what files a user has interacted with and what activities they may have carried out on the system. Whilst this information is useful for a user, these retained records also provide insight into the user's behaviour for a digital forensic practitioner and can often support an interpretation of how a device has been used and by whom. Consider:

- When would evidence from an operating system be valuable?
- Is data from recently wiped devices retrievable?
- How would a digital lawyer establish the recreation of evidence from a devices that has been wiped?

At the end of this activity, you should start to question the sorts of digital evidence that is useful and the risks associated with digital evidence, including the questions that may be useful for a digitally proficient lawyer to consider.

DIGITAL LAWYERING AND DIGITAL FORENSICS

In common law jurisdictions such as England and Wales, criminal cases are established on the standard of proof that is beyond reasonable doubt. In civil disputes, the standard of proof is the balance of probabilities. Philosophical, ethical and legal constructs of fairness and justice are applied over the entirety of the case as a whole, whilst scientific and technical evidence is a particular aspect of the whole matter.[27]

Why do you, as a law student and potentially a future digital lawyer, need to know about digital forensics? The answer is simple: To determine the admissibility of evidence and the weight that is to be given to that evidence.

Digital evidence is vital in court proceedings. However, it can only be utilised if it is deemed to be admissible by the courts. A digital lawyer will benefit from being aware of the rules and guidance governing the admissibility of digital evidence. These will help to determine the accuracy, authenticity and integrity of the evidence in any particular case. They will also assist the lawyer to ask the right questions to determine its effectiveness during the court proceedings.

The process of determining the admissibility of evidence is complex. There is a legal set of requirements and a procedural set of requirements.

Evidence is generally legally admissible when:

- It is offered to prove the facts of a case;
- The manner in which it was obtained meets the legal requirements of searches and seizure of information;
- It does not violate other laws; and
- The process in which it was collected, examined and analysed are forensically sound and can be justified.

The judge in a case determines the admissibility of the evidence. Considerations include the following.

THE EXAMINATION OF AUTHORISATION TO LEGALLY CONDUCT A SEARCH AND SEIZURE OF DEVICES AND INFORMATION

The digital forensics investigator has the responsibility for ensuring that the evidence-gathering process, and the evidence gathered through it, adhere to any relevant guidelines and best practice protocol. This is to

27 J. I. Thornton, 'The General Assumptions and Rationale of Forensic Identification' in D. L. Faigman, D. H. Kaye, M. J. Saks and J. Sanders (eds), *Modern Scientific Evidence: The Law and Science of Expert Testimony* (Vol. 2, St. Paul, MN: West Publishing Company, 1997).

ensure it will be admissible in court. Prior to commencing any form of investigation, collection or retrieval of digital evidence, it must be established by the digital forensics practitioner that the means used to achieve the evidence are in fact legal. It must be legally obtained with authorisation and a search warrant. The most common reason why digital evidence becomes inadmissible is because it has been obtained without the necessary legal authorisation, such as a warrant to carry out the search and seizure. The challenge within the digital sphere is the nature of networks and infrastructures which are interlinked with each other. A warrant with specificity may not always allow for the wide span of networks such as where the IoT comes into play.

Many criminal investigations are multidisciplinary, requiring input not just from multiple forensic areas (e.g. a crime scene where physical trace and digital evidence is present), but also from investigatory and legal contexts. As a result, all those involved in the criminal investigation process must understand the value that specific evidence types can bring to an inquiry, including any digital evidence involved. However, it is not simply about understanding the value of the evidence; it is also important to understand the evidential chain and the legal and professional challenges which exist around it.

In England and Wales, Rule 19.2 of the CPR confirms that an expert's duty is to "help the court to achieve the overriding objective" that criminal cases be dealt with justly, through providing objective, unbiased opinion within the expert's area of expertise, regardless of who they are being instructed by. Therefore digital forensics experts are not "hired to support a particular belief"' by any given party; instead they are required by law to remain independent, producing findings which may support the court in their overriding objective under Rule 1.1 of acquitting the innocent and convicting the guilty.

One of the preliminary challenges for law enforcement lies with recognising the value that any digital device may have to an investigation by acknowledging their capability, capacity and relationship to an offence. Whilst this may seem straightforward, the pace of technological change now means that any one individual is unlikely to recognise all available devices and their abilities. An issue of paramount importance is that much cloud-based data can transcend different jurisdictions, with data hosted outside of the jurisdiction that the digital forensics practitioner and the court may operate in. This may make it difficult to obtain access to the data and its use may be governed by different legal rules.

A full description of the legal obligations placed upon forensic science experts in England and Wales is provided by the Forensic Science Regulator (2020); however, it should be stressed that experts are required to assess and pursue all avenues which lead both to and away from any suspect in question.[28] In 2020, the Criminal Procedure and Investigations Act 1996 (Code of Practice) Order 2020 introduced a revised code of practice under the Criminal Procedure and Investigations Act 1996.[29] Further key sources of best practice guidelines come from the Scientific Working Group on Digital Evidence, the UK Association of Chief Police Officers and the US National Institute of Justice. These best practice guidelines set out principles based upon which digital forensics practitioners and investigators undertake the process and procedure of establishing digital evidence.

In Sync 3 you will be able to spend some time considering the rights of those from whom digital forensics practitioners may retrieve data for evidence from personal artefacts such as personal computers, mobile devices and other forms of digital devices where personal data is stored. In some jurisdictions, this gives rise to a potential conflict between Article 6 of the European Convention on Human Rights (the absolute right to a fair trial, confirmed by the Criminal Procedure and Investigations Act 1996 (Code of Practice) Order 2020 in England and Wales) and Article 8 of the European Convention on Human Rights (the right to respect for private and family life, home and correspondence).

Sync 3: The challenge of creating a code of ethics

You should allow around 30 minutes for this activity.

Taking into consideration the balance between the right to a fair trial and the right to respect for privacy, make some notes on what you would include if you were creating a code of ethics for digital forensic practitioners who are undertaking the collection and retrieval of data from electronic devices.

28 Forensic Science Regulator, 'Legal Obligations' (2020) <https://assets.publishing.service.gov.uk/government/uploads/system/uploads/attachment_data/file/882074/FSR_Legal_Obligations_-_Issue_8.pdf>

29 The House of Lords Library, 'The Criminal Procedure and Investigations Act 1996' (Code of Practice, October 2020) Order 2020 <https://lordslibrary.parliament.uk/the-criminal-procedure-and-investigations-act-1996-code-of-practice-order-2020/>

In developing your initial thoughts, consider the following:

- What specific behaviours would be covered?
- What themes would the code address?
- What agency or organisation would enforce the code?
- To whom would the code apply—all practitioners involved with digital evidence or just those processing it?
- How do you balance the principles of trust, justice, freedom, privacy and fairness?
- What other principles will you include in your framework?

At the end of this sync, you should start developing some critical thinking around the ethical issues that surround digital forensics process and examination. You should be able to make a strong case towards the fine and fair balance between the right to a fair trial and the right to respect for privacy in this process, including how privacy can be balanced and protected at the same time as carrying out the absolute right to a fair trial.

Digital lawyering skills: critical thinking

The reference to "critical thinking" in relation to Sync 3 is no accident. Critical thinking is an important skill for all lawyers, including digital lawyers, to possess. Indeed, there is evidence that law firms are increasingly testing for critical thinking within their recruitment processes.[30] These tests commonly look for a number of abilities, including:

- Being able to deduce whether a conclusion follows on logically from a statement.
- Being able to infer a conclusion from a set of statements.
- Being able to interpret statements to justify whether or not a conclusion is accurate.

30 The Lawyer, 'The Watson Glaser and BCAT Critical Thinking Tests' (*The Lawyer*, 28 April 2015) <https://www.thelawyer.com/watson-glaser-test/> accessed 29 April 2021.

- Being able to recognise assumptions and whether or not there is evidence to support them.
- Being able to evaluate arguments to assess their strengths and weaknesses.

All of these are skills which law schools commonly encourage their students to develop. For example, when discussing a topic in an essay you are encouraged to not just describe the viewpoints of academics, but also to critique them and evaluate their validity and strength for yourself. Avoiding simply accepting facts and information, and instead questioning the thinking behind them, is an important way of thinking for an aspiring digital lawyer to develop.

THE EXAMINATION OF THE TECHNICAL AND SCIENTIFIC PROCESS, TOOLS, TECHNIQUES AND PROCEDURE TO CONDUCT DIGITAL FORENSICS

Understanding the process, tools, techniques and procedure to conduct digital forensics are key elements of a proficient digital lawyer's toolkit. Figure 8.3 summarises the essentials. In this section, we explore in more detail how the digital lawyering process and digital forensics process become vital in establishing admissible evidence in court. During the investigation, collection, examination and analysis of digital evidence, the evidence should never be altered, deleted or tampered with. It should be a complete and accurate copy of the digital evidence and remain unchanged since its collection. There are no exceptions to this guideline. Furthermore, the digital forensics process will be questioned by lawyers during court proceedings to ascertain whether there were probabilities of any alteration to the evidence from its original form and the form in which it is presented at court. Some of the questions a digital lawyer will be keen to find out answers to include the manner in which any deleted data was reconstructed, whether there was any manipulation of the data during the reconstruction phase, the security of the equipment that contained the data to avoid tampering, and any contamination of information in safeguarding the data and establishing its authenticity. It is also useful to establish whether the digital artefact from which the evidence was collected was functioning in the way it should. Errors within the digital artefacts

Figure 8.3 Key points about the digital forensics process

and devices could lead to mistakes in date stamps, timestamps and locations as examples. As such, further evidence to support the examination and conclusion of the digital forensics process would be useful. In the absence of any evidence to the contrary, the courts will automatically presume that the digital artefacts and devices were in proper working condition at the time of the digital forensics collection and retrieval of evidence.[31]

The competency of the investigator of the digital evidence could be questioned in court proceedings. Therefore, it must be someone who is a qualified digital forensics practitioner. Again, no exceptions are available to this guideline even if the process and evidence collection and analysis were time constrained. Challenges here could include use of equipment which may be outdated and the lack of national and international standards for identifying, retrieving and examining digital evidence. As such, two different investigators might reach different conclusions about a particular piece of evidence because they used different equipment or had divergent training. An awareness of these challenges is crucial for a digital lawyer, as they can cause evidentiary issues around the reliability and integrity of the evidence presented in court. The examination of the digital evidence will be of interest to a digital lawyer. To pre-empt questioning by the court or the other party's lawyer and to establish reliability, authenticity and integrity of the examination, the lawyer may want clarification around the sort of data that is being presented at court, its location and its manner of collection and examination. This again helps to establish that the data could not have been changed or modified. If another party in a case is using digital evidence, a digital lawyer may well want to ask their legal representatives similar questions.

The process of the investigation and the process of obtaining digital forensics must be auditable so that the process can be evaluated. Another expert digital forensics practitioner should be able to repeat the process documented in the hope of replicating the result to demonstrate the integrity and credibility of the process where necessary. This means that its reliability and validity can be peer-reviewed where necessary.[32] The audit trail will also help the investigator to justify the use of the technical and scientific aspects of the admissibility of evidence and demonstrate that these aspects are forensically sound and can be used by another investigator to establish and corroborate

31 Law Commission, 'Evidence in Criminal Proceedings: Hearsay and Related Topics' (1997) *Law Commission Report* 245.

32 European Network of Forensic Science Institute, 'Best Practice Manual for the Forensic Examination of Digital Technology (*ENFSI-BPM-FIT-01*, 2015) <http://enfsi.eu/wp-content/uploads/2016/09/1._forensic_examination_of_digital_technology_0.pdf>; US National Institute of Justice, 'Digital Evidence in the Courtroom: A Guide for Law Enforcement and Prosecutors' (2004) <https://www.ojp.gov/pdffiles1/nij/211314.pdf>

the reliability and integrity of the evidence.[33] The audit trail is particularly beneficial to review the methodologies, tools and techniques used in the digital forensics process to help determine the reliability of digital evidence and the strength of the analysis and conclusion. Limitations to the process, procedure, tools and techniques used must be disclosed, including any factors which could have contribute to any potential bias.

A digitally proficient lawyer may want to understand how evidence has been produced for the court. Documentation provided by digital forensics professionals helps to demonstrate the authenticity of the evidence presented in court, such as how and where the evidence was collected and retrieved from and establishing the reliability and integrity of the evidence including its original form. Language use within the reporting and documentation is critical, as these could cause certainty or doubt over the way in which the evidence is being presented. Therefore, a digitally proficient lawyer should question the documentations to establish the level of certainty in the conclusion of the reporting, establishing different possibilities and scenarios through questioning.

Examples of situations where digital evidence were used in determining the conduct of the parties involved include the following.

Using Internet search history

Lusha was arrested based on his Internet search pattern. Activities on his laptop showed that he had downloaded a substantial amount of information on how to make detonators, explosives and associated belts from online sources. Searching his apartment, the police found large volumes of products to make explosives and associated devices. He had also been corresponding online through chat sites such as MSN, and these conversations were retrieved from his computer and used as digital evidence in the court. Lusha was found guilty based on these evidence of terrorist offences.[34]

33 A. Antwi-Boasiako and H. Venter, 'A Model for Digital Evidence Admissibility Assessment' in G. Peterson and S. Shenoi (eds), *Advances in Digital Forensics* (Cham, Springer, 2017), 23–38.

34 *R. v Lusha* (*Krenar*) [2010] EWCA Crim 1761; BBC News, 15th December 2009, Man jailed over suicide bomb book <https://news.bbc.co.uk/2/hi/uk_news/england/derbyshire/8414527.stm>

Using Internet search history

In a distressing case, the Internet search history of Mikayla Munn gave substantial evidence to support a conviction of neglect and homicide and she was subsequently convicted. According to her Internet history, she had searched for "at-home abortions" and "ways to cut the umbilical cord of a baby" prior to giving birth to and immediately drowning her baby in a bathtub, which helped to establish evidence around how the child had died.[35]

Using data from a pacemaker[36]

Data from a pacemaker served as evidence in court. The data consisted of information such as heart rate and corresponding pacer demand. This information helped the courts establish that in fact the information provided by the defendant included fake medical documentations and that he had committed insurance fraud and arson of his home. The defendant had claimed that he was asleep when his house caught fire. He quickly packed some essentials and leapt from his bedroom window to safety. However, the data from his pacemaker before, during and after the fire took place were inconsistent with his account of events.

In this case, whilst the defence argued that the search and seizure violated the defendant's privacy around his medical information collected and used to provide medical care, the courts allowed the data from the pacemaker to be submitted as evidence against his testimonial. This in turn raises wider questions within the forensics and law enforcement disciplines around wearable and health technologies and when data can be collected and used in legal proceedings.

Using data from a Fitbit

Wearable technology information was used in court to determine the truth in the defendant's testimony. A Fitbit device is capable of establishing the wearer's heart rate, sleep patterns, steps taken, distance travelled and location via GPS tracking. Data from Fitbits and most wearable technologies can be synchronised with other digital artefacts and platforms and data can be collected

35 The Indiana Lawyer <https://www.theindianalawyer.com/tags/mikayla-munn?__cf_chl_jschl_tk__=pmd_3a38ebf9bc89d30130627ffa18fc85682499f3ef-1627493748-0-gqNtZGzNAeKjcnBszQji>

36 *State of Ohio v. Ross Compton* <https://www.journal-news.com/news/arson-suspect-unique-case-featuring-pacemaker-data-back-custody/dn6JyzsOemZovpayJMZLNJ/>

from the device itself or the platforms which contain the data.[37] In establishing the truth of the defendant's claim and the time of death of the victim, evidence collected from Connie Debate's Fitbit showed that she had been in the house at the time the defendant, her husband, had claimed that she was out of the house. When he sounded the alarm, which he claimed was caused by an intruder, the Fitbit data showed that Connie had already stopped moving before the alarm went off.

Using network data

Analysis of data from servers and other networking infrastructures such as routers can help to trace and monitor network activity and investigate user activity.[38] An engineer who worked for Apple's autonomous car division had been downloading vast amounts of company information and design blueprints and trade secrets from databases which held secret and sensitive information according to network forensics, which led to him being indicted for theft of trade secrets.

Conclusion

Drawing on the legal requirements and technical and scientific requirements to establish the admissibility of evidence produced for a digital forensics investigation, this conclusion sets out some key principles to ensure the ethical and admissible collection, retrieval, examination and analysis of evidence from electronic devices.

Whilst there are no competency definitions for digital forensics and no standardisation and framework to demonstrate competency, the court must establish that the investigator is competent to report on their investigation and to be able to give evidence explaining the

37 NBC News, 'Fitbit Murder Case: Richard Dabate Pleads Not Guilty in Wife's Death' (29 April 2017) <https://www.nbcnews.com/news/us-news/fitbit-murder-case-richard-dabate-pleads-not-guilty-wife-s-n752526>; In a similar case where Fitbit data was used to establish murder, the BBC Tech News Reports, 'Fitbit Data Used to Charge US Man with Murder' (4 October 2018) <https://www.bbc.co.uk/news/technology-45745366>

38 Sean O'Kane, 'A Second Apple Employee Was Charged with Stealing Self-driving Car Project' (*The Verge*, 30 January 2019) <https://www.theverge.com/2019/1/30/18203718/apple-self-driving-trade-secrets-china-titan>

process and decisions they have made, the relevance of the evidence and the implications of their actions. Therefore, as you read each of the principles in the following table, consider carefully, as a digital lawyer, what sorts of questions you would ask the digital forensics practitioner to establish the reliability, authenticity, accuracy and integrity of the digital evidence and the procedures and process conducted prior to the evidence being presented at court.

Principles	**Ethical considerations and reflections**
In any investigation, an investigator is expected to pursue all reasonable lines of inquiry, whether they favour the case or not, and whether they point towards the existing suspect or not. The investigator's role is neutral. They have a particular responsibility to perform, one that is unbiased throughout the digital forensics process.	This is an area of utmost concern in the digital forensics sector right now. Considerations include: • Does the investigator understand that they are under this obligation? • Is it typical practice for the digital forensics investigator to overlook this duty and side with the party who requested the investigation? • How does the lawyer in a trial determine whether relevant content has been missed or whether there was a deliberate overlooking of lines of inquiry, where does the burden of proof lie and how can this issue be determined? • How do digital forensic investigators evidence that they have considered inculpatory/ exculpatory evidence? • How does the lawyer determine if elements from the investigation could be missed? • How does the investigator know where to being their investigation and follow-up? • What happens if you get a poor evidence examiner? No two examiners are equal. There is a real risk that the same case examined in two different police forces might not come up with the same results.

During the collection and retrieval phase, the investigator is responsible for deciding which material it is reasonable to inquire into, in what manner and to what extent.	Considerations here include: • What is the extent of the legal permission for search and seizure? • Has the extent of the permission been explained clearly to the investigators so that they understand the parameters of the search? • What were the sorts of explanation and documentation that led to someone consenting to a search? • How has the investigator managed the balance between privacy and search? Recent mobile device examination recommendations published in 2019 by the Information Commissioner's Office[39] and the College of Policing also have a consultation out for making sure that devices and their data is not "over-processed".
The investigator should comprehensively record all information.	Case notes are also an issue. Courts in England and Wales have mandated the need for robust case notes as part of the admissibility procedures of digital evidence. Comprehensive notes should be seen as a support mechanism for the practitioner: They record what they have done, when they have done it and why they have done it. Also, this should allow a third party to repeat their processes and get the same result.[40] The lawyer should determine that the notes presented in court have been written with the necessary attention to detail and account for all elements of the process and decision-making.

(*Continued*)

39 Information Commissioner's Office, 'Mobile Phone Data Extraction by Police Forces in England and Wales Investigation Report' (June 2020) <https://ico.org.uk/media/about-the-ico/documents/2617838/ico-report-on-mpe-in-england-and-wales-v1_1.pdf>

40 *R v. Smith* [2011] EWCA Crim 1296, see discussion by D. H. Kaye, 'R. v. Smith: Court of Appeal Rebukes Latent Fingerprint Identification in Britain for Being Out of Step with Modern Forensic Science' (June 2011) <http://for-sci-law.blogspot.com/2011/06/displaying-grave-dissatisfaction-with.html>

Forensic Science Regulator, 'His Honour Judge Andrew Goymer, The Importance of Forensic Science to the Courts' (March 2014) <https://www.gov.uk/government/publications/his-honor-judge-andrew-goymer-oral-transcript>

	The investigator is expected to investigate all relevant persons linked to the chain of evidence if there is a belief that persons may be in possession of material that may be relevant to the investigation. Investigative decision-making is key.[41]
All information gathered must be marked accurately. Sensitive material should be recorded but marked as such, warning others of the nature of the content.	Some content must only be viewed in controlled environments under the right conditions—for example, indecent images of children,[42] where a digital forensics practitioner has legal protections in some instances but must not stray beyond them.
An audit trail of all the processes followed and decisions applied to the digital evidence should be recorded.	Considerations here include: • An exploration of the digital forensic practitioner's digital evidence strategy and how it was formed prior to the examination of evidence. A digital evidence strategy would help to show their methodological approach to a case and also evidence the work that has been undertaken to others who may wish to evaluate it. It also helps to determine what the examiner has done and whether it is sufficient to address all lines of inquiry. • How was it evaluated? • How was information integrity maintained throughout the process?
The audit trail should enable another investigator to undertake the same process and use the same decisions to arrive at the same outcome and result.	Considerations here include: • Sufficient details provided in the audit trail so that method validation can take place. Method validation is vital if results are to be relied upon. The complexity of cases is so great that it should be transparent to all involved what a practitioner has done and has not done as a quality assurance and control mechanism. • Has the digital evidence strategy been sufficiently articulated with a clear audit trail to bring it to life?

41 Supra n. 19.
42 Protection of Children Act 1978.

ADDITIONAL RESOURCES

Scientific Working Group on Digital Evidence <https://www.swgde.org/>

The Forensic Science Regulator <https://www.gov.uk/government/organisations/forensic-science-regulator>

National Institute for Standards and Technology <https://www.nist.gov/programs-projects/digital-forensics>

The European Union Agency for Cybersecurity (ENISA) <https://www.enisa.europa.eu/>

The European Network of Forensic Science Institutes (ENFSI) <https://enfsi.eu/>

Horsman G, "ACPO Principles for Digital Evidence: Time for an Update?" (2020) 2 *Forensic Science International: Reports* 100076.

Horsman G, "Raiders of the Lost Artefacts: Championing the Need for Digital Forensics Research" (2019) 1 *Forensic Science International: Reports* 100003.

Horsman G and Sunde N, "Part 1: The Need for Peer Review in Digital Forensics" (2020) 35 *Forensic Science International: Digital Investigation* 301062.

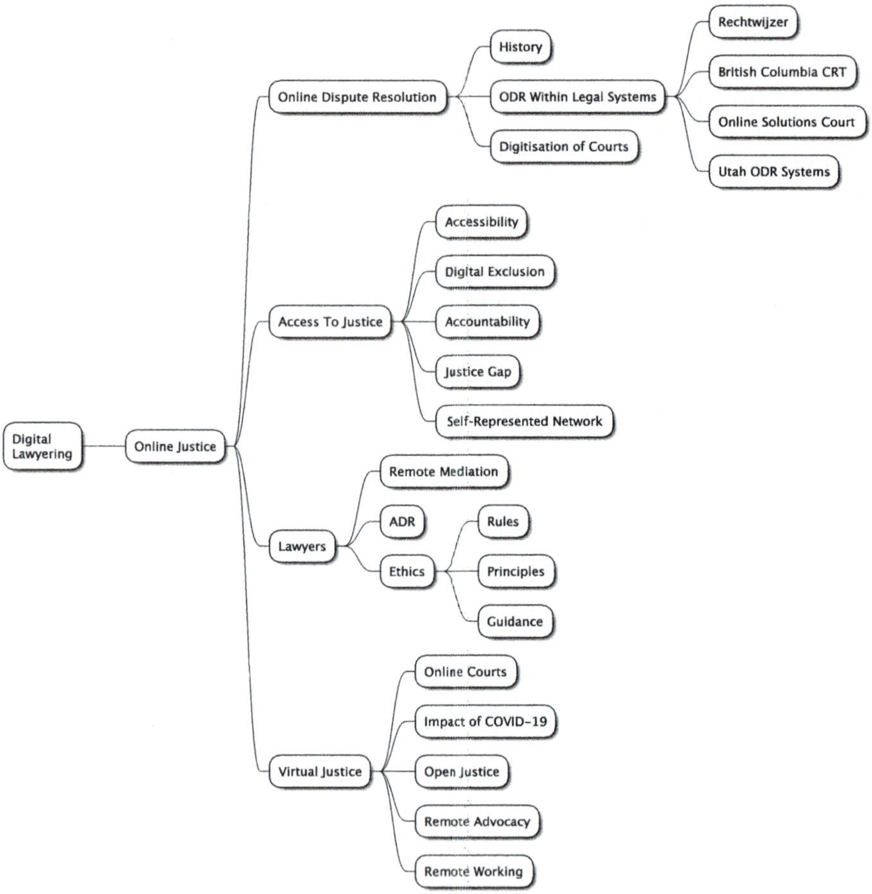

Mind Map 9.1 Chapter topics

9

ONLINE JUSTICE

Francine Ryan

INTRODUCTION

Technology is driving the administration of justice. Online dispute resolution (ODR) is providing an alternative method of resolving legal issues, and virtual courts are now an integral part of the legal system. This chapter will consider how legal disputes are resolved via web-based systems and examine a variety of different ODR systems. It will discuss the development of online and virtual courts and consider how the COVID-19 pandemic has accelerated the use of remote courts. You will consider the opportunities and challenges that arise from delivering justice online and reflect on how, as we progressively adopt technology, there are increasing opportunities to promote access to justice that does not create a digital divide.

Chapter hot spots

When reading this chapter, questions to think about include:

- What is online dispute resolution?
- How is technology transforming the administration of justice?
- How will online courts work?
- What lessons have been learned from the COVID-19 pandemic on the use of remote courts?
- How do we ensure there is not a digital divide?

Having read the title and introduction, you can add any other questions you want to explore here:

DOI: 10.4324/9780429298219-9

Online courts

In his book *Online Courts and the Future of Justice*, Richard Susskind argues that online courts will become an essential element of our legal system.[1] There is some confusion over what is meant by the term "online court" because there is no agreed definition. It may refer to online procedures for resolving disputes provided by the state, or it may be an online service where the case is resolved through the system by a judge without any form of hearing.[2] As you will discover, different forms of online courts already exist in different jurisdictions.

What is ODR?

> Eventually ODR may be the way we resolve most of the problems in our lives, with algorithmic approaches even more trusted than human powered resolutions.[3]

If there is a greater use of technology to resolve disputes, then we need to understand what constitutes ODR. This is the settlement of disputes between the parties through the use of technology. It is a concept that has emerged over a number of years from alternative dispute resolution (ADR) and involves elements of negotiation, mediation and arbitration. It has been described as "technologically assisted dispute resolution".[4] In order to mediate disputes, it uses different forms of technology such as chat, email, online forms, automated decision-making tools and video conferencing. ODR can resolve disputes entirely or partly online and it concerns disputes that arise both online and offline. It is used both formally and informally. This means that what is considered to be ODR is very broad and can include a wide range of processes for resolving disputes including online debt collection, online tribunals and automated decision-making systems where the computer is the adjudicator. ODR is used in different legal systems and across different areas of law

1 Richard Susskind, *Online Courts and the Future of Justice* (Oxford, Oxford University Press, 2019).

2 Ibid., p. 6.

3 Ethan Katsh and Colin Rule, 'What We Know and Need to Know About Online Dispute Resolution' (2016) 67 *S.C.L. Rev.* 329, 343.

4 Colin Rule, 'Is ODR ADR?' (2016) 8 *Online Dispute Resolution* 8.

to resolve consumer, family, civil and commercial disputes. One of the interesting aspects of ODR is that it is being used outside of legal systems to resolve complaints before they become legal problems.

There are many examples of ODR, and each one works slightly differently and incorporates a variety of different tools. In this chapter we will explore some examples of ODR to get a better understanding of how it works and how it can assist parties to resolve their disputes. We need to consider what types of disputes are most suitable for ODR and how processes can be developed to improve the use of ODR. ODR systems are evolving, so we need think carefully about the expansion of ODR and consider whether using an online platform to resolve an online purchase of a few pounds is more beneficial than resolving a civil claim for a few thousand pounds. As ODR systems develop, each platform has different strengths and weaknesses. Although there may be many benefits of ODR, we need to decide whether they apply equally across all forms of ODR.

The range of technological options for resolving disputes is expanding, but it is essential to examine and question these changes to ensure that technology is developed in a way that improves the resolution of disputes for everyone. It is important we question the use of technology so we are not blinded to the potential issues and challenges that might emerge with the growth and expansion of technology solutions. A digital lawyer needs to be a critical lawyer to challenge the thinking around technology.

Sync 1: Online dispute resolution: opportunity or threat?

You should allow around 15 minutes for this activity.

1 What are the benefits to ordinary citizens with the increased use of ODR?

2 What are the barriers to the adoption of ODR within legal systems?

Several reports have been published that argue ODR can improve access to justice for ordinary citizens. The costs of instructing a lawyer and issuing court proceedings are very expensive and prevent many people enforcing their legal rights. ODR could be designed to be more affordable and accessible for people who would ordinarily find it difficult to engage with the court process. A well-designed ODR system that is simple to use could allow people to represent themselves at no disadvantage and make the process of resolving disputes quicker and more efficient.

Although public bodies such as courts and governments are more open to the idea of ODR, there are barriers to adopting technology within current legal systems. In most jurisdictions current court rules and procedures are not designed to support ODR. A significant investment from the state is required to develop and introduce ODR into the administration of justice. Lawyers are naturally conservative, and many of them are concerned about the risks of making such significant changes to the court system. Many lawyers worry that a lack of sufficient investment from the state will result in ODR systems not being fit for purpose and not delivering on improved benefits such as access to justice. Although some lawyers view ODR as an opportunity to deliver new legal services, other lawyers, such as litigators, may be concerned that ODR will reduce the need for their specialist skills.

ODR: THE BEGINNING

In 1995, eBay[5] launched; its original name was AuctionWeb. Most people are familiar with how eBay works: It is a platform that brings buyers and sellers together to trade goods. By 1997 eBay had over 700,000 users, and many of them had disputes over their transactions. At first the company attempted to resolve complaints via email, but with the growing number of users it was evident that was not going to be feasible, and they needed to develop a more cost-effective and efficient system. eBay contracted SquareTrade to develop an ODR system that could help them address a significant number of disputes. The first stage of the SquareTrade system was an online form where the user could make an initial claim that set out their demands. Then, if a settlement could not be reached, a human mediator would become involved to resolve the dispute. The system was revolutionary because the software replaced the functions of humans. In 2003, eBay started developing the system internally, and by 2011 they were handling over 60 million disputes a year.

The way in which eBay chose to resolve disputes was the beginning of the journey for ODR. eBay demonstrated it was possible to resolve disputes at scale using specialist software systems. It was and still is an informal and voluntary system that sits outside the legal system. The intention of eBay's system is to resolve problems before they escalate

5 <http://www.ebay.co.uk>

into legal disputes, and it is perhaps the most widely known ODR system. Other companies such as Amazon, Airbnb and Uber have all adopted similar processes for resolving consumer complaints. The eBay system pioneered the development of ODR. The success of ecommerce providers utilising ODR systems encouraged public bodies such as governments and courts to explore the potential for ODR within their legal systems.

Figure 9.1 represents the essential elements of an ODR system which are required to ensure it works and persuades users to sign up.[6]

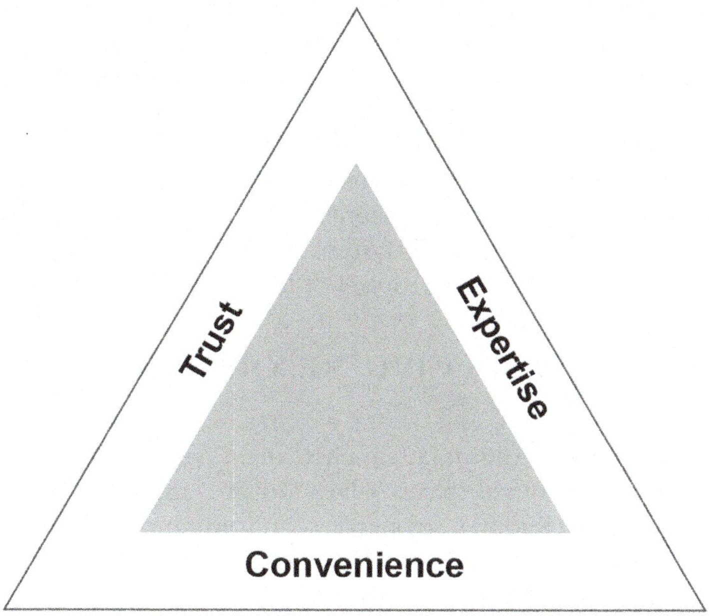

Figure 9.1 Essential elements of the ODR system

RECHTWIJZER: ODR WITHIN A LEGAL SYSTEM

The first example of an ODR within a legal system was Rechtwijzer. *Rechtwijzer* ("signpost" in Dutch) it was developed by a group from the Dutch Legal Aid Board, the software company Modria, and the Hague Institute for the Internationalism of Law (HILL) to support

6 Ethan Katsh and Orna Rabinovich-Einy, *Digital Justice* (Oxford, Oxford University Press, 2017).

people with the legal process of divorce. It was dissolved in July 2017 after three years in operation. There were two versions of Rechtwijzer. Version 1 was an interactive pathway designed to meet the individual needs of the user; it helped the parties work out agreements on issues connected to their divorce (e.g. children, housing, money). Version 2 incorporated ODR to allow the parties to negotiate agreements.

The major challenge for Rechtwijzer was that it was funded through social investment and could not be made financially viable. Nevertheless it was an innovative project that demonstrated the potential of digital solutions to provide interactive advice coupled with ODR integration. The learning from Rechtwijzer influenced the development of other systems across the world, and it demonstrated the importance of having government support to succeed. Although it was disappointing for many that Rechtwijzer was dissolved, it has now been replaced by Uitelkaar.nl, which is based on the original platform and offers a paid service that provides customised divorce plans. The learning and innovation that was pioneered with Rechtwijzer was built on in the next iteration of an ODR system developed in British Columbia (Canada) called the Civil Resolution Tribunal.

BRITISH COLUMBIA CIVIL RESOLUTION TRIBUNAL

In July 2016, British Columbia launched the Civil Resolution Tribunal (CRT),[7] an online tribunal that resolves motor claims (up to $50,000), small claims (up to $5000), property (condominium) disputes of any amount, and society and co-operative disputes of any amount. At the time of writing, the CRT deals with eight types of small claims, including disputes about construction work, employment, personal injuries and accidents. The CRT was established by the Civil Resolution Tribunal Act [SBC] 2012. One of the interesting features of the CRT is that it sits outside the court structure in British Columbia. There is a four-stage process (Figure 9.2).

The first stage of the process is the solution explorer, which is very important because it allows the parties to ask questions about their dispute and, based on their answers, provides free legal information and tools to assist the user. It allows the user to understand their legal issues, guides them through the process and provides them with options to

7 <https://www.civilresolutionbc.ca>

Figure 9.2 The four-stage process

help them resolve their problem. After receiving information and guidance about their legal problem, if the user still wants to continue, the next stage allows them to make a claim with CRT. The parties are encouraged to negotiate to try to resolve the issues, but if that is not possible, a case manager attempts to facilitate an agreement; if that is not possible, then an independent decision is made by an adjudicator. Agreements can be made into orders which can be enforced in a similar way to a court order. The role of lawyers is limited to allow parties to be able to represent themselves.

The five principles that underpin the CRT are timeliness, flexibility, accessibility, affordability and efficiency. The CRT was designed in collaboration with and continues to work with community partnership organisations in British Columbia. From 1 April 2019 to 31 March 2020, 5880 applications were made to CRT.[8] Since its creation, the number of people using CRT has increased and the feedback from users appears positive. CRT has demonstrated that ODR systems work and have the potential to resolve small claims.

The success of CRT has led to other jurisdictions exploring ideas to incorporate ODR into their legal systems, and new models of ODR are being developed. In 2016, there was a proposal to develop an Online Solutions Court for England and Wales. What was different about this solution from CRT was that it would incorporate ODR into the court and tribunal structure rather than be developed separately to the court system.

Models of online dispute resolution: England and Wales

In 2016, the Lord Chancellor, the Lord Chief Justice and the Senior President of Tribunals published a report titled *Transforming Our Justice System*, which set out a new vision for the justice system.[9] The

8 Civil Resolution Tribunal, 'Annual Report 2019/2020' <https://civilresolutionbc.ca/wp-content/uploads/2020/07/CRT-Annual-Report-2019-2020.pdf> accessed 25 April 2021.

9 Lord Chancellor, the Lord Chief Justice and the Senior President of Tribunals, 'Transforming Our Justice System' (2016) <https://assets.publishing.service.gov.uk/government/uploads/system/uploads/attachment_data/file/553261/joint-vision-statement.pdf> accessed 19 April 2021.

report proposed an online system for starting and managing cases with the use of virtual hearings and, more controversially, some cases being resolved entirely online. It offered a radical vision for the justice system in England and Wales, bringing together ODR and virtual hearings to resolve civil cases. Lord Briggs suggested that it should be called the Online Solutions Court, and not the Online Court, because there were plans for aspects of all court processes to be conducted online. However, most people still refer to it as the "online court". The plan was that the online court would deal with civil claims up to a value of £25,000 through a three-stage process (Figure 9.3).

Stage 1

Preventative justice - users will be given information and advice to help them determine whether they have a viable legal issue.

Stage 2

Case officers will provide a mixture of case management and conciliation to try to narrow the issues or resolve the dispute.

Stage 3

Decision stage - a judge will either hear the case on paper or order a hearing which could be via telephone, online or in person.

Figure 9.3 The three-stage process

Stage 1 of the process is similar to CRT. Its purpose is to help users better understand their legal problems to help them decide whether they should start court proceedings. The provision of information and guidance at the first stage is meant to try and filter out spurious cases. The use of case officers is designed to reduce the number of cases that need to proceed to the decision stage, as it is hoped they will be able to resolve a significant number of the disputes. One of the overriding factors in the design of the online court is to create a process that removes the need for lawyers. The vision was to create an efficient and simplified system that could deal with straightforward civil claims and improve access to justice.

The legislation to create the online civil court was contained in the Prison and Courts Bill published in 2017. However, the legislative process has not been straightforward. The Prison and Courts Bill never made it into law because the then Prime Minister Teresa May called a general election and the bill lapsed. In the Queen's Speech in June 2017, the government said it intended to bring in legislation to modernise the court system, and it was thought this would include the online court. However, it was not until May 2018 that the Courts and Tribunals (Judiciary and Functions of Staff) Bill was published. It became law in December 2018 but it did not contain most of the provisions in the original Prison and Courts Bill, including the online court.

The legislation did start the process of digitally transforming Her Majesty's Court and Tribunal Service (HMCTS). The HMCTS £1 billion court reform project began with a remit to close and centralise the court estate and to digitalise the process for civil, family and probate cases. Although the process of court reform continues at the time of writing, there is still no legislation to operationalise the online civil court.[10] The recent priorities of the UK government have been the UK's departure from the European Union and the COVID-19 pandemic. The online court may feature in future legislation. However, there is an issue around funding for the online court because it does require significant investment. It is not yet known what the cost of the COVID-19 pandemic to the UK economy might be, and, if there is a return to austerity, the government may not want to commit to the future development of the online court.

10 In 2019, the government introduced some of the previous provisions from the original Prison and Courts Bill into a Bill called the Courts and Tribunals (Online Procedure) Bill which included online procedure rules to simplify the rules for online proceedings. However, the Bill also lapsed when a general election was called for 12 December 2019.

DIGITISATION OF COURTS

Although we still don't have a fully integrated ODR and an online court in England and Wales, technology is being incorporated into the court system in a variety of different ways. One example is being able to start court proceedings online.

Case study: Money Claim Online[11]

Money Claim Online (MCOL) is an HMCTS service in England and Wales that is Internet based. It can be used by those bringing a claim (claimant) and those defending a claim (defendant). The service is designed to allow a claimant to bring an action online in the county court for a fixed amount of money that is less than £100,000. The online system takes the claimant through the eight steps that are required to issue a claim through MCOL. Once the claim has been issued, the defendant can file a response online. If the defendant admits the claim, then the claimant can make a request for judgment online; if the defendant makes a payment straight away, then the claimant can mark the claim as settled online. If the claimant has a judgment against the defendant but the defendant does not pay, a warrant for payment can also be issued online. If the case is defended, it can no longer be dealt with by MCOL and is transferred to the local County Court Hearing Centre. The cost of issuing proceedings through MCOL is less than issuing proceedings through the County Court Money Claims Centre, and the online service works well for straightforward cases that are not disputed. MCOL also demonstrates the potential for resolving claims online.

HMCTS[12] is part of the Ministry of Justice and is responsible for the administration of civil, criminal and family courts and tribunals in England and Wales. HMCTS has piloted and recently launched several online services, including online divorce and the digital probate service. The court system in England and Wales is centralised, but that is not the same in other jurisdictions. Some countries have state or federal systems, which means the digitalisation of the court system is

11 HMCTS is piloting a new service called Online Civil Money Claims which is in addition to MCOL. This is an online service for members of the public to issue claims of up to £10,000. HMCTS is currently piloting a number of other services in the County Court. <https://www.moneyclaim.gov.uk>

12 <https://www.gov.uk/government/organisations/hm-courts-and-tribunals-service/about>

not necessarily the same across the country. There are many examples worldwide of technology being used in different courts to assist with the resolution of legal disputes.

THE WORLDWIDE DEVELOPMENT OF ODR

Other jurisdictions are also incorporating online platforms into their legal systems. Courts in New South Wales (NSW, Australia) use online systems for interlocutory hearings and messaging between lawyers and the judge. In the supreme and district courts, the judge can decide to resolve civil law matters that are not contested in an online courtroom.[13] Singapore has an online system that allows for virtual negotiation to resolve small claims matters.[14] The court website contains much information to support court users, including a chat function. China has been at the forefront of technological innovation; it has incorporated ODR platforms, Internet courts and emerging technologies within its justice system. The West Lake Court in Hangzhou uses virtual courtrooms, and a robot provides support for court users. Several regions in China have Internet courts that have been created specifically to resolve Internet disputes, such as domain name or copyright infringements.[15] China is also developing AI tools to help litigants draft court proceedings and understand their legal issues.

UTAH ODR SYSTEM

In 2018, the US state of Utah launched the first version of an ODR platform created by the Utah Administrative Office of the Court (AOC). The platform is available for use in three jurisdictions within Utah, and its focus was on debt collection and payday loans where the amount in dispute is less than $11,000. The plan was to extend the platform across the whole of the state in 2020, but there have been some issues with the wider launch. A report was prepared by the Innovation for Justice programme, which stated:[16]

13 <https://courts.nsw.gov.au/>

14 <https://www.statecourts.gov.sg/cws/Pages/default.aspx>

15 <https://www.netcourt.gov.cn/>

16 Stacey Butler, Sarah Mauet, Christopher L. Griffin Jr and Mackenzie S. Pish, 'The Utah Online Dispute Resolution Platform: A Usability Evaluation, and Report' (September 2020) <http://law.arizona.edu/sites/default/files/i4J_Utah_ODR_Report.pdf> accessed 19 April 2021.

> [Online dispute resolution] is this emerging approach to access to justice that is at the intersection of law and technology and has so much hope and promise.

One of the important lessons from this project is the importance of user testing in the design of these platforms, which is something that we explored in Chapter 4. Stacey Butler said:

> But I was fascinated that no one has run a [user experience] test on an online dispute resolution platform in the U.S. to evaluate whether it was going to work for the people who use it.[17]

If there is going to be an expansion of new platforms, there must be more research and engagement with stakeholders into the design and development of ODR to ensure that it meets the needs of end users.

Case study: Self-represented litigation network[18]

In the United States, each state has its own procedures for dealing with civil legal issues. The Self-Represented Litigation Network (SRLN) estimates there are 30 million people per year who are unrepresented in America's state and county courts. It believes there are even more who represent themselves in municipal courts and in administrative proceedings. Legal Aid in America is limited. According to the Legal Service Corporation 2017 report,[19] between 62% and 72% of those who apply for legal aid are unable to receive help. The growing number of self-represented litigants led to the creation of SRLN in 2005. It brings together judges, court managers, lawyers, librarians, academics and community organisations to develop resources, education and training to help support people navigating the court system alone.

17 Emma Cueto, 'Online Court Pilot Gets Low Marks Ahead of Wider Launch' (*Law 360*, 13 September 2020) <http://www.law360.com/access-to-justice/articles/1309437/online-court-pilot-gets-low-marks-ahead-of-wider-launch?nl_pk=77322a31-1bbc-4e35-8532-8a4ef2d22451&utm_source=newsletter&utm_medium=email&utm_campaign=access-to-justice&read_more=1> accessed 19 April 2021.

18 <http://www.srln.org>

19 Legal Services Corporation, 'Justice Gap Report: Measuring the Civil Legal Needs of Low-income Americans' (2017) <https://www.lsc.gov/media-center/publications/2017-justice-gap-report> accessed 19 April 2021.

Sync 2: Self-help resources

You should allow around 20 minutes for this activity.

1 Go to <http://www.lawhelp.org/find-help>

2 You will see a map of the United States. Click on the state of New York and have a look around the website, in particular the self-help tools.

The Lawhelp.org website contains a wide range of resources and information. Technology solutions are being designed to help someone represent themselves; for example, on the New York website a self-represented individual can create a debt verification letter.[20] There is also a link to the NYcourts.gov website that allows someone to use the do-it-yourself forms to process their case if they do not have a lawyer. A HP Action can be started in New York City through an app called JustFix, which is a free and confidential service to force a landlord to make repairs.[21] There are certain claims such as housing repairs and landlord harassment that use aspects of ODR.

ACCESS TO JUSTICE

One of the main drivers for ODR has been the need to improve access to justice for ordinary citizens. In Chapter 4 you learned about the impact of cuts to funding for legal advice and how many people are not able to afford the services of lawyers. Despite the lack of access to specialist advice, many people still have to navigate the court system. Doing this alone means that the process is often distressing and confusing. Many parts of the justice system are making the case that access to courts must be more accessible and more affordable. There is an expectation that ODR will be a part of the solution, but that will only be possible if the platforms are accessible and easy to navigate.

20 A debt verification letter is a person's legal right to request information about a debt from the debt collector.

21 A tenant can bring a case against their landlord to require them to take action or perform repairs; this is called an HP action <https://app.justfix.nyc/en/ehp/splash>

Sync 3: Justice gap

You should allow around 20 minutes for this activity.

Consider the strengths, weaknesses, opportunities and threats (SWOT) of ODR systems in relation to addressing the justice gap by completing the SWOT analysis (Figure 9.4).

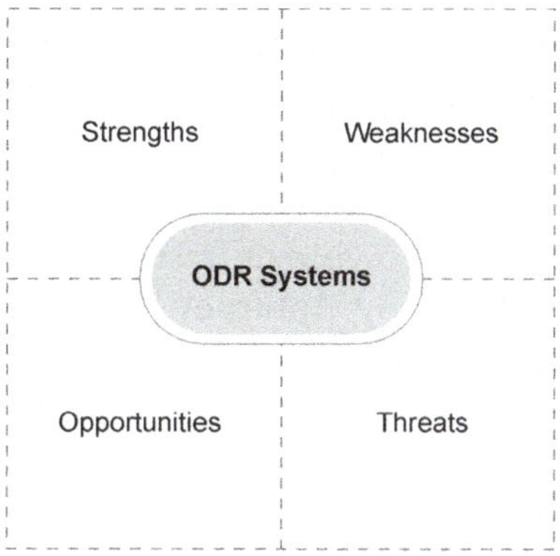

Figure 9.4 ODR systems SWOT analysis

You may have included some of these points in your SWOT analysis.

Strengths

- To provide faster and cheaper options than those currently existing.
- To provide a more flexible system to resolve legal disputes by negotiation and through online hearings rather than having to attend court in person.

Weaknesses

- A perception that ODR platforms provide second-rate justice which is not comparable to current systems.
- It requires users to have access to and be able to engage with technology.

Opportunities

- To engage more users in the legal system.
- To improve court efficiency.

Threats

- A lack of investment will impact on the viability and performance of the platforms.
- Government or state support is required, the current economic situation is challenging and modernising court systems may not be an investment priority.

Although there is considerable potential for ODR, it is important to recognise the challenges of developing and incorporating these platforms into existing legal systems. There are significant barriers to overcome before they can become widely adopted. ODR is gaining wider acceptance and there is a growing infrastructure around these platforms. The more people using Internet technology may lead to a greater desire to leverage the benefits ODR can offer.

THE ROLE OF LAWYERS

Some parts of the legal profession have been resistant to ODR because it excludes lawyers from the dispute resolution process. ODR has primarily been considered for low value claims. However, due to COVID-19 aspects of ODR have been explored for use more widely and, in particular, in complex commercial claims. In these types of cases the term "ODR" has been replaced with "remote mediation", and we have seen more substantial disputes being resolved online. Because COVID-19 has forced lawyers to work from home, there has been an increased level of acceptance and confidence in using remote mediation. The time- and cost-saving benefits achieved using remote mediation mean it is very likely it will continue. Remote mediation replicates face-to-face mediation through video conferencing platforms such as Zoom. There is now a plethora of conferencing platforms to choose from and they are including features that particularly support mediation.

A mediator hosts the meeting and uses breakout rooms for each of the parties. The mediator visits the breakout rooms and has private discussions with each of the parties. The parties then come together in a joint session and through a collaborative process come to a resolution and agreement on the issues. There is already a trend towards ADR from court-based litigation. Future lawyers will need an understanding of remote mediation and the skills to successfully support clients through the process. It is important to have a practical understanding of how remote mediations are conducted to ensure it goes well. There are number of technology-related issues that need to be considered in advance of a remote mediation.

REMOTE MEDIATION TIPS

- Agree with your client in advance how you will communicate in a joint session.
- Have the bundle on a second device so you have the documents you need readily available.
- Check your hardware and make sure you have good connectivity before the meeting starts.
- Do not leave your client in the breakout room; use the time you have with your client during the mediation effectively.
- If there is a chat function, ensure that it is only used for non-confidential and non-private messages.
- Have a video pre-meeting discussion with the mediator to make sure everyone fully understands the process.
- Make sure there is good lighting: It is more challenging to read non-verbal clues online and even more difficult when there is poor lighting.

It is important to be aware of the changes that are happening within legal practice. Lawyers are increasingly going to be participating in mediations rather than in trials. Many law schools are now offering training in advanced negotiation and mediation, providing students with the opportunity to acquire the practical skills and techniques required for facilitating negotiations. Mediation training can support the development of effective listening, conflict management and negotiation skills. Mediation is becoming a preferred approach to conflict resolution in many jurisdictions. Many lawyers are now also trained mediators. The range of disputes mediated online is also expanding including complex commercial cases, employment and family law disputes, so it is therefore relevant to all parts of the legal profession.

ETHICAL PRINCIPLES

As the potential for ODR increases, we need to consider the ethical principles that underpin the design and developments of ODR systems. There needs to be an awareness of both the positive and negative benefits that emerging technologies can bring. Although ODR may hold the promise of increasing access to justice, there are risks in relation to data security, privacy and (as discussed) later lack of access and power imbalances with the adoption of more technology-enhanced solutions. We need to consider whether there are appropriate standards and regulations governing ODR platforms now and in the future. The National Center for Technology and Dispute Resolution has developed the Ethical Principles for Online Dispute Resolution.[22] These are not enforceable rules but act as guidance around the shared values that should be incorporated into the design and development of ODR systems. The purpose of these principles is to assist ODR designers, practitioners and public bodies to more effectively respond to some of the ethical issues and challenges that arise with the development and implementation of ODR systems.

In the United States, the International Council for Online Dispute Regulation promotes standards for worldwide adoption of ODR systems.[23] It builds on the previous work of the National Center for Technology and Dispute Resolution and has a simplified set of standards. ODR systems should be:

- Accessible
- Accountable
- Competent
- Confidential
- Equal
- Fair/Impartial/Neutral
- Legal
- Secure
- Transparent.

22 The National Center for Technology and Dispute Resolution, 'Ethical Principles for Online Dispute Resolution' (2016) <http://odr.info/ethics-and-odr/> accessed 18 April 2021.

23 International Council for Online Dispute Regulation, 'ICODR Standards' <https://icodr.org/standards/> accessed 18 April 2021.

There is a recognition that with the expansion of ODR, more robust forms of regulation are going to be required. Lawyers and future lawyers must work towards ensuring that ethical principles of confidentiality, fairness, transparency and accountability are central tenets of the regulation of ODR systems. Lawyers are going to be required to understand these issues from a global perspective because the increase in technological enhanced dispute resolution will be across borders. The globalisation of dispute resolution is going to have a significant impact on the way in which digital lawyers of the future practice law.

WHAT IS THE FUTURE FOR ODR?

The expansion of ODR systems is becoming possible through developments in machine learning and AI. You learned about AI in Chapter 7. The increased use of ODR in the private sector and improvements in technology are going to drive the expansion of ODR in the next few years in the public sphere. We may see ODR platforms moving from handling low-value claims to more complex disputes. As new forms of technology emerge, we are going to see the further development of ODR systems. Perhaps we are going to become more accepting of algorithms and AI negotiating and making decisions on our behalf. ODR also has the advantage that it can be used to resolve cross-border disputes, and this is a significant selling point in an increasingly globalised world. Technology can be leveraged to ensure that ODR is an effective dispute resolution mechanism, but it is no panacea. There are still significant challenges to the future development of ODR systems. Although the move online has been accelerated during the COVID-19 pandemic, significant investment is required in order to realise the benefits of ODR.

In the first part of this chapter, we considered the relationship between online courts and ODR systems. The next part of this chapter will explore virtual justice and the move to online hearings.

VIRTUAL JUSTICE

The introduction of online courts is having a significant impact on the way in which millions of people engage with the justice system, not just in the UK but across many jurisdictions. The trend towards virtual hearings is not a recent phenomenon but something that has been happening in courts for a while. Prior to COVID-19, hearings would take place in a physical courtroom with some parties joining virtually, such as in bail hearings where the defendant would join from prison by a video link. What has been less common is virtual hearings, where all the parties attend remotely and there is no physical courtroom in place.

In England and Wales, the £1 billion modernisation of the justice system has led to around 80 courts being closed. There are further court closures planned, and by 2025/7 an additional 77 more courts will be closed.[24] Part of the decision to close courts is because the current court architecture is old and under-resourced. The focus of the modernisation programme is to improve the court system by moving to digital services and to recoup the investment by selling court buildings. As a result of the court closures, many people have to travel much further to attend court, and there is concern about access to justice. It is important to think about the effect of this policy on court users who have a disability, are on low incomes, live in rural areas, are reliant on public transport or have caring responsibilities, because the impact for them maybe more significant. There is also another interesting issue about whether not having physical court buildings will undermine public confidence and diminish the rule of law.

However, proponents of online courts argue that courts are intimidating places for non-lawyers and that the provision of virtual courts means that it will be easier and cheaper for people to access courts and legal services. It is argued that this will improve access to justice, particularly for those people who cannot afford the services of a lawyer. The increasingly capability that technology can deliver will result in a more seamless journey for the court user through the justice system. Prior to COVID-19 there was an ongoing debate around the digitisation transformation process. As a result of lockdown during the pandemic, physical events were no longer possible, and therefore the only way to continue court hearings was virtually. This has resulted in an unprecedented opportunity to collect data on the engagement of court users in virtual hearings.

24 Owen Bowcott, '77 More Courts in England and Wales to Close' (September 2019) <http://www.theguardian.com/law/2019/sep/13/77-more-courts-in-england-and-wales-to-close> accessed 26 April 2021.

Case study: The impact of COVID-19 on court users

Prior to COVID-19, in England and Wales 60 crown courts and 93 magistrates' courts were using the Cloud Video Platform (CVP) for remote hearings. In March 2020 court buildings were closed and in-person hearings were suspended. In July 2020, as part of the recovery plan, the use of the CVP platform was extended to the civil and family courts to ensure that the justice system could continue to hear cases. CVP works through a secure web browser and can be accessed by mobile devices.

Judges ordinarily have discretion over the use of digital technologies; however, during the pandemic there was an emergency move to remote hearings. A remote hearing is defined as a hearing that is conducted by either telephone or video conference.

On 19 March 2020, the Lord Chief Justice of the Courts of England and Wales stated:

> The default position now in all jurisdictions must be that hearings should be conducted with one, more than one, or all participants attending remotely.[25]

COVID-19 provided a unique opportunity to gather evidence on the move to remote hearings. Several reports have been published that have examined the impact of the pandemic on the court users and the court system.[26]

The findings suggest that lawyers using remote hearings were broadly satisfied with their experience but believe that some types of hearings, such as interlocutory hearings[27] and where both sides are legally represented, are more suited to being heard remotely.

25 Lord Chief Justice, 'Coronavirus (COVID-19): Message from the Lord Chief Justice to Judges in the Civil and Family Courts' (*Judiciary.Gov*, 19 March 2020) <http://www.judiciary.uk/announcements/coronavirus-covid-19-message-from-the-lord-chief-justice-to-judges-in-the-civil-and-family-courts/> accessed 19 April 2021.

26 Dr Natalie Byrom, Sarah Beardon and Dr Abby Kendrick, 'Rapid Review: The Impact of COVID-19 on the Civil Justice System' (2020) <http://www.judiciary.uk/wp-content/uploads/2020/06/FINAL-REPORT-CJC-4-June-2020.v2-accessible.pdf>

27 Interlocutory hearings are those that take place in the course of the legal proceedings but before the trial takes place, and may include a directions hearing, for example. For more information on different types of hearings, see <https://www.gov.uk/guidance/designs-disputes-resolution-hearings>

Lay users face a number of barriers to accessing remote hearings:

- The inability to access the technology and be able to participate fully in the hearing.
- The challenge of creating bundles to be submitted online.
- The use of technology coupled with an unfamiliar process causes anxiety that may exacerbate issues of participation.

At the height of the crisis many cases were adjourned and the number of new claims being issued was reduced; this meant that the participation of laypeople in remote hearings may have been lower than in "normal" times. It is therefore important to recognise that these studies may not present a complete picture on how laypeople engage with remote hearings. The pandemic has for many people exacerbated welfare, housing and employment issues and as a result has led to an increased need for legal services. Many people do not have access to paid legal advice because legal aid is not available for these areas of law, and this may lead to an increase in the number of people representing themselves in legal proceedings.

The research indicated that there were some issues with remote hearings:[28]

- Technical issues, such as people not being able to access the hearing.
- Poor connections, causing people to drop out of the hearing or lose video or sound or experience a delay in sound.
- A lack of technical support, so there was no one to try to resolve technical issues.
- Time wasted at the start of hearings: A lot of time was spent trying to deal with technical and connection issues.
- Interruptions: During COVID-19 more people were working from home, so hearings could be interrupted by children, animals or the doorbell.
- Difficulties using e-bundles.
- Lack of process: There were no agreed standards of what would happen if connections were lost or what the ground rules for the hearing would be.

28 Supra n. 25, p. 22.

- Difficulty of lawyers being able to communicate with their clients during the hearing.
- Multitasking was challenging: Laptops were often used to access the hearing; another screen was needed to view the documents as well as a mobile phone to communicate with the client.

The research investigated how remote hearings compared with physical hearings. In relation to interlocutory hearings and fast-track trials where there were no witnesses, remote hearings are seen as helpful as they have brought benefits including reducing travel and waiting time, improved efficiency, and improved work/life balance. In complex cases that are contested and involve laypeople, remote hearings were considered not to be suitable.

Sync 4: Article 6(1) European Convention on Human Rights

You should allow around 15 minutes for this activity.

The right to a fair trial is enshrined in law, and this includes the right for a party to be heard "either in person or through his/her own legal representative with whom s/he can freely communicate".

1 What impact might remote hearings have on laypeople being able to communicate freely with their legal representative?

2 What implications does that have for access to justice?

One of the difficulties that laypeople have is accessing suitable technology to connect to a remote hearing. There is often a presumption that everyone has access to a computer or a tablet, but for many people they may only be able to join the hearing via their mobile telephone. If they are using their mobile telephone to access the hearing, during the court proceedings they have no other way of communicating with their representatives. Interpreters are often required in court hearings, and this may complicate matters further if there are challenges in translating what is happening. There is also a perception problem: One of the dangers of remote hearings is that they may been seen as a poor substitute to a physical hearing, and laypeople may feel that justice was compromised. It is important these issues are addressed in the future design of online courts to ensure they do not undermine the faith in our justice system and the rule of law.

As a result of COVID-19, remote hearings have become an integral feature of legal proceedings, and it is likely they will now have a more prominent place in the judicial system. In response to the pandemic and the closure of courts around the world, a new website was set up to support jurisdictions moving to remote hearings.[29] The purpose of the website is to encourage discussion around remote hearings, share good practice and prevent unnecessary duplication of effort. The site includes experiences from across the world that demonstrate how different jurisdictions have adapted their court system in response to COVID-19. There is also a research project being undertaken to explore the use of remote hearings on a worldwide basis.

COMMON LAW AND CIVIL LAW JURISDICTIONS

When the courts were forced to close due to the pandemic, some jurisdictions were more able than others to respond to move proceedings online. England and Wales, Australia and Austria already had some form of technology in place to support remote hearings. However, many other jurisdictions had no infrastructure to accommodate virtual hearings; this was not just in less wealthier countries but also included EU member states.[30] In Spain emergency legislation was passed at the end of April to allow for virtual hearings, and in Italy all court proceedings were suspended except for those considered urgent.

One interesting question is whether the type of legal system may be relevant for the expansion of virtual hearings. In the inquisitorial system, which is typical in countries such as Italy and France, the court is actively involved in directing the investigation of the case. The judge plays a key role in the trial, and evidentiary hearings in civil law systems are often shorter. In comparison, the adversarial nature of the common law system means that hearings are often longer and involve much more oral argument and cross-examination. The adversarial system has theatrical aspects which are not easily replicated online.

29 <https://remotecourts.org>

30 Jean-Pierre Douglas-Henry and Ben Sanderson, 'Empirical Evidence from our Global Experience: Virtual Hearings' (2020) <https://www.dlapiper.com/~/media/files/insights/publications/2020/05/virtual-hearings-report.pdf?la=en&hash=9917A7A0EC9368965CFC25932075237514284C4F> accessed 19 April 2021.

During the pandemic, virtual hearings were required because of necessity and, whilst it is likely that virtual hearings will continue, there needs to be more research to examine whether they offer an effective replacement for in-person hearings. It may be that inquisitorial systems are better placed to adapt to virtual hearings. A blanket introduction of virtual hearings in common law systems without some review of the process may be problematic. Conducting more substantive hearings virtually may cause issues with cross examination of witnesses and the parties' ability to challenge more complex aspects of the case. Although the pandemic accelerated the use of remote hearings, both common and civil law systems will need to think carefully about the role virtual hearings have to play in the future of court systems. Irrespective of the legal system, it is important that we ensure that the public understand the processes that underpin the justice system. In addition, when decisions are taken, we must make sure that all court users are heard. We need to understand the implications of moving from face-to-face to online and factor in the impact of digital exclusion on our justice system.

CRIMINAL TRIALS

In England and Wales, all criminal trials were suspended on 23 March 2020 because of the pandemic. As a result, those people remanded into custody were unable to have their cases heard and remained in prison until such time as trials could commence again. While criminal trials were suspended, it meant that the existing backlog of cases kept growing. On 11 May criminal trials started again in the Central Criminal Court in London and Cardiff Crown Court. The trials could only proceed if social distance measures were in place; to facilitate this, multiple courtrooms were used linked via closed-circuit TV. Although it was important that trials resumed, the requirement for socially distanced trials meant fewer could take place, causing an increased backlog of cases.

During the pandemic the non-governmental organisation, JUSTICE,[31] started testing the idea of fully remote jury trials. In a fully remote jury trial, all participants join the virtual court via video link and the case is live-streamed to a virtual public gallery.

31 <https://www.justice.org.uk>

Sync 5: Virtual Crown Court

You should allow around 20 minutes for this activity.

1 Go to <https://www.avmi.com/news-and-resources/avmi-develop-and-pilot-hybrid-virtual-mock-jury-trial-service-with-justice/>

2 Watch the video on the introduction to the Virtual Crown Court, which explains how the process works.

3 Write down your reflections on your thoughts on the benefits and challenges to virtual jury trials.

You can watch the full trial, although we should point out that it is just over three hours long. If you do decide to watch the trial, you might want to think about whether it changes your initial thoughts on virtual jury trials. Are you more convinced or less convinced about the benefits of this approach and how would you feel as a participant? You might also want to consider whether, as a practising lawyer, you need different skills to conduct advocacy in a virtual hearing compared with a physical hearing. Do you think you need to take a different approach to planning and conducting the case? What do you think are the differences between building rapport with the jury in a virtual hearing compared with a physical hearing?

OPEN JUSTICE

The principle of open justice is fundamental to the rule of law, and it is one of the mechanisms that ensures accountability, scrutiny and the adherence to professional standards in the administration of justice. Lord Shaw of Dunfermline quoted Jeremy Bentham in *Scott v Scott* [1913] AC 417, 477: "Publicity is the very soul of justice. It is the keenest spur to exertion and the surest of all guards against improbity. It keeps the judge himself while trying under trial". Open justice allows the public and the press to participate in the justice process and ensures that there is public oversight of court proceedings.

The use of remote hearings for court cases poses challenges for the principle of providing open access to courts for the public. Prior to COVID-19, the public and the media could access courts by sitting in the public gallery and watching the proceedings. Access to virtual courtrooms often requires the permission of the court. In Australia, the Federal Court allows members of the public to request access to hearings, and the District Court of NSW has a process to allow the media to request and attend virtual hearings. In England and Wales, Schedule 25 of the Coronavirus Act 2020 gives the court discretion to determine whether proceedings will be broadcast "for the purpose of enabling members of the public to see and hear the proceedings". One of the complexities of remote hearing is balancing openness and confidentiality. Family courts allow accredited journalists carrying press cards to access hearings. In those hearings restricted material may be discussed which the press is not allowed to report on but which does not prevent their attendance. The courtroom is therefore a protected space where complex issues can be explored freely in the knowledge that those discussions will not leave the room. The difficulty is how to achieve this in a remote courtroom and still protect open justice. This is an issue that courts and tribunals across the world will need to consider if there is an increased use of remote hearings.

Digital lawyering skills: remote advocacy

The pandemic forced lawyers to adapt at pace to remote hearings; however, in the future it is likely virtual hearings will be commonplace. Some of the skills that you will need to develop may include learning to handle electronic documents. In advance of a hearing, you can use Acrobat or PDF Expert to mark up the documents. It is important to understand data protection legislation, which is explored in Chapter 6. All documents have to be stored remotely (compliant with the General Data Privacy Regulation), not directly on your device. In a remote hearing face-to-face communication is reduced, and you will not be able to pick up the same verbal clues you would see in a face-to-face hearing. In a hearing it is important to be able to identify whether the witness is not following the line of questioning or whether you are "losing" the judge. Advocates will be required to adapt their style of advocacy, so questions will need to be shorter and arguments made clearer and more concise; this is especially critical if there are issues with sound and video quality. The professional skills in communication and persuasion that advocates develop in the course of their practice remain the same, but they need to be adapted to be effective in remote hearings. We are likely to see an increase in the use of remote hearings for interlocutory matters and trials; these skills are going to be essential for law students as they move into legal practice. There will also be opportunities to work in geographically dispersed teams on virtual hearings. Lawyers will need to have remote collaboration skills to be able to discuss strategy, develop arguments and prepare documents.

Sync 6: I am not a cat!

You should allow 20 minutes for this activity

1 Watch these videos <https://www.youtube.com/watch?v=qcnnl6HD6DU> and <https://www.ncsc.org/newsroom/public-health-emergency/tiny-chats>

2 What checks should you have in place before you start a remote hearing?

3 What did we learn about access to justice from the chat?

In the chat, Judge Roy Ferguson (394th Judicial District, Texas) discusses some of the benefits of remote hearings for improving access to justice. However, there are also challenges to moving hearings online.

DIGITAL EXCLUSION OR DIGITAL POVERTY?

Although there are many benefits of ODR and virtual courts, the efforts to move legal services online does risk impacting on disadvantaged income groups, older people or those with disabilities. As discussed in Chapter 4, there are parts of our society that are either unable to operate online or struggle to do so. As more of our legal services are digitally transformed, it is important to consider how digital exclusion impacts on people and also more broadly on the rule of law.

INTERNET ACCESS

In the run-up to the election in 2019, the Labour party made a pledge to provide all UK citizens with free Internet access.[32] At the time, the policy came in for a considerable amount of criticism, but when COVID-19 and the lockdown hit, the need for high-quality Internet access across all communities was clearly demonstrated. According to OFCOM (the UK's regulator of communication services), 190,000 UK properties had no access to decent broadband in 2020, and 11% of

32 BBC News, 'General Election 2019: Labour Pledges Broadband for All' (*BBC News*, 15 November 2019) <http://www.bbc.co.uk/news/election-2019-50427369> accessed 19 April 2021.

the population had no Internet access at home.[33] The lack of access to the Internet subjects many individuals to further exclusion, with many lower-income households unable to afford to pay for Internet access. There is a direct link between income and Internet access. Only 51% of households earning between £6000 and £10,000 had home broadband compared with 99% of households with an income of £40,001 or more.[34] Digital exclusion is further compounded by many households not having access to a computer. The issues with access to justice which arise as a result are similar to those seen in the pandemic in relation to lack of access to education. Online access to a computer is required to engage with court services, but many people only have a mobile phone. It is very challenging to navigate court services or attend remote hearings with a small screen and mobile data. Digital exclusion was an issue prior to the pandemic, but, if technological transformation is accelerated without proper support services in place, it is only going to become harder for those who are digitally excluded.

DIGITAL LITERACY

Chapter 4 discussed the importance of digital skills because to navigate digital services, people need the necessary skills and levels of digital literacy. This concept will also be discussed further in Chapter 11. The way in which online platforms and services are designed is an essential part of ensuring that users can easily navigate websites and find accessible information. Chapter 4 explored the importance of human-centred design which is critical with more services moving online.

Case study: Good Things Foundation

The work of the Good Things Foundation[35] is to promote digital inclusion. They have a network of centres in the UK and Australia, providing community-based learning to support the development of digital skills. The foundation is

33 OFCOM, 'Connected Nations 2020 UK Report' (2020) <http://www.ofcom.org.uk/__data/assets/pdf_file/0024/209373/connected-nations-2020.pdf> accessed 19 April 2021.

34 Office for National Statistics, 'Exploring the UK's Digital Divide' (2019) <http://www.ons.gov.uk/peoplepopulationandcommunity/householdcharacteristics/homeinternetandsocialmediausage/articles/exploringtheuksdigitaldivide/2019-03-04> accessed 19 April 2021.

35 <https://www.goodthingsfoundation.org>

working with HMCTS to deliver the HMCTS-Digital support pilot. As discussed earlier in the chapter, many courts and tribunal services are moving online as part of the reform programme. The purpose of the pilot is to provide support in accessing digital services for those people who need help and assistance to move online. The people they support are often in the most vulnerable and socially excluded groups in our society.

The service is delivered face-to-face and via telephone. It supports users to access online services which include civil money claims, divorce, help with fees, probate, and social security and child support appeals processes. The service was designed for people who do not have digital skills, the capability to access online platforms and/or access to a digital device or Internet connection. It support users to understand and complete online forms, particularly those users who have a physical or learning difficulty or face a language barrier. The 2020 Good Things Foundation report[36] identified multiple barriers for users accessing HMCTS online services, and it is clear that without this type of support many users would not be able to be able to exercise their legal rights. For the rule of law to be effective, there must be access to courts and tribunals; therefore it is essential that through the processes of digitalisation we focus on ensuring digital inclusion.

REMOTE WORKING

The pandemic forced the wholescale move to remote working including law firms and also the free advice sector, including law centres and Citizens Advice. The Good Things Foundation alongside Advice UK, Law Centres Network, Law for Life, Citizens Advice and Legal Advice Centre started a fundraising campaign: Devices for Justice. This project was to provide equipment to specialist advice agencies to be able to respond to the increased demand for legal advice and to protect access to justice. COVID-19 has accelerated the development of digital services that many of these organisations offer. The free advice sector has an important role in ensuring that the digital transformation that is happening across many jurisdictions does not exclude certain groups within our society. As the administration of justice is digitalised further, they will have a greater role in ensuring access to justice.

36 HMCTS and the Good Things Foundation, 'HMCTS Digital Support Service: Implementation Review' (2020) <https://www.goodthingsfoundation.org/sites/default/files/research-publications/digital_support_service_implementation_review_evaluation_report_-_september_2020.pdf> accessed 19 April 2021.

CONCLUSION

This chapter has explored the development of ODR both outside and inside the legal system. COVID-19 has unlocked the potential of technological enhanced justice. However, it is not just the pandemic that has made this possible. As law firms face increasing global competition, the cost savings that can be achieved through virtual proceedings have also become more important. The justice system and lawyers have responded well to the changes forced upon them in the pandemic. It is likely that virtual hearings are going to become a permanent fixture and that there is going to be an increased use in ODR platforms to resolve disputes. This is not the future; this is happening now. Law students need to understand the importance of online dispute resolution across all areas of legal practice and have the skills to confidently work in remote teams conducting remote hearings.

ADDITIONAL RESOURCES

Remote Courts Worldwide <https://remotecourts.org>

Susskind R, *Online Courts and the Future of Justice* (OUP, 2019).

Wing L, Martinez J, Katsh E and Rule C, "Designing Ethical Online Dispute Resolution Systems: The Rise of the Fourth Party", (2021) <https://doi.org/10.1111/nejo.12350>

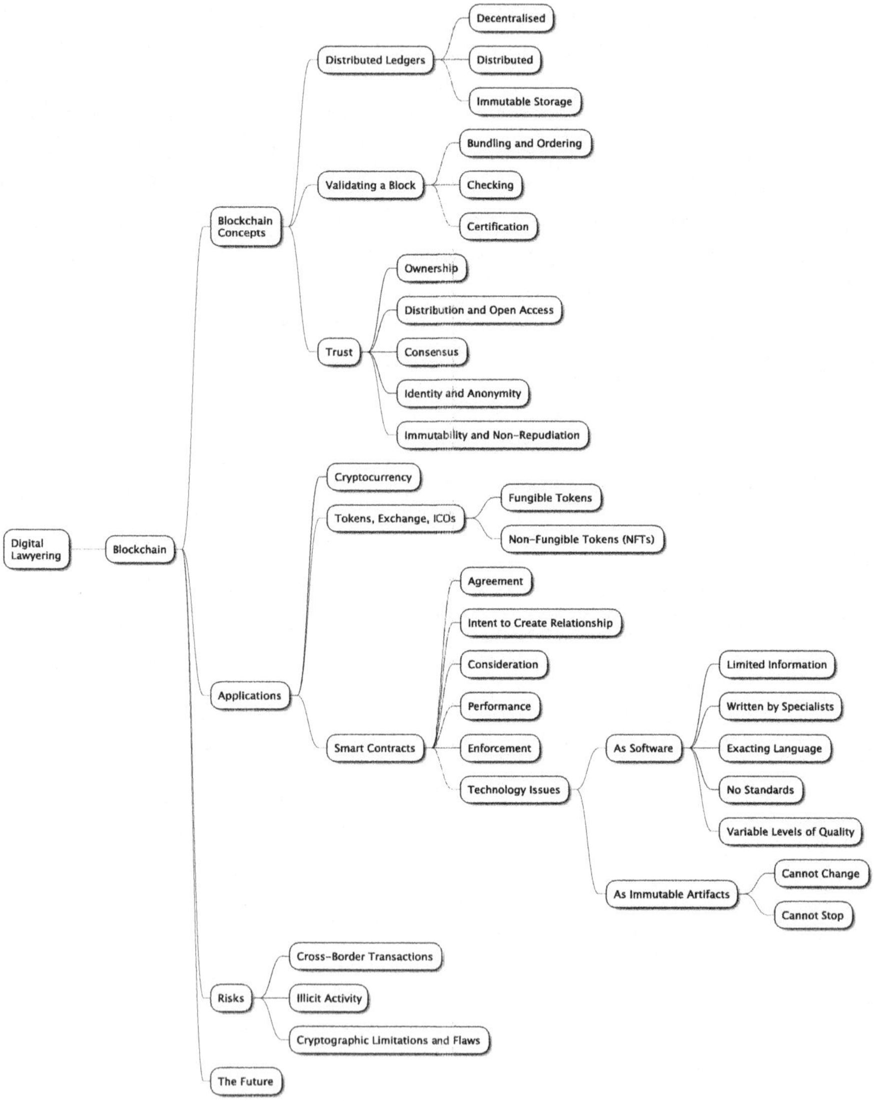

Mind Map 10.1 Chapter topics

10 Blockchain

Terry Wong

Introduction

This chapter will introduce blockchain technology, highlighting key characteristics that make it the foundation of trust for a growing variety of commercial and legal applications. Going beyond the use of blockchain as the basis for various forms of digital currency, we explore these applications and the options the technology offers for anonymity, privacy protections and legal positioning. Questions of regulation, jurisdiction and compliance applying to the use of the technology will be considered together with the implications of increasingly important features like smart contracts and distributed execution.

Chapter hot spots

When reading this chapter, questions to think about include:

- As a vehicle for conducting commerce and legal exchange, what are the characteristics of blockchain (beyond currency) that are most important for a lawyer to keep in mind?
- What are the challenges facing governments with blockchain applications, who cannot fully control the operation of distributed blockchains beyond their borders, even as their citizens increasingly use such technologies? What is the role of international cooperation in such cases?
- How might a lawyer advise clients seeking legal protections for activity conducted using blockchain technologies, where the basis of trust is primarily technological, and is legal in nature only when legal regimes are current and practicable?

  Having read the title and introduction, you can add any other questions you want to explore here:

DOI: 10.4324/9780429298219-10

Illustration: An Urban Power Microgrid

The New York City (US) borough of Brooklyn has a community project for electricity generation by homeowners with solar panels, and the sale and transfer of excess power to other participating members of the community. An electronic marketplace for community power facilitates the bidding process for power, tabulates the flows of electricity from producers to consumers on the community grid, and allows payment in the form of exchange credits purchased with US dollars. Users start participating by downloading a mobile application and registering. To sell power, one must have or install solar panels meeting a minimum generation capacity and install a smart meter that also serves as a node on the marketplace network.

Local generation and peer-to-peer provision of power is a significant break with power delivery through traditional, centralised public utility monopolies, made possible using blockchain technology. Whereas traditional marketplace approaches would rely on a centralised authority for setting prices, accepting bids, matching counterparties and finally clearing transactions, a blockchain supporting applications that implement each of those steps allows the decentralised marketplace to function, addressing a number of key concerns:

- *Timely gathering and processing of marketplace information.* If this was done by a central authority, it would introduce significant communications delays between parties. The data flows made possible by blockchain technology will include real-time power capacity and demand from each of the participants as well as bid and ask prices.
- *Fair pricing.* A central authority could change the prices of electricity for its own benefit. Open and auditable pricing data ensures transparency and fairness in marketplace pricing.
- *Cost-effective transaction processing.* Processing exchanges through a central authority would require additional payment infrastructure, with the possible involvement of financial intermediaries and the introduction of additional costs for processing and handling. Direct value exchange between participants in the network using credits not only speeds transactions but also lowers costs. The availability of transaction data on the blockchain ensures that participants can audit and trust the chains of transactions occurring on the network.

A key theme with blockchains in operation is trust. The trust assurance mechanisms built into blockchain technology and its applications make such marketplaces possible, as we will see in other examples to follow.

A BLOCKCHAIN PRIMER

Sync 1: What is blockchain?

You should allow around 10 minutes for this activity.

Make some initial notes on what you understand by the term "blockchain". You can review these at the end of this chapter to see how your understanding has changed and developed.

What is blockchain? Is it currency? Is it a database? Is it a replacement for the Internet? These are the questions that arise when considering the technology or supporting those doing so in a lawyerly capacity, trying to make sense of its varied applications and the incomplete explanations of its nature.

Blockchain technology has, in mainstream media, been primarily associated with cryptocurrencies[1] like Bitcoin, and, to a lesser extent, with application-oriented hybrid implementations like Ethereum and Hyperledger Fabric. While it is possible that some emerging applications will make it as important or even more important than the Internet (as some enthusiastic commentators have asserted),[2] the technology represents a significant advance in the decoupling of applications and control, to a decentralised model combining high trust, resilience, and privacy. As we will see, these characteristics give blockchain technology and its applications both great appeal and a risk profile that business, regulators and lawyers will be challenged to understand, harness and manage in the years to come.

1 In this book, we will always refer to cryptographic currency applications on blockchain, such as Bitcoin, as "cryptocurrency" rather than the imprecise and sometimes incorrect usage "crypto" popularised in mass media. We feel that "crypto" is vague, conflating two very broad and important concepts: cryptography with cryptocurrency. The former is a more mature but still evolving foundation technology with exceedingly broader application in communications, commerce and so forth, while the latter is a narrower application of exchange enabled by the former.

2 J. Ito, N. Narula and R. Ali, 'The Blockchain Will Do to the Financial System What the Internet Did to Media' (*Harvard Business Review*, 2017) <https://hbr.org/2017/03/the-blockchain-will-do-to-banks-and-law-firms-what-the-internet-did-to-media>; 'Could Blockchain Have as Great an Impact as the Internet?' <https://www.jpmorganchase.com/news-stories/could-blockchain-have-great-impact-as-internet>; John. Naughton, 'Is Blockchain the Most Important IT Invention of Our Age?' (*Guardian*, 24 January 2016) <https://www.theguardian.com/commentisfree/2016/jan/24/blockchain-bitcoin-technology-most-important-tech-invention-of-our-age-sir-mark-walport>

Blockchain technology serves as the basis for many new decentralised applications in commerce, finance, utilities, manufacturing, law and other sectors of the economy. A blockchain can be thought of, in the fundamental sense, as a decentralised, distributed data storage technology. The term "distributed ledger" is also used when describing blockchain. Indeed, blockchain is now the most used type of distributed ledger. Let us examine each of these important aspects of the technology:

- *Decentralised.* The network of participants in a blockchain-based application act without a single central point of control. Central points of control generally provide the function of ordering and recording information, serving as the reference or source of truth for application data. Blockchains are designed to operate with multiple points of activity, sharing control through consensus, achieved through several operations relying on rigorous, provable algorithmic methods.
- *Distributed.* Multiple points of activity operating through consensus each have a full copy of the application's data. This sort of redundant distributed system means that the data on the application network is resilient and highly available, and very difficult to destroy. Because members have access to all the application data, the data is open to inspection and validation, offering opportunities for greater trust.
- *Storage.* Many blockchains can store application data of varying size, though a balance must be struck between storing rich application data and processing speed and data size, affecting the willingness of participants to join the network.

The word "blockchain" conjures an image of a linked sequence of blocks, which is in fact an effective way to visualise its structure. Blockchain is thus, technologically speaking, a sequential block implementation of a distributed ledger (Figure 10.1).

The basic unit in a blockchain is a parcel of application data, the block, containing the details of a transaction, such as the transfer of value, goods or real property. In cryptocurrency applications, the block would concretely contain records of transfer transactions in the cryptocurrency. In addition, the block would contain coordinating information which members of the network would need to treat the data as part of the blockchain. Most important is a cryptographic signature of the previous block that it proposes to follow. In blockchain applications, members on the network running applications conducting transactions would submit transaction data to the network, to be received by members engaged in transaction validation.

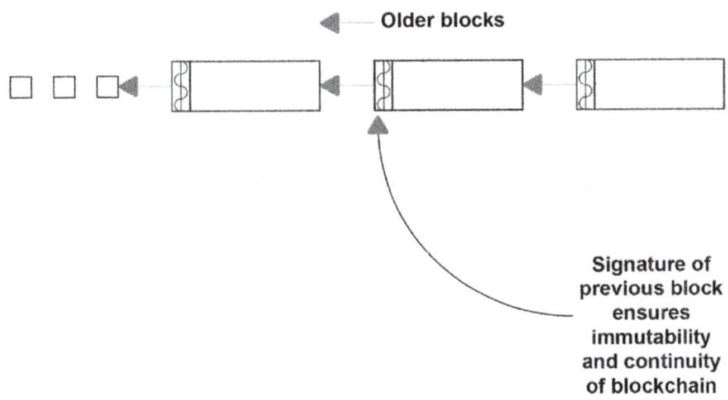

Figure 10.1 Illustration of a blockchain

Validating a block (in cryptocurrency applications, the process is called "mining") involves several steps:

1 *Bundling and ordering.* The records submitted to the network within a given time window are bundled together and sorted into submission-time order.
2 *Checking for consistency and conformity to application rules.* Individual records are checked for consistency; for example, transfer quantities between cryptocurrency wallets are in balance, or only the power that is currently available and stored at a node on a microgrid network may be transferred to a consuming member
3 *Certification.* Correct, in other words, consistent and conforming blocks are certified by computing a cryptographic hash function whose result can be used at any later time to ensure the integrity of the contents of the block (in other words, that the records cannot and have not been altered in any way once accepted). Specific applications have additional rules that are validated during the certification process (e.g. the hash must meet certain conditions set by the network for cryptocurrencies like Bitcoin).

You will note that the cryptographic hash value—a very large, unique number computed for certifying a block—is also used as part of the contents of the following block. That following block is thus able to assert its own order in the chain, ensuring the ordering of other blocks in the blockchain and ensuring immutability by precluding the alteration of blocks already accepted and committed. In other words, they cannot be changed. Arbitrary reordering and alteration of any committed correct block is not known to be possible in a blockchain, hence the technology's name.

By design, the computation of cryptographic hash functions used in certifying blocks in a blockchain is an expensive operation involving substantial calculations that consume time and energy in the form of electricity. In early 2021, the BBC reported that Bitcoin mining alone consumed over 121.36 TWh (terawatt-hours) a year, greater than the power consumption of a country like Argentina or the United Arab Emirates for the same period.[3] This power consumption, and the results of the calculations themselves used in ensuring the integrity of the blockchain, represent some of the economic value rewarded in turn to members who validate transactions or mine cryptocurrency.

Members of the network performing validation or mining who successfully complete the operation on a block will submit the result to the network. The first member who successfully submits a correct and conforming result according to the rules of the application will, in the case of cryptocurrencies, be awarded a certain quantity of that cryptocurrency as a reward, representing the incentive for participating and expending the time and resources needed to validate transactions. This process is illustrated in Figure 10.2.

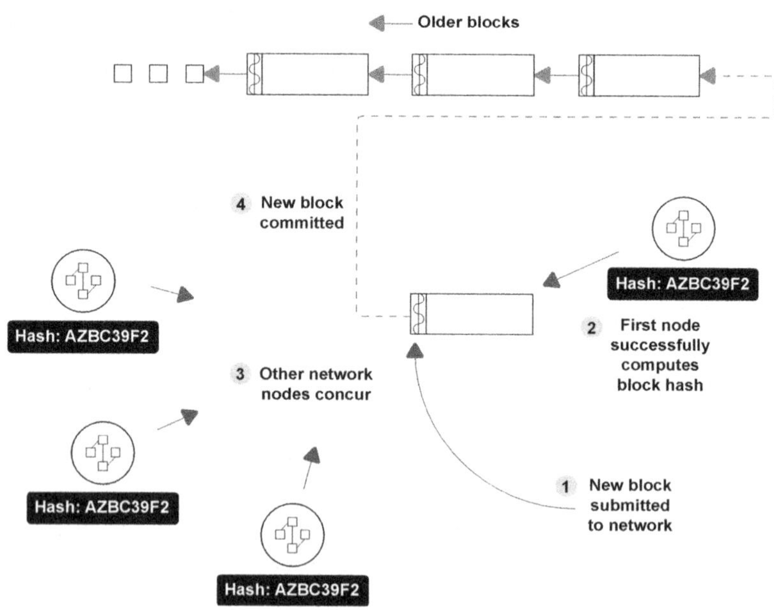

Figure 10.2 Validation by consensus/proof of work

3 'Bitcoin Consumes "More Electricity than Argentina"' (*BBC News*, 10 February 2021) <https://www.bbc.com/news/technology-56012952>

TRUST IN BLOCKCHAIN

Research in the early 1980s combining cryptographic techniques in contexts of mutual distrust led to explorations that would come to fruition with the emergence of Bitcoin. This was the first widespread blockchain application and first successful decentralised cryptocurrency, created in the aftermath of the 2008 financial crisis. Many observers assert that Bitcoin was developed as a direct response to the loss of trust in the world financial system, combining in its blockchain desirable characteristics that build trust:

- *Decentralised.* No longer could a financial institution, central bank or network of banks act individually or in concert against the interests of individuals.
- *Distributed.* Members and actors on the network contribute to its operation and are rewarded for doing so.
- *Immutable storage.* The unchangeable, redundant storage of transaction data open for inspection allows members to realise a level of transparency and reliability heretofore unknown with traditional banking and exchange.

Other views assert that Bitcoin's enigmatic creator, Satoshi Nakamoto, had been developing the technology for some time, simply choosing an opportune time for its release and the publication of the seminal paper describing its theory of operation.[4]

While it may be debatable whether Bitcoin was a response to the great loss of public trust in the financial system in 2008, it is clear that its characteristics by virtue of being a blockchain application were critical to its early success. Let us examine some aspects of trust and the ways blockchains address those aspects in various contexts and with operational methods that do not of themselves engender trust among parties, including:

- Ownership
- Distribution and open access
- Consensus
- Identity and anonymity
- Trust across borders
- Immutability and non-repudiation.

4 Satoshi Nakamoto, 'Bitcoin: A Peer-to-Peer Electronic Cash System' (31 October 2008) <https://bitcoin.org/en/bitcoin-paper>

OWNERSHIP

A particularly difficult characteristic of some blockchain applications is the nature of ownership of the data and the network on which the application runs. For some applications like the Bitcoin cryptocurrency, there is no single operator or central authority controlling the network. There is likewise no privileged member who has the ability on the network to approve or "correct" transactions. This lack of a single operator or central authority controlling the network is critical for the success of a cryptocurrency serving as a decentralised means of exchange. It provides strong protections by design against a possibly corrupt central authority manipulating volumes and prices.

DISTRIBUTION AND OPEN ACCESS

A common criticism levelled by opponents and non-promoters[5] of blockchain technologies is the common understanding from anecdotes and experience with Bitcoin that all blockchain data is open and publicly available, and therefore inherently insecure and not suitable for storing confidential and personally identifying information. One must unpack the concerns and assumptions embedded in those objections:

1 *That a lack of a trusted intermediary like a bank, government, or some similar organisation is an indicator of less than 100% trustworthiness.* This assumes that a trusted intermediary is 100% trustworthy, which is not true. Centralised intermediaries are not 100% reliable in practice, as it has been seen that actors in banks and governments can and sometimes do alter and withhold information for their own benefit.

2 *That distributed copies of data in a blockchain are inherently insecure.* While it is true that all application data is openly available for inspection by participants on the blockchain network, it is also true that a large number of full copies of the data distributed to all participants, updated by consensus, ensures that attempts to tamper with, falsify or destroy application data will in all likelihood be unsuccessful.

5 A healthy, substantial population of sceptics is necessary. Sceptics open to new facts and information ensure that a technology trend garnering such an enormous level of hype and interest, with such far-reaching implications on commerce and on society overall, is adopted or as the eventual case may be, put aside for better alternatives.

While it is true that participants on public blockchains can read the bytes committed to those blockchains, it is also true that in practice only the critical metadata necessary to verify the transaction and the integrity of supporting documents and data are committed and made publicly readable from the blockchain. Many applications will store the supporting data—which may be large—in privately controlled cloud storage, with encrypted storage and access control suitable for their particular use cases. Cryptographic signatures taken of the data must match those stored on the blockchain, thus ensuring the integrity of the off-blockchain supporting data. Figure 10.3 illustrates this transaction recording and data storage strategy.

Blockchains will tend to have several, if not countless more copies of their data on their networks, ensuring that data and metadata committed to them cannot change, sometimes even with the computing

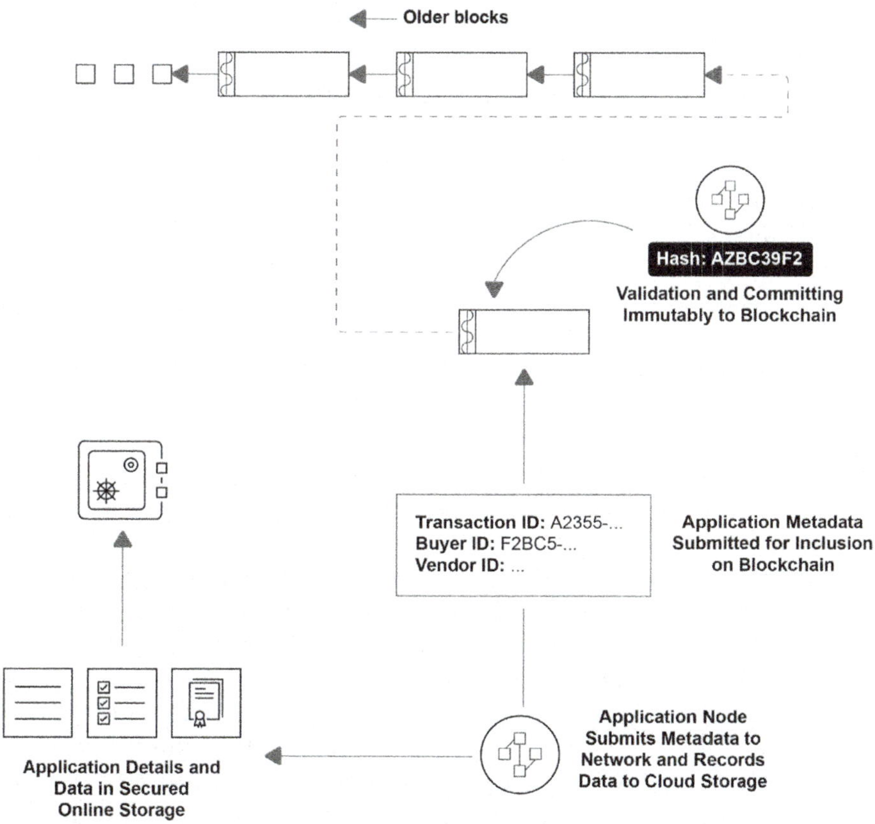

Figure 10.3 Recording transactions with blockchain

resources of state actors. The distributed, decentralised data of blockchains is thus a significant assurance of trust.

CONSENSUS: THE ENABLER OF TRUST

The assumption built into consensus-based decision-making is that the consensus (agreement) of a larger group is more reliable than that of a single individual or smaller group of individuals. While this mode of decision-making and ascertainment of truth is not always desirable (e.g. for abstract problem-solving), some systematic ways of computing by consensus work at large scale for blockchains.

Blockchain applications use one of the numerous commonly accepted protocols (sets of rules) to achieve consensus on their networks, examples of which include:

1. *Proof of work* (PoW). Certain cryptographic functions take large amounts of time and resources to execute, thereby obtaining a result that is usually a large number (a very long sequence of digits), mathematically proven to conform to certain specifications. It is considerably less expensive, if not trivial, to validate the correctness of such a number than to compute it. Because of this property, it is possible to present PoW as a means to ensure that, for example, a Bitcoin transaction is valid and complete. This is because it is necessary to present a valid PoW in order to assert that a specific block of transactions is valid in the act of mining.
2. *Proof of stake* (PoS). Participants on a network must prove that they are invested in a network for a certain period of time prior to being able to operate in validation or mining operations on a cryptocurrency network. Members must hold a certain amount of an asset of value on the network, such as a cryptocurrency, for a verifiable period in order to be consider for selection to create the next block on the blockchain. In this way, actors have an incentive to participate as reliable actors, since the stake is put up as collateral, with penalties for behaviour detrimental to the system ranging from the loss of the stake to rejection of the block or replacement of the block (Figure 10.4).
3. *Practical Byzantine fault tolerance* (PBFT). The Byzantine Generals Problem is a well-known systems problem, the solution to which specifies an upper bound to the number of bad actors that a system can withstand. The example in the paper describing the problem involves a number of Byzantine generals besieging a city who may

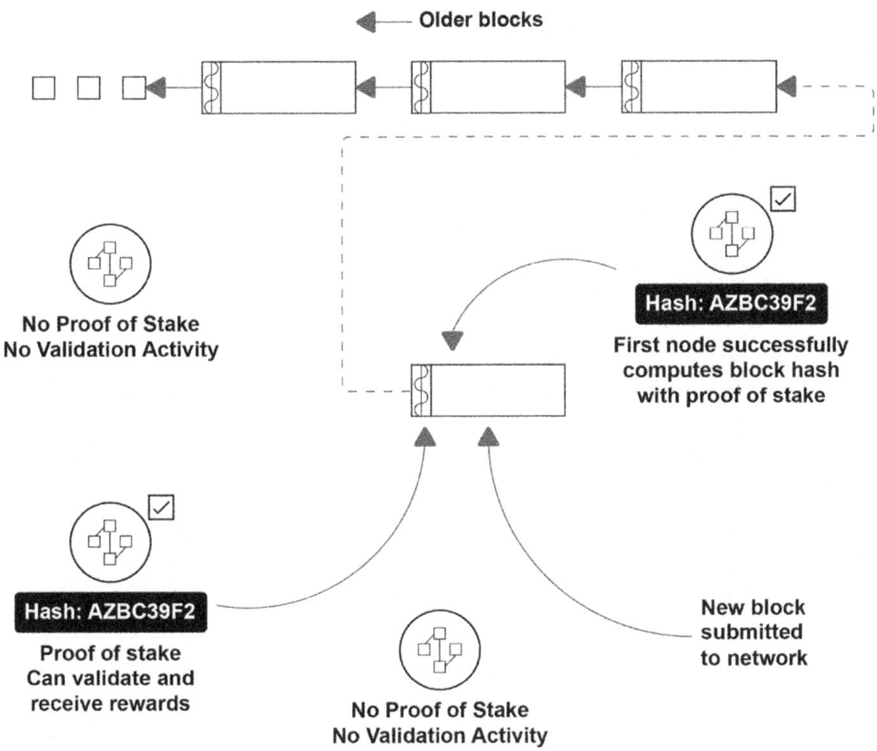

Figure 10.4 Proof of stake

only communicate via messenger. An indeterminate number of the generals are disloyal, possibly issuing misleading or malicious instructions to betray the army laying siege.[6] The solution is also directly applicable to blockchain applications, in which the actors are not trusted by design. Using Byzantine fault tolerance, a network can have up to one-third of its actors be unreliable, go missing because of hardware or communications failure, or have malicious intent and still be able to function reliably. The two-thirds majority will allow consensus to be reached.

The foregoing is by no means a comprehensive list of all the consensus mechanisms being used. Innovation in this area continues, with new methods being developed and tested regularly, as both speed of

6 L. Lamport, R. Shostak and M. Pease, 'The Byzantine Generals Problem' (1982) 4 *ACM Transactions on Programming Languages and Systems* 382.

computation and reliable means of achieving consensus are sought-after characteristics in blockchain development and operations. The former characteristic (speed) enables higher throughput and volumes, while the latter (reliability) maintains the critical factor of trust.

IDENTITY AND ANONYMITY

When conducting a transaction, the ability to trust that we are dealing with a counterparty on whom we can rely to complete the transaction is a prerequisite to successful exchange. In traditional transaction contexts, legal traditions, legislation and case law establish penalties for the breach of an agreement. A generally necessary part of the contract is the ascertainment of the identities of the parties to an agreement such that their obligations and performance may be ensured and penalties for breaching the agreement enforced. What happens, however, when one or both parties wish to remain anonymous, even to one another, yet still enjoy strong protections against each other as to performance under their agreement? As we will soon see, the distributed, decentralised, cryptography-reliant nature of blockchains provide the means by which such requirements may be fulfilled.

How can one establish the identity of another party for the purpose of conducting a transaction, while omitting all other identifying data (personally identifiable information [PII]), such that it would be impossible to connect that transaction with a natural person? Blockchain-mediated transactions offer a viable solution for such transactions, reliant as they are on strong cryptographic methods. Such methods involve the exchange of cryptographic public keys, which are long unique numbers generated through the computation of functions. These public keys support two important capabilities:

1 *Security of transmission*, whether of a message or a unit of cryptocurrency. Only the owner of the private key matching a given public key can decode a message encrypted with that public key.
2 *Validation of transmission*. A message signed with a user's private key can be authenticated using a published public key, again ensuring that the message was sent from the owner of the private key. There is an assumption that the owner follows good practice in physically securing copies of his or her keys, limiting access to them with passwords or biometric locking mechanisms such as facial recognition or fingerprint locking.

An example of an anonymous transaction

Let us consider an example where a freelance marketing analyst offers services with a blockchain-based matching service. A buyer looking for research to support evaluation of a possible market opportunity will pay a certain amount of cryptocurrency for a report quantifying the demand for a specific class of products in the freelancer's country, together with a list of key brands and the distributors of those brands. Because the buyer is considering entering that market, and does not wish to disclose its plans, it withholds its identity when posting the brief and requirements for the job on the matching service's online platform. In addition to protecting its identity, the buyer hopes to minimise possible bias in its research results, which may result if the freelancer were to know for whom the research is being conducted.

Under the terms of the matching service, half of the full amount is to be paid by the buyer and held in escrow in the researcher's cryptocurrency wallet on the matching service until the final deliverables are posted to the service's online document sharing area. At that time, pending a verification of the general nature of the deliverables by the service, the initial payment is released. Upon final payment, the deliverables are released to the buyer, and the balance of the funds less the online service's fees is released to the freelancer's wallet, available for conversion to traditional currencies, to other cryptocurrencies, or for use by the freelancer in another transaction but in the role of a buyer.

TRUST ACROSS BORDERS

In our previous example, we saw how a blockchain-based work-matching service could facilitate a successful transaction involving substantial contracting of work and exchange of value in cryptocurrency. In many traditional transaction contexts, the exchange is governed by a set of regulations in the jurisdictions hosting the service. Such regulations are applicable and enforceable not only because of geography but especially because payment in the local currency or commonly used hard currencies such as the US dollar or British pound is used. This provides mechanisms and pathways that traditional banking providers can use to track and mediate the exchange.

As the basis of transaction is in the end the means of payment, which in the traditional case is in the ultimate control of the banks licenced by the jurisdiction's regulator, a government has a range of highly effective tools to regulate these exchanges if it so chooses or requires to do so in order to meet policy objectives. The use of cryptocurrencies that does not require government-sanctioned banking services for transmission and clearing of payment could raise some concerns, especially when transactions occur across borders.

Some users may view the complete removal of government and banking involvement in the conduct of commerce as a beneficial feature, but in the end, there is a need to establish trust in some way so that exchange may take place. There are two options:

1 *Rely on other intermediaries.* These include exchanges or other third-party services who offer mechanisms for establishing trust. Some services are built using certain blockchain technologies that rely on cryptographic key and identity management tools managed by trusted authorities that issue certificates, known as certificate authorities (CAs), which serve as the source of trust in a given application network.[7] These parties take the place of governments and banks, and in some contexts, particularly in developing countries or countries with corruption and weak banking systems, may be preferable.
2 *Rely on technological features.* These are built into certain blockchain technology implementations. They allow the technology itself to supply and operate the mechanisms for trust. Smart contracts are the best known of these approaches, allowing application operators ways to execute programs that run in the context of blockchain operations themselves. Some of these programs can even perform gatekeeping and payment release functions when those conditions are met, as specified by the application or the particular transaction. We will examine smart contracts in more detail later in this chapter.

In general, the use of government-sanctioned means of exchange is preferable not only for compliance with local laws but also for recourse in case of problems or disputes. Resolution mechanisms and existing legal processes provide at least some levels of protection and established process for seeking redress when transactions go awry.

We might, with some optimism, anticipate the eventual development of international trade agreements covering exchange and commerce using cryptocurrency and blockchain-mediated transactions as

7 At the time of this textbook's writing, the most prominent example of such an implementation in general use is Hyperledger Fabric.

local and international law catches up with the rapid developments in technology.

IMMUTABILITY AND NON-REPUDIATION

A significant feature of blockchains is their immutability. This is to say that records committed and accepted through consensus mechanisms onto a blockchain may never be altered, thus providing a permanent, reliable record of activity and exchange. Unlike with traditional data storage mechanisms, such as databases or file-sharing mechanisms, there is no privileged mechanism that would allow some party to "correct" or in any way alter records committed to a blockchain.

A distributed asset exchange application built with a blockchain would provide a significant assurance of reliability, even in the absence of a regulator or trusted exchange operator or clearing entity. The exchange can be trusted because not one of its transactions can be altered in any way without being detected. It is impossible to give the privileged with access on a centralised network the ability to alter results in favour of certain parties retroactively after market close. In the blockchain application context, many objections to the privilege of a central authority and its manipulative potential simply do not exist.

The property of immutability also prevents participants on a network from denying or retroactively trying to cover up their participation in specific transactions. Reliable recording with consensus and the strong encryption protocols used to sign network requests for blockchain applications assure the validity of even anonymous transactions. It is a small irony that while regulators and would-be detractors of blockchain applications decry the ability of blockchains to operate without government oversight, the non-repudiation (inability to challenge the validity of a signature) built into blockchain technology ensures reliable attribution of transactions if identity can be established through other means, as might happen in far-reaching criminal investigations.

The immutable and distributed nature of blockchain transactions, with their numerous cryptographically signed copies of application data, ensures that non-repudiation is also a survivable fact, so long as there is a sufficiently large enough number of participants on the network. It would be extremely difficult, if not physically impossible, for a well-funded actor or even a state operator to eliminate all traces of a transaction from a large enough blockchain network.

Sync 2: Blockchain and trust

You should allow around 15 minutes for this activity.

Select one of the features discussed earlier (ownership, distribution and open access, consensus, identity and anonymity, and immutability and non-repudiation). In your own words, write a paragraph explaining its importance.

For digital lawyers dealing with sometimes complicated technological concepts, it is important that they can explain information in a clear and accessible way. This is vital to ensure that clients, colleagues and third parties who are less familiar with such ideas can understand the relevance of such concepts and any advice based upon them.

APPLICATIONS OF BLOCKCHAIN

In this section we present several blockchain applications to offer a general sense for the student of the range of possibilities. This exploration is by no means exhaustive but merely reflecting the state of market and technological development in early 2021.

CRYPTOCURRENCY

It is inevitable in an introductory discussion of blockchain that we have already gone into some detail about Bitcoin and its underlying technology, uses and regulation. In the years since its introduction, an explosion in innovation has occurred, with cryptocurrencies emerging to fit into every conceivable space and application. In March 2021, CoinMarketCap, a website tracking cryptocurrency capitalisation, listed over 8795 cryptocurrencies in its directory.[8] You are recommended to visit the CoinMarketCap site, or find a similar listing in an Internet search, to see the range of cryptocurrencies that have emerged.

Some governments have hastened to prohibit certain cryptocurrency-related activities within their borders. China did so in 2017, ostensibly to address energy consumption concerns with transactions and mining

8 'Cryptocurrency Prices, Charts and Market Capitalizations'. CoinMarketCap <https://coinmarketcap.com/> accessed 22 March 2021.

activities.[9] Since 2019 the Chinese government has banned the first public sale of several new cryptocurrencies (known as initial coin offerings [ICOs]) and cryptocurrency exchange activities that could, in the eyes of the government, result in speculative and economically destabilising activities.[10] Most importantly, financial institutions are prohibited from handling cryptocurrencies, pending the issue of a government-backed sovereign cryptocurrency.

In contrast to the situation in China, US and European jurisdictions have not prohibited financial institutions from handling cryptocurrencies. The Bitcoin boom of the late 2010s and early 2020s saw many online financial technology start-ups and established banks all offering services related to the cryptocurrency, adding momentum to the meteoric rise in the market value of a single Bitcoin.

Not all cryptocurrency is used for pure exchange. The second largest cryptocurrency in use, Ether (ETH), is used with Ethereum, a decentralised, open source blockchain used for general applications requiring the execution of smart contracts. The execution of the code in a smart contract requires payment from the parties in the form of Gas, a fractional portion of a unit of Ether, whose value is determined by the supply and demand relationship in time between contracts to be executed on the Ethereum network and the computing resources available.

TOKENS, EXCHANGE AND ICOS

Cryptographic tokens, or simply tokens,[11] are a type of cryptocurrency that are used, as their name implies, to represent an asset. Often the asset is a physical asset, such as a piece of art or other item of property. The token can be used accomplish the exchange for payment or other value, whether in tokens representing other assets or other cryptocurrency acceptable in the context of a transaction.

9 'Bitcoin Mining in Northern Chinese Province to Be Halted amid Energy-Saving Push. *South China Morning Post* <https://www.scmp.com/economy/china-economy/article/3123633/bitcoin-mining-northern-chinese-province-be-halted-amid> accessed 22 March 2021.

10 L. Zhang, 'Regulation of Cryptocurrency' (June 2018) <https://www.loc.gov/law/help/cryptocurrency/china.php> accessed 14 March 2021.

11 Sometimes also called crypto tokens, though we also discourage the use of "crypto", as it is vague, and especially imprecise when discussing tokens.

Tokens are divided into two classes, according to the type of application. If the tokens are used to represent unique items that are not replaceable, for example, original works of art or pieces of real property such as a parcel of land, the token used is a non-fungible token, not replaceable by another token, just as the represented item is not replaceable. Non-fungible tokens can be said to serve a certification function for ownership or proof that an exchange or other critical event took place. These tokens can also, because of their unique nature, serve as digital identity records for things and for individuals.

Tokens representing commodities such as units of agricultural products or energy are traded using fungible tokens. It should be noted that cryptocurrency units are themselves examples of fungible tokens.

Tokens are sometimes created and issued in ICOs for raising funds for a venture or new blockchain application, at which time a fixed set of tokens are minted using a suitable algorithm and offered for sale for legal tender or cryptocurrency. When fully funded, the tokens could represent underlying assets such as a stake in a start-up company, rights to its future cash flows or some other item of value.

While tokens may be used to represent ownership of an asset and record that ownership in a decentralised way on a public blockchain, some applications of non-fungible tokens have gone further and become pure digital assets. Digital art can be registered and, in some cases, stored directly on a blockchain as a non-fungible token. While the item can be examined and viewed by anyone with access to blockchain data, the ownership record is also visible, without the need for maintenance by a central clearinghouse or registry of valuables. In March 2021, the auction house Christie's reported the sale of EVERYDAYS: THE FIRST 5000 DAYS,[12] a digital collage by the artist Beeple, in the form of a non-fungible token. The sale price of $69,346,250 was paid in the market equivalent form of Ether cryptocurrency.[13]

12 <https://www.christies.com/features/Monumental-collage-by-Beeple-is-first-purely-digital-artwork-NFT-to-come-to-auction-11510-7.aspx>

13 S. Reyburn, 'The $69 Million Beeple NFT Was Bought with Cryptocurrency' (*New York Times*, 12 March 2021) <https://www.nytimes.com/2021/03/12/arts/beeple-nft-buyer-ether.html> accessed 20 March 2021.

Some use cases for blockchain

Provenance of goods for human consumption

Outbreaks of disease resulting from the consumption of contaminated raw vegetables can be costly in terms of lost goods, lost consumer confidence and exposure to liability. Agricultural producers, from vegetable growers to winemakers, are turning to blockchain to ensure quality in their products and to provide the means to trace the production and supply chain for those products. The retailer Walmart implemented a blockchain application for suppliers of leafy green vegetables to record every step of production, harvesting, processing, packaging and delivery. Instead of discarding every package of produce on its shelves, as it has done in previous outbreaks, the application supplies enough information to pinpoint the location of contaminated packages for removal. The system allows Walmart to work more closely with public health officials to contain outbreaks caused by contaminated produce while providing greater control over loss.

Know Your Customer

Know Your Customer (KYC) verifications required by financial and legal organisations before taking on clients are time-consuming and expensive to conduct. A common application of blockchain is KYC, taking advantage of distribution and non-repudiation to firmly establish a person's identity and their key financial and legal profile information. Some scenarios have customers unlocking access to their data stored on a public blockchain, with the requesting institutions paying the network for accessing the released data.

Diamond provenance certification

The provenance of diamonds is of great concern to consumers and the commercial members of the diamond trade. There are particular concerns over the trade in blood diamonds, stones mined in war-torn countries in Africa and often obtained with modern slave labour and sold to finance war efforts, insurrection and terrorism. Their trade raises not only ethical concerns but also serious issues of legal compliance at every step in the supply chain. Given the high stakes and risk, it follows that solutions to address the issue of diamond provenance have emerged. It also follows that blockchain-based solutions should figure prominently in a solution, considering the key benefits of the technology and the objectives:

- *Distribution.* Multiple industry partners cooperating on a network provide more trust than a single, possibly corrupt central authority or clearing organisation. Cooperation of key players in the trade lays a core of trust in the network, leading smaller players to join and participate as well. The increasing activity in the network further strengthens its acceptance as growing numbers use it. Instead of relying on a mandated standard or central authority, cooperation and convention may yet lead to an even stronger, more trusted, decentralized network as a positive collective foundation for the future of the trade.
- *Auditable.* Open accessibility of data to all network participants, not just a central authority, supports transparency in reporting, while security protocols allow protections of proprietary information related to sourcing and pricing.
- *Immutability.* Strong guarantees that records cannot be altered support trust in the system's information, guaranteeing compliance to ethics and law in the trade and supporting the confidence of the final purchaser.
- *Non-repudiation.* Should there arise questions or issues, players cannot deny transactions, and thus have the incentive to comply with and ensure good practices in trade.

It is illustrative to note that multiple efforts have emerged in the industry, one from the dominant diamond supplier DeBeers and another spearheaded by IBM and backed by a consortium of mining, distribution and retail players. The two solutions reflect contrasting approaches and, in some respects, the dynamics of the diamond trade.

SMART CONTRACTS

Perhaps the application of blockchain technology that is most associated with the legal profession, and which attracts the most attention from it (if just for the name), is smart contracts. Building upon blockchain technology and its key features of decentralisation, distribution, immutability and non-repudiation, smart contracts offer lawyers and technologists working together many options to implement structures for agreement and exchange. These new structures represent new approaches that are simpler, faster and in some cases more trustworthy than those implemented using traditional contracts.

One illustration of this is in the field of media licencing. Publishers working in print and online media often have the need to obtain licences to use images and illustrations in their works. The process is sometimes managed using paper forms mailed, faxed or more often emailed or uploaded to an intermediary organisation such as a clearing house or stock agency, depending on the intermediary's preferred or supported mechanisms for conducting business. Intermediaries often have websites that support the purchase of licences, but in fact the websites are merely e-commerce mechanisms, offering little in the way of certification of ownership, certification of licence, or access control and metering of access.

Using an existing website to initiate a transaction and support the creation of a smart contract, intermediaries or media owners may use the smart contract to receive confirmation of payment from a banking system or directly from a cryptocurrency's blockchain, following which access to the media would be granted. The media would contain watermarks or have their digital fingerprint recorded on a public blockchain to prove ownership. The media may be delivered to end users from a web service that counts digital impressions or views, much like an online advertising server. The smart contract may be written in such a way as to demand payment from the licensee at certain view count levels, allowing licence use, compliance and payment to take place all at once, without intervention from either party.

A SMART CONTRACT PRIMER FOR LAWYERS

A critical question that arises when considering smart contracts is whether they are, in fact, legal contracts. Let us examine their qualities in more detail, in light of the elements of contracts.

AGREEMENT

While traditional contracts may be memorialised in writing, and in many cases, use language open to human interpretation, such as "the parties undertake to. . .", smart contracts encode the conditions of an agreement using software code evaluated by a computer with specific inputs that represent conditions expected by the parties to yield a specific, deterministic result. Because of the specificity of computer code, it is often difficult, if not impossible, to render an agreement made between humans with the level of flexibility that a computer may take and operate upon, much less interpret. Smart contracts have been used to express contracts that have a limited set of conditions and interpretations, in contexts with high volumes of transactions, such as financial transactions or low-unit-value, high-volume settings such as automated consumer sales.

A middle ground is often taken with smart contracts, in which an external, traditional contract is made between parties, sometimes called a wrapper, that either defines the terms of the agreement in its entirety (in which case the smart contract is a mere accessory to performance, and not the contract itself), or which defines certain terms, and the outcome of executing the smart contract's code as the balance of the terms of the agreement. The parties may or may not place limitations on the smart contract, in some cases defining terms of recourse, should there prove to be errors in the execution of the smart contract's code.

INTENTION TO CREATE A RELATIONSHIP

Many have argued that, given the nature of blockchains and the use of encryption keys in the control of the parties, smart contracts do in fact capture the intention to create a relationship. Where traditional contracts use verbal agreement, handshakes and, in the case of contracts in writing, wet signatures and notarisation to certify the creation of the relationship, a smart contract comes into force (becomes legally binding) when the smart contract is committed to a blockchain with submissions signed using the encryption keys of the parties involved. Many of the precedents established in earlier generations of technological change with electronic signature have been applied to the use of cryptographic keys and signatures in smart contracts.

CONSIDERATION

Whether using cryptocurrency or tokens representing virtual or real assets, smart contracts display the characteristics of an exchange of assets or value. Legal scholarship has asserted the validity of the element of consideration, given that the automated nature of smart contract exchange resembles other online transaction methods in traditional electronic commerce resulting in the formation of contracts.[14]

14 M. Giancaspro, 'The Consideration Myth About Smart Contracts' (2020) 1 *ANU Journal of Law and Technology* 11.

PERFORMANCE

Whereas traditional contracts leave the matter of performance to the parties to a contract, a smart contract's code may be delegated the task of execution, ensuring that both parties fulfil their part of the agreement. The code may execute and fully complete in the same instance of time in which it is recorded on a blockchain, particularly if it is created to facilitate an exchange of virtual assets.

Other smart contracts will need inputs from outside sources, called "oracles" in technological terms. These inputs may be provided by the parties or other automated applications at the time of contracting or at points during the lifetime of the contract. The data is evaluated by the systems running the smart contract code on the network hosting the blockchain application. An application on a blockchain network incorporating a smart contract is sometimes termed a decentralised application ("DApp"), executed by numerous members of the network in duplicate, as the transaction records are committed to the blockchain in the act of mining or committing blocks. As we have mentioned, certain blockchains, such as Ethereum, may charge a certain amount of cryptocurrency as payment (Gas, in the case of Ethereum) for the processing of the source code in the smart contract and the recording of the result to the blockchain.

It is in the performance of a contract that many find significant, even compelling, value in smart contracts. If written correctly and trusted by all parties, the exchange may happen frictionlessly, with little attention from human principals. Whereas traditional contracts may involve numerous third parties to certify and validate a transaction, the secured automation provided by the smart contract and the blockchain offer the potential to streamline the transaction while maintaining trust, unlocking value in one transaction, and more and more as others conduct similar transactions at scale.

ENFORCEMENT

The complexity embodied in the full scope of a non-trivial traditional contract can be considerable. The need for arbitration and litigation in the case of disputes that are not resolved through negotiation is indicative of the level of difficulty in drafting contracts that can withstand the rigors of the real world. The complexity is not reduced in the transformation of contracts from natural language to computer languages. It can be argued that this reality is a testament to the enduring indispensability of human lawyers.

A common concern raised when considering smart contracts is the recourse parties to a smart contract may have in the event that the results of executing the contract code are not what some or all of the parties intended. This area of law is evolving. Some legal scholars have argued that the need for a traditional contract continues to exist,[15] and that smart contracts as they currently exist should only be trusted as a way of automating the performance of a contract. Wrapper contracts sometimes include terms to override the results of a smart contract under certain conditions, acknowledging that it is currently difficult to ensure complete reliability in the code of certain smart contracts.

Technologists sometimes argue that, especially in cross-border transactions or in transactions occurring outside the borders of a jurisdiction, the smart contract is the law, in an expansion of a new subset of law recalling the early days of the Internet called *Lex Cryptographia*.[16] Such assertions may in time be tested. Perhaps simpler questions regarding the legality of smart contracts used in the exchange of property will ground much of the near- to medium-term discussion of smart contract legality.

The conveyancing of property is an area where much activity and speculation has occurred. Proponents of property applications with blockchains and smart contracts hope for a simplification through the use of technology, while incumbent interests assert the reliability and resilience of processes based on traditional contracts, open to negotiation and adjustment. The important point to consider with the introduction of smart contracts as tools or outright replacements for traditional contracts is that the matter of those contracts must themselves be legal. In other words, it must be legal for that contract to be formed and executed under the law, regardless of whether it is done with a traditional contract, or a smart contract with the exchange of cryptocurrency and a non-fungible token representing ownership of a piece of land. A title that cannot be recognised by a court would not be recognised, regardless of the form of the contract used in the transaction.

15 M. K. Woebbeking, 'The Impact of Smart Contracts on Traditional Concepts of Contract Law' (2019) 10 *JIPITEC* 8.

16 A. Wright and P. De Filippi, 'Decentralized Blockchain Technology and the Rise of Lex Cryptographia' (*Social Science Research Network*, 2015) SSRN Scholarly Paper ID 2580664 <https://papers.ssrn.com/abstract=2580664> accessed 21 March 2021.

In November 2019, the LawtechUK Panel, established by the UK's Ministry of Justice, published a *Legal Statement on Cryptoassets and Smart Contracts* through its UK Jurisdiction Taskforce. It offers a more detailed set of guidance and points for lawyers to consider as they work with clients and technologists to navigate the selection and guide the implementation of blockchain applications, with particular attention to smart contracts and their consequences in application. The publication was put out as a proactive action by the government, recognising the importance of this rapidly growing area of technology and the need for government to have robust frameworks for understanding, negotiating and promulgating guidance and policy.

Sync 3: Smart contract legal concepts

You should allow around 90 minutes for this activity.

Download and carefully read the *Legal Statement on Cryptoassets and Smart Contracts* from the UK Jurisdiction Taskforce[17] to familiarise yourself with the task force's thinking on the issues likely to arise at law when applying blockchain technologies. This is an opportunity for exposure to some critical points for understanding blockchain, cryptocurrency, tokens and smart contracts in the context of legal thinking by leading members of the UK legal community.

Consider the following questions:

1 Are cryptocurrencies, tokens, and other virtual assets, which have no physical form and are distributed in sometimes countless copies in a blockchain application network, to be treated as property?

2 Is it legal to use blockchain applications in the conveyancing of property? What are the various approaches to answering this question in England and Wales?

3 If a transaction carried out by smart contract on a blockchain takes place on a network in jurisdiction A, conducted between parties in two separate jurisdictions B and C, exchanging property in a fourth jurisdiction D, what laws apply to the transaction? What reasons do you give for your assertion?

17 'The LawtechUK Panel' (*Tech Nation*) <https://technation.io/lawtechukpanel/> accessed 21 March 2021.

As you read through the *Legal Statement*, and examined some of the cases in the sync, you should have found that in near-term practice as smart contracts are adopted, people will rely on hybrid arrangements using traditional contracts as wrappers or catch-all solutions until more experience is gained in mainstream use of smart contracts. We hope that you will have noted that English law is capable of supporting the view of smart contracts as enforceable contracts, provided the subject of the contracts is legal matter for a contract (i.e. a traditional contract on equivalent terms would be enforceable).

TECHNOLOGICAL ISSUES WITH SMART CONTRACTS

As computer programs, smart contracts present all of the challenges associated with developing, running and maintaining software:

1. *Limited information.* It is developed according to certain specifications made by persons working with the knowledge at hand.
2. *Written by specialists often removed one or two degrees from the business.* Software is written by persons knowledgeable in the practice of computer programming. The software engineer writing the code is not necessarily the person who gathered and documented the requirements, who in turn is not a party using the smart contract.
3. *Require languages demanding high precision.* Computer software code must be written in highly constrained languages and must express the intended process steps or desired result with great precision, allowing for little ambiguity if strict correctness is required.
4. *No standards mandated by law.* As we noted in Chapter 3, software engineering is a relatively young discipline and is yet to develop codified standards for quality and practice, enforced by regulations. While good software practice and high-performing software development and operations organisations exist, there is no single applicable standard.
5. *Highly variable levels of testing for quality and reliability.* Software is tested to varying degrees and to varying levels of certainty, as a function of the skills available in the organisation developing the software, and the time and resources allocated to the task.

Smart contracts, recorded immutably on a blockchain at the time of creation, present two additional problems:

1 *They may not be changed.* Software code executing the smart contract must be correct and capture the intent of the parties perfectly, unless the parties have made provisions in a wrapper agreement in case of error.
2 *They may not be stopped.* When a smart contract begins execution on a blockchain application network, there is no way to terminate or reverse its execution. If the parties to the contract intend the contract to be the only memorial and means of executing and enforcing the contract, then any fail-safe mechanisms must be built into the code and tested to the satisfaction of the parties, or the intention of the contracting parties is not in fact realised.

Lawyers working with clients and software developers building applications with blockchains and smart contracts will be well-served to keep these challenges in mind when giving guidance and advice.

Sync 4: Developing a blockchain concept

You should allow around 60 minutes for this activity.

Consider pairing up with a classmate for this exercise. Identify an existing process in commerce, legal procedure or property transfer that requires a trusted third party such as a government or clearing organisation to complete.

Drawing on some of the examples we have presented in the chapter so far for background knowledge, sketch two diagrams on a piece of paper:

1 Draw a diagram showing the existing process, and the steps to complete the process, highlighting the steps requiring trust and trusted intermediaries such as a government, bank or service operator.

2 Draw a diagram imagining a transformed process, identifying one or more opportunities for the application of blockchain technology, where its use may enhance trust, reliability, processing speed, user adoption or other factors.

Assess your two diagrams and consider the following questions:

- What were the difficulties you had in drawing the diagrams? Was it difficult to choose the level of detail of the diagram, such that you could draw it to communicate to your classmates?

- Why did you choose a particular step for transformation with blockchain technology?
- What regulatory or cross-border legal concerns might be raised by your transformed process? What options might you suggest in order to address those concerns, or how would you go about learning what you need in order to come up with options?

As an additional, advanced step, consider finding a technologist friend and discussing this exercise! This activity is a brief version of the type of work that participants in legal technology hackathons and ideation sessions go through, to learn more and to develop new, innovative solutions, advancing the state of the art.

Digital lawyering skills: creativity

Sync 4 is a good example of the importance of creativity to a digital lawyer. You are creating a transformed process in a way which requires new and innovative thinking. Although this is a skill which you may not be expressly taught in law school, it is a skill that can be developed in a huge variety of different ways. Many hobbies, from writing stories and poetry to drama, from dance to sewing and knitting, and from painting and playing a musical instrument all require creativity. Although you may be used to being creative in areas seemingly far removed from the law, this skill can be transferred to all different types of settings.

Even if you do not feel you are creative in an artistic sense, it is still possible to be creative intellectually and with technology. Writing a piece for a law and/or technology journal or blog, setting up your own website or podcast or simply answering the syncs within this textbook are all ways to develop your creative flair!

Risks of blockchain

As with many promising technologies approaching mainstream adoption, there are risks to be aware of in relation to blockchain, especially as a lawyer advising clients or working with technologists to develop innovative new legal applications. We have already discussed issues of enforceability and technology risks with smart contract applications. The following risks also apply to smart contracts and more generally to blockchains and distributed ledger applications:

- *Cross-border and extraterritorial transactions.* While the UK and many Commonwealth jurisdictions that may follow its lead will develop legal frameworks and reasoning applicable within their borders, much similar work will have to be done in jurisdictions from other legal traditions, and protocols and treaties developed to regulate trade and transactions between jurisdictions. The directions recommended by the UK task force with regard to the treatment of virtual assets and the application of existing law to activities taken with blockchain-enabled applications should inform eventual policies.
- *Illicit activity.* The anonymity that is possible with blockchain applications may allow them to support illicit activities in plain sight or hidden away in DApps deployed on dark web nodes. Outlawed activities, trade in illicit goods such as drugs or endangered animals, human trafficking and other activities may be supported through the use of blockchain technology.
- *Cryptographic limitations and flaws.* Blockchains rely on cryptographic suites that may be proven mathematically to be extremely difficult to break. History has shown that cryptographic suites either have flaws that are revealed through persistent analysis by motivated, skilled cryptographers or are made obsolete by technological advances. In the latter case, increases in computational speed have made some previously strong cryptography obsolete. Advances in quantum computing or other computation methods yet to be discovered may render the current generation of blockchain technologies vulnerable and possibly unusable.

A digital lawyer will take the risks we have highlighted and work with technologists to develop guidance for clients seeking advice that balances technological and legal realities, offering the balance that best meets the client's risk tolerance and optimising compliance with applicable law.

Sync 5: Challenges to law enforcement

You should allow around 30 minutes for this activity. Please note that this activity contains reference to images of child sexual abuse.

Blockchain technologies enable a class of highly distributed computer applications with network participants spread around the globe, operating at the fringes of regulation or even beyond it. They are often deployed and operating in jurisdictions that have widely varying regulatory regimes, in some cases trading between two jurisdictions whose governments have poor or non-existent diplomatic relations, let alone treaty frameworks for negotiating solutions.

Consider a scenario where there is exchange in illicit digital property, such as the exchange of images of child sexual abuse, conducted using multiple cryptocurrencies. While the material itself is not committed to a blockchain, the anonymous sales and purchase transactions are. Illicit vendors operating on the dark web monitor these transactions to provide one-time access for downloading the material.

Governments around the globe have enacted legislation prohibiting the creation, sale and consumption of such material, while international efforts have resulted in a number of protocols in various stages of implementation and enforcement. Given the challenges in legislation and international cooperation, what other challenges does government face in enforcing such legislation and protecting minors with its jurisdiction, given the additional nuances of blockchain technology?

Consider the following questions:

1. How could a law enforcement agency establish possession of illicit digital material, given there are few publicly visible records of the material itself?
2. What necessary steps would agents and police need to take in order to establish a chain of custody?
3. How would a publicly visible blockchain help or hinder such efforts?

Despite the technical and legal challenges of enforcement across borders, it is possible to start with vigorous enforcement within a jurisdiction, with the cooperation of international law enforcement partners and digital forensics practitioners who can develop protocols for evidence gathering in these contexts. As you did this activity, you may have found that there are views that blockchain-based exchange with cryptocurrency are a boon to law enforcement, in as much as all transactions are immutable and there is a quality of non-repudiation, making it much more difficult to destroy evidence.

The Future of Blockchain

ENVIRONMENTAL IMPACT AND SUSTAINABILITY

A common criticism of blockchain applications focuses on the substantial consumption of computing power and the electrical energy required to operated PoW consensus mechanisms needed by many of those applications. As we saw earlier in this chapter, consumption of energy for a PoW-reliant cryptocurrency such as blockchain will only grow as more coins are mined and more users conduct transactions. While some players have located themselves in areas where there are lower-cost power sources for the sake of economic viability,[18] few have explicitly addressed operations with renewable or carbon-neutral sources. Certain blockchain technology implementations already contribute in substantial ways to global warming.

GROWTH OF SMART CONTRACT USE AND STALE, IRREVOCABLE CONTRACTS

It is possible to write smart contract templates without specifying time limits for the execution of the code pertaining to instances of smart contracts created from those templates. Such contracts may live on and either pose risks for economic loss or lead to enforcement issues requiring adjudication. Old, still-running software from previous eras, possibly no longer maintained because the original software developers or vendors have retired or gone out of business, may in the coming decades pose challenges to businesses reliant upon so-called legacy code. Smart contracts may become the legacy code of the future, with all the business, technological and legal challenges that come with aging technology with no means of replacement. Well-reasoned legal frameworks for handling such situations fall outside of the highly regulated parts of the financial sector. The precedents set there may prove useful but perhaps not completely prescriptive for what forms of regulation may be required for aging blockchain solutions.

18 'Soaring Bitcoin Prices Put Central Washington Electrical Utilities on Alert' (*The Seattle Times*, 9 January 2021) <https://www.seattletimes.com/business/technology/sunday-buzz-soaring-bitcoin-prices-put-central-washington-electrical-utilities-on-alert/> accessed 22 March 2021.

BREAKDOWN OF EXPENSIVE COMPUTING MODEL WITH QUANTUM COMPUTING

We have mentioned briefly the possible vulnerability of cryptographic software suites used to build blockchain technology. Advances and upgrades in cryptographic technology based on new computing capabilities like quantum computing may bring enhanced features to future blockchain implementations, including real-time, high-performance execution beyond the minute or multiple minutes required for current solutions, enhancing adoption and enabling applications yet to be conceived.

CRIMINALISATION AND REGULATION

The near-term future will likely bring regulation or criminalisation of certain blockchain applications in many jurisdictions, particularly involving cryptocurrencies and tokenised assets. Other applications may be deployed and see widespread adoption with little regulation until a major incident involving a data breach or a catastrophic event involving major loss of value or life spurs policymakers into reacting. Digital lawyers who have advised clients and technologists as the technology matures will be well-positioned accordingly to act for their clients or to influence policy.

ADDITIONAL RESOURCES

"Beeple's Masterwork: The First Purely Digital Artwork Offered at Christie's". Christie's <https://www.christies.com/features/Monumental-collage-by-Beeple-is-first-purely-digital-artwork-NFT-to-come-to-auction-11510-7.aspx>

"China's Courts Use Data Analytics and Blockchain Evidence Storage on the Way to First AI-Integrated Legal System" (*South China Morning Post*) <https://www.scmp.com/news/china/politics/article/3124815/chinas-courts-use-data-analytics-and-blockchain-evidence>

Corkery M and Popper N, "From Farm to Blockchain: Walmart Tracks Its Lettuce" (*New York Times*, 24 September 2018) <https://www.nytimes.com/2018/09/24/business/walmart-blockchain-lettuce.html>

"Distributed Ledger Technology: Blackett Review" (GOV.UK) <https://www.gov.uk/government/publications/distributed-ledger-technology-blackett-review>

Kolb J and others, "Core Concepts, Challenges, and Future Directions in Blockchain: A Centralized Tutorial" (2020) 53 *ACM Computing Surveys* <https://doi.org/10.1145/3366370>

Lipton A and Levi S, "An Introduction to Smart Contracts and Their Potential and Inherent Limitations" (*The Harvard Law School Forum on Corporate Governance*, 26 May 2018) <https://corpgov.law.harvard.edu/2018/05/26/an-introduction-to-smart-contracts-and-their-potential-and-inherent-limitations/>

Nakamoto S, "Bitcoin: A Peer-to-Peer Electronic Cash System" (31 October 2008) <https://bitcoin.org/en/bitcoin-paper>

Ramamurthy B, "Blockchain in Action" (*Manning*, 2020) <https://www.manning.com/books/blockchain-in-action>

Reyburn S, "The $69 Million Beeple NFT Was Bought with Cryptocurrency" (*New York Times*, 12 March 2021) <https://www.nytimes.com/2021/03/12/arts/beeple-nft-buyer-ether.html>

"What Is an NFT and Why Should Photographers Care?" <https://petapixel.com/2021/03/12/what-is-an-nft-and-why-should-photographers-care/>

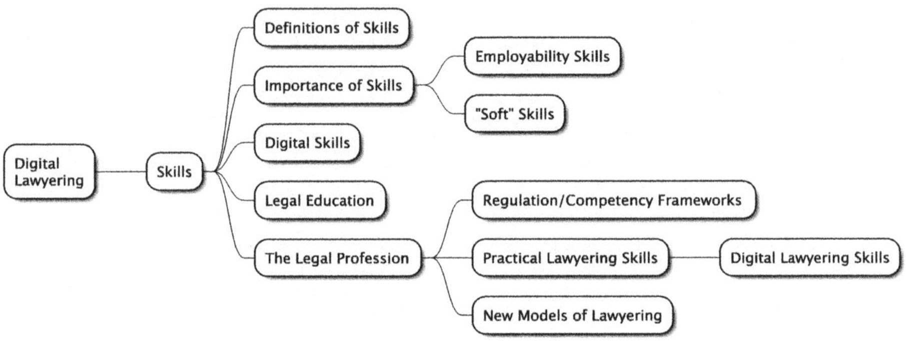

Mind Map 11.1 Chapter topics

11

DIGITAL LAWYERING SKILLS

Emma Jones

INTRODUCTION

This chapter will begin by exploring the importance of skills and the idea of "digital skills". It will discuss the extent to which these skills are acknowledged and developed in legal education. The chapter will then move on to consider the key skills currently valued within the legal profession and contrast these with the skills required to become a successful digital lawyer. It will conclude by considering a number of models of lawyering which encompass a broad range of skills.

Chapter hot spots

When reading this chapter, questions to think about include:

- Do the skills legal professionals are currently required to demonstrate equip them for digital lawyering?
- What skills are necessary to be a successful digital lawyer?
- Can and should legal education include digital lawyering skills?
- How can you develop your own digital lawyering skills?

Having read the title and introduction, you can add any other questions you want to explore here:

DOI: 10.4324/9780429298219-11

THE IMPORTANCE OF SKILLS

The term "skills" is frequently used, but it can be difficult to define. It is often used interchangeably with terms such as "attributes", "abilities" or "competencies". One way to define it is as an ability to perform or execute a job or task well. This could range from knitting a scarf to coding a computer programme to memorising a very long piece of poetry. In this chapter we will be using the term broadly to capture all of the above terms as appropriate.

In today's society, skills are increasingly viewed as important and valuable. It is often not enough to simply know something; it is about being able to apply that knowledge in practical settings. In universities, the focus has traditionally been on cognitive (or thinking) skills. For example, when you are asked to write an essay, it is not enough simply to know lots of facts about a topic; you also need to be able to understand what the question is asking, select the most relevant points to include, synthesise information from different sources and analyse and evaluate arguments made in articles and books.

However, in recent years, there has also been an increasing focus on employability skills within universities—in other words, developing the skills that are required within the workplace. A number of employers have criticised universities for not producing graduates who are prepared for the world of work, with a recent survey of UK human resources managers suggesting one in five graduates is not "workplace-ready".[1] Similar concerns have also been raised in other countries, including the United States, Australia and Hong Kong.

Government policies often emphasise the importance of universities producing skilled graduates who can contribute to the economy and assist in future economic growth. For example, the website of the UK Government's Office for Students states, "We want all students to gain the skills they need to succeed in future employment or further study".[2] This emphasis on employability skills can be controversial, as many people would argue that learning is a good in itself and should not be about the eventual economic outcomes. They also argue that

1 Anna Britten, 'Graduate Employability: One in Five UK Graduates Not Workplace-Ready' *University Business* <https://universitybusiness.co.uk/news/graduate-employability/> accessed 26 November 2020.

2 Office for Students, 'Supply of Higher Skills Levels' <https://www.officeforstudents.org.uk/advice-and-guidance/skills-and-employment/supply-of-higher-level-skills/> accessed 26 November 2020.

developing strong cognitive skills is important training for any form of employment.[3]

Despite this controversy, in reality there is now a significant focus on employability and more practical skills within universities. For law students, one example of this is the common use of problem questions, where you are given a scenario and asked to apply legal principles to that particular set of facts. By doing so, you are applying your legal knowledge in a way which demonstrates a number of skills, such as identifying key facts, analysing how the law will apply to these and writing in an accessible and concise manner. Often the idea is that these problem questions mirror the situation where a legal professional has a new client and has to try and unpack their issues and give appropriate advice. Other examples include the increase in clinical legal education provision, where students gain opportunities to provide legal advice in law clinics, produce resources and/or presentations to schools and community groups and undertake other "real-life" legal work.

In addition to the focus on skills within university education, there is also a growing emphasis on lifelong learning and the idea of people developing new skills or transferable skills to assist them to adapting to changes in the labour market or to aid them in moving into new areas of employment when they need to (e.g. due to a downturn in the economy). A 2017 report from the UK Government's Office for Science explains: "Those entering the labour market now can expect to work longer and may need to change careers more frequently. Economic security will not come from having a job for life but from having the ability to maintain and renew the right skills through lifelong learning".[4] It also explains that technology is one of the factors driving these changes, with the automation of tasks and the use of artificial intelligence removing some job roles and creating demand for others.

3 See, for example, Anthony Bradney, *Conversations, Choices and Chances the Liberal Law School in the Twenty-First Century* (Oxford and Portland, Oregon, Hart Publishing, 2003).

4 Government Office for Science, 'Future of Skills and Lifelong Learning' 5, <https://assets.publishing.service.gov.uk/government/uploads/system/uploads/attachment_data/file/727776/Foresight-future-of-skills-lifelong-learning_V8.pdf> accessed 26 November 2020.

Sync 1: Key employability skills

You should allow around 15 minutes for this activity.

Using your university's website (or, if you are not a current university student, the web page of your local university), find out what information it includes on employability skills. They may well have a list of graduate attributes or details of the employability skills your degree will assist in developing. Based on these, think about the following:

1 What does the website suggest are the key employability skills a degree will assist in developing?

2 How many (if any) involve digital technology?

You may have identified a number of different employability skills. A 2016 UK report surveying 187 pieces of research conducted between 2011 and 2016 identified a wide range of skills, from emotional intelligence and resilience to professional knowledge, research skills and time management.[5] Different subject areas may also refer to specific skills (and we will consider these in relation to legal education further on in this chapter). What is clear is that the range of skills which graduates are required to display is becoming far more diverse than traditional cognitive skills and often now refers to skills more commonly associated with the workplace, such as oral communication, teamwork and collaboration. In addition, there is an increasing awareness of the need for graduates to be digitally literate and have the skills to thrive in a digital workplace. Figure 11.1 presents a word cloud illustrating a number of the skills often identified as key attributes for graduates.

5 Jane Artess, Tristram Hooley and Robin Mellors-Bourne, 'Employability: A Review of the Literature 2012 to 2016 A Report for the Higher Education Academy' 17 <https://www.advance-he.ac.uk/knowledge-hub/employability-review-literature-2012-2016> accessed 26 November 2020.

Figure 11.1 Key skills and attributes for graduates

THE RISE OF DIGITAL SKILLS

In Chapter 4 you were introduced to the term "digital literacy". Describing this term in 1997, Paul Gilster argued that it was "the ability to both understand and use digitised information".[6] A range of other terms such as "information literacy" and "computer literacy" also developed in the same period. The focus was largely upon the use and management of digital information in an appropriate manner.

Around the same time, it also became common to find the idea that the younger generation (born after 1980) were "digital natives"—in other words, people who had grown up with digital technology and whose work and personal lives were all heavily influenced by technology, from socialising online to using the Internet for research to the way they access news stories and music. As one book put it: "They all have access to networked digital technologies. And they all have the skills to use those technologies".[7] This was often contrasted with older generations who were perceived as struggling to adjust to digital technologies. This could lead to the assumption that younger lawyers

6 Paul Gilster, *Digital Literacy* (New York, Wiley, 1997), 2.

7 John Gorham Palfrey and Urs Gasser Born Digital, *Understanding the First Generation of Digital Natives* (New York, Basic Books, 2008), ii.

would find it easier to adapt to technological advances, whereas older lawyers would struggle with the transition.

Since then it has also been recognised that it is too simplistic to divide people between so-called "digital natives" and those of older generations. A range of other factors also influence levels of digital literacy, including socio-economic status and geographic location. In 2020 the Lloyds Bank UK Consumer Digital Index (referred to in Chapter 4) estimated that 16% of the UK population (16 million people) cannot undertake basic digital activities such as switching on a digital device and connecting it to the Internet. Although they found age to be a significant factor, with only 7% of over 70s able to manage their money and shop online, they also found that benefit claimants, people with lower household incomes and people with disabilities were significantly less likely to be digitally literate.[8] In 2018 it was estimated that 16% of US adults (31.8 million people) had no digital literacy.[9] This report noted that these adults were "less educated, older, and disproportionately Black, Hispanic, and foreign born".[10] In 2020 in Australia it was estimated that over 2.5 million people have no Internet access, with significant differences between rural and city areas.[11]

Alongside the evolution of a more nuanced approach to the question of who is digitally literate, a more pluralistic way of looking at the skills involved has also developed. This means that the term "digital literacies" is now sometimes used to illustrate the wide range of different skills encompassed. It is also recognised that which skills are included within this definition may vary depending on the context the term is used in; for example, a law student may need a very different set of digital skills from someone employed by a business selling goods online. It may also be that some people struggle to transfer their digital

8 Lloyds Bank, 'Lloyds Bank UK Consumer Digital Index 2020' <https://www.lloydsbank.com/assets/media/pdfs/banking_with_us/whats-happening/lb-consumer-digital-index-2020-report.pdf> accessed 26 November 2020.

9 National Centre for Education Statistics, 'A Description of U.S. Adults Who Are Not Digitally Literate' <https://nces.ed.gov/pubs2018/2018161.pdf> accessed 26 November 2020.

10 Ibid., p. 6.

11 J. Thomas, J. Barraket, C. K. Wilson, I. Holcombe-James, J. Kennedy, E. Rennie, S. Ewing and T. MacDonald, 'Measuring Australia's Digital Divide: The Australian Digital Inclusion Index 2020, RMIT and Swinburne University of Technology, Melbourne, for Telstra' (2020), 6 <https://apo.org.au/sites/default/files/resource-files/2020-10/apo-nid308474.pdf> accessed 26 November 2020.

skills from one setting to another; for example, someone may use social media frequently but may have little or no experience with word processing programmes.

The notion of digital literacy now implies that digitally literate individuals will have the skills needed to use technology in an appropriate and effective manner in settings which are relevant to them. For digital lawyers, this means being able to use technology within their legal practice in a way which enhances their work and their service to clients whilst taking account of practical and ethical issues.

Equality, diversity and inclusion and digital literacy

The preceding discussion demonstrates that the level of digital literacy you have can be influenced by socio-economic status and geographic location. For example, if you have a low income or live in a rural area, you may not be able to afford or access an Internet connection at all. If you are able to obtain a connection, it may not be able to run at a high enough speed or quality to enable you to use online services or information effectively.

Other personal and practical factors may also be relevant; for example, if you experience social anxiety or are working from home in a very crowded household, you may not be able or willing to put on your webcam, or even to use the microphone, in meetings or workshops. There may also be cultural and legal issues; for example, some countries have strict censorship policies in relation to Internet usage.

Individuals with disabilities may be unable to access certain types of technology. Conversely, they may have different skills in using specialist software. For example, an individual may be unable to use a keyboard to type into word processing programmes, but may instead be skilled at using voice recognition software to input information.

When considering digital literacy, it is therefore important to think about how this relates to issues of equality, diversity and inclusion. Such issues can have negative impacts, as in some instances people may not be able to develop certain digital skills or may not be able to apply them in certain settings. However, they can also have positive impacts; for example, a client with physical disabilities may be able to receive legal advice online, making it more accessible.

MODELS OF DIGITAL LITERACY

A number of different models have developed to try and captures the core skills involved within being digitally literate. One of these, developed by Jisc for use in higher education, refers to seven different elements, including media literacy, information literacy, digital scholarship, learning skills, information and communications technology (ICT) literacy, career and identity management, and communication and collaboration.[12] Another, developed by Doug Belshaw, has eight "C" elements, including cultural, cognitive, constructive, communicative, confident, creative, critical and civic.[13] For the cultural element, Belshaw uses the example of "digital natives", suggesting that although they may be confident using their smartphones to socialise, they may not be comfortable using technology in other settings, such as the classroom and workplace. This is because they may not have developed the skills allowing them to move easily between the application of technology in different environments. It is therefore necessary to be able to adapt the use of technology to different cultural contexts. The cognitive element refers to the need to have a broad perspective, enabling individuals to adapt to different technologies and become fluent in navigating them (e.g. the types of menus commonly used on websites). For a digital lawyer, this could involve being able to navigate the menus and files involved in a case management system.

The constructive element relates to being able to use technology in different ways, building upon what has already been done and using it in innovative ways; for example, when applying algorithms to case law to more accurately predict the likely outcome in future cases. The communicative element refers to the need to be able to communicate in a way that demonstrates an acknowledgement and use of appropriate assumptions and norms; for example, including an appropriate digital signature when using email. The confident element refers to people being able to manage their own learning and solve problems in the digital environment; for example, by lawyers adapting to new technology and seeking out training to assist them in using it effectively. The creative element involves doing new things in new ways to

12 Jisc, 'Developing Digital Literacies' <https://www.jisc.ac.uk/full-guide/developing-digital-literacies> accessed 26 November 2020.

13 Doug Belshaw, 'The Essential Elements of Digital Literacies [pdf]' (Self-published, 2014), 11–12

uncover and identify new problems requiring solutions; for example, creating e-discovery systems which can also deal with means of electronic communication. The critical element involves looking beyond the technologies to question their basis and assumptions; for example, a lawyer questioning how accessible new technologies are for their client base. The civic element refers to the need to use technology to support the development of society more generally. One example of this is the use of online law clinics to provide free legal advice to people in need, particularly those who may find it difficult to physically travel to access help.

Sync 2: Elements of digital literacy

You should allow around 10 minutes for this activity.

Using an Internet search engine, locate two different models of digital literacy or literacies. This could be models that are used within higher education, the workplace or more generally.

1 What do you think are the strengths and weaknesses of these models?

2 Based on these models and your reading so far, what would you say are the essential elements of digital literacy?

You may have found a variety of models. Some may be more focused on technical know-how and abilities (e.g. being able to code), whereas others may be broader and focus on wider elements, such as Belshaw's reference to culture. In the next part of this chapter, we will move on to consider the skills currently required from legal professionals and to what extent these include elements of digital literacy.

SKILLS AND LEGAL EDUCATION

As many digital lawyers begin their careers as law students studying within law schools, it is useful to look at which skills are currently emphasised within legal education and to what extent digital lawyering skills are included within these.

In the UK and Australia, law schools are largely able to identify and emphasise whichever legal skills they believe to be most appropriate, taking into account the general skills students are expected to develop through studying a degree. In Australia, a 2017 report by the New South Wales Law Society identified the importance of technology in the future development of the legal profession. In relation to legal education, it suggested that more consideration needed to be given to whether aspects of technology should be included when teaching core legal subjects and to what extent lawyers need to be trained in technology.[14]

In the UK, the Quality Assurance Agency has produced the "Benchmark Statement for Law", which tries to capture some of the key skills a graduate in law should have. These include the "ability to apply knowledge and understanding to offer evidenced conclusions, addressing complex actual or hypothetical problems" and "self-management" and communication skills.[15] Nowhere in the statement is digital lawyering expressly mentioned, but it does refer to the need for universities to provide adequate resources, including "information and communications technology", to consider exposing students to online environments and to ensure that "learning, teaching and assessment strategies" reflect "advances in . . . information technology".[16]

In the United States, the American Bar Association (ABA) requires the law schools it accredits to establish a programme whose learning outcomes require students to be competent in "legal analysis and reasoning, legal research, problem-solving, and written and oral communication in the legal context" and "other professional skills needed for competent and ethical participation as a member of the legal profession".[17] Once again, there is no express mention of technology, although it could fall under "other professional skills".

At present, therefore, digital lawyering skills are not required within law school curriculums, although many law schools do include reference to these and even offer optional modules or courses on lawtech and digital lawyering. In terms of incorporating digital skills in existing modules, some examples can be found by looking at the recent

14 The Law Society of New South Wales, 'The Future of Law and Innovation in the Profession' 78 <https://www.lawsociety.com.au/sites/default/files/2018-03/1272952.pdf> accessed 30 November 2020.

15 Quality Assurance Agency, 'Subject Benchmark Statement Law November' <https://www.qaa.ac.uk/docs/qaa/subject-benchmark-statements/subject-benchmark-statement-law.pdf?sfvrsn=b939c881_16> accessed 30 November 2020.

16 Ibid., pp. 6, 7.

17 American Bar Association, '2020–2021 Standards and Rules of Procedure for Approval of Law Schools' <https://www.americanbar.org/groups/legal_education/resources/standards/> accessed 26 November 2020.

winners of the Thomson Reuters Teaching Law with Technology Prize in the UK. In 2020, one of the finalists used an online module using the technology to help students provide public legal education and legal advice to members of the community. Another finalist used Padlet in large trust lectures to enable students to ask anonymous questions and have them answered quickly. The winner was the creator of an escape room, where students had to enter a room and use a range of technology, including virtual reality headsets, to solve a range of puzzles and challenges relating to data protection law.[18]

In terms of modules and courses, several UK universities run master's (postgraduate) programmes in law and technology, for example, the University of Law offers an MSc in law and technology. In the United States, an example is the University of California, Berkeley, which offers a range of courses via its Center for Law and Technology. In Australia, an example is the University of Melbourne, which offers a range of courses on digital law and technological innovation. However, some of these offerings are more focused on technology law (e.g. regulating cyberspace) than on digital lawyering. Such provisions are also not offered to all law students and in all law schools.

It has been argued that a much greater focus on technology within legal education is now needed. The US legal academic Dyane O'Leary captures the argument well:

> Today's farmers use moisture sensors for soil, drones to monitor crops, self-driving GPS wielding tractors to seed, and even wearable trackers on cows to check their vitals (yes, really!)—all to make farming more profitable and efficient. But what if I told you apprentice farmers were not introduced to these things? That they were too busy being shown how to tend to oxen pulling plows. Too busy being trained to navigate crops with their handheld hoe. Too busy being taught the art of kneeling to the soil to gauge moisture. That's crazy, right? How can a student prepare for their future if instruction is based on their teacher's past? But that is the approach many law schools take in the required curriculum.[19]

18 Kirsten Maslen, 'Teaching Law with Technology Prize 2020—Finalists Announced' (*Thomson Reuters*, 6 March 2020) <https://blogs.thomsonreuters.com/legal-uk/2020/03/06/teaching-law-with-technology-prize-2020-finalists-announced/> accessed 16 March 2021.

19 Dyane L. O'Leary, '"Smart Lawyering": Integrating Technology Competence into the Legal Practice Curriculum' (2020) <https://ssrn.com/abstract=3671632> accessed 21 February 2021.

O'Leary argues that, instead of being viewed as optional, technical competence should be integrated fully into the curriculum of law schools as a core professional skill and ethical requirement. This could help students prepare to enter the legal profession and also give them digital skills they can use in other careers, such as project management or marketing, and in other areas of their lives. However, it does require law schools to invest time and money to develop the curriculum in this way. It may also require hiring additional staff (or retraining current staff) with the appropriate knowledge and skills in this area.

Of course, legal education is not all focused upon training aspiring lawyers, and not all law students will go on to be lawyers. However, if (as seems likely) law schools do gradually increase their focus on digital lawyering and technical competence, then this in turn may have an impact on the legal profession. Legal employers may begin to look for a higher level of digital skills and prioritise them more when recruiting trainees. This in turn could accelerate the impact of digital technologies on the legal profession more widely. However, before considering which digital skills may become increasingly prized, the next question to consider is what skills the legal profession currently requires from its members.

SKILLS AND THE LEGAL PROFESSION

Working in the legal profession requires a range of different skills, from those involved in client care to those involved in administration and management. To identify which skills are currently viewed as important within the legal profession, a good starting point is the requirements of the bodies who regulate different parts of the legal profession. They will often specify key skills or competencies which individuals are required to possess before they can obtain entry to the legal profession.

Sync 3: Skills in the legal profession

You should allow around 30 minutes for this activity.

Using the Internet, research what legal skills legal professionals are currently required to display for entrance into the legal profession.

If your legal profession is divided into a number of roles, you may wish to focus on one (e.g. attorney, solicitor, barrister, or advocate), or you can compare and contrast different roles to see whether similar skills are required. You should base your research on whichever jurisdiction you are currently located within.

Make a note of your answer so that you can revisit it later in this chapter.

If you are located in England and Wales, a useful starting point is the 2013 Legal Education and Training Review.[20] This looked at what is required for a legal professional to be competent—in other words, to be able to perform their role appropriately. As part of its work, the review conducted research into the knowledge, skills and attributes required within the legal profession at that time and what respondents thought would be required in 2020.

Based on the Legal Education and Training Review, the Solicitors Regulation Authority (SRA) and the Bar Standards Board (BSB) introduced competency statements. These set out the skills and abilities a solicitor or barrister must be able to demonstrate to work in their role.

The SRA's Statement of Solicitor Competence covers "ethics, professionalism, and judgment", "technical legal practice" (in terms of skills such as researching and drafting rather than technology), "working with other people" and "managing themselves and their own work". Under "managing themselves and their own work", there is a requirement that solicitors make appropriate use of information management systems, both in hard copy and electronically, which includes storing and retrieving information. They must also comply with requirements relating to data protection, confidentiality, security and file management (e.g. guidelines on how long to keep a file when a matter is concluded). The reference to electronic information management systems is the only clear reference to the use of technology in the work of solicitors. However, it is arguable that some of the competencies listed could require solicitors to use technology. For example, solicitors must maintain an appropriate and current understanding of practice, policy and the law and communicate in a style and method that best fits the circumstances and the person receiving

20 Legal Education and Training Review, 'Setting Standards. The Future of Legal Services Education and Training Regulation in England and Wales' (2013) <https://letr.org.uk/index.html> accessed 27 November 2020.

the communication. They must also record and present findings and information in a clear and accurate way.[21]

The BSB's Professional Statement for Barristers covers "legal knowledge, skills and attributes", "practical knowledge, skills and attributes", "advocacy", "professional standards", "values characteristics and behaviours" and identifies aspects of "working with others" and "management of practice". When referring to skills relating to research, it requires barristers to use appropriate and up-to-date methods and resources (including electronic resources). As with the SRA statement, there are some skills that could imply an engagement with technology; for example, a requirement to use the form of communication most suited to its content and the recipients. However, overall, there is a little explicit reference to technology.[22]

In contrast to the above, CILEx Regulation, the regulatory body of the Charted Institute of Legal Executives (CILEx, a body of legal professionals who perform functions similar to solicitors) are introducing "technical competence" as a required competency for individuals to demonstrate before being awarded membership of CILEx.[23]

In the United States, the ABA does not provide a single statement setting out the skills required from lawyers. However, in 2009 the ABA set up a Commission on Ethics 20/20 to consider the ABA's Model Rules of Professional Conduct (the rules governing the behaviour of lawyers in the United States) and the way lawyers are regulated in light of developments in technology and global changes to the way law is practised. The Commission noted that technology had changed legal practice in ways which were both fundamental and irrevocable and that, as a result, lawyers must understand its role to ensure that they can provide the client care and service that is required.[24] The notes to

21 Solicitors Regulation Authority, 'Statement of Solicitor Competence' <https://www.sra.org.uk/solicitors/resources/cpd/competence-statement/> accessed 30 November 2020.

22 Bar Standards Board, 'Professional Statement for Barristers' <https://www.barstandardsboard.org.uk/uploads/assets/0279b209-dab6-40c9-a554af54994e2566/bsbprofessionalstatementandcompetences2016.pdf> accessed 30 November 2020.

23 Vicky Purtill, 'Lawtech: Standards for the Lawyers of the Future' <https://www.regulationmatters.uk/features/legal-tech-for-the-lawyers-of-the-future/> accessed 22 February 2021.

24 ABA Commission on Ethics 20/20, 'Introduction and Overview' https://www.americanbar.org/groups/professional_responsibility/committees_commissions/aba-commission-on-ethics-20-20/ accessed 27 August 2021.

Rule 1.1 of the Model Rules of Professional Conduct, which set out the standards required from legal professionals, state that a lawyer must stay informed of legal changes and changes within legal practice, including the risks and benefits connected to relevant technologies.[25] This was also referred to in Chapter 5.

In Australia, one acknowledgement of the importance of technology was the 2017 report on the Future of Law and Innovation in the Profession by the Law Society of New South Wales.[26] This was the result of a commission of an enquiry set up by the Law Society to investigate changes within the profession.

There are also other examples from different countries which indicate that there is a gradual acknowledgement of the increasing importance of digital technology within the legal profession. For example, in 2013 a section of the Canadian Bar Association called the CBA Legal Futures Initiative produced a report discussing the future of the Canadian legal profession and emphasising the importance of technology in transforming both the profession and wider society. It identifies a wide range of possible disruptions as a result, from the potential need to change or update regulation of the profession to monitor online transactions appropriately to the way in which law firms brand and promote themselves. The report suggests that individual lawyers will need to adapt their existing skills; for example, applying negotiation and advocacy skills to online dispute resolution. It also suggests they will need to develop new non-legal skills (such as managing projects and risk and keeping up to date with innovations in technology).[27]

The preceding discussion demonstrates that many countries see digital skills as increasingly important within the legal profession. However, to date, the ways these skills are acknowledged and

25 ABA Comment to the Model Rules of Professional Conduct <https://www.americanbar.org/groups/professional_responsibility/publications/model_rules_of_professional_conduct/rule_1_1_competence/comment_on_rule_1_1.html.> accessed 7 December 2020.

26 The report is only available to members of the Law Society of New South Wales at <https://www.lawsociety.com.au/about-us/law-society-initiatives/flip/flip-documents-resources>. However, it is discussed in detail in Michael Legg, 'The Future of Australian Legal Education' (*Thomson Reuters*, 2018) [2018] UNSWLRS 51 <http://www5.austlii.edu.au/au/journals/UNSWLRS/2018/51.pdf> accessed 22 February 2021.

27 Canadian Bar Association, 'The Future of Legal Services in Canada: Trends and Issues' <https://www.cba.org/CBAMediaLibrary/cba_na/PDFs/CBA%20Legal%20Futures%20PDFS/trends-isssues-eng.pdf> accessed 16 March 2021.

incorporated into legal education and legal practice are somewhat piecemeal and fragmented. There is no single comprehensive digital skills framework against which legal professionals (and their regulators) can judge their competency in this area. It is therefore perhaps unsurprising that a recent UK report on the digital lawyering landscape identified concerns over a skills shortage, stating "it could be difficult to find lawyers with the sufficient skills and experience to fully understand the technology".[28] The next sync asks you to consider whether having a digital skills framework for use across the legal profession could help to address some of these challenges.

Sync 4: A digital skills framework

You should allow around 10 minutes for this activity.

What would be the advantages and disadvantages of having a common digital skills framework for the legal profession?

You may find it useful to make a note of the key arguments you identify.

You may have identified a range of arguments. Some advantages could include a framework raising the legal profession's awareness of the importance of technology and digital skills and assisting aspiring lawyers to identify the digital skills required in legal practice. A framework could also be used to assess the suitability of individual's existing skills and identify gaps where further training and development are required. Disadvantages could include the fast-moving nature of technology, meaning that skills identified now could be obsolete in a few years (or even months). It may also be that different parts of the legal profession require very different digital skills; for example, whereas a lawyer in private practice may need to be competent in using time recording and client management systems, an in-house lawyer may instead require expertise in using their company's online business systems.

28 Alan Cunningham, Andrew D. James, Paul Taylor and Bruce Tether, 'Disruptive Technologies & Legal Service Provision in the UK: A Preliminary Study' (7 December 2018) <https://ssrn.com/abstract=3297074> accessed 16 March 2021.

WHAT DIGITAL SKILLS DO LAWYERS NEED?

The next question to consider is what digital skills lawyers actually need to have now, and what digital skills they will need to have in the future. As noted earlier, there is no single digital skills framework for the legal profession, perhaps reflecting the fact that different roles within practice will have different digital requirements (see Chapter 12 for more discussion). However, there is a wide range of suggestions over what should be considered as key digital skills within the legal profession generally. This section will consider some of these, but it is necessary first to consider an underlying debate in this area; namely, whether lawyers should learn to code.

Should lawyers learn to code?

A question that has often arisen, particularly in the legal press, is whether lawyers should actually learn to code—in other words, to be able to use computer programming language to design software. Some people have argued that lawyers should learn to code to enable them to understand the technology they are using, to give them important employability skills and to set them apart from their competitors when working with clients involved in digital businesses. A recent article in the *Legal Technologist* suggested that a knowledge of coding could be applied to help lawyers work out simple solutions to some issues; for example, where they had a lot of information to record and organise online. It also indicated coding would be useful in dealing with many of the digital platforms now available for the legal profession, by assisting individuals to become familiar with digital structures and approaches, such as algorithms.[29] Therefore, it is perhaps unsurprising that a number of law firms now offer their staff training in coding.

At the same time, others have argued that lawyers learning to code is not a productive use of their time and expertise. Writers such as Richard Susskind suggest that it is more important for lawyers to understand the function and purposes of technology and how that interacts with the law rather than develop detailed technical skills themselves.[30] This is particularly

29 The Legal Technologist, 'Why Lawyers Should Learn to Code, But Not for the Reasons You Think' (25 November 2020) <https://www.legaltechnologist.co.uk/why-lawyers-should-learn-to-code-but-not-for-the-reasons-you-think/> accessed 22 March 2021.

30 Richard E. Susskind, *Tomorrow's Lawyers an Introduction to Your Future* (Oxford, Oxford University Press, 2017).

the case when coding can change and evolve rapidly, so such skills could quickly become outdated. For example, it is very unlikely that a lawyer who has undertaken an introductory coding course will be able to design software sophisticated enough to assist with client issues. Instead, a better business model is for them to work as a team with software developers to ensure solutions meet clients' technological and legal issues. A qualified software designer is likely to be able to undertake the coding work more quickly and cost-effectively and does not have the issue of having to justify chargeable hours spent on coding activities the way a lawyer would.

Of course, it is possible that there is a middle way, in which lawyers understand the basics of coding but use that to work with software developers and others to ensure they can work together productively and understand the terminology used and any issues raised. As we discuss the various digital skills which lawyers should or could develop, it is worth thinking about what your position is on this debate and whether or not you think legal professionals should learn to code.

Thinking about digital skills which lawyers require, a fundamental skill (or group of skills) is around the everyday use of technology in the legal workplace. One of my co-authors, in an article proposing a digital lawyering framework for students, describes this as "Collaborating & undertaking legal services using digital tools & software articulated by appropriate e-practice & project management".[31] Chapter 2 discussed the changing face of legal practice and the ways in which digital technology has now become an integrated part of the workplace; for example, word processing information, sending emails to colleagues and clients, recording chargeable time online and conducting legal research using online databases. This means that any legal professional will now require a basic level of technological competence to enable them to practice effectively. It is hard to imagine a lawyer who wholly relied on handwritten letters, the postal service and a local law library being able to work efficiently and obtain and retain a large number of clients! Of course, some individual lawyers may rely upon support staff, such as legal secretaries, to undertake much of the work involving digital technology. However, this is unlikely to be cost-effective in the long term, and some level of technical competence would still

31 Ann Thanaraj, 'Making the Case for a Digital Lawyering Framework in Legal Education' (2017) (3) *International Review of Law* 17, 32.

be required; for example, to forward relevant emails or cope when a member of staff was on annual leave.

Understanding how to use such technology goes beyond just knowing which button to press to send an email or working out how to log on to a video call, for example. Part of "appropriate e-practice"[32] also includes understanding the relevant etiquette involved. You looked at a humorous illustration of this type of issue in Sync 6 of Chapter 9, which referred to the recent case of the so-called cat lawyer. A Texan lawyer appearing at an online court hearing had a cat filter on his screen which he could not remove. The video of him saying "I'm here live, I'm not a cat" went viral globally.[33] Although this was seen as an entertaining mistake, failures to use technology appropriately could have more serious consequences. Sending kisses at the bottom of an email to an important client or appearing in a video call in your pyjamas or during a shopping trip to the supermarket is likely to seem unprofessional and could mean you lose the confidence of clients and colleagues.

This leads to another area where digital skills are required, which is to take part in digital marketing and networking, when lawyers and law firms are looking to obtain new clients and retain existing clients. Although a range of networking is carried out face-to-face, the pandemic has demonstrated the importance of digital marketing and networking. Having a Twitter, Facebook or other social media account can be an important way to connect with clients or potential clients and spread the word about your services (as discussed in Chapter 5). Running or joining in webinars, conferences and other online workshops and discussions can also be valuable. It is also important to be aware of the wider digital environment and the broader changes advances in technology are making to the legal sector; for example, it may be more attractive to clients and profitable if your workplace moves to an alternative business structure or adopts a virtual law firm model (examples given in Chapter 2).

The reference by Thanaraj to project management in this context also suggests a wider range of skills than just being able to master using specific forms of technology. As an individual, it is important to understand how to manage your time effectively when working with

32 Supra n. 28.

33 BBC News, 'Lawyer Gets Stuck with Cat Filter During Virtual Court Case' (9 February 2021) <https://www.bbc.co.uk/news/av/world-us-canada-56005428> accessed 22 March 2021.

technology. This can include everything from avoiding getting distracted by googling irrelevant points, to ensuring your email inbox is well organised so you can find important messages easily, to ensuring you back up information saved on your laptop.

So far, the digital skills discussed could be largely viewed as the basic digital skills that all lawyers will now need. However, for many legal professionals the skills needed will go beyond this. Thanaraj refers to the need to "acquire the knowledge and skills to use digital tools and software to deliver alternative forms of technology-driven legal service" as another key area.[34] For individuals, this could involve participation in online dispute resolution (see Chapter 9), developing new skills to deal with the requirements for evidence-gathering and e-discovery in the digital age (see Chapter 8) and adjusting to and/or applying the use of machine learning artificial intelligence (AI), such as predictive coding software, as part of legal practice (see Chapter 7). When working in a team and/or incorporating digital technology into a project, there is likely to be an even wider range of wider skills required (digital and otherwise). The International Institute of Project Management divides such work into four stages: define, plan, deliver and close.[35] Figure 11.2 gives some examples of the work involved in each stage (you may notice some similarities with the stages of design thinking illustrated in Chapter 4).

Sync 5: Project managing a lawtech project

You should allow around 10 minutes for this activity.

Imagine you are a lawyer working for a large firm. One of your clients is a large company that manufactures televisions. Your company wants to launch a new website selling its products online. It asks you to lead a team considering the potential legal implications. The team will consist of in-house lawyers, several of the company's directors, members of its IT department and representatives from a marketing agency, all of whom are based in different countries.

Consider each stage of the project management process. What issues might arise that you need to deal with? You may want to make some notes for your own reference.

34 Supra n. 28, p. 33.

35 International Institute of Legal Project Management, '4-Phase LPM Framework' <http://www.iilpm.com/wp-content/uploads/2020/05/IILPM-LPM-Framework-English-Version_2020.png> accessed 26 March 2021.

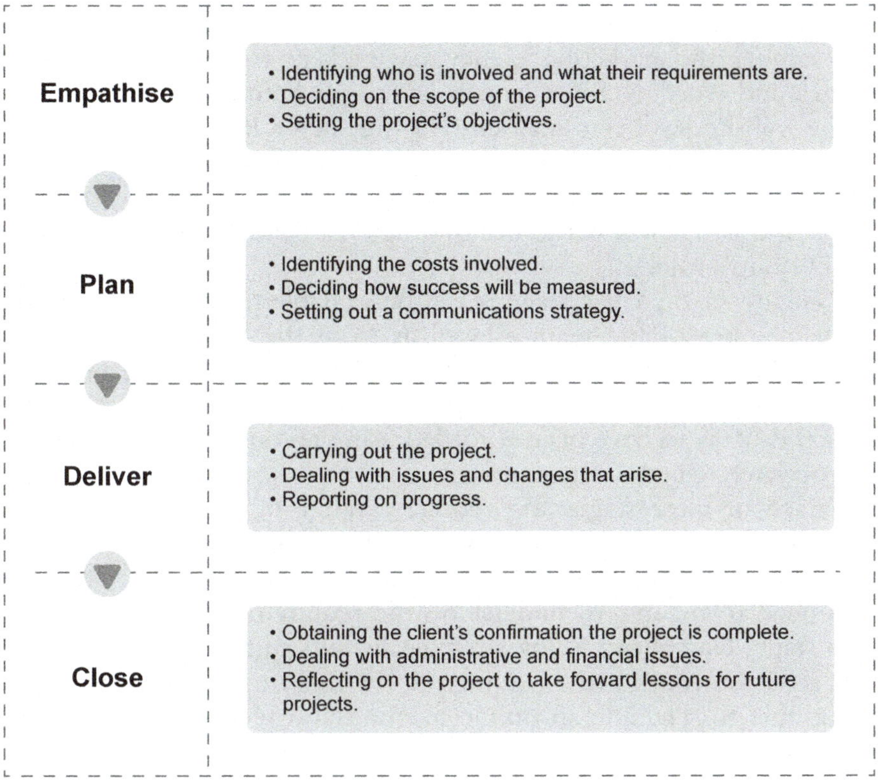

Figure 11.2 The stages of project management

You may have thought of a range of ideas. In relation to the define stage, it will be important to understand the technical side of the company's plans, such as whether or not the website will be a bespoke design; whether there will be an agreement with a host server; who is providing the content and images; and what system will be used, or developed, to collect payments. With so many people involved, it would be vital to know who has what role and what expectations each individual has about their involvement. It will also be important to know what the overall objectives are; for example, is it to have the website successfully launched, or simply to provide a written piece of advice on the legal implications?

Moving on to the plan stage, organising a communications strategy will be key. Even arranging a meeting can be complicated when the attendees are in different time zones, so it will be vital to agree the best ways to communicate as a team, as well as knowing who else in the company you will need to report to (and when).

In relation to delivery, a range of potential challenges could arise; for example, the marketing agency may be keen to decide upon specific images and wording for a launch campaign before the overall design of the website has been finalised. Having such a large team also means there is potential for misunderstandings and miscommunications, such as the IT team assuming the in-house lawyer is dealing with cyber-protection issues whilst the in-house lawyer believes this to be part of the IT team's role.

Finally, at the close stage it will be valuable to gain feedback from every member of the team as well as from the company as a client. There will be a need to ensure that all records are up to date and stored appropriately and that your time and that of any others in your firm (which is likely to have been recorded using an online system) has been appropriately billed to the company.

Each of these stages will require a range of skills, from planning and organisation to communication and collaboration to an ability to respond appropriately to feedback (and possibly criticism). There will be a need to be able to understand the requirements and demands of each stage, plan ahead, think strategically and anticipate any issues that may arise. Of course, this is alongside the more technical skills, such as being able to schedule an online meeting and record your chargeable time accurately.

Digital lawyering skills: innovation and entrepreneurship

Lawyers have often been perceived as risk-adverse and cautious. In contrast, innovators and entrepreneurs have been portrayed as forward-thinking pioneers, identifying new markets, introducing new business models and exploiting gaps and opportunities that arise.

However, in recent years a new brand of "legal entrepreneurs" has begun to emerge.[36] These are people who have recognised the opportunities arising from the developments in digital technology, the deregulation of the legal profession and the emergence of new models of legal practice such as alternative business structures (discussed in Chapter 2). Although these

36 Mark A. Cohen, 'The Golden Age of The Legal Entrepreneur—Why Now and Why It Matters' (*Forbes Magazine*) <https://www.forbes.com/sites/markcohen1/2018/06/01/the-golden-age-of-the-legal-entrepreneur-why-now-and-why-it-matters/?sh=5a4496447803> accessed 29 April 2021.

individuals often do not have a traditional legal background as lawyers, they are an increasing presence in the legal world.

For lawyers to be able to compete with such legal entrepreneurs and remain relevant in the legal market, they are increasingly having to develop their own skills of innovation and entrepreneurship; for example, partnering with other professionals to offer a more comprehensive range of services to clients, redesigning the management structures of law firms and rebranding their services.

As a student, there are a range of ways you can begin to develop your skills of innovation and entrepreneurship. This could include volunteering to lead on projects, putting forward proposals for new innovations (e.g. the creation of a new student society or a new journal or magazine), starting your own part-time business (such as selling on Etsy or eBay) or perhaps finding a mentor who can offer support and guidance. All of these have the potential to assist you in transitioning into the world of digital lawyering.

BROADENING THE SCOPE

The final principle Thanaraj identifies when discussing a digital lawyering framework is "the knowledge and skills to consider the safety, security, confidentiality, privacy, appropriateness and ethical issues before using digital tools for legal practice".[37] This demonstrates once again that purely technical skills in isolation are not sufficient for a digital lawyer. Instead, it is important to be able to consider the wider issues that arise when using such technology. Thanaraj explains that "this principle includes understanding the repercussions of unprofessional and unethical behaviour online, taking into consideration issues of safety, privacy, and digital footprint in online interactions. Specific to lawyering and professional skills, students will need to develop an understanding of the roles of technology, privacy, and security and how they affect the online practice of law".[38] A number of these issues have already been discussed within this textbook; for example, Chapter 5 looked at the ethical issues that can arise as a result of lawyers' use of social media, and Chapter 6 discussed the implications of breaches of data protection laws for law firms. Being able to identify such potential issues, avoid them where possible and respond appropriately where that is not possible requires a range of skills.

37 Supra n. 28, p. 33.
38 Supra n. 28, p. 33.

To demonstrate this, imagine you are a trainee lawyer in a small law firm specialising in employment disputes and you are asked to create a new monthly electronic newsletter updating existing and potential clients on changes and developments in employment law. Your first thoughts might be about what content to include (such as recent cases and legislation) and also which word processing and publishing programme(s) would be most suitable to use to produce the newsletter. These are both important issues, but they are not the only ones to consider. You will also need to think about points such as whether your existing clients have consented to their email addresses being used for the purposes of newsletter circulation, how you will obtain consent from prospective clients and how and where you will store the data being used for these purposes. You will also need to bear in mind ethical issues, such as how to ensure your readers understand that you are giving generic summaries of the law and not offering legal advice in your articles. If you want to write about a recent case your firm has been involved in, you will need to consider how you can do this without breaching client confidentiality in any way.

To tackle all of these potential issues, you are going to need to have a range of skills, including (but certainly not limited to):

- Organisational and administrative skills (e.g. setting up or directing the setting up of a mailing list).
- Legal research skills (e.g. to look into questions of data protection and client confidentiality and to identify relevant newsletter content).
- Commercial awareness (e.g. if your law firm intends to use the newsletter as a form of marketing, you need to be aware what type of content will be of interest to prospective clients to encourage them to use the firm's services).
- Legal writing skills (e.g. to draft a suitable disclaimer to go on the newsletter explaining that it does not contain legal advice).

Underpinning all of these will be a need for critical thinking to help you in identifying such issues in the first place.

Sync 6: Identifying relevant digital skills

You should allow around 30 minutes for this activity.

The preceding section has considered a wide range of digital skills. However, it is not intended to be comprehensive. What eight digital skills would you see as being most important for a digital lawyer and why?

To answer this question you can use the preceding section, your wider knowledge and reading and perhaps your own experience (e.g. if you have undertaken a clinical legal education module or legal work experience). To help you narrow down your ideas, you may wish to focus upon one role or practice area, perhaps one you are interested in being involved in during your career.

There is no single right answer to Sync 6. Instead, the skills you choose are likely to be influenced by any particular role or practice area you focused upon, together with your own experiences and research. However, hopefully your list reflected the fact that digital skills are not the same as technical skills. Instead, they include a much wider range of skills, such as project management, which are adapted to and applied within the digital environment. Another illustration of the width of this range of skills is the growth of interest in what are sometimes called "soft skills".

SOFT SKILLS

The earlier discussion about digital lawyering skills demonstrates that technical skills cannot be considered in isolation. To apply technical skills effectively in the legal workplace requires a range of other skills, including organisational and time management skills, critical thinking and communication skills. In addition, the growth of digital technology has also lead to an increased emphasis on so-called soft skills within the legal profession. These are non-technical skills which relate to how you regulate yourself and your relationship with others; for example, being able to understand and control your emotional responses to situations appropriately, demonstrating empathy with clients and using patience and tact to work well within a team. As you can see from these examples, they often involve what are termed social and emotional competencies or social and emotional intelligence.[39] The term "soft skills" is used here because it is a commonly used shorthand. However, it is a

39 Daniel Goleman, *Emotional Intelligence* (London, Bloomsbury, 1996); Peter Salovey and John D. Mayer, 'Emotional Intelligence' (1990) 9 (3) *Imagination, Cognition and Personality* 185.

contentious term because there is a strong argument that such skills are equally important to "hard skills" within legal practice, such as analysing problems and evaluating courses of action. Despite this, soft skills have traditionally often been ignored or undervalued because they often involve social and emotional competencies which sometimes appears to conflict with traditional legal values of objectivity and rationality.[40]

To think about the place of soft skills in legal practice, imagine that you are a junior lawyer who has received an email from a client complaining in quite an aggressive manner that you have not responded to their last email for over 48 hours. Your first thought might be to feel cross and feel the client is being unreasonable; alternatively, it might be to apologise straight away to avoid any further complaints. Rather than respond immediately, a good starting point is to pause and think about what lies behind the wording of the email. It could be that the client is anxious and worried about their case, or that they have little understanding of the usual etiquette for email writing, or that they have low levels of literacy generally. Using empathy to put yourself in the client's shoes will help you to understand the background behind this email. In turn, this understanding will enable you to respond in a sensitive way which can potentially enhance your relationship with the client; for example, rather than dashing off an email response you may choose to telephone the client to reassure them that the work they require is in progress and explain the usual timescales involved.

It is also worth reflecting upon your own response. If you are angry, is it because you react defensively to criticism or that you find it hard to build a rapport with that particular client? If you immediately want to apologise, is it because you are scared of making a mistake or just want the situation to go away? None of these responses is wrong, but understanding what lies behind them will enable you to regulate your responses and learn from them for the next time a similar situation arises.

The growth of interest in and importance of soft skills is inextricably linked to the rise of digital technology. There have been fears that the automation of a range of legal processes and the offering of cheaper online platforms for legal services will result in the traditional lawyer role becoming redundant, or at least much reduced. As a result, law firms have sought to demonstrate that they can offer personalised

40 Emma Jones, 'Making Practice More Affective: Emotional Intelligence as a Legal Meta-competency' (2018) 24 (1) *European Journal of Current Legal Issues.*

and responsive individual services in a way technology cannot—in other words, providing a human touch within legal practice. This demands a high level of skills including "a delicate blend of empathy and detachment, approachability and boundary setting".[41] Unfortunately, there are arguments that current legal education and training has tended to ignore these types of skills or dismiss them as irrelevant to law. This means that lawyers may not always be well-equipped to demonstrate these skills in their practice. Even the different competency frameworks and statements which govern different parts of the legal profession tend to largely imply such skills (e.g. by discussing client care), rather than explicitly identifying the different skills involved and their importance. However, there is some evidence that this approach is gradually changing; for example, in England and Wales the Chartered Institute of Legal Executives is introducing the idea of emotional competence within their educational standards. There is also a range of models of lawyering that have been developed to try and capture the much broader range of skills now required from legal professionals, including digital lawyering skills and soft skills (which arguably form a part of digital skills in any event).

Do lawyers come in all shapes and sizes?

The growth in importance of soft skills has contributed to a number of different models of lawyering designed to demonstrate that it is not enough for a lawyer to simply have a narrow skill set; for example, focusing on either technical skills or problem-solving abilities. Instead, they emphasise that a lawyer must have a wide range of skills and abilities. This is in contrast to the traditional "I-shaped" model, where lawyers have a narrow focus on legal expertise. Several of these more recent models are briefly described here and shown in Figures 11.3–11.5:

- *The T-shaped lawyer*

In this model, the vertical bar of the "T" represents traditional, in-depth legal knowledge, and the horizontal bar represents other knowledge, expertise and skills; for example, in technology, project management, leadership and teamwork. The idea of a T-shaped professional has been used widely outside of law. It is increasingly being used within law to acknowledge the fact that many lawyers now have to work together with a range of non-lawyers on

41 Emma Jones, 'Digital Lawyering and the Growing Importance of the Human Touch: Implications for Wellbeing' (October 2019) 7 *The Legal Technologist* 25.

projects, and as a result they need a much broader range of skills and abilities to enable them to adapt and work appropriately.[42]

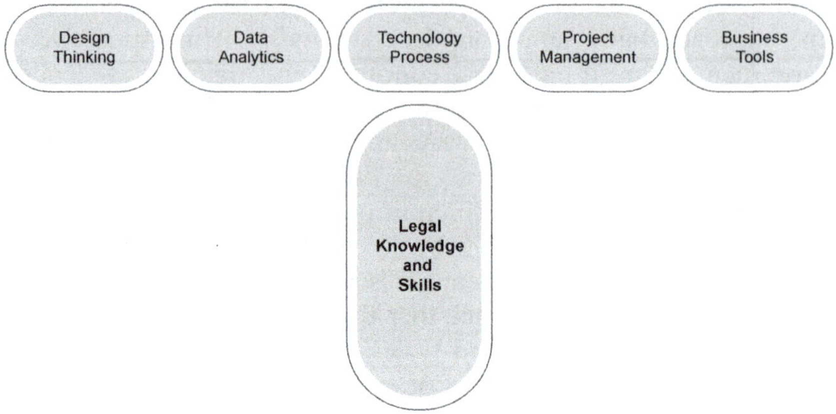

Figure 11.3 The T-shaped lawyer

- *The delta model*

The delta model is based on the T-shaped lawyer model and is still evolving, based on the work of a group of legal academics in the United States.[43] It conceptualises legal practice in the form of a triangle, with each side representing a different area of competency required from lawyers. Like the T-shaped lawyer, there is a need for the more traditional in-depth legal knowledge and skills ("the law"). However, the other areas are "business and operations" and "personal effectiveness". Business and operations covers technical and commercial skills whilst personal effectiveness is about having the self-awareness and skills to work well with others.

- *The O-shaped lawyer*

In this model, which was designed in the UK by an in-house lawyer, the focus is on lawyers being rounded and demonstrating a range of skills, behaviours and mindsets.[44] These are divided into five components: optimism, ownership, open-minded, opportunistic and original. The focus of these components

42 Elaine Mak, *The T-shaped Lawyer and Beyond: Rethinking legal professionalism and legal education for contemporary societies* (The Hague, Eleven International Publishing, 2017).

43 Design your Delta, 'Developing the Delta Model' <https://www.designyourdelta.com/about> accessed 27 August 2021.

44 The O Shaped Lawyer, 'The O Shaped Lawyer Programme' <https://www.oshapedlawyer.com/about> accessed 27 August 2021.

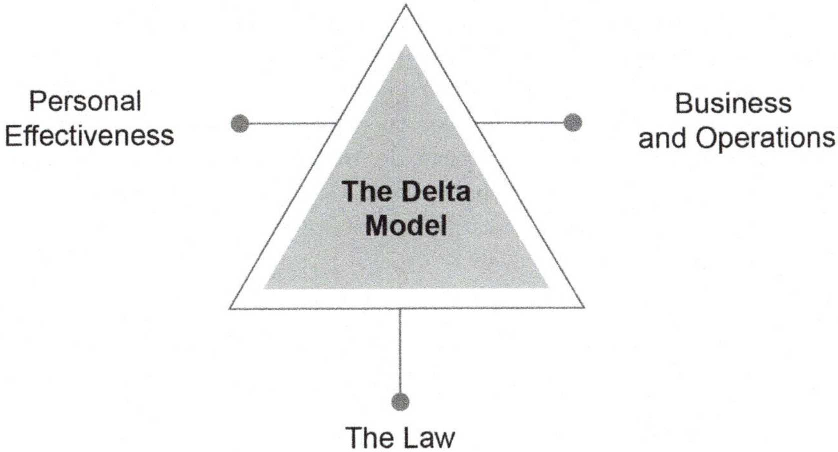

Figure 11.4 The delta model

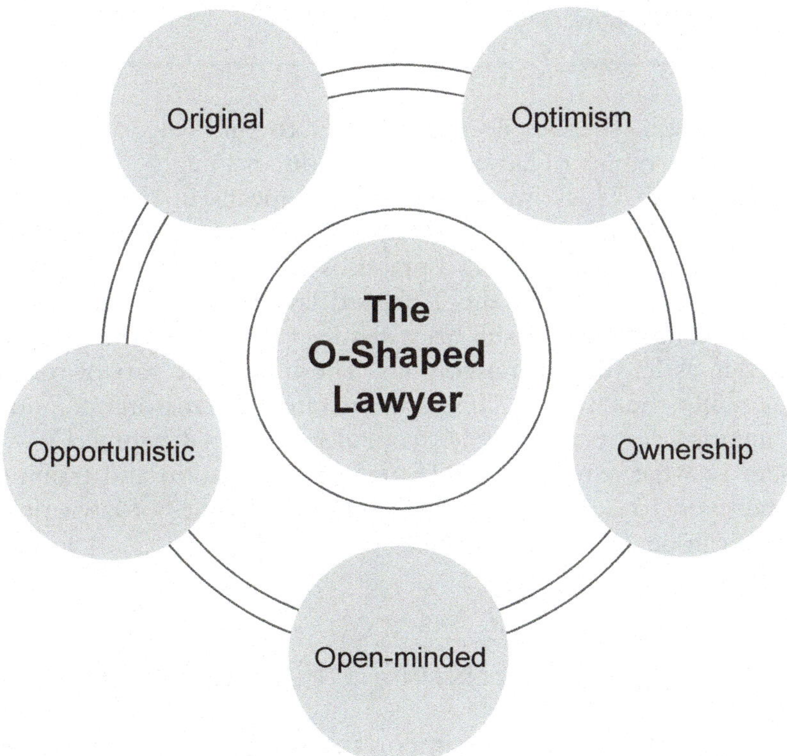

Figure 11.5 The O-shaped lawyer

is on encouraging lawyers to be more positive, proactive and creative in their approach in a way which enables them to add greater value in commercial situations. Although this model does not expressly refer to digital lawyering within it, the components it includes do seem to mirror many of the skills required by digital lawyers; for example, being open to trying new digital solutions for issues, using opportunities to incorporate digital technology in new and innovative ways and thinking more widely about the broader implications of such technologies.

Sync 7: Evaluating the models

You should allow around 10 minutes for this activity

Consider each of the three models in the preceding box (you may also want to look at the additional information given in the Additional Resources section at the end of this chapter). Which model do you think is the most appropriate and why?

Once again, there is no right answer to this sync, as each of the models has a range of advantages and disadvantages. You may also have questioned what "most appropriate" means in this context. For example, you could view the O-shaped lawyer as more applicable to a corporate lawyer than one who practices family or criminal law. Conversely, you may feel that the T-shaped lawyer is a simpler and more achievable model given it still has a significant focus on traditional legal knowledge as its supporting column. The important part of this question is really the "why". This demonstrates the reasoning (and critical thinking) you used to reach your decision. In Chapter 13 we will consider to what extent you feel your legal education and training has equipped you to demonstrate these different models of lawyering and how you can develop relevant skills.

Conclusion: defining digital skills

This chapter has explored the importance of skills in society generally and within higher education, the growing employability agenda and the type of skills required within legal practice. It has considered the type of digital skills which are becoming an increasingly important part of legal practice and emphasised that this is not just about being able to use certain types of technology. Instead, digital skills are much broader, encompassing project management and more besides. As a part of this, soft skills are also increasingly acknowledged as a vital part of legal practice. This has led to the development of new models of lawyering. For the digital lawyer of the 21st century, it is crucial to be aware of the digital skills that are needed and to consider ways to develop these. In Chapter 13 we will develop this theme further.

ADDITIONAL RESOURCES

For a recent UK report on lawtech and regulation, see <https://www.legalservicesboard.org.uk/wp-content/uploads/2020/04/LSB-Technical-Perspectives-FINAL.pdf>

For resources on the T-shaped lawyer, see <http://elainemak.com/the-tshaped-lawyer-and-beyond>

For resources on the delta model, see <https://www.alysoncarrel.com/delta-competency-model>

For resources on the O-shaped lawyer, see <https://www.oshapedlawyer.com/>

For resources on lawyer wellbeing, emotional competence and professional resilience, see <https://www.fitforlaw.org.uk>

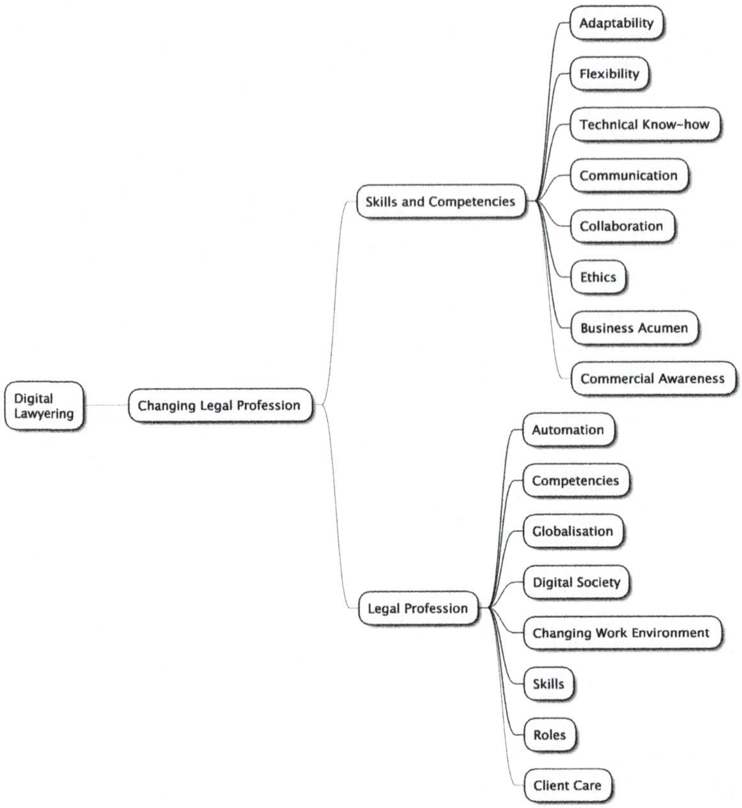

Mind Map 12.1a Chapter topics

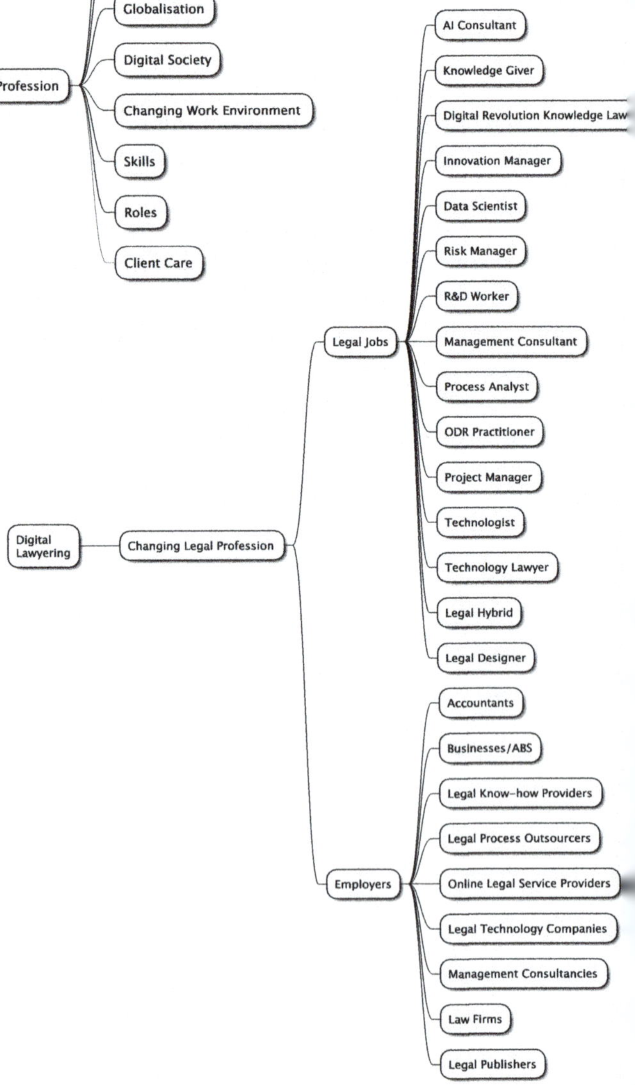

Mind Map 12.1b Chapter topics

12

The Changing Legal Profession

Francine Ryan, Ann Thanaraj and Emma Jones

Introduction

This chapter considers how the impact of technology will bring about the development of new demands and innovations which will change the practice of law. It explores emerging careers in law and the new business and employment structures these involve. It also encourages you to think about the different skills these new and changing roles will require and ways in which you can begin to develop them. What it means to be a lawyer is changing; lawyers will have different career opportunities available to them, and some key roles for the future have probably not been created yet. It is an exciting time to be considering a legal career, and those students who understand how legal practice is changing and can develop the skills required for a very different workplace will find themselves in demand from employers.

Chapter hot spots

When reading this chapter, questions to think about include:

- Is knowledge or skills more important?
- What will the legal profession look like in 10 years?
- Who will be the key stakeholders in the future of the legal profession?
- What skills will the legal practitioner of the future require?
- When, where and how can these skills be developed?

Having read the title and introduction, you can add any other questions you want to explore here:

DOI: 10.4324/9780429298219-12

THE CHANGING LEGAL PROFESSION

> Around 85% of the jobs that today's learners will be doing in 2030 haven't been invented yet.[1]

> We are living through a fundamental transformation in the way we work. Automation and "thinking machines" are replacing human tasks and jobs, and changing the skills that organisations are looking for in their people.[2]

If you are reading this book, it is likely that you are as a Millennial and/or part of Generation Y or Generation Z. These are terms commonly used to describe people born from the early 1980s up to the mid-2000s who have grown up alongside rapid technological advances. From smartphones to smart televisions, from social media to virtual learning environments, from the World Wide Web to virtual reality, from travel apps to fitness monitors, it is likely that technology is integrated into many (if not all) aspects of your daily life. Other generations have also had to adapt to what is now commonly termed the "digital society". These developments are intertwined with other key changes across the globe, including globalisation, demographic shifts and scarcity of resources.

As you saw in Chapter 2, the working environment is no exception to this increasing emphasis on technology, with emails, online meetings, chatbots, virtual assistants and many other innovations changing how and where people work. At a more fundamental level, it is also having an increasing impact on the types of work that people do. Although a few of the headlines about this may be somewhat exaggerated, there is clear evidence that jobs are changing and new roles are emerging. This leads to a demand for different skills and competencies as employers look to fill these vacancies, as well as new opportunities for entrepreneurs.

The legal sector is not immune from these changes, and there have been a number of headlines in the legal press suggesting that artificial intelligence (AI) and automation may pose a threat to people's

1 Institute for the Future for Dell Technologies, *The Next Era of Human Machine Partnerships* (2017), 14 <https://www.delltechnologies.com/content/dam/delltechnologies/assets/perspectives/2030/pdf/SR1940_IFTFforDellTechnologies_Human-Machine_070517_readerhigh-res.pdf> accessed 3 October 2018.

2 C. Stubbings, 'Foreword' in Price Waterhouse Cooper, 'The Workforce of the Future. The Competing Forces Shaping 2030' (2018), 3 <https://www.pwc.com/gx/en/services/people-organisation/workforce-of-the-future/workforce-of-the-future-the-competing-forces-shaping-2030-pwc.pdf> accessed 17 October 2018.

jobs. If many of the more routine tasks, such as reviewing and sorting documents, can be done electronically, the suggestion is that this will reduce the need for human input and therefore the job vacancies on offer within law. To combat this, there has been an increased emphasis on the need for law firms to provide personalised and high-quality client care with a "human touch" to ensure that their services cannot be easily replaced and that clients value the personal relationship with their advisor. However, it is arguable that over the next 20 years there will also be more fundamental changes to parts, at least, of the legal profession.

The market for legal services (in other words, the type of legal work being demanded by clients and employers) is shifting in light of the increased role of technology. For example, clients need lawyers who can protect their intellectual property in the digital content they create, advise on technologically innovative methods of production and delivery and deal with the consequences of potential cyberattacks. The legal profession must respond to these demands to remain relevant and competitive. Technology is disrupting legal practice by changing what is required from lawyers and the ways in which they themselves work.

The term "legal profession" has typically been defined to include solicitors and barristers (commonly termed "lawyers", depending on which jurisdiction you are in). It can also include other roles, such as that of a chartered legal executive or paralegal, which often involve performing many similar tasks to those of traditional members of the profession. However, it is questionable whether this definition of the legal profession captures the new jobs and roles beginning to emerge.

Sync 1: What is a legal professional?

Using your general knowledge, and your reading of this textbook so far, how do you define the term "legal professional"?

We will return to this question later in this chapter (in Sync 6 and Sync 7) so you may wish to make some notes to remind yourself of your ideas.

Of course, the existing legal profession covers a wide range of different types of firms and individuals, ranging from very large, international law firms to small firms offering local services to individuals in towns and villages. Therefore, the impact of technology is likely to differ greatly even within the legal sector. For example, while a number of firms have legal technology and innovation departments[3] dedicated to developing advanced technological solutions, others may still be heavily reliant on posting out letters and sending faxes. However, as discussed in Chapter 2, even the least technologically advanced firm is likely to be using emails and online legal databases, demonstrating that no part of the legal profession is immune from change.

While thinking about the opportunities digital lawyering presents, it is important to consider the varied and broad wider impact on the legal profession. For some legal practitioners, this could be negative. For example, individuals undertaking routine legal work that can be automated may become surplus to requirements. This could particularly impact on parts of the profession where there is less protection and stability, such as the work of paralegals. If they are seen as easily expendable, then this could mean this route to entry into law becomes even more difficult. For those already working within law, the demands to "upskill" and develop new competencies could also place a heavy burden on people in terms of time, resources and well-being. These points should not detract from the opportunities available, but it is important to consider them critically as you work through this chapter.

Any changes within the legal profession are also likely to impact on legal education. In the UK, although only a minority of law students actually go on to qualify as a solicitor or barrister, many law schools do try (at least to some extent) to prepare their students for these roles. In other jurisdictions, such as the United States, a large majority of law graduates go on to work as lawyers and expect to graduate "practice-ready". Law schools therefore need to think carefully about what their students will need to enter the legal profession in the future. As discussed in Chapter 11, this can mean focusing on developing skills rather than knowledge; for example, ensuring students know how to use legal databases to find cases rather than learning a large list of cases. If you are a law student, as you read this chapter you may find it interesting to reflect on how well your studies are preparing you for the world of digital lawyering.

3 See Addleshaw Goddard as one example: <https://www.addleshawgoddard.com/en/>

LEGAL JOBS IN THE DIGITAL WORLD

As the market for legal services is changing, the traditional model of delivery is being disrupted by technology and globalisation. Over the past ten years, technology has altered legal practice and these shifts will accelerate with the pace of technological change. The COVID-19 pandemic has also changed the legal profession. Traditional ways of working were dispensed with, and remote working created a new and different dynamic within the culture of many law firms. Home working and virtual meetings has become the norm, and the use of technology has been amplified in these new ways of working. Law firms are also investing in AI, and it will be used to support the work of lawyers. AI will not replace lawyers, but it will change the way in which legal services are delivered. Innovation is driving change in law firms, and technology enables change. Future lawyers will be required to work with a range of technological applications and have the digital skills to successfully operate in this new world of work. Those future lawyers who embrace change, are curious and are interested in learning new skills will be able to respond to new opportunities as they emerge. The future law firm will offer alternative career paths for lawyers and new jobs will continue to be created which reflect the shifting legal market. This will lead to opportunities but also challenges, as you will be expected to demonstrate new skills and competencies. Understanding how the job market is changing will prepare you for a competitive marketplace where innovation and technology are central to the practice of law.

Sync 2: The changing legal services market

Watch this video to learn more about how technology is changing the legal services market <https://www.youtube.com/watch?v=vyjWIHHUXNo>

The video in Sync 2 demonstrates that the future is already here; there has been a proliferation of new technologies with law firms adopting automated legal tools.

Analysts predict the need for fewer lawyers because technology will automate many routine legal tasks.[4] However, a technology-enabled future

4 A Deloitte study argued that 114,000 jobs in the legal sector are likely to be subject to automation in the next 20 years: Deloitte, *Developing Legal Talent: Stepping*

also offers the possibility of a greater range of roles and opportunities connected to legal practice. In 2017, Richard Susskind[5] identified ten "new" jobs for lawyers. In fact, these are no longer new jobs, as many already exist.

THE NOT-SO-NEW JOBS!

What are these not-so-new jobs?

Sync 3: Thinking about different roles

Consider the ten jobs in Figure 12.1. In the first column, indicate whether this is a job you are familiar with, and in the second column, consider whether it's a job you may be interested in. We will revisit this later in the chapter to consider whether any of your answers have changed.

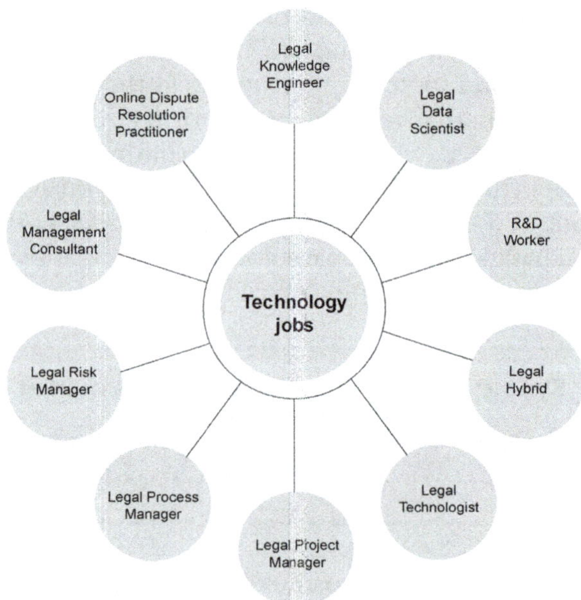

Figure 12.1 The not-so-new jobs

into the Future Law Firm (February 2016) <https://www2.deloitte.com/content/dam/Deloitte/uk/Documents/audit/deloitte-uk-developing-legal-talent-2016.pdf> accessed 12 October 2018.

5 R. Susskind, *Tomorrow's Lawyers* (Oxford, Oxford University Press, 2017), 133.

New jobs	Yes/no	Interested/not interested?
Legal knowledge engineer		
Legal data scientist		
Research and development worker		
Legal hybrid		
Legal technologist		
Legal project manager		
Legal process analyst		
Legal risk manager		
Legal management consultant		
Online dispute resolution practitioner		

WHAT ARE THESE JOBS?

When you are reading about these jobs, consider what relevant skills and competencies you may already have to undertake these roles, and what skills and competencies you might need to develop.

LEGAL KNOWLEDGE ENGINEER

The legal market is becoming increasing more competitive, and law firms need to utilise technology to enhance their productivity and become more efficient. Increasingly, law firms are looking at legal processes and thinking about ways to innovate to create new legal products and services. A legal engineer is someone with both legal knowledge and technological expertise who can find creative solutions to optimise existing legal processes and find technological solutions to address the needs of clients. The role requires someone who is technologically proficient and has knowledge of legal practice to understand the problems.

Most importantly, a legal engineer needs to be creative, as they need to be able to use technology to solve legal problems.

LEGAL DATA SCIENTIST

A data scientist is "someone who can bridge the raw data and the analysis—and make it accessible".[6] Predictive analytics, machine learning and data mining are all buzzwords in data science. Law firms are using analytic tools in e-discovery. Data science is furthering our ability to predict what will happen, but this raises many legal and ethical implications around how data is stored and used. A legal data scientist needs to understand the data collection process and be able to curate and analyse it for many different purposes and considering the implications of these methods and uses. Technical knowledge is required but communication skills are also essential to present data in a clear and usable way to lawyers. Several universities now offer a postgraduate master's degree in data science, which indicates this is an area for growth.

RESEARCH AND DEVELOPMENT WORKER

In many sectors research and development (R&D) departments are commonplace, but they have not featured within many law firms. Jordan Furlong[7] identifies four R&D activities law firms could engage in:

- New products and services
- New delivery mechanisms
- New pricing systems
- New management systems.

Investment in R&D is going to be important to the success and competitiveness of legal practice. It will create new opportunities to develop innovative ways to shape the business of law firms. If you would like to be challenged to consider new ways of developing legal services, R&D is an interesting field to be involved in.

6 S. Rogers, 'What Is a Data Scientist?' (*Guardian*, 2012) <https://www.theguardian.com/news/datablog/2012/mar/02/data-scientist> accessed 12 October 2018.

7 J. Furlong, 'Why Law Firms Need R&D Investment' (*L21 Blog*, 2014) <https://www.law21.ca/2014/08/law-firms-need-rd-investment/> accessed 12 October 2018.

LEGAL HYBRID

As explained in Chapter 2, complex legal matters often require a multidisciplinary approach and clients need lawyers to work with other professionals. For example, family lawyers work with mediators, psychologists and social workers. Corporate lawyers liaise with consultants, brokers, bankers and accountants. Changes to the way legal services are being delivered has led to many lawyers gaining additional professional qualifications and offering a broader range of services to clients. Already many family and civil lawyers are trained mediators, as it gives them the opportunity to add new services to their practice. As clients seek multifaceted support, the demand for legal hybrids will grow.

LEGAL TECHNOLOGIST

Technology is transforming the capability of law firms. It is now an integral part of the practice of law and the administration of justice. The expansion of IT and technology departments has provided new opportunities for lawyers with an interest in technology to transfer into legal technology roles. The rapid pace of change has resulted in the growing demand for legal technologists to such an extent that it is now recognised as a career in its own right.

With the development of new technologies, it is no longer a generalist role; instead there are growing opportunities to specialise in different technological applications. Understanding how lawyers use technology, with the ability to explain it in a way that is accessible, is key to the role. A passion for technology with a willingness to learn about different applications and develop expertise will be important for anyone pursuing a career as a legal technologist. Technological innovation is the future of legal practice, and there are exciting opportunities to engage in developing legal services.

LEGAL PROJECT MANAGER

You were introduced to the importance of project management in Chapter 11. The International Institute of Legal Project Management state:

> Legal Project Management is the application of project management principles and practices which enhance the delivery of legal services. In practice, our research confirmed that it also encompasses technology

enablement, process improvement and the people dynamics that brings greater success to legal service delivery.[8]

Once the legal service has been designed, a project manager will plan, allocate resources and prepare a budget to ensure the successful delivery of the project. These roles already exist and there is a growing legal project management community.[9] The Institute offers certification as a legal project associate or legal project practitioner.[10] There is significant potential in legal project management, and it offers the opportunity to work in conjunction with other roles such as legal management consultants and legal process analysts.

LEGAL PROCESS ANALYST

Legal process analysts review the legal processes and systems to identify and analyse issues that limit efficiency and devise solutions to improve the central process. They may work in in-house legal departments to map the process of legal work and ensure the efficiency of the operation. They may work independently and offer their services on a consultancy basis to law firms. They will focus on making changes to strategy, operating models and business processes to optimise the performance of the organisation and support future growth. Jobs are emerging in this field and they require individuals who can identify how technology can be used to innovate and shape the practice of law.

LEGAL RISK MANAGER

With increasingly amounts of regulation in areas such as privacy and data protection,[11] law firms and their clients face multiple risk and compliance issues. Legal risk needs to be managed systematically with an

8 A. Smith and T. Hutchinson, 'Building Legal Project Management Skills and Organisational Capability' (2017) <https://gallery.mailchimp.com/ef0907072acfd9dfa8857ea40/files/d4eb13ae-8896-4b27-81ca-3ad6cf48e5ad/Building_LPM_Skills_Organisational_Capability.pdf>. Sourced from: <https://legalprojectmanagement.co.uk> accessed 12 October 2018.

9 See <https://www.iilpm.com>; <https://www.linkedin.com/groups/13509439>; <https://www.facebook.com/groups/legalprojectmanagement>

10 <https://www.iilpm.com>

11 See, for example, the Solicitors Regulation Authority Code of Conduct; Bribery Act 2010 c.23, and The Money Laundering, Terrorist Financing and Transfer of Funds (Information on the Payer) Regulations 2017.

identifiable risk management framework. It is complex and challenging work, involving the ability to not only to identify legal risk but also to analyse and evaluate it. The role of a legal risk manager will involve integrating different processes using technology to proactively manage risk and add value to their law firm.

LEGAL MANAGEMENT CONSULTANT

In January 2018, Deloitte Legal[12] launched its legal management consultancy, stating "LMC is a new approach and a new discipline, developed for lawyers by lawyers and other experts. . . . LMC focuses on operating models, technology, work-sourcing and cost management".[13] Legal management consultancy offers clients a range of different services, but an important aspect is to work in partnership with clients to develop strategies to respond changes in the legal market. This is an area that will develop as law firms focus on how to use technology to contribute to their growth and need specialist support to embed technology within their organisations.

ONLINE DISPUTE RESOLUTION PRACTITIONER

As you learned in Chapter 9, there is an increasing number of online dispute resolution (ODR) systems, particularly in civil mediation and consumer redress.[14] ODR platforms provide an alternative to traditional court-based litigation. In the UK and elsewhere, the courts themselves are also becoming increasingly digitalised with the introduction of online court systems. Digital solutions to resolve legal problems have the potential to create new opportunities for lawyers and add value for clients. A dispute resolution professional will need to understand how to successfully support and work with clients online. As a result of the COVID-19 pandemic, collaborating and working online has now become commonplace, and therefore we may see accelerated growth in this area.

12 <https://www2.deloitte.com>

13 Deloitte Legal, 'A Changing World Requires a New Approach to Law' (2017) <https://www2.deloitte.com/content/dam/Deloitte/global/Documents/Legal/dttl-legal-deloitte-approach-legal-management-consulting.pdf> accessed 12 October 2018.

14 See, for example, the European Union's ODR platform for resolving consumer problems <https://ec.europa.eu/consumers/odr/main/index.cfm?event=main.home2.show&lng=EN> accessed 12 October 2018.

Although Richard Susskind identified ten new jobs, there are other roles emerging. There might be some overlap between these jobs, or organisations may have slightly different names for similar roles (Figure 12.2).

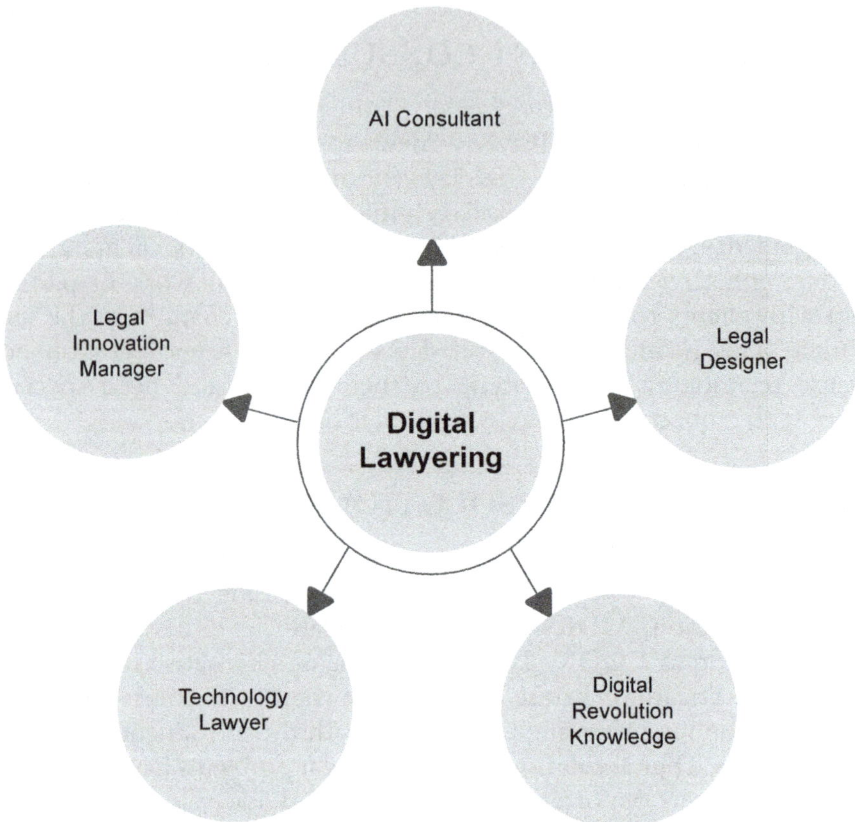

Figure 12.2 Emerging jobs

LEGAL INNOVATION MANAGER

Law firms with legal technology and innovation departments view these as important to ensure that the firm can respond and innovate to stay at the cutting edge of legal practice. These departments need managers who have responsibility for the strategic development of the team. The managers act as a bridge between the team and the rest of the organisation, sharing knowledge of new technologies and identifying and promoting the use of technological solutions.

DIGITAL REVOLUTION KNOWLEDGE LAWYER

Law firms already employ professional support lawyers (non-fee-earning positions) to support knowledge management in their practice areas. The nature of the role varies but may include research, professional development and leading the firm's know-how activities. Lawyers are required to understand about all aspects of digital transformation and the impact technological disruption will have on them and their clients. A new type of professional support lawyer is required who can provide lawyers with this type of insight and support.

AI CONSULTANT

In Chapter 7 you explored AI and learned how it can automate tasks that would have been undertaken by junior lawyers. Proponents of AI argue that it will free up lawyers to focus on more complex work. Orlando Conetta,[15] former head of R&D at Pinsent Masons LLP,[16] has degrees in law and computer science. He was responsible for developing TermFrame, which is the basis of the firm's legal AI process platform. AI is being used in discovery and legal contracts and provides significant benefits to clients to solve legal problems more efficiently. Knowledge of AI will be highly prized, offering opportunities within law firms to incorporate AI into existing processes but also in consultancy roles to provide AI expertise.[17]

LEGAL DESIGNER

> Legal design is the application of human-centred design to the world of law, to make legal systems and services more human-centred, usable and satisfying.[18]

The legal designer works to embed technology and innovation within an organisation without impacting on its current ways of working. This is achieved through the creation of legal design maps to visualise the process of integrating technology and human interaction. A design

15 <https://twitter.com/termframe>

16 <https://www.pinsentmasons.com>

17 Infographic taken from <http://ai.lawgeex.com/rs/345-WGV-842/images/LawGeex%20-%20The%20In-House%20Counsel%27s%20LegalTech%20Buyer%27s%20Guide%20-%202018%20Edition.pdf> accessed 13 October 2018.

18 M. Hagan, 'Law by Design' (2014) <https://www.lawbydesign.co/en/legal-design/>

approach starts with the end user, focusing on solving legal problems in a clearer, and more user-friendly way. Technology is viewed as a resource to support human-centred design. In other words, the people within the system or process are viewed as at the heart of legal design. Thinking like a designer can lead to improvements in current processes and innovative new products and services.

TECHNOLOGY LAWYER

We are seeing the rise of the technology lawyer, with new opportunities being created within legal practice. Advice on the legal implications of specialised and emerging technologies is required by clients; for example, intellectual property protection, e-commerce, contracts, data protection and privacy. In August 2018, Addleshaw Goddard announced it was offering a new training seat in its legal and technology group. It already has a secondment option for its qualified lawyers to gain experience of new technology platforms and develop digital skills.[19]

Sync 4: Finding out more

Now that you have had the opportunity to read more about the emerging roles in the legal profession, would you change any of your original answers in Sync 3? Has this discussion piqued your interest in finding out more? Choose a role and search the Internet to see what you can find out, or have a look at the example job adverts in the Appendix at the end of this chapter.

Also take some time to reflect on the challenges involved in these roles. For example, accessing relevant training may take time and money, and competition for such jobs can be fierce. Weighing up the opportunities against the challenges involved can help you to consider your own future career direction.

Each of the not-so-new and emerging jobs discussed in this chapter offers a range of challenges but also new opportunities. For someone with a passion for technology, they offer alternatives to traditional routes into the legal profession to explore.

19 <https://www.legalcheek.com/2018/08/addleshaw-goddard-to-offer-six-month-lawtech-seat-to-trainee-lawyers/> accessed 12 October 2018.

Digital lawyering skills: flexibility

A few generations ago, people tended to focus upon finding a job, or at least a career, for life. It is still not uncommon for individuals to have decades-long careers in one industry or profession. However, it is also becoming increasingly usual for people to have a range of careers within their working lives. Some will also have what is sometimes termed a "portfolio career", working in several different roles; for example, as a part-time professional support lawyer and part-time legal consultant, or as a part-time fee-earning lawyer and part-time life coach. Even within one profession, it is now more common for people to move between jobs, and this is likely to increase as digital technology changes and develops, leading to changes in the roles required.

These shifts mean that individuals have to be flexible to cope with and adapt to the changes that occur. This can sound daunting, but you have probably already learnt ways to be flexible; for example, by changing from school or college to university and by changing your study style according to the demands of individual modules.

Some tips to help with flexibility include:

- Distinguish between what you can and cannot change. If something is outside of your control, there is no point in worrying about it. You need to focus on the things you can change.
- Be aware of your own values and ethics. This will help you to understand when and why you may find some types of change stressful.
- Take measured risks. Not all change is bad. It is important to realise some change is positive and can lead to types of challenge that motivate or even inspire you.
- Keep your eyes on the bigger picture. Sometimes change can seem overwhelming, but if you rationalise it, usually it is only one small part of a much bigger picture. For example, even if you change jobs and find you do not enjoy it, you will still have your family, friends and hobbies.

TYPES OF EMPLOYERS

Now you have a better understanding of the types of roles that are emerging, let's consider where you might work. What is exciting is that alongside law firms there are a range of other employers who will recruit for these roles. You may be familiar with some of them, like accountants, but less so with others, like legal publishers, so there is a lot to learn. Figure 12.3 summarises the range of potential employers.

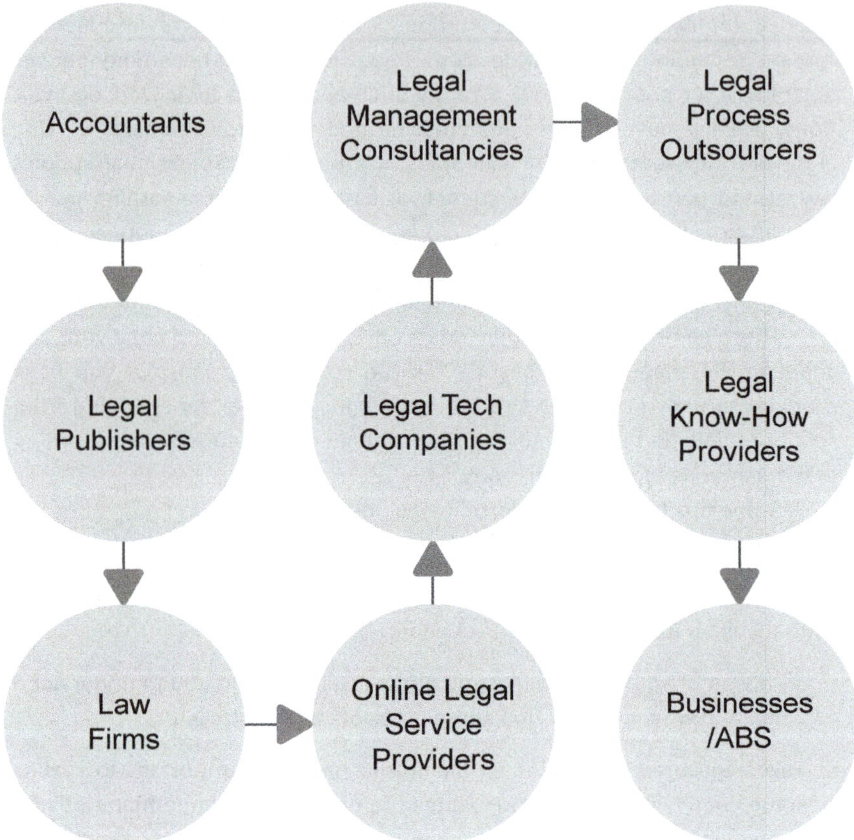

Figure 12.3 Employers past and present

ALTERNATIVE LEGAL SERVICE PROVIDERS

As technology disrupts existing markets, the legal marketplace will see a growth of alternative legal service providers (ALSPs) offering a range of legal services, creating opportunities for lawyers and law related jobs. The following table[20] outlines what ALSPs offer and examples of key

20 Adapted from 'Alternative Legal Service Providers: Understanding the Growth and Benefits of These New Legal Providers' (2017) <https://static.legalsolutions.thomsonreuters.com/static/pdf/Alternative-Legal-Service-Providers_Long.pdf> accessed 13 October 2018.

players. More information about these providers is explained as you progress through this chapter.

	Accountants	**Legal process outsourcing connected to law firms**	**Legal process outsourcing**	**Managed legal services**	**Contract lawyers**
What do they do?	Deliver legal services; developing a wider legal consultancy service.	Owned by law firms; located in lower cost area-volume work.	Independent of law firms; project-based work; managed by in-house departments or law firms.	Organisations that provide part or all of the legal function of an in-house department.	Provide lawyers and paralegals on a contract basis.
Examples of organisations	Deloitte EY PwC KPMG	Clifford Chance Eversheds Allen & Overy	Thomson Reuters Mindcrest Integreon LDiscovery	Thomson Reuters Axiom Riverview Law Elevate	FLEX Axiom LOD Halebury

ACCOUNTANTS

The Big Four global accountants in the UK[21] already employ significant numbers of lawyers in their legal practices. Deloitte Legal has over 2000 legal professionals in 80 countries; PwC has 3600 lawyers worldwide; and in 2014 EY launched EY Law.[22] As discussed previously, Deloitte is not just offering legal services; they have a legal management consultancy that targets in-house legal departments to support them with digital transformation. The team consists of 100 professionals across the world offering a range of services including risk manage-

21 This term refers to the largest and most influential four accounting companies globally: Deloitte, PWC, KPMG and Ernst & Young.

22 In September 2018 EY <https://www.ey.com/en_gl/who-we-are> acquired Riverview Law <https://www.riverview.law> Riverview Law is a leading innovative legal services firm with a strong technology practice.

ment, analysing and reviewing processes to achieve efficiencies through the optimisation of technology. The Big Four are global operators and are putting legal technology at the core of their business. They recruit talent across a range of different disciplines and are an attractive option for law students and lawyers who want to pursue a career outside a traditional legal practice.

LEGAL PUBLISHERS AND KNOW-HOW PROVIDERS

LexisNexis[23] and Thomson Reuters[24] provide news, information, software solutions and analytic tools relating to legal, regulatory and tax changes using technology to support legal professionals. Thomson Reuters is working in close collaboration with Legal Geek[25] to support the tech start-up ecosystem. Both companies have R&D divisions, and Lexis has a tech hub in Chancery Lane, London. Danielle McCormick, UK director of solutions at LexisNexis, said "Lexis wants to be lawyer-led and it's sending a bit of a signal out by putting me—a lawyer not a techy—in charge, I know what I would have wanted in practice".[26] Both companies offer a variety of different roles, but this demonstrates that there is a demand for both legal and digital skills.

LEGALTECH COMPANIES

Sync 5: Legal Geek

1 Visit the Legal Geek website and access their start-up map <https://www.legalgeek.co/startup-map/>. Read in the FAQs the question 'How is the legal tech startup map categorised?'

2 Research three companies from this map to find out what they do and the positions they are recruiting for. The companies on the map are situated across many jurisdictions and therefore give you the opportunity to find out what is happening both within and outside your own jurisdiction.

23 <https://www.lexisnexis.com/en-us/home.page>
24 <https://www.thomsonreuters.com/en.html>
25 <https://www.legalgeek.co>
26 D. McCormick, 'Legal IT Insider Newsletter' (2018) <https://www.legaltechnology.com/wp-content/uploads/2018/09/Sept-Insider316.pdf> accessed 13 October 2018.

It is a good idea to think about what areas of legaltech interest you. For example, if it is AI, Kim[27] is a great place to start, as it has a platform that uses AI concepts to allow a user with no software expertise to automate processes and workflows. It has won several awards, including the *Financial Times* Innovative Lawyers Europe Award. The company is based in the United States and the UK and has seen significant growth.

Online legal services providers are also part of the legaltech revolution. For example, Rocket Lawyer[28] allows you to create legal documents, ask a lawyer and register your company online. The driver for online legal service providers is to harness technology to make legal services more affordable.

LEGAL MANAGEMENT CONSULTANCY

Consultancy firms like OMC Partners[29] offer a wide range of services to law firms, in-house legal departments, and newly formed alternative business structures (ABSs), including legal process analysis, legal spend management, legal technology advice and alternative resourcing. Legal management consultancies will recruit for many of the new jobs identified earlier in this chapter as demand increases for these types of services.

LEGAL PROCESS OUTSOURCING

Legal process outsourcing (LPO) involves delegating work to another organisation to carry out work such as litigation support services or services in specialised areas such as risk and compliance. Integreon[30] is an example of a LPO provider. Other examples of LPOs were provided in the table at the start of this section. Law firms have also created LPOs which they own to offer their clients better value for money for

27 <http://ask.kim/about>
28 <https://www.rocketlawyer.co.uk>
29 <https://www.omc-partners.com>
30 <https://www.integreon.com>

generally high-volume work. Ownership of the LPO allows them to retain control over the quality of the work. Freshfields[31] in Manchester, England, and Herbert Smith Freehills[32] in Belfast, Northern Ireland, are examples of law firms that have an LPO.

LAW FIRMS

Law firms are creating different opportunities within their legal practices. There are roles within innovation departments but also within specialist law firms. Digital Law[33] started in 2014 and is the only UK law firm to specialise in online, data and cyber law. Change is also happening to the way in which lawyers work. Flexible Legal Resources is a consulting business of PWC;[34] it has a bank of specialist lawyers with a range of different backgrounds including risk and compliance. Lawyers work on projects on a consultancy basis within in-house departments. As discussed in Chapter 2, virtual law firms are also starting to emerge; Vlaw Limited[35] is an example that offers lawyers an alternative option to traditional legal practice. Lawyers are self-employed and collaborate on matters together virtually. F-LEX[36] is an online platform which connects law students to law firms to work as paralegals. It is a lawtech start-up which is using a tech-enabled platform to disrupt traditional legal recruitment.

BUSINESSES

A range of different business will recruit digital lawyers, from large global corporations to high street banks. High street brands may continue to challenge traditional high street law firms by offering services such as conveyancing and wills and probate but using technology to optimise the process of delivery. Large corporations are likely to retain in-house legal support, but with an expectation that cost efficiencies will be achieved through using technology and perhaps outsourcing

31 <https://www.freshfields.com>
32 <https://www.herbertsmithfreehills.com>
33 <https://www.digitallawuk.com>
34 <https://www.pwc.co.uk/careers/experienced-jobs/opportunities/flexible-legal-resources-html>
35 <https://www.virtuallaw.eu>
36 <https://www.flex.legal>

some provision to other providers. There are myriad opportunities going forward to explore in this area.

Sync 6: Changes to the legal profession

Reflect on these questions:

1. What type of legaltech will most radically change the way in which lawyers will work in the next five years?
2. Do we need a new definition of the "legal profession" considering these changes?
3. What is one thing you should do to prepare for legaltech changes in the next five years?

RETURNING TO DIGITAL SKILLS

With the emerging new uses of technology in the delivery of legal services, and the way in which existing laws are being applied as solutions to digital living, you will need a variety of skills and competencies, including knowledge of substantive laws, awareness of technology and its uses and an appreciation for the changing trends in the ethics and professional responsibility for lawyers.

As Chapter 11 illustrated, a broad range of skills are required for an individual to be considered digitally competent, and this captures an important shift in thinking about competent 21st-century lawyering. Historically, competency in legal practice was very much focused on gaining and demonstrating competency in the foundations of legal knowledge and other substantive areas of law, and the ability to represent your client in accordance with the codes of conduct and professional rules.

Sync 7: Which digital skills?

Based on your reading of Chapter 11, the "digital lawyering skills" boxes in each chapter and the reading you have done about jobs in this chapter, make a note of the five skills you think are essential for working as a digital lawyer. Take time to reflect on how this differs from the skills and competencies currently required within the legal profession.

We have identified several broad areas of skills and competencies we see as crucial, including:

- Technical know-how
- Communication and collaboration
- Understanding ethics and confidentiality
- Business acumen
- Commercial awareness and entrepreneurship
- Adaptability and resilience.

These are not necessarily "new", but they will need to be applied in very different ways.

TECHNICAL KNOW-HOW

Substantive legal knowledge is the foundation of our core competency to deliver a fit-for-purpose legal service. This also requires the continued acquisition of the types of key legal skills referred to in Chapter 2. However, the knowledge we need is also changing as technology evolves and emerges. For example, in handling contractual matters, blockchain technology, digital currencies and smart contracts are a few relevant areas of study. Within civil procedure rules, learning about ODR and electronic discovery are necessary topics of study. In criminal law, learning about digital theft or digital ownership in property law are key foundations of our legal knowledge. As technology evolves and its use becomes ubiquitous, every aspect of legal practice will require an awareness and basic knowledge of technology's impact—in other words, as discussed in Chapter 4, a level of digital literacy and digital competence. Knowledge of how technological developments would be addressed by existing law and whether that law is adequate becomes an integral part of a future lawyer's competency.

As much as there is no expectation on lawyers to know how to code, yet a digitally competent professional will be confident in choosing solutions for online tasks for a particular purpose or audience. To do this you must understand what the technology does, how it functions, and what it is capable and not capable of doing, whilst having a clear objective of what you are setting out to achieve and what the technology is capable of offering. Acquiring the knowledge and skills to use digital tools and software to deliver alternative forms of technology-driven legal service requires you to learn continually about the developments in technology.[37]

This means that being considered digitally competent is more than being able to source information online; it means possessing the understanding, knowledge and skills required to enable the effective use of technology, keeping abreast of the changes in the law and its practice, the influence of technology on both domains, and acquiring knowledge continually about the benefits and risks associated with relevant technology, coupled with the necessary confidence and adaptability required to learn and utilise new technologies. This does not mean that you will need to become a technology expert, but there is an obligation to have a basic understanding of different technologies, including their affordances, limitations and potential use in legal services. As the uses of AI, blockchain technology and other innovative tools are rolled out, lawyers will be expected to know how those tools affect their clients too. Keeping yourself up to date on suitable technology for the delivery of legal services is necessary, including best practices for the use of these delivery models.

COMMUNICATION AND COLLABORATION

Working online requires excellent collaboration, communication and the sharing of tasks and goals with each other. The knowledge and skills relevant to communicating and undertaking legal services online include the need to be flexible in communicating and listening because each client and colleague they encounter will have a different concept of accessibility and varying levels of comfort in communicating online. You will need to be aware of acceptable etiquette when working online with clients and other professionals and how to collaborate effectively utilising individual's strengths in an online team. As discussed in Chapter 3, legal teams will increasingly be interdisciplinary in nature, requiring the ability to collaborate with a wide range of people, communicating clearly and effectively.

37 Some of the legal services already using technology include automated document assembly, electronic court scheduling and file share technologies—technologies used within law practices include digital means of communicating with clients and third parties and transmitting information, electronic research and software applications for document generation, electronic calendaring, and docketing and much more.

UNDERSTANDING ETHICS AND CONFIDENTIALITY

A focus on codes of conduct, professional responsibilities and legal ethics is important for online delivery of legal services, especially for ensuring that all forms of communication and data handling are safe and encrypted. As discussed in Chapter 5, you will require the knowledge and skills to consider the safety, security, confidentiality, privacy, digital footprint and ethical use of digital tools for legal practice.

Further, within the practice of law, ethical and professional responsibility are key elements of codes of conduct, and as such, data security in the form of safeguarding electronically stored client information and communications is crucial. Whilst you need not master the security rules and features of a piece of technology, as this will evolve as the technology changes, you will be expected to continuously keep abreast of digital security practices. This means being aware of the benefits and risks of emerging technologies that can be used to deliver legal services and safeguards to ensure your client's information and data is held confidentially, with the appropriate security in place to protect it from disclosure, access or acquisition. This is for information that is privileged between the lawyer and client and any other information held about the client. Further, the obligation to competently maintain client confidentiality requires an understanding of data encryption and its purpose in transmitting data electronically; safe ways of communicating confidential data is essential, alongside being aware of the risks associated with using public wireless access to view clients' files and undertake communication.

Maintaining privacy and security over data becomes a bigger challenge when data is held in the cloud. This means that data and information relating to a client and case files will be stored on virtual servers owned by third parties outside the relevant law practice. The duty to keep information safe and confidential still remains the professional responsibility of the lawyer even if the data is stored elsewhere. In fact, this places even more of a burden on verifying and ensuring that the cloud host has an enforceable service level agreement on how data held in the cloud will be preserved and handled, methods of data retrieval, and backup and storage of data.

Given the abundance of retrievable data online, there is a need to develop one's ability to evaluate content found online and make informed judgements on its reliability for the handling, sharing and safe storage of data. Electronic discovery is the preservation, retrieval, review and production of electronic information as evidence in court. Skills such as problem-solving and critical and analytical thinking skills are exercised when discussing practical e-discovery issues. You will require an understanding of the various e-discovery processes to be able to challenge or critique the results of the discovery if necessary, such as because of biases or reliance on incomplete data. Knowing about ethical sources of information is useful to ensure the quality, reliability and credibility of data gathered.

BUSINESS ACUMEN

Business acumen and an understanding of business intelligence are significant and necessary skills in our data-driven world. The practice of law remains a profession, a vocation and a business. Alongside the traditional key skills of a practising lawyer such as substantive legal knowledge, professional and practical client-facing skills and legal skills, the business world requires that a lawyer can run a legal practice business with excellent customer service and client care aided using appropriate technology. The ability to understand financing, budget handling, and reporting on cost and benefit is important. In this regard, project management is becoming a fixture in many law courses. Your ability to scope, schedule and cost legal work, accompanied by resourcing, managing and monitoring progress on work with a view to delivering that legal work in an efficient and effective manner that balances the expectations of clients and business objectives, is deemed an essential skill in legal practice business. As discussed in Chapters 8 and 10, there is also a need for critical thinking and creativity to enable you to be proactive in both identifying and addressing client issues.

COMMERCIAL AWARENESS AND ENTREPRENEURSHIP

It is essential that you understand the environment in which law firms and clients operate. Lawyers are trusted advisors, and the legal advice they give must support the needs of their clients. Clients will expect their lawyers to use technology as part of their operating model and advise them on the legal implications of emerging technologies. This requires a digital lawyer to be both a systematic thinker and also a problem finder and problem-solver (as discussed in Chapters 6 and 7).

ADAPTABILITY AND RESILIENCE

There is a need for a competent lawyer's skill set and knowledge to evolve along with the emerging technologies being used for the delivery of legal services and in the use of technology across our personal and professional lives.

A willingness to continually learn is much needed in a disruptive and innovative fast-paced environment. The not-so-new jobs in legal services require you to develop an appreciation for a global perspective on the law and legal practice. Many disputes and transactions are more frequently giving rise to cross-border issues, particularly enabled by technology, so that a purely domestic legal practice is becoming rarer. Further, the digital age gives rise to the need for cross-disciplinary awareness as legal services become more often unbundled, requiring lawyers to work with other professions and occupations. This requires the types of flexibility referred to earlier in this chapter.

The COVID-19 pandemic is a recent illustration of the need to adapt and be resilient. It required legal professionals to change their ways of working almost instantly; for example, by switching to the forms of remote advocacy discussed in Chapter 9. However, this pandemic also illustrated the ways in which demands to adapt can also be stressful and sometimes harmful to wellbeing. It is important that individuals are able to adapt and show resilience in healthy ways, rather than feeling a pressure to change and succeed at all costs.

Sync 8: Analysing digital lawyering careers

Based on this chapter, and any wider reading you have undertaken, complete the following table to form a SWOT analysis which identifies the strengths, weaknesses, opportunities and threats involved in a career as a digital lawyer. You can focus on yourself personally or on the legal profession as a whole and choose a specific role or look at digital lawyering more broadly.

Strengths	
Weaknesses	
Opportunities	
Threats	

Conclusion

The legal profession in 20 or 30 years' time is likely to look very different than today. There are going to be more career options available for qualified lawyers. Many of you will work in roles that have yet to be created. COVID-19 has accelerated change, and the role of the lawyer will change faster than many could have predicted. Lawyers will need to use their legal knowledge and apply it across a range of different industries. It is an exciting time to be a law student; there are myriad opportunities connected to a future legal career. It is important to think about these changes critically and reflect on both the opportunities and challenges that might be involved. Before moving on, look back at this chapter's hot spots and take time to complete Sync 8; pause and reflect on how these changes could also impact on you and your future career.

Additional resources

Here are some ideas on how to find out more:

- Join professional associations like the Society for Computers and Law (SCL) and the International Legal Technology Association. Many offer free membership and resources and they often have events you can attend where you can make connections.
- Educate yourself. There are lots of free courses where you can learn about technology: try Future Learn.
- Subscribe to *Legal IT Insider*,[38] which produces a free monthly legaltech newsletter.
- Use social media: Follow and engage with industry experts on Twitter and LinkedIn.
- Participate in a Tech Challenge or a Hackathon: The SCL Junior Lawyers' Group organises one each year, but there may be other ones you can participate in.

38 <https://www.legaltechnology.com>

- Look for work experience: Firms are now offering placements in law and technology.[39]
- Keep up to date with legal technology: Stanford CodeX created a searchable database where you can find companies providing different legal technology to the legal market.

39 Reed Smith in April 2018 launched its Summer Technology Associate programme which combines work experience with a technology focus <https://www.reedsmith.com/en/news/2018/04/reed-smith-launches-summer-technology-associate-program>

APPENDIX 1 TO CHAPTER 12

Here is a selection of job adverts that have been created based on recently advertised roles that have been discussed in the chapter. They provide details of the experience and skills required to perform these jobs. We recommend you search for similar jobs on recruitment sites to find out more about these types of opportunities.

Legal Innovation Manager
Purpose of the Role This is considered a Senior Manager role, with the person contributing to the strategic development of the team with line management and work allocation responsibility.
Duties • Managing technical projects undertaken by the Legal Technology and Innovation Team and acting as a key contact. • Responsible for how the team assess, prioritises and delivers work, from initial enquiry through to delivery, and defining and implementing more effective ways of working through the better use of people, process and/or technology. • Line-managing members of the Team, including day-to-day management and regular appraisals. • Delivering a programme of training and development within the Legal Technology and Innovation Team. • Supporting the development of technology platforms used by the team and sharing that knowledge more widely across the Firm. • Engaging across the Firm to promote Legal Technology and Innovation, including attending internal and external meetings and proactively identifying and promoting opportunities to use technology to solve problems.

- Liaising with other departments within the Firm to make sure the team can react quickly to change whilst operating within Firm guidelines for security.
- Understanding and applying principles of the IT strategy to deliver innovative solutions which support the Firm's longer-term technology strategy.

Knowledge, Skills and Experience Required

- Prior experience of working within the legal sector.
- Project management experience.
- An understanding of the challenges impacting on law firms and the changing legal services market.
- An understanding of legal work.
- People management experience required.
- Ability to work well in a challenging, fast-paced environment.
- Organised and able to prioritise workload according to business needs.

Qualifications

- Degree level qualified.
- Project management qualification preferable.

Legal Project Manager

The Legal Project Manager is a client-facing role and acts as the business partner between designated teams within the Firm and our clients.

The Legal Project Manager will report to a Senior Legal Project Manager. You will work closely with lead Partners and their teams to lead the project management activities and to coordinate delivery of the legal work to meet clients' needs to an agreed timeline and budget. You will have client contact from the outset to define and document scope, advise on and set up internal matter management structure and governance, resourcing and budgeting, tracking transaction and financial progress, managing risk and identifying efficiencies throughout the life of the project.

The focus of the Legal Project Manager team is to lead and implement change by improving on delivery, process improvement and innovation, to increase efficiency and provide excellent client service on the most complex matters through effective legal project management.

Main Duties and Responsibilities

- Providing Legal Project Management support.
- Working alongside the lead Partner and core legal team to support on project delivery.
- Coordinating work effort, scoping, pricing, planning, monitoring and reporting, liaising with clients, tracking changes, and working with specialist departments within the Firm. The work on each project will depend on the size and type of project.
- Working with Legal Project Management technology to set up and track the status of each project.
- Researching and developing working processes through discussions with members of the Firm.
- Analysing work products to identify any tasks that could be done by different/other resources.
- Introducing new working efficiencies where appropriate and developing improved processes, tools and systems.
- Delivering improvements and solutions through coaching and training sessions.
- Supporting fee-earners to ensure they have accurate information and support available to them.
- Developing strong working relationships with other departments and teams.

Skills and Attributes

- Experience of leading projects, preferably within a law firm.
- Project management qualification such as Prince 2 or equivalent.
- Analytical and strategic mindset.
- Excellent attention to detail.
- Technology savvy; able to use various other IT tools to support efficient working processes.

Legal Process Analyst

Legal Process Analysts are part of our legal team, working across the Firm.

Key Responsibilities

- Conducting document review, due diligence or other practice area–specific fee-earning work.
- Providing general support to personnel within the Firm.
- Maintaining an up-to-date knowledge of relevant areas of law to the team you are allocated to.
- Ensuring compliance with financial regulations on matters.

Skills, Experience and Qualifications

Essential

- Law graduate (2:2 or above) or a postgraduate qualification in law with a minimum of three A levels (ideally B grades and above).
- Ability to review, analyse and organise documentary and factual evidence.
- Attention to detail.
- Aptitude for learning the use of technology, ability to use large databases/ document management systems.

Key Competencies

- Professional integrity
- Self-development
- Develops resilience
- Legal capability
- Delivers good-quality work
- Delivers outcomes
- Teamwork and communication
- Develops networks
- Contributes to the Firm
- Understands the client experience
- Innovates to support the Firm

Legal Technologist

The Legal Technologist will work within the team to identify and harness innovative ideas and new solutions that will challenge current structures and help develop the legal service delivery. The successful candidate will have an understanding of legal practice and knowledge of legal technology. The candidate will also encourage our lawyers to understand the benefits of legal technology and will work with them in designing innovative approaches and processes for the benefit of our clients.

Key Responsibilities

- Working with our lawyers develop an understanding of legal work and existing processes in order to implement the use of legaltech tools which best meet the requirements of our lawyers and improve our client service delivery.
- Providing an understanding of the legal market and technology trends and investigating new solutions and technologies, to determine how we better tackle the challenges faced by lawyers.

- Developing strong relationships with our lawyers across various practice areas.
- Assisting in designing new methods of delivery using technology, to refine processes which create efficiencies and which deliver against our clients requirements.
- Promoting the use of our existing legaltech to our lawyers and encouraging use.
- Identifying requirements for new legaltech solutions.
- Assisting with the introduction and embedding of new legaltech solutions.
- Coordinating and delivering training, presentations and demonstrations to our lawyers and clients.
- Assisting in the preparation and deliver of pitches to clients.

Skills and Experience

- Ability to problem-solve and design innovative solutions to achieve the desired outcomes.
- Ability to communicate effectively, develop relationships and clearly explain legaltech solutions' benefits accessibly for non-technical experts.
- Strong organisational skills and an ability to manage, prioritise and complete multiple projects.
- Knowledge of technology and IT literate.
- Educated to degree level in a law or computer science discipline or equivalent.
- Legal training.

Key Competencies

Desirable

- Previous legal experience or legal technology experience.
- Experience of and interest in new and emerging technologies.
- Experience using legaltech solutions.

Legal Management Consultant

The candidate will have a degree in law and have a postgraduate qualification in law. We are recruiting for a Legal Management Consultant who will have responsibility for maintenance of the legal database and work as a Data Protection Officer (DPO) for clients.

Key Responsibilities

- Managing the in-house database.
- Analysing new legislation to extract the legal requirements applicable to businesses and presenting them in plain English.
- Supporting clients with the interpretation of specific legal requirements.
- Preparing briefings and updates on legislation.
- Providing DPO services to clients.

Qualifications and Experience

- Minimum 12 months post-qualification practical legal experience.
- Direct experience working with specific practice areas within the business.
- Experience of contract review.

Personal Qualities

- Conscientious.
- Keen attention to detail.
- Works with minimal supervision and takes responsibility.
- Ability to work to and maintain high standards while working under pressure.
- High levels of professionalism.

Legal Automation Consultant

Role

In this role you will provide customer support on how to use the product, resolve issues and create automated legal content. You will need to be able to communicate between the technical and non-technical staff to address clients' questions in a professional manner. You will develop relationships with the clients and provide them with a professional and competent service.

Major Responsibilities

- Develop content for the document assembly solution based on legal documents.
- Create precise designs for automation.
- Support customers with automation and resolve queries.
- Provide help and support designing and developing automated legal templates.
- Deliver customer training on content creation.
- Support internal teams within the business.

Key Skills and Experience

- Good knowledge of information systems.
- Excellent communication skills.
- The ability to work in a fast-paced environment.
- Customer focused.
- Capable of learning, understanding, and communicating higher-level technical information.
- Maintain a positive attitude with the ability to support customers.
- Ensure customer satisfaction and the success of the business.

Desirable Skills and Experience

- Experience with document assembly solutions.
- Experience of working in a legal environment.
- Ability to work with virtual teams to successfully deliver projects.
- Knowledge of project management.
- Problem-solver who is self-motivated and a good team player.

Education

- 2:1 degree in either law or technology.
- Deep knowledge of Microsoft Office technology.

Risk and Compliance Lawyer

The successful candidate will be delivering in-house legal guidance to our clients on regulatory and compliance issues facing financial services, helping clients with change management and regulatory implementation.

Previous experience with developing risk mitigation strategies is required. You will need to work across all parts of the business to identify, manage and report on these risks. You will be involved in drafting, reviewing and implementing mitigation strategies and internal compliance policies.

Requirements

- Excellent academic background.
- At least two years of relevant post-qualification experience in an in-house legal department or law firm.
- Demonstrate deep knowledge of the regulatory and compliance issues in the financial services sector.
- Ability to develop close and positive client relationships.
- Deliver high-quality client service.
- Highly organised and attentive to detail.

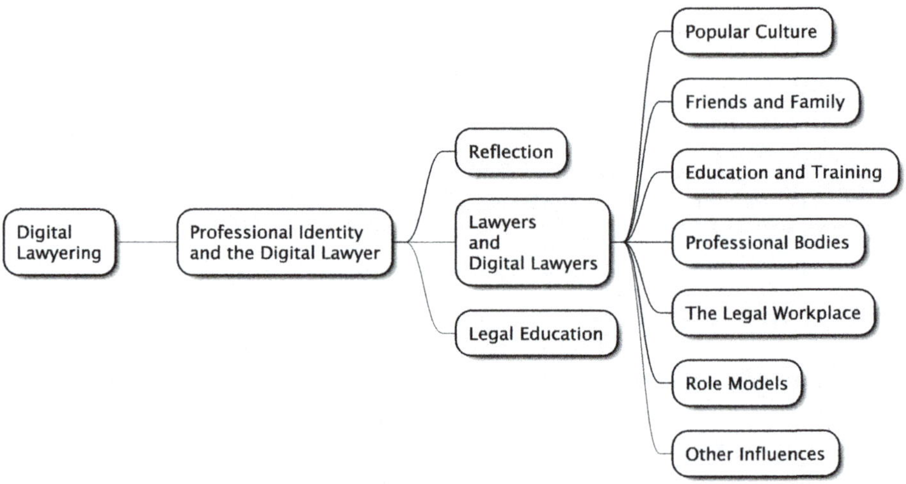

Mind Map 13.1 Chapter topics

13 PROFESSIONAL IDENTITY AND THE DIGITAL LAWYER

Emma Jones

INTRODUCTION

Throughout this chapter there will be an emphasis on you, as the reader, reflecting upon your own professional identity and how this can influence your future career as a digital lawyer. To assist you in this reflective process, this chapter will begin with a brief discussion of what reflection is and why it is so important for all legal professionals.

This chapter will then consider what the term "professional identity" means, and how this idea is currently applied within the legal profession. It will explore the existing tensions around professionalism in the legal profession and discuss how these may translate into the digital environment. It will identify which potential elements could be included in a new form of professional identity for digital lawyers before concluding by discussing the possible implications for the law schools of the future.

Chapter hot spots

When reading this chapter, questions to think about include:

- What is your image of a traditional lawyer?
- What is your image of a digital lawyer?
- If these two images differ, how and why is this?
- What is your professional identity as a law student?

Having read the title and introduction, you can add any other questions you want to explore here:

DOI: 10.4324/9780429298219-13

THE REFLECTIVE PRACTITIONER

> To be prepared to face a myriad of interconnected and complex challenges, twenty-first century legal professionals need a reflective legal education that emphasizes self-assessment and self-efficacy, develops metacognition, supports and diversifies life-long learning, promotes innovative and critical thinking, strengthens legal professionalism, and builds a stronger aptitude for problem-solving and tackling "wicked problems". An increased capacity for individual, critical and collective reflection—beginning in law school—could help to ensure that the legal profession is better equipped to provide responsive leadership in the face of dire predictions of a future of unrelenting and disorienting change.[1]

Reflection is a way to process your thoughts and feelings about an incident or situation. Reflecting upon something gives the opportunity to come to terms with the experience and the actions, responses, thoughts and feelings it has generated. For example, as a student you may receive some critical feedback on an assignment that you initially find confusing ("but I thought I had done that") or upsetting ("I did my best, but it wasn't good enough"). One approach could be to try and put the feedback behind you by putting it out of your mind and moving on to your next piece of work. However, another approach would be to spend some more time thinking about the feedback and your reaction. You may end up realising that some of the criticism was valid and raised points you can work on in future. You may realise your initial confusion was because you had skimmed the feedback comments rather than reading the full detailed explanation. You may end up making an action plan for how you are going to tackle your next piece of work. Each of these potentially positive outcomes would arise from you spending time reflecting upon the original feedback. Doing so could enable you to build on your mark in a subsequent assignment, resulting in more positive comments. It could also assist you in identifying any comments you still felt confused or unsure over, so that you could discuss those with the person who had marked your work.

Reflection is not just important for students; it is valuable in all walks of life. This means it is important for all lawyers, including digital lawyers, to be what is known as a "reflective practitioner".[2] This term

1 Michelle M. Leering, 'Integrated Reflective Practice: A Critical Imperative for Enhancing Legal Education and Professionalism' (2017) 95 *The Canadian Bar Review* 47, 49.

2 Donald A. Schön, *Educating the Reflective Practitioner: Toward a New Design for Teaching and Learning in the Professions* (Jossey-Bass, 1987).

was coined by Donald Schön, a professor who conducted research into the ways in which professionals think. He describes two different kinds of reflection: "Reflection-in-action" and "reflection-on-action". The first of these, reflection-in-action, refers to reflecting during a particular incident or situation. This can result in your adapting your behaviour or approach to deal with the scenario more appropriately. For example, if you are conducting an interview with a new client, you may begin to realise that the client is very emotionally invested in a particular issue, leading them to become agitated and repeat points several times and not answer your questions. Having been focused on listening patiently and building a rapport with your client, you may then wish to become more assertive about redirecting the conversation to move the client on to other topics.

The other form of reflection, reflection-on-action, refers to when you look back over a particular incident or situation to think about how you responded and what you can learn from it. This is the sort of reflection a student can engage in when they receive feedback on their assessments. Taking the example from legal practice discussed above, after your interview with a client you could spend some time thinking over what happened. You may realise that you omitted to set clear ground rules for what the interview would cover at the start and that you missed some indications the client was beginning to get agitated. As a result, you may make a note of ground rules to put in place at the start of interviews in future and resolve to focus more on interpreting the client's reactions to your questions.

One important point to note is that reflection is not just about what you thought or how you acted in a particularly incident or situation. You can also reflect on your emotional responses too. This can help you to become more self-aware and understand your responses better, which in turn can help you to regulate them appropriately in future. Returning to the client interview again, you may have felt yourself becoming cross or upset when the client did not answer your questions. On reflection, you could realise that this is not about the client but about your difficulty with the feeling of being "ignored" which stems from an experience in your past. Alternatively, it may be that you realise what you thought was anger actually stems from worry and concern that you have mishandled the interview and that the client will be unhappy with your approach. All of these realisations could help you to understand and respond appropriately to future emotional reactions and to adjust your approach to similar situations that arise.

This chapter will largely focus upon the idea of reflection-on-action. One way to incorporate this reflective process into your own situation is set out in a learning cycle designed by the educational researcher David Kolb.[3] He identified four stages to work through. The first stage is "concrete experience", where you live through an incident or situation. The second stage is "reflective observation", where you think over what happened and review it. This can involve recalling what happened and how you reacted and felt during it. The third stage is "abstract conceptualisation". This is about learning from your reflections and asking yourself questions such as "Am I happy with my response?" and "Is there anything I could do differently next time?" The final stage is "active experimentation". This involves taking the lessons you learnt and applying them when another appropriate incident or situation arises. Of course, once you do that, you have another "concrete experience" and the whole cycle begins again (Figure 13.1).

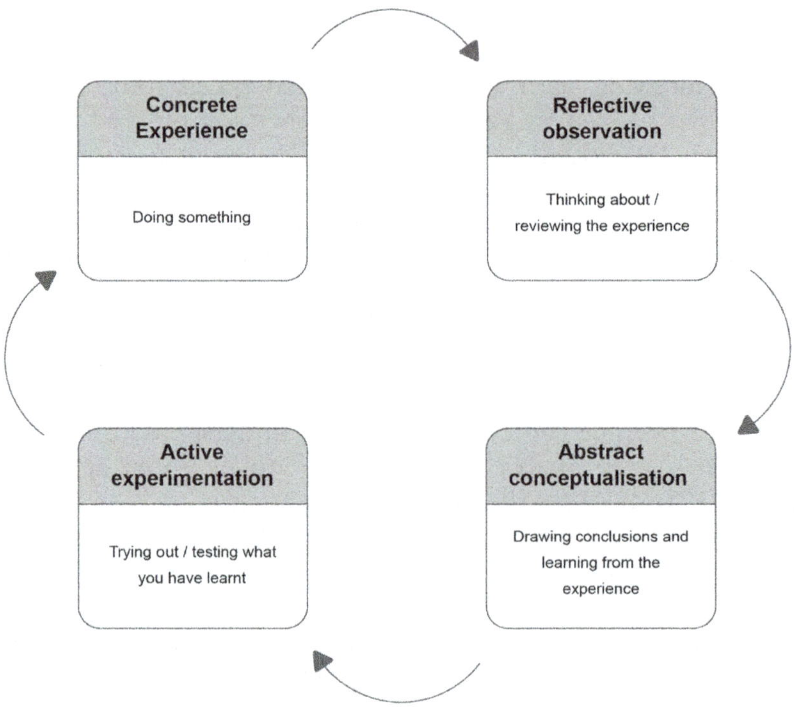

Figure 13.1 Kolb's cycle

3 David A. Kolb, *Experiential Learning: Experience as the Source of Learning and Development* (Vol. 1, Englewood Cliffs, NJ: Prentice-Hall, 1984).

Sync 1: Practising reflection

You should allow around 15 minutes for this activity.

Think of a recent incident or scenario. It could be something that has happened relating to your study or work, or your personal life (e.g. a discussion with your parents, siblings or children). Using this as your "concrete experience", spend some time in "reflective observation" and make some notes about it. Then practice "abstract conceptualisation" and write down at least three learning points you can take from the experience. This could be something you did well, something you would change next time, or anything else you think it useful.

Keep your learning points somewhere safe so that you can refer back to them in a few weeks or months and see if they were helpful when you faced a similar incident or situation.

So far this section has emphasised the importance of individual reflection and suggested that it can be divided into two types. The legal academic Michelle Leering (writing in relation to legal education and legal practice) takes a somewhat different approach.[4] She refers to "reflection-on-practice" (which is similar to Schön's reflection-on-action). However, she suggests this largely focuses on reflecting upon your skills and performance. For example, in Sync 1 you thought about your reactions to a particular incident or scenario.

Leering also argues that there is a need for two other types of reflection. The first of these is "critical reflection". This involves reflecting on, and critiquing, your knowledge and questioning any underlying assumptions. For example, you may assume that digital technology is a huge benefit for the legal profession, but in doing so you could fail to acknowledge the disruption and the change it can bring, and how this may impact the wellbeing of individual legal practitioners. More broadly, you may want to reflect upon the impact of digital lawyering upon society and justice as a whole. The second additional type of reflection which Leering identifies is "self-reflection". This is about reflecting on your values and asking questions about why you are doing certain things and what meaning lies behind them. For example, for

4 Michelle M. Leering, 'Conceptualizing Reflective Practice for Legal Professionals' (2014) 23 *Journal of Law and Social Policy* 83, 94.

some people their interest in digital lawyering is driven by a desire to improve access to justice.

She also emphasises the need for "reflecting in community". In other words, sharing your reflections with others to open up discussions and debates and help you (and others) to develop their thinking further. You may be aware of the old proverb, "Two heads are better than one". This captures the idea that sharing thoughts and reflections can help you take on new perspectives and ideas and reframe your thinking on issues. As digital lawyers often have to work collaboratively with others, often in interdisciplinary teams, this type of reflection can be a valuable way to foster trust and closer relationships with colleagues.

Having considering the importance of reflection, and how to approach reflection, this chapter will now move on to discuss the notion of professional identity. As you work through this chapter, there will be more opportunities to develop and apply your skills of reflection in other Syncs.

THINKING ABOUT PROFESSIONAL IDENTITY

When individuals join a profession, such as the legal profession, it is not just about applying their skills and knowledge in a new environment. At the same time, individuals will also develop a sense of professional identity. This refers to how you see yourself as a professional and how others see you as a professional. Individuals will have ideas about how they think about and see themselves as professionals and how they should appear to others within that particular role. This will then shape the ways in which they think and act within their role (and perhaps more generally in life). In particular, an individual's professional identity will involve certain attributes (characteristics or features), beliefs, values, motives and experiences.[5]

Hilary Sommerlad, a legal academic, conducted an experiment a few years ago where she asked aspiring solicitors in England and Wales who were undertaking the vocational stage of their studies to write and draw what came into their mind when they thought of solicitors.[6] Despite the participants being both male and female and from a range of backgrounds and ethnicities, the figures they drew were all white,

5 Herminia Ibarra, 'Provisional Selves: Experimenting with Image and Identity in Professional Adaptation' (1999) 44 *Administrative Science Quarterly* 764, 765.

6 Hilary Sommerlad, 'Researching and Theorising the Process of Professional Identity Formation' (2007) 34 (2) *Journal of Law and Society* 190.

mostly male corporate lawyers—wealthy and powerful. This suggests that the participants had a particular view of solicitors in their mind. Given this view, it seems likely that a number of them would seek to adopt some of the attributes, beliefs, values, motives and experiences they viewed these figures as possessing (although some did indicate they wished to challenge these stereotypes).

This experiment also shows that professional identity begins to be shaped before an individual actually enters a profession. Factors contributing to these ideas about professional identity for traditional lawyers could include (Figure 13.2):

Figure 13.2 Factors influencing professional identity

- *Legal education.* The time people spend at law school is often described as an important part of their professional identity formation.[7] Law students will absorb messages about the law and lawyers

7 See, for example, Susan L. Brooks, 'Fostering Wholehearted Lawyers: Practical Guidance for Supporting Law Students' Professional Identity Formation' (2018) 14 *University of St Thomas Law Journal* 412.

throughout their studies. Some of these may be expressly taught to them (e.g. if they undertake a course on professional ethics). However, other messages will be hidden (knowingly or unknowingly) in the ways law is taught and discussed more generally. For example, law students may discover displaying an emotional reaction to a case they are studying is often frowned upon in the classroom. Instead, they are expected to suppress their emotional response and instead focus on a legal analysis of the principles involved.

- *Professional bodies.* Most, if not all, parts of the legal profession will be regulated and/or represented by one or more professional bodies. Regulation refers to a body having powers to grant or refuse entry into the profession, set the standards required within the profession and discipline individuals or organisations which fall below those standards. Representation refers to supporting, protecting and advocating for the rights of a particular part of the legal profession. For example, solicitors in England and Wales are regulated by the Solicitor Regulation Authority and represented by the Law Society of England and Wales. In the United States, each state has its own body known as a bar association. In some states these both regulate and represent lawyers. In others, they may just represent lawyers. The American Bar Association is also a national association, with voluntary membership, which represents lawyers. Similarly, in Australia, different territories have their own bodies, but there are nationwide bodies such as the Law Council of Australia (who represents solicitors).

  An important part of the work of regulatory bodies is to set the standards required of legal professionals. This usually involves a code of conduct, or similar, setting out the ethical rules governing the work of members. For example, most will contain a provision around "conflict of interest", stating that you cannot represent a client if you already work for a client who has a potentially conflicting interest, such as a buyer and seller of a particular property. Chapter 5 included a range of examples of codes of conduct dealing with the use of social media. These codes will help determine how individuals behave and act within legal practice, assisting in forming their professional identity.

  It is likely that professional bodies will also contribute to professional identity formation in other ways; for example, by holding workshops, discussions and webinars on specific topics, by showcasing the work of specific organisations or individuals and by setting the agenda for debate on key topics within legal practice.

- *The legal workplace.* There is evidence that a lawyer's professional identity will be significantly influenced by their workplace.[8] Each individual workplace is likely to have its own working practices and culture—a set of ways of working and behaving—which a new joiner will be expected to adhere to in order to fit in. It has been identified that there are certain aspects of culture which are common in many law firms and other organisations, including a competitive atmosphere and an emphasis on long working hours.[9]

  In a traditional law firm, it is likely that the partners who lead the firm will have a significant influence on the working practices and culture within it. This may be by having express policies and rules on various issues (e.g. not using the Internet for personal purposes) but also by the ways in which they behave (for example, not leaving the office until 9 pm). However, it is also likely that the behaviour and attitudes of those you work most closely with, such as your line manager, will also influence your professional identity. In other legal settings (e.g. barristers' chambers, which are groups of self-employed barristers who work together), the approach of colleagues is likely to be even more influential.
- *Popular culture.* From watching *Suits* on television to reading John Grisham books and following law firms on social media, lawyers are often portrayed in popular culture using a range of stereotypes; for example, as somewhat dull and bland individuals with no sense of humour surrounded by piles of old law books, or as rich, successful and glamorous people working in the corporate world, or as passionate campaigners fighting for a specific cause.
- *Role models.* If you have friends or family members in the legal profession, you are likely to have developed some of your ideas around professional identity through speaking to and observing them. However, you may also have had a range of other role models, from a lawyer in your local town to a legal author whose work you find inspiring to a professor at law school who you admire.

8 See, for example, Vivien Holmes, Tony Foley, Stephen Tang and Margie Rowe, 'Practising Professionalism: Observations from an Empirical Study of New Australian Lawyers' (2012) 15 (1) *Legal Ethics* 29.

9 Emma Jones, Neil Graffin, Rajvinder Samra and Mathijs Lucassen, *Mental Health and Wellbeing in the Legal Profession* (Bristol, Bristol University Press, 2020).

By contributing to peoples' ideas around professional identity, these factors also help shape what is seen as "professionalism"—in other words, the conduct, behaviour and attributes that are viewed as part of being a professional. However, it is important to be aware there are also other broader factors that contribute to notions of professional identity and professionalism. This includes the range of factors identified in Chapter 2 as impacting upon the legal profession more generally. For example, Chapter 2 referred to the marketisation of the legal profession with a move towards seeing practising law as less of a public service and more as a form of business. This could contribute towards lawyers seeing viewing themselves as business people rather than as public servants, potentially encouraging them to measure their success more in terms of chargeable hours rather than whether they have helped someone.

In fact, there have long been tensions between different, often seemingly opposing, visions of lawyers. For example, in the novel *Bleak House*, author Charles Dickens portrays the legal profession as greedy and grasping, using their knowledge of the law purely for financial gain.[10] However, some contemporary authors such as the academic Anthony Kronman have argued that previous generations of lawyers were focused upon the acquisition of understanding and insights into human nature.[11] Other authors, such as the UK legal academic Donald Nicolson, argue that a return is needed to an emphasis on a passion for justice and a desire to contribute to promoting the ideals which follow from this.[12]

The next sync gives you an opportunity to think about your perceptions of a lawyer and also to consider what the professional identity of a digital lawyer in particular might involve.

Sync 2: Who are "lawyers" and "digital lawyers"?

You should allow around 30 minutes for this activity

This activity is based on Sommerlad's experiment (described earlier). You need to draw two pictures:

- A traditional lawyer.
- A digital lawyer.

10 Charles Dickens, *Bleak House* (London, Bradbury and Evans, 1853).

11 Anthony T. Kronman, *The Lost Lawyer: Failing Ideals of the Legal Profession* (Cambridge, MA, Harvard University Press, 1993).

12 Donald Nicolson, 'Calling, Character and Clinical Legal Education: A Cradle-to-Grave Approach to Inculcating a Love for Justice' (2013) 16 (1) *Legal Ethics* 36.

Next to both images, write five words or phrases to describe the person you have drawn.

When you have finished, spend some time thinking about the following questions:

- Are either or both of your images similar to the description of the images in the Sommerlad experiment?
- What factors influenced your images and choice of descriptions?
- Do your two images and descriptions differ? If so, in what ways and why?

You may have come up with a range of drawings and descriptions, based on your personal experiences (and perhaps even some of the content of this textbook!). You may have felt it was artificial to make a distinction between "lawyers" and "digital lawyers" because virtually all legal professionals today use digital technology in some form. Alternatively, you may have felt that a digital lawyer is likely to be quite different than a traditional lawyer. In the next section, we will consider the potential differences between a traditional lawyer and digital lawyer and what elements may form part of a digital lawyer's professional identity.

THE DIGITAL LAWYER AND PROFESSIONAL IDENTITY

In the previous section we considered a range of factors which could influence the professional identity of a traditional lawyer. Each of these is also likely to impact on the professional identity of a digital lawyer, but within these there may be significant differences.

- *Legal education.* A digital lawyer may have undertaken a traditional form of legal education, but they may also have taken other routes into the legal profession; for example, by starting out with a first degree in computer science or digital and technology solutions. In England and Wales, the introduction of the Solicitors Qualifying Examination means that individuals can take two examinations to become a solicitor regardless of what degree they have previously studied, potentially making alternative routes more likely.

Even if a digital lawyer has studied a law degree, they may well have chosen options focused on digital technology. These could be specifically on digital lawyering; for example, Monash University in Australia has a unit titled Legal Tech Studio, where students work with industry experts to design solutions to real-life business and legal issues.[13] In the United States, the Legal Design Lab at Stanford Law School and d.school encourages law students to design and build a wide variety of legal services and products,[14] including a new online platform to provide help for individuals facing eviction or other landlord-tenant issues.[15]

Alternatively, or in addition, digital lawyers may have focused on modules looking at the ways in which the law regulates different types of technology (e.g. the Internet) or the implications for traditional areas of law (e.g. intellectual property). An increasing number of law schools also offer either extracurricular activities involving technology for students to undertake; for example, the University of Sheffield (UK) offers an optional certificate in legal technology. Sometimes this type of activity is linked to clinical legal education, such as The Open University's Digital Justice project, in which students design and create apps and chatbots capable of providing legal information on specific topics to the general public.[16]

- *Professional bodies.* Digital lawyers may be required to be members of particular legal bodies, depending upon which role they have within the legal profession. However, they may also be involved in a range of different bodies which give them different perspectives and networks. For example, the Society of Computers and Law[17] offers a range of events and special interest groups, and the UK organisation

13 Monash University, 'Legal Tech Studio' <https://www.monash.edu/study/courses/find-a-course/2021/legal-tech-studio-pdl1031> accessed 12 April 2021.

14 Legal Design Lab, 'Stanford Legal Design Lab' <https://www.legaltechdesign.com/> accessed 12 April 2021.

15 Legal Design Lab, 'Legal FAQ' <https://legalfaq.org/> accessed 12 April 2021.

16 The Open University, 'Digital Justice' <https://www.open.ac.uk/open-justice/public-understanding-law/digital-justice> accessed 15 April 2021.

17 <https://www.scl.org/society>

BIMA is open to anyone working within digital, tech and creative industries.[18]

- *The legal workplace.* Digital lawyers may work in more innovative and cutting-edge environments which have the resources and the dynamism to embrace new ways of working and practising law. Chapter 2 referred to the growth of alternative business structures and NewLaw, all of which are closely related to technological developments. These challenge many traditional elements of the legal workplace; for example, how often would such a law firm have a secretary? It is quite possible a form of virtual assistant may well become more prevalent to reflect the norms of work in lawtech. It is also possible that more interdisciplinary, collaborative and design-led approaches will be integrated into the work of digital lawyering and that this will be reflected in the professional identity of individuals. For example, a digital lawyer may not relate to the hierarchical structure of traditional law firms. Instead of measuring success in terms of promotion to partner or having a secretary working for them, they may use alternative measures such as the prestige of the organisations they have worked in partnership with and the ways in which they have innovated within a particular sector.
- *Popular culture.* Images of people working in digital technology are often different from the ways in which members of the legal profession are depicted. If a digital lawyer views themselves more as a technologist or an entrepreneur than a legal professional, they may identify more with these images and attempt to align themselves with them. This could be a deliberate attempt to remove themselves from images of lawyers as perhaps rather bland or boring and/or perhaps part of an attempt to market themselves to potential clients as someone who is at the cutting edge of digital lawyering.
- *Role models.* Following on from the ideas of digital technology in popular culture, rather than identifying with a partner in a law firm or a judge as a potential role model, a digital lawyer may have different role models. This could be figures such as Richard Susskind or Elon Musk (to take two quite different examples!) or other individuals working within the fields of technology and law. This may influence their behaviour and approach to their role and their career aspirations.

18 <https://bima.co.uk/>

Sync 3: Other influences on the digital lawyer

You should allow around 10 minutes for this activity.

What other influences do you think may influence the professional identity of the digital lawyer? You may draw on your own experiences, or those of others around you, as well as any reading and research you have previously conducted.

You may have thought of a range of influences. You may have also identified that these influences will probably vary significantly between individuals depending upon their role within the workplace, experience, interests and background. One idea could include experience within non-legal workplaces; for example, an individual could have used their digital skills within a different profession or as an entrepreneur before moving into law. This could mean that they are used to different professional standards and norms around issues such as confidentiality and privacy. They may find it challenging or even frustrating to adapt to a legal environment, which has traditionally been viewed as highly regulated and potentially as stifling to creativity. They may see themselves as an entrepreneur or innovator rather than predominantly as a legal professional (although as discussed in previous chapters, the two are not mutually exclusive!). It is also interesting to consider what values these individuals may hold. Are they motivated by a passion for justice, a desire for profit or perhaps something else; for example, a love of technology and a belief in its transformative potential?

The client role in shaping identity

When thinking about the professional identity of both lawyers and digital lawyers, it is important to acknowledge the role that clients can play in shaping this. In fact, this could be existing clients or even potential clients which an individual or firm are seeking to attract. This can affect people's professional identity in a range of ways, from altering your dress (e.g. feeling obliged to wear a suit when meeting with a corporate client) to seeking to align yourself with a large client's values and motivation.

It is important for a legal professional to consider who they are working with and to what extent they are willing or able to adjust some of their professional attributes to work with those clients. Sometimes this may involve assessing whether you feel ethically and morally comfortable with what you are being asked to do. At other times, it may simply be a case of ensuring that you put strict lawyer-client boundaries in place from the start of your relationship. What is crucial is that you are aware of how such relationships can impact on your professional identity and professionalism.

LEGAL EDUCATION AND DIGITAL LAWYERING

THE ROLE OF LEGAL EDUCATION

> A legal educator's duty goes beyond teaching the law and shaping analytical minds; one additional responsibility is to model behavior desired in the profession.[19]

The term "legal education" is in fact very broad. It encompasses topics such as citizenship in schools and colleges, as well as the more formal academic and vocational training that law schools commonly offer. To some extent, the purpose of legal education will vary depending on what type we are referring to. Within law schools there often exist tensions over whether the law degree should be viewed as purely intellectual or as vocational in nature (in other words, the start of preparing students for life as a lawyer). Different jurisdictions and law schools take a variety of approaches to this; for example, in the United States the law degree is postgraduate and therefore more commonly associated with forms of vocational training. In jurisdictions where the law degree is undergraduate, such as the UK and Australia, there has traditionally been a tendency to focus more on purely intellectual development. However, many law schools aim for some combination of the two approaches. Given the growing recognition and emphasis on employability skills in higher education (as discussed in Chapter 11), there is also arguably increasing pressure on law schools to at least acknowledge the requirements of the legal workplace. Whether or not this is the right approach is heavily debated in law schools, particularly given that not all law students want (or are given the opportunity) to pursue a legal career. However, the reality is that most law schools and law degrees will try—at least to some extent—to prepare or shape students for legal practice.

19 Christine Cerniglia Brown, 'Professional Identity Formation: Working Backwards to Move the Profession Forward' (2015) 61 *Loyola Law Review* 313, 314.

This means that notions of professional identity and professionalism do form a part of legal education within law schools. Sometimes this may be through specific modules on topics to do with lawyering, digital lawyering or legal practice. At other times, it may be through extracurricular activities to do with employability, such as talks from local law firms and help preparing for job interviews. Even if the law school is not actively trying to take such steps, it is arguable that students will absorb ideas about professional identity and professionalism in any event (as demonstrated by Sommerlad's experiment). This may be through their reading and research, participating in clinical legal education, interacting with fellow students who aspire to become lawyers or by observing and absorbing ways of behaving from staff. Staff who have themselves worked in the legal profession may well have become used to doing things or acting in certain ways which are the norm within the profession. They are therefore likely to demonstrate this in their teaching and interactions with students.

Sync 4: Your experience of law school

You should allow around 15 minutes for this activity.

Reflect on your own experience of law school and think about the following questions:

- What was your "professional identity" as a student?
- To what extent is your law degree preparing you to become a member of the legal profession?
- To what extent (if any) is your law degree preparing you to become a digital lawyer?

If you are not studying law, you can still think about these questions, as it might well be that your degree has given you valuable transferable skills and knowledge. Alternatively, you may want to compare your studies with what you have learnt about legal studies in this textbook: How similar do you think your study experience is to that of a law student?

Thinking about your professional identity as a law student can help you identify elements which you are likely to take forward into the legal profession. It can also help you understand what has influenced your perceptions of law, the legal profession and digital lawyering to date.

Although being a student is not commonly referred to as a "profession", when people begin law school they are likely to develop a new identity. This will partly be shaped by the fact that they are transitioning into higher education and a new phase of their life. However, it is also likely to be influenced by the fact they have specifically chosen to study law, and whether or not they aspire to enter the legal profession. When thinking about your professional identity as a law student, you may have felt that as a student you have more freedom than a legal professional with a greater focus on socialising and having fun. Alternatively, maybe your focus was on your intellectual development and ensuring you absorb as much knowledge and learning as possible. Another option is that you may have felt that you were using your studies to prepare you for the workplace and to develop the types of characteristics (e.g. being conscientious and reliable) that you are likely to need to display in a working environment. Perhaps you thought of some combination of the three, or something else entirely! Figure 13.3 identifies some of the potential influences that could shape the professional identity of a law student and their journey onwards into the legal profession.

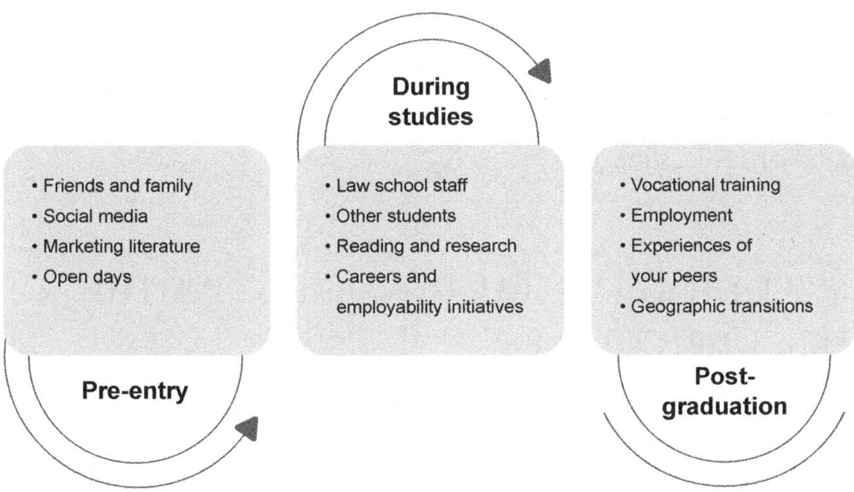

Figure 13.3 Factors influencing the identity of a law student

Just as you probably had ideas about the legal profession before studying law, you are also likely to have had some ideas about what being a law student was likely to entail. This may have been from your family and friends, social media (e.g. following students or universities on Instagram or joining relevant Facebook groups) or from your initial contact with law schools on open days or through their prospectuses. It may also be that you had previously studied law at school or college as well. As discussed previously, once you begin law school, that is when it is likely that staff, students and your study experience will begin to impact on your ideas. After graduation, it is likely that further training, the experience of your fellow graduates and your subsequent employment will change and develop your professional identity, so you move away from seeing yourself as a student and begin to see yourself as a professional. Often students have moved for university and end up moving again for work; this type of physical move can also have a psychological impact in distancing yourself from aspects of your previous identity.

When answering Sync 4, you may have found that your law degree focused more on preparing you for the legal profession generally, but not so much for digital lawyering in particular. This probably reflects the background and interests of the staff within your law school, which in turn shapes the curriculum that is offered. It may also be a result of the constraints on resources (both in terms of finance and time) that all universities have to face. However, it is likely that the current focus will change over the next few years as an acknowledgement of digital lawyering becomes increasingly common. It will be interesting to see whether this impacts upon the professional identity of law students and whether they begin to view themselves in new ways, for example, as digital citizens or innovators.

EMBEDDING DIGITAL LAWYERING WITHIN THE CURRICULUM

Preparing law students to participate and contribute to legal practice in the digital age will require an awareness of the application of law in a digitally networked society and digital living and practices. As such, it is likely that the study of how law interacts with technology, the breadth of technological influence on the law and gaps in the application of current laws on technology will increasingly become an important part of the curriculum. The ways in which this happens are likely to differ between law schools and jurisdictions. The following are some examples of how this could happen, drawing upon some commonly taught subjects from the law degree.

LEGAL SYSTEMS

A law degree will introduce you to the legal system of the jurisdiction in which you are studying and will often also encourage you to compare and contrast this with other legal systems. Some ways in which digital lawyering may be incorporated include:

- Questioning the current interpretations of various pieces of existing laws for application in a digital landscape; for example, the impact of social media on regulations around reporting upon court cases.
- Discussing the adequacy of public policy in regulating the digital world; for example, the application of the Universal Declaration of Human Rights and the European Convention on Human Rights.
- Identifying gaps where there is a need for the development of new legal doctrine as a result of developments in technology; for example, the increased collection by the state of biometric data (such as fingerprints and facial images).
- Developing a detailed understanding of the relationship between ethics, law, technology, and public policy and questioning the doctrine of justice when administered online.

CONTRACT LAW

A law degree will usually cover the law of obligations as a fundamental element required for the smooth running of society. Some ways in which digital lawyering may be incorporated include:

- Considering the functionality and impact of blockchain technology, its affordances across a wide variety of industries and its formation of smart contracts (as discussed in Chapter 10).
- Encouraging a deep understanding of smart contracts and how and when they operate, including the differences between traditional contracts and smart contracts.
- Raising awareness of the multi-jurisdictional locality of blockchains giving rise to complex jurisdictional issues.
- Determining the difference in contractual relationships, legal certainty, applicable laws, rights and obligations between smart contracts and traditional contracts.
- Understanding how blockchain commands operate and leave room for errors and omissions.

CRIMINAL LAW AND EVIDENCE

Criminal law is seen as essential for regulating the relationship between individuals and society and is therefore a key component of law degrees. The law of evidence is also critical in legal practice, although it is perhaps less frequently studied at the undergraduate level. Some ways in which digital lawyering may be incorporated include:

- Developing an appreciation for the multidisciplinary components which make up the subject area, such as components of law, criminology, ethics and forensics.
- Discussing the ways in which the rapid advancement of technologies is changing the types of crimes to be investigated, the ways in which evidence is collected and disclosed, and the ways of working in the law enforcement and criminal justice services.
- Exploring the challenges to the rule of law and the limitations on jurisdictional application of the law given that online crimes lack physical and geographical borders.
- Considering how law enforcers manage our obligations under the new data protection directives for the police, balancing the rights and freedoms of the public whilst protecting them, along with issues such as the use of algorithms and artificial intelligence and its ethical impact on decision-making in law enforcement.
- Identifying that because all activities online have a digital trail, digital evidence features prominently in many investigations.
- Encouraging a detailed understanding of how technologies have been used to determine evidence; for example, a case heard in the United States where the prosecution requested and obtained access to a conversation at home recorded by Alexa on Amazon Echo. This offers an introduction to the legal and technical aspects of digital forensic investigation, including techniques of extracting, preserving and analysing digital evidence retrieval via digital footprints. It balances the study of computing science with legal issues such as cross-border location, accessibility and relevance of material to better prepare students to handle evidence in digital form when in practice.
- Understanding the role of digital evidence in court processes. Evaluating theoretical principles of admissibility of evidence and how these principles apply to digital evidence, how digital evidence is used in trial, methods of extracting and handling of evidence using admissible methods for use in court, the significance and use of the metadata contained in digital evidence and the methods of recovering deleted evidences via a digital trail.

- Considering broader issues also raise awareness of how evidence can be collected across jurisdictions and the transfer of evidence between different jurisdictions.

Sync 5: Design your own curriculum

You should allow around 60 minutes for this activity.

Imagine you are a member of staff at a law school who wants to design a curriculum which incorporates digital lawyering. Using the preceding examples for inspiration, pick three existing subjects commonly found within the law school curriculum; for each one, write down at least five ways in which you could integrate digital lawyering.

If you are struggling to think of a subject, you could choose from tort law, family law, public law, land law and equity, and trusts.

The ways that you choose could relate to the content of the module and identifying topics and issues that relate to digital technologies. They could also be related to the way in which the module is taught, using digital technologies to enhance its delivery.

You may have identified a wide range of ideas. If you are currently studying any of these modules, perhaps you could share your ideas with your tutor or the module convenor.

Other examples of aspects of legal education which can be used (and already are) to integrate digital technologies with the law degree include:

- *Skills and legal education.* Chapter 11 highlighted that law schools today do not just focus on legal knowledge; they also emphasise the importance of developing a range of skills, including employability skills. Throughout this textbook we have highlighted a range of skills which can be developed during your legal education and which are valuable skills to apply to legal practice and digital lawyering. These were drawn together into some key themes in Chapter 12.
- *Clinical legal education.* An important aspect of legal education which affords significant opportunities to encourage the incorporation and discussion of digital technologies is clinical legal education, whether this is through using online case management systems, communicating with clients remotely, or using technology

to organise documents and information and conduct research. Various examples have been given throughout this textbook, and these are likely to become more common in the next few years.

The COVID-19 pandemic has also required law schools (and universities more widely) to think about the role of technology within their provision. Just as law firms shifted to remote working, legal studies were also moved online. This provided new challenges in terms of students and staff learning to use different forms of technology quickly, ensuring individuals had access to the equipment and Wi-Fi to participate, and thinking about the best ways to facilitate learning remotely. However, it has also brought new opportunities; for example, instead of sitting in a crowded lecture theatre, students were able to access pre-recorded lectures at a time of their choosing, listening and taking notes at their own pace. The ways in which both students and staff have been forced to upskill and adapt could have significant long-term consequences for legal education and accelerate shifts towards a focus on digital technologies and digital lawyering.

Thinking like a lawyer

The term "thinking like a lawyer" is commonly used to describe the types of thinking that students are introduced to within law school. This is sometimes referred to as a process of socialisation—in other words, familiarising students with the culture and attitudes that commonly exist within law and the legal profession. It has often been associated with a very rigid form of legal analysis,[20] the type of analysis you often see applied in problem-style questions during assessments.

The discussion of skills which runs throughout this textbook has demonstrated that the lawyers of the future will need a broad range of skills to not only survive but also thrive in the digital world. Although thinking like a lawyer will always have a place, it is increasingly being recognised as just one element of the skill set needed to practice law successfully. The types of changes that are and will occur within the law school curriculum are likely to begin to challenge the concept of thinking like a lawyer so that it will widen (e.g. to include the forms

20 Colin James, 'Lawyers' Wellbeing and Professional Legal Education' (2008) 42 (1) *The Law Teacher* 85–97.

of technical knowledge referred to in Chapter 3 and the types of soft skills referred to in Chapter 11). Alternatively, it may wither away to be replaced by a new notion of "thinking like a digital lawyer".

Sync 6: Thinking like a digital lawyer

You should allow around 20 minutes for this activity.

Drawing on your reading of this textbook and your wider reading and research, write a brief summary of:

- Your definition of digital lawyering.
- Your explanation of what "thinking like a digital lawyer" would entail.

Hopefully, Sync 6 will help you to draw together some of the ideas and themes you have identified as you have worked through this textbook. In the next chapter, as authors, we will explain our own understanding of these. Your answers can also form part of the reflective process, as you can continue to develop and enhance your understanding and insight as you continue to learn more about digital lawyering.

CONCLUSION: FUTURE IDENTITIES

Professional identity is important. It shapes how we behave, act and even think within the workplace. It can also affect our personal lives, as few people can entirely compartmentalise their work and home personalities and attitudes. Professional identity is formed by a range of factors and shapes the notions of professionalism which become accepted (and largely complied with) throughout the profession.

Within law, professional identity begins to be shaped even before a student enters law school. Their legal studies are likely to have a significant influence upon this. Once they enter the legal workplace (assuming they choose to do so), their professional identity will also continue to develop and evolve, depending upon their roles, workplaces and experiences.

The changes and shifts within the legal profession caused or influenced by the development of digital technologies will impact on the professional identity of both law students and lawyers. They will challenge some long-held assumptions and norms within the legal profession and require new skills and ways of thinking. The traditional notion of thinking like a lawyer will no longer be fit for purpose, and both legal education and the legal profession will need to adapt and evolve to exploit the new opportunities offered.

ADDITIONAL RESOURCES

- For a discussion on the ethical identity of law students, see Moorhead R, Denvir C, Cahill-O'Callaghan R, Kouchaki M and Galoob S, "The Ethical Identity of Law Students" (2016) 23 (3) *International Journal of the Legal Profession* 235–75.
- For a discussion of professional identity among US law students and lawyers, see <https://thepractice.law.harvard.edu/article/the-professional-identity-formation-of-lawyers/>
- For an influential report on lawyering and professionalism in the United States, see <http://archive.carnegiefoundation.org/professional_graduate_education/legal-education-study.html>
- For a consideration of the role of technology in clinical legal education, see Noone MA, "Innovation and Disruption: Exploring the Potential of Clinical Legal Education" (2020) 27 (3) *International Journal of Clinical Legal Education*.

14 CONCLUSION

SHAPING THE FUTURE OF DIGITAL LAWYERING

Emma Jones, Francine Ryan, Ann Thanaraj and Terry Wong

INTRODUCTION

This chapter concludes our exploration of digital lawyering in the 21st century. It begins by drawing out key themes that have emerged through the previous chapters within this textbook. These include the concept of the digital lawyer; technology, innovation and regulation; ethics and conduct; challenges and critiques; and skills and opportunities. Drawing upon these themes, it then moves on to consider what the future of digital lawyering might look like. To do so, each author takes one theme (digital lawyering and the legal profession, the effects of technology development and innovation, dispute resolution and ethics, and legal education and skills) and considers what the position may be 30 years into the future.

Based on your reading of this textbook, we hope that you will feel able to critique these visions of the future, and the themes they draw upon, by applying your own knowledge and understanding. Have we missed any key themes? Are the views of the future we present realistic, or overly optimistic or pessimistic? What challenges and opportunities do these ideas present? As a potential digital lawyer of the future, this is an opportunity for you to develop your skills of evaluation and critical thinking as you work through this chapter.

KEY THEMES IN DIGITAL LAWYERING

THE CONCEPT OF A DIGITAL LAWYER

The digital lawyer is a digitally fluent professional thriving in their legal practice. They flourish in a professional environment that is a hybrid of

DOI: 10.4324/9780429298219-14

face-to-face and online setting, using various digital solutions to communicate in compelling ways and engaging with clients seamlessly using tools that have the most impact. They will be working with a wide spectrum of individuals, drawing on interdisciplinary knowledge and methodologies. To do this will require a lifelong commitment to one's own professional and personal development and reflection, and evolving their mindset, skills, and knowledge as digital solutions develop in fast-paced environments. Although other professions, industries and sectors are also changing and adapting to the technological revolution, the ongoing transformation of the legal profession is arguably particularly radical, reshaping existing roles, careers, ways of working and even fundamental notions of professional identity and professionalism. This textbook has included considerations around how these roles are changing due to the advancement of technologies in the profession and also of the types of new roles being developed within it. At the heart of this change is the question of how the study of law and digital literacies and fluencies can be merged to create dynamic roles to serve clients.

A digital lawyer has a unique ability to thrive in the changing workplace, particularly in the legal profession, with agility, creativity, confidence and adaptability. This enables them to learn and utilise new technologies and to work in ways which are augmented by technology and legal expertise. They need to be equipped with a foundational understanding of some of the complex and disruptive changes brought about by technologically mediated practices, and their impact in the current and fast-developing future of legal practice. To do this, they will need to use a blend of legal knowledge and interdisciplinary knowledge and methodologies beyond the components of subjects and modules that make up a traditional law degree to flourish in legal practice. The digital lawyer will need to be prepared with an understanding of the art and science of lawyering and the needs of legal practice but should also have a focus upon the digital transformation of practice, delivery and user experience.

The fluency of the digital lawyer is captured through their deep understanding of core technologies, their features and functionalities, how they are being utilised and the impact of these technologies on the role of legal professionals. A second dimension of digital lawyering lies in understanding the gaps in the profession and the opportunities to merge law with technology towards creating hybrid professions within the legal sector. A third dimension is in exploring the limitations and gaps in legislation and how these can be interpreted more broadly to capture the physical and digital worlds and the intersection between technology, law and society. With a need for horizon scanning, a digital lawyer will be expected to become aware of the current and emerging trends in the delivery of legal services and how to use the new technologies required to meet those demands through the use of appropriate, safe, and effective digital technological innovations and techniques for delivering legal services. This will also require being self-aware through online collaboration with clients, peers, instructors, and other professionals, developing judgement skills and professional responsibility and evaluating professional identity and values, including an examination of one's own personal standpoint when delivering services online.

Digital lawyers are also leaders, equipped with the leadership needed to shape the conversation around regulating in the digital age, using new and existing laws and the notion of the rule of law to shape the (digital) transformation of social, economic, democratic, political and ethical structures which are being reimagined in the landscape of the Fourth Industrial Revolution. Drawing on solid legal knowledge, a digital lawyer frames the discussion of technologies, innovation and law around use and impact in legal services, grounded in one's values, ethics and professional responsibilities in a rapidly evolving legal profession and practice.

Success as a digital lawyer, or any digitally proficient professional, is less about the technology itself and more about understanding what technology works best in a given situation and how to optimise and use it within that situation. This means that the digitally proficient lawyer understands a legal or business problem, can appreciate the transcending boundaries of their client's problem across the physical and digital worlds, and has innovative ideas about how to solve it through the medium of technological tools and solutions where appropriate. This is where old legal problems can be approached in new ways by working out which tasks are repetitive or time-intensive, which require express legal knowledge, and which are most important to the client. A digital lawyer embraces lifelong and continual learning, which is absolutely necessary in today's fast-paced world to develop a new and improved understanding of the benefits and limitations of particular technologies and an appreciation for a digitally networked environment.

TECHNOLOGY, INNOVATION AND REGULATION

In this book, we have offered an introduction to the foundations of modern computing technology in Chapter 3. In subsequent chapters we have illustrated the role of networks, Big Data, analytics, machine learning and artificial intelligence (AI), as well as emerging distributed ledger applications on blockchain technology (Chapters 6, 7, 8 and 10). Each of these technologies presents significant, even transformative opportunities to clients and the lawyers who advise them.

The digital lawyer faces three challenges with respect to technology:

1 *Technology itself.* With many varied branches of practice, technology is complicated, jargon-filled, and apparently arcane and unusable for the average person. New technologies often require new ways of use, compel new ways to relate to technology and in some cases, present challenges to safety and privacy. A lawyer, bearing an already great cognitive load in meeting the tasks of understanding rules and regulations, drafting documents and navigating the vagaries of human interaction, might find reason to question the utility or relevance of most technology and technology-related learning to the daily practice of law. We hope that we have demonstrated the connections to legal practice and the advantages that can be realised within this textbook.
2 *Rapid innovation.* The change and evolution of technology continues to accelerate, rendering many tools and ways of working increasingly dated, if not obsolete. Significant shocks such as the COVID-19 pandemic forced many to accept and apply many technologies long avoided by the legal profession, such as video conferencing and other remote working technologies, with astonishing rapidity. Before the pandemic, the attitude was one of "wait and see", if not of deep reservation or outright rejection. Continued acceleration of change is an inescapable reality against which we have offered the reader some techniques for understanding and formulating personal and professional strategies.
3 *Regulation.* New technologies and new applications bring new uses. As we have seen with distributed ledger applications using blockchain, such as cryptocurrencies, non-fungible tokens and smart contracts, new applications raise many questions in real life. The legality of certain transactions, the concrete conception of smart contracts under the law, their enforceability, and the validity of exchange conducted with them are all questions we have examined. We have highlighted areas of development in the law as well as resources for understanding. We encourage a sort of legal agility akin to agile technology practice, in which collaborating teams

observe systems in action and adjust their tactics in an iterative fashion, based on experimentation and interpretation of new information.

Staying abreast of technological developments need not mean abandoning the lawyer's calling for one of a technologist or data scientist, but rather following developments with healthy curiosity, basing one's views on emerging evidence as the technology is adopted and used in real-world applications. It means engaging and relying on the help of technology specialists to understand the opportunities and risks, all the while asking hard questions in the interest of the client or of one's own practice. As with all lawyerly pursuits, good relationships and open, mutually respectful dialogue in pursuit of facts and acceptable options will serve one well in learning and problem-solving.

While technologies can support trust, they cannot necessarily prevent breaches of privacy in highly complex modern systems, regardless of the care put into their engineering and implementation. This reality exists because such systems are built by humans with limitations, often labouring under conditions where scope, schedule and budget are traded off in a sometimes blind calculus of economic viability. Operating with technology will always involve three forces, each in a state of tension and yet complementary to the others: Innovation, risk management and continuous improvement. It is said that lawyers are trained first and foremost in risk management, but that they do better when they also support innovators by questioning and examining shortcomings in improvement activities, even as they serve as a line of defence in risk management.

The legal profession has until recently been slow to adopt technologies, though it has at times appeared keen, rightly or wrongly, to call itself the "legal industry" despite (in a sweeping generalisation) casting itself in many settings as an individual craft, holding up the superiority and excellence of the individual legal mind over "mere machines" in sometimes self-limiting expressions of legal professional exceptionalism. While we do not debate the merits of this sentiment here, we can highlight the opportunity for lawyers to take advantage of emerging technologies that they learn about and trust to gain advantage in their daily practice: To use technology as a force multiplier for the excellence of the legal mind.

Technology can now reduce the time spent on background research and identify relevant material more accurately and more thoroughly than large teams of lawyers. This fact is cited in a negative, backward looking manner when viewing technology as a threat to the profession, stoking fears that "AI will destroy the legal profession" and turn it into a dystopian manifestation of the "legal industry". We assert that both positive and negative aspects of emergent outcomes in the struggle for change are in the hands of energetic, informed members of the profession, theirs to shape with care, informed deliberation and a spirit of humility.

The empowered digital lawyer will see technology allowing all of those lawyers previously fated to toiling on research free to spend more time thinking more deeply about the problems they are trying to solve on behalf of their clients. As clients look to manage their legal expenses more closely in the context of the hourly billing model, technology could be viewed to support more, not less, value delivered to the client per billable hour. Viewed as a tool, even a partner, technology and technologists working side by side with digital lawyers have many opportunities to remake the profession and professional practice into forms that better serve society, clients and lawyers.

ETHICS AND CONDUCT

Ethics goes to the very heart of what it means to be a lawyer. Legal ethics covers a range of matters such as confidentiality, upholding the rule of law, competence, acting with integrity, acting in the best interests of clients, and professional judgement. Lawyers are regulated by the relevant codes in their jurisdiction, and they must be committed to acting ethically based on those particular standards and requirements.

Lawyers will face difficult situations and dilemmas in their professional lives, and ethical principles help lawyers know how to respond when they have these challenges. Lawyers owe their clients ethical obligations and can be brought to account by their regulatory body if they do not meet those responsibilities.

Lawyers have a fundamental duty to deliver legal services competently and need to have the required legal knowledge and skills to discharge this duty. As discussed in Chapter 11, in 2012, the American Bar Association introduced the ethical duty of "technological competence" to Model Rule 1.1, which states that for lawyers to effectively represent their clients, they have a responsibility to be competent in technology.[1] Lawyers have a professional responsibility to be familiar

1 American Bar Association, 'Model Rules of Professional Conduct' <https://www.americanbar.org/groups/professional_responsibility/publications/model_rules_of_professional_conduct/> accessed 30 April 2021.

with and understand the workings of technology. Although there isn't an equivalent standard set out in the SRA Code of Conduct for Solicitors, you could argue that technological competence falls within Rule 3.3, which provides that lawyers must keep their knowledge and skills up to date.[2]

There is a difference between being confident using technology and understanding how technology is deployed within legal practice. It is not sufficient for lawyers to be comfortable using applications such as PowerPoint and Microsoft Teams. All lawyers, irrespective of their jurisdictions, need to ensure that as new technologies emerge, they have the knowledge and skills to understand the implications for their practice. Lawyers are not required to be technology experts, but they have a responsibility to ensure as part of their continuing professional development that they have the requisite knowledge to understand the impact technology is having on the practice of law.

In this textbook we have discussed the professional workings of lawyers and the ways that technological competence is required across all areas of practice. Chapter 7 identified myriad ethical issues that arise out of the use of AI, from data privacy and bias to automated decision-making. AI will continue to raise new and challenging legal and ethical questions, and lawyers will need to know how to navigate these as technology advances. It is not yet clear how the law will evolve and respond to these questions, and it is likely to be different across jurisdictions. Lawyers must be prepared to raise and discuss the ethical dimensions of technology innovation.

The consequences of the lack of physical and geographical borders were highlighted in Chapter 8 in the discussion on policing in a digital age. Lawyers are already involved in, and advising across, jurisdictional borders. With increasing connectivity, law firms are going to want to take further advantage of global developments and leverage the benefits from globalisation. Lawyers are going to be required to understand legal and ethical issues from a global perspective. Technology and globalisation are going to have a significant impact on the way in which law students of the future practice law.

In Chapter 9 we discussed how technology is changing the way in which courts resolve legal disputes. The increased adoption of online dispute resolution (ODR) systems means that we must consider the ethical principles that should underpin the design and implementation

2 Solicitors Regulation Authority, 'SRA Code of Conduct for Solicitors' <https://www.sra.org.uk/solicitors/standards-regulations/> accessed 30 April 2021.

of ODR. The National Center for Technology and Dispute Resolution has been developing a framework that outlines the ethical principles that should be adopted for ODR. As jurisdictions across the world explore the increased use of technology within different forms of dispute resolution, it is increasingly incumbent on lawyers and law students to be aware of the ethical challenges that arise within the field of ODR. Chapters 4 and 9 highlighted the issue of digital exclusion and marginalisation of vulnerable parts of our society; we have to ensure that those with less access and power are still able to exercise their legal rights, and that requires paying particular attention to ethics in developing ODR systems.

In Chapter 5 we discussed ethics and social media. There are important ethical issues for lawyers in their personal and professional use of social media. Lawyers are required to understand social media and how social media platforms work so they can competently advise their clients. The content from social media sites is now a feature of legal proceedings, and lawyers need to be able to advise their clients on their social media presence. The rules on spoliation and preservation of evidence will be different across jurisdictions, but wherever you practice law you need to understand how social media evidence can be used in legal proceedings. Beyond the ethical issues that are raised with social media in legal matters, there are also professional competence issues, such as how a lawyer maintains their own social media networking sites. Law students must also be aware of the risks and consider very carefully how they conduct themselves on social media. There are high standards of conduct that apply to lawyers, so it is essential that the duty to act professionally permeates all social media activity to ensure that professional conduct rules are not breached.

As technology further impacts on the practice of law, lawyers will need to leverage a new digital lawyering skill set which will include developing new ethical and professional competencies to respond to a disrupted legal environment.

CHALLENGES AND CRITIQUES

Each of the chapters within this textbook has highlighted the potential of existing and future technological developments, and the role of digital lawyering. However, we have also been careful to emphasise the challenges and critiques involved in such changes and shifts. It is important to take a balanced approach when assessing the benefits and challenges of digital technology within the legal profession and not seek to view it as a form of panacea or assume that its impact will be wholly positive.

At the most basic level, there is the impact of individual perceptions and preferences. As human beings, we have to learn to adapt to new digital technologies and the new ways of living and working and even being that they bring. We may feel unwilling, unable or reluctant to embrace such change. For example, a partner or principal in a law firm may be reluctant to invest in new technology because they feel "things are fine as they are". There are also some fears around the consequences of incorporating technology, which can lead to suspicion and resistance. These are understandable when it is acknowledged that, for some sectors of the legal profession, there may be negative consequences for individuals. For example, the adoption of AI is likely to bring a reduction in the need for paralegals for routine tasks which can be automated. This can lead to people feeling that their income and job security is under threat.

There is also a need for lawyers to understand clients' wants and expectations. For example, you may be used to communicating with people via emails and assume that clients are also happy with this means of communication. However, a client may prefer a telephone call or even a letter. There be a sense of mistrust from some clients if processes they expect to be done "in person" are instead automated. Conversely, some clients may expect a high level of technological input and may struggle to see the value that can sometimes be added by a "human touch" in legal practice.

There is also the possibility of human error impacting on the adoption and use of digital technologies. This could involve practical issues around lack of digital literacy, digital poverty and digital exclusion. It can also be related to a plethora of ethical issues where inappropriate conduct and poor decision-making impact on clients and colleagues and have possible repercussions for the career and reputation of the individual involved. The examples given in Chapter 5 relating to social media demonstrate the challenges involved in applying professional codes of conduct and ethical standards to new issues raised by digital technologies. The blurring of lines between personal and professional lives is also highlighted by this.

The affordances of digital technology can also lead to challenges. The process of legal design should uncover these, and lead to potential solutions, at an early stage. However, this process itself can take considerable resources in terms of expertise, time and finance. It often requires interdisciplinary work with expert input from a range of professionals and involves an iterative process of testing and refining. It may be that emerging digital technologies are not yet well enough developed to meet the needs of the legal profession. The stringent regulatory requirements in most, if not all, jurisdictions may mean that lawyers may not always be able to act as early adopters of innovative new technologies. There is also the potential for errors and biases (e.g. an algorithm which is inaccurate in its predictions). This requires the individual(s) using the technology to have the knowledge and understanding to be able to assess the affordances of technology and adapt their working practices accordingly.

The use of information generated and processed via digital technologies also raises significant issues which need to be considered. In an era of Big Data, questions over how to securely and appropriately collect, store and destroy data have become increasingly important. The need to comply with data protection regulations and be able to advise clients upon the implications of these are now important parts of legal practice. The balance that often needs to be struck with privacy issues also raises ethical issues and adds complexity to the way information is handled.

There are also broader challenges relating to the wider role of the legal profession in society. Questions such as how we can utilise digital technologies to promote access to justice are key. ODR and legal advice and assistance provided without the input of lawyers can all promote better access. However, this is not always the case. As discussed in Chapter 4, issues such as digital poverty and a lack of digital literacy can exacerbate barriers to access, potentially for those groups who need it most. This raises vital questions about how we can best use technology to promote values which are crucial to the rule of law and the flourishing of society.

SKILLS AND OPPORTUNITIES

Although Chapter 11 focused specifically on digital skills, in fact the importance of understanding and developing the appropriate skills for digital lawyering have been emphasised in several chapters. We have highlighted some of these skills which digital lawyers will be expected to use within legal practice and which you can also begin to develop as a law student and whilst reading this textbook. Although these can involve technical know-how, many are much broader in scope, such as creativity and the ability to communicate clearly with clients via a range of mediums. As digital technology becomes more prevalent in legal practice there has also been a move towards lawyers demonstrating increasing soft skills to ensure that the client care they provide is individualised and involved building rapport and empathy in ways which (as yet!) cannot be emulated by AI or other machine learning.

This textbook has noted the general issues around digital literacy within wider society. Although these levels have been increasing, it has also been emphasised that (as discussed earlier) there are areas of digital poverty and problems with digital exclusion. It cannot be assumed that law students themselves have all the digital skills that may be required within legal practice (perhaps you noticed this in the skills audit within Chapter 4). There are a range of digital skills frameworks which can be used to identify and assess relevant skills, but these are not specific to law. Even within the legal profession, the type and extent of digital skills required have not always been fully acknowledged or understood. Different jurisdictions demonstrate different levels of engagement with digital lawyering skills. The extent to which such skills are embedded within skills and competency frameworks also varies.

It should also be acknowledged that different digital skills will be required within different legal roles. Although the contemporary lawyer, however "traditional", will require some level of digital literacy, this may be very different from those skills required by those who work within digital lawyering, or those who are involved in the types of new legal roles referred to in Chapter 12. As such skills become increasingly specialised, this raises interesting questions around whether and to what extent they can be fostered within legal education and training.

These changes in "legal skills" will also impact more widely upon notions of professional identity and professionalism within law. People's perception of themselves as digital lawyers may challenge existing notions of what makes a good or successful lawyer. This may alter or adapt the influences which currently shape ideas of lawyering both within the legal profession and more widely within society and popular culture. This may in turn impact on the aspirations and perceptions of law students and other aspiring entrants into the legal profession.

At the heart of these changes and developments around skills is an understanding that digital technology offers great opportunities and potential for the legal profession. Despite the challenges and critiques presented above, the transformative potential of digital lawyering should not be overlooked. In fact, aspects of the legal profession and lawyering have already been transformed. Examples within this textbook range from the use of smart contracts in conveyancing and other fields to the ways in which law firms have transformed in terms of communications, staff, strategy and working methods. The COVID-19 pandemic has illustrated the capabilities of technology to transform many aspects of law and the workplace. Although for many this increased reliance on digital technology was from necessity rather than choice, it has demonstrated its potential in a way which will shape the legal profession long into the future.

OUR VISION FOR 30 YEARS IN THE FUTURE

In this section, each author sets out their vision of the future of digital lawyering, drawing on the themes previously discussed within this chapter and the content of their individual chapters.

DIGITAL LAWYERING AND THE LEGAL PROFESSION (ANN THANARAJ)

In 30 years, the profession will be unrecognisable. From the manner of operating to the roles and responsibilities of practising lawyers, I believe that everything we do as lawyers in the very near future will be creative, with a move away from a heavily laden knowledge sector with highly specialised skill sets to an industry that operates a service model based on creativity in problem-solving for clients. Much of the work paralegals and junior lawyers do will be automated. Hybrid careers in legaltech and in other professional business sectors will emerge. Creativity will be in the art and craft of the legal professional and digital lawyer.

More interdisciplinarily qualified lawyers will exist. The world faces a host of wicked and grand challenges that cannot be addressed by any one discipline in isolation. This is a powerful beginning in my reimagination of the future of the legal profession: To survive and thrive in a disruptive yet opportune world. This is also where creativity integrates with how the legal services industry will evolve and thrive.

There will be much more automation with technologies such as different aspects of AI (for example, natural language processing [NLP], chatbots and sophisticated knowledge database search engines) tailored to niche areas of problems with legal and practical solutions. These will help clients find answers to their questions. The ability to research and understand one's route to a legal claim and compensation can be automated reasonably easily with high levels of accuracy as AI technology develops, which is trained with data sets to recognise patterns and draw from its machine learning and predictability functionalities about things such as family law, traffic tickets and contracts. Outsourced companies are building affordable legal solutions using technology to do this at a fraction of the cost, including niche areas such as contracts drafting. Opinion writing (providing legal advice on an issue) can be made much easier through predictions technology and automatic research databases.

Litigation will continue, but it will be about handling certain pieces of large, high-stakes cases which will require interdisciplinary knowledge, legal knowledge and skills of persuasion and asking different questions with alternative solutions to problem-solving across a variety of domains. Perhaps the role of a lawyer will change to one that has specialist and niche expertise to advise on unique and complex matters in creative ways requiring high-end specialisms that technology cannot automate. The ability to advise in this way may require experience and knowledge of working in other industries, acquiring grounding in understanding the practice of that discipline to bring expert knowledge which can be integrated with law. For example, advising on a criminal matter may require experience of previous work in digital forensics or IT security to demonstrate an understanding of new and emerging threats in the digital world and an appreciation of the application of law on people from other dimensions. Ethics and digital technologies will play a fundamental role in the work lawyers do. All areas of the law will be involved in dimensions of the digital world, and there will be a need to seamlessly transfer legal knowledge and acumen between problem-solving for the physical and digital worlds. As new technology is rolled out, litigation around those technologies and its impact on the digital and physical worlds will be on the rise.

Lawyers will also develop and improve the legal processes to regulate technologies and other innovations, to adapt to changes in technologies and interpretation of the law. They will also be fine-tuning the data sets that are used by algorithms that are producing outcomes for and solutions to problems, so that the AI can support in the less complex work that can be easily automated and does not require human intervention or special consideration.

More hybrid careers will exist. Legal services will be delivered alongside other professional services that offer multidisciplinary business advice. They will be delivered by those qualified as lawyers and by those qualified in a variety of service industries, such as in banking and accountancy. Professional services, particularly those with a global footprint putting legaltech at the forefront of their offering, will be leading the way in how the delivery of legal services will operate. Agility and seamless and integrated automated services will be in high demand at low cost. Therefore, more packaged business services with streamlined processes that do not require specialist skill set will be on the rise.

Creativity will be at the heart of a thriving legal profession. Creativity is something that is misunderstood occasionally. It is the ability to demonstrate an approach or methodology in a unique and new way, thereby solving problems differently. The knowledge of law needs to be coupled with other disciplines such as science, ethics, humanities and philosophy, applied in a new way within the context of solving legal problems, taking an exploratory approach that extends beyond devising clever legal arguments to think about what alternatives might exist for solving their problems, bringing changes to the way the law operates in contexts that require innovating and regulations. Creativity becomes an indispensable trait, and one that is not capable of automation.

THE EFFECTS OF TECHNOLOGY DEVELOPMENT AND INNOVATION (TERRY WONG)

In the coming decades, we can expect to see continued acceleration in the development of technology, with a greater focus on its application to augmenting human experience and performance. More and more, technology will be seen as a set of indispensable tools. In nearly all aspects of daily life, including legal practice, the condition in which digital technology is interwoven with everyday practice has already lost its novelty. Perhaps counterintuitively, improved technology will become less visible, as human-computer interfaces become more capable and more fluid, achieving a sought-after state in interface design parlance known as ambience.

Ambient interfaces are so functional and so fitted to their use that they cease to be novel and assertive in their presence, receding into the background and supporting their delivery of function in as fluid and intuitive a manner as possible. Put in other terms, "they get out of the way". While we do not care to speculate as to the exact nature and manifestation of these developments, we can say that some believe that natural language interactions with spoken word and text-chat interfaces will become more and more the primary mode of everyday interaction with computing technology.

Blockchain and cryptocurrencies around the world and in space

In the coming years, we will surely see case law, if not legislation, adjudicated or enacted to settle significant questions of law regarding the validity and execution of smart contracts, as well as clarifications of their role as the memorial of agreement or even active arbiter in resolving disputes. We can look for the clarification of the limits of recourse in case of dispute, or codification of the process of finding by the parties or a competent authority that they are in some way deficient or defective.

We will also see the consolidation of cryptocurrencies, with dominant solutions or emerging leaders and subsequent consolidation in the market. Governments will enact policy, clarify regulatory positions and set limits on the use of various cryptocurrencies and related technologies such as tokens. Some may even ban mining, handling or using cryptocurrencies within their borders, creating significant challenges for compliance or enforcement in some cases.

Legal clarification, mainstream adoption of technologies, and trust will also fuel another movement in technology. This will be a culmination of trends in trust, encryption technologies, and hardware evolution: the continued decentralisation—one may go as far as to say atomisation—of applications. This atomisation will be enabled by and rely upon the dispersal of computing power through the Internet away from central servers to devices "at the edge"—in other words, to webs of devices that include not only mobile phones and personal computing devices but also devices such as cameras and household smart devices (such as locks, alarms and thermostats). Such applications will continue to build on the foundations of technology we have discussed in this textbook, enabling uses and opening opportunities yet unforeseen.

Quantum computing and huge data

Advances in quantum computing, a computing technology harnessing the properties of nature at the scale of atomic particles, may lead to a possible breaking of encryption algorithms which much of the current Internet relies upon for security and authentication. This will represent a crisis moment for not only technology and technologists but for society as a whole, if a range of new algorithms and methods are not developed and proven successful ahead of such an event.

Data continues to grow at exponential rates. The emergence of Big Data sets enabled astonishing advances and the realisation of previously inaccessible predictive capabilities. Recent years have begun to show that the frontiers of technology problem-solving lie not where there is a dearth of data but where there are poor methods. Indeed, if data sets and data generation trends continue, Big Data will certainly become Huge Data. The current crisis in methods and training in the disciplines of data management, data science, machine learning and AI will likely continue, if not continue to compound. While the legal issues may remain the same, the focus on training and growing talent to serve the demand for data and data-dependent applications in industry will continue—if not greatly increase—the demand for lawyers able to navigate the issues for technology and technology management, with a savvy approach to creating options for their clients and their collaborators and service providers.

Law in space

As we see the resurgence of space flight, its commercialisation and the establishment of a more permanent human presence in low Earth orbit and beyond, it is clear that issues of jurisdiction and applicable law will be raised among the new pioneers in space. As settlements beyond the Earth's gravity eventually take root and develop, difficult questions of governance, independence and changes in legal tradition may arise. Enormous distances preventing real-time communications will require new protocols for the observance of proper legal forms, or perhaps they will require society to return to wisdom, courtesies and even protocols left behind with the inventions of the telegraph and telephone.

For now, even simple practical questions of law will arise, with the paths to resolution possibly unclear. For instance, there has already been a report of a crime alleged to have been committed in space aboard the International Space Station. Science fiction literature has many rich speculations for the future of life in space, with varying suggestions with respect to the law. As always, in periods of great change, the genre provides ways to define, debate and understand the issues that emerge. It is likely that some readers of this text, enjoying now the contemplation of that future, will in time become involved as leaders in the lawyering that will be critically needed.

DISPUTE RESOLUTION AND ETHICS (FRANCINE RYAN)

Dispute resolution

Over the next 30 years we are going to see exponential growth in ODR, but we are also going to see how technology can be used for conflict prevention. Court systems are expensive, slow and difficult for self-represented litigants to navigate. Emerging technologies have the potential to find new ways to help people resolve their problems before they escalate into legal disputes. ODR is already firmly embedded within the private sector and resolves millions of disputes online with minimal human interaction. These platforms have demonstrated how technologies can be leveraged to provide quick and efficient resolution of disputes. We already have examples of ODR being used in court services, but over the next decade ODR is going to become an integral part of the court system. The expansion of ODR will also include the creation of online courts, and there will come a time when we cannot imagine there was ever much resistance to them.

The pandemic accelerated the use of online hearings: It allowed the courts to keep functioning when court buildings were closed. It also shifted attitudes towards technology and has provided opportunities for research into the strengths and weaknesses of technologically assisted justice. It will also afford opportunities to build that learning into the future direction of dispute resolution. If we envision the future, technology will have transformed the court system. Disputes will be categorised in relation to complexity and value and allocated accordingly to an online process. Some of those processes are likely to be fully automated where all the interaction with the court is digitalised. ODR is currently considered particularly suitable for low-value claims where automation can support users to navigate the process, including systems to draft court documents and where decisions can be made through a form of online judging. If the predictions about ODR are right, ODR will be expanded to resolve higher value claims. With the development of AI, there is further scope for the expansion of ODR and there is potential for a global platform that can be enabled for different jurisdictions.

Lawyers are already conducting litigation online, but we need to ensure that we are equipping our future lawyers with the right skills and competencies to succeed in ODR. By 2051 our court systems will be unrecognisable, and emerging technologies will displace current ways of working and replace them in ways we cannot yet imagine. At The Open University we are developing a virtual reality courtroom, and there are other similar projects around the world that are harnessing the benefits of virtual reality to train future lawyers, but there is potential for the use of virtual reality in court proceedings. The future of dispute resolution will be radically different to our current traditional court system, but there needs to be careful consideration of how we create a system that is fair, efficient and accessible to all. Technological innovation must ensure access to justice and strengthen the rule of law.

Ethics

Ethics is an integral part of being a lawyer, but as technology further evolves lawyers must have an ethical tech mindset. Lawyers will need to have a robust understanding of the potential ethical issues that arise with the use of technology and will need to be able to design systems and policies to be able to respond. Over the next 30 years we will see a rapid rate of technological innovation which will give rise to greater ethical challenges, and lawyers and law firms will need to think carefully about the development and utilisation of technology. Technology has consequences, some of which have been explored in this textbook and some that are only starting to emerge. Lawyers have responsibilities around decisions that are made about the use of technology and will need to have the required skills and competencies to scrutinise and challenge decisions to ensure they are ethically grounded.

Technology is going to permeate all aspects of law and the practice of law. Lawyers will be required to advise clients on the ethical challenges that arise from the development of machine learning and the algorithms that underpin these systems. There are significant issues in the development of AI in how to respond to the challenges of minimising bias. It is likely that those who design and develop new technologies are going to be responsible for the legal and ethical issues that might arise. There are myriad ethical issues that relate to emerging technologies such as privacy, trust, values, rights and risk, all of which will underpin their future development and use. The regulatory and legal landscape is going to change, and lawyers are going to require a sufficient grounding in technology to effectively advise their clients.

In addition to advising clients, technology will have an impact on the future of employment. Automation is going to impact on the delivery of legal services, and over the next 30 years the future work opportunities for lawyers will change. AI is already being used in legal practice, legal research, document management, predictive analytics, e-discovery, and contract and litigation management. The traditional work done by lawyers is going to be different; lawyers will still have important roles to play, but they will change and will not reflect what has been done in the past. This will have an impact on the composition and economics of legal practice. Law firms are going to face ethical challenges about the meaning of legal work and around the place of work. It is likely that there will be a further shift to remote working, which raises ethical issues that will have to be addressed. Cybersecurity will become a greater concern for law firms; they will need to have robust policies in place around data access and security. As more and more work is conducted online, new threats from attackers will emerge and lawyers are going to face increasing obligations and responsibilities to ensure they protect the data of their clients.

Over the next 30 years we will see the emergence of new types of legal service delivery, increased use of technology and AI leading to ethical challenges. It is therefore essential that ethical obligations are not overlooked and that ethical integrity remains a core attribute of a lawyer and a digital lawyer.

LEGAL EDUCATION AND SKILLS (EMMA JONES)

Legal education

The law student of the future is likely to face changes in content and delivery, both significantly influenced by the continued development of digital technology. In terms of content, it is inevitable that digital lawyering and law and technology will increasingly become mainstream parts of the curriculum. They will move from being often regarded as "extras" into integrated parts of teaching and learning throughout a law degree. If such degrees remain largely broken down into courses or modules, the likelihood is digital technology will be acknowledged within each and every subject, from smart contracts in the law of obligations to data protection and privacy in human rights law.

However, it may well be that more law schools begin to move away from the current form of the modularised system. Instead, there is likely to be a shift towards approaches which avoid rigidly separating out different legal subjects and instead integrate them into an overall approach. For example, the University of York (UK) takes a problem-based learning approach, where students' study is based around a series of problem scenarios that each incorporate a range of different legal topics and areas.[3] The range of topics covered within digital lawyering suggests endless possibilities for adopting this type of approach. This could not only involve combining a range of legal topics but also working with staff and students from other disciplines.

Digital lawyering is an interdisciplinary topic involving insights from technology, business, sociology and other subjects. This could well involve students from, for example, computing, marketing and communications, sociology and law all working together on long-term problems and projects. Such a process has already started within some law schools, particularly within law clinics (see Chapter 13). However, in 30 years it is likely to have become far more deeply embedded across law schools and jurisdictions as a central part of a law degree.

Of course, there will be barriers and challenges in adopting this type of approach. For example, staff may feel more comfortable and well-equipped to deliver "traditional" forms of law teaching. Law schools and universities more widely may find difficulties arise in finding the resources (including finance and time) to facilitate the transition to a different mode of delivery (not to mention the paperwork involved!). It may well be that law schools which adopt this approach decide to use these in their marketing strategies as a unique selling point to encourage students to join them. This in turn will promote the profile of digital lawyering even further.

In terms of delivery of teaching and learning, it is likely that there will also be an increasing reliance on technology. Forms of blended learning, combining online and face-to-face learning, are already becoming more common. For example, traditional lectures are now often being converted into a series of shorter online videos which are easily accessible to students. This then frees up face-to-face teaching time to focus upon interactive activities and group work. The COVID-19 pandemic has forced most law schools to move their teaching and learning wholly online and, although this is a temporary measure, it is likely to accelerate the focus on technology in the delivery of teaching. The new skills and insights it has equipped teaching staff with are unlikely to be simply discarded or ignored by law schools moving forward. The incorporation of these is likely to benefit students interested in becoming digital lawyers by putting them on a sound footing

3 University of York, 'LLB (Hons) Law' <https://www.york.ac.uk/study/undergraduate/courses/llb-law/> accessed 28 April 2021.

to transition to workplace environments where technology is at the forefront.

So far, this vision of legal education has focused upon law schools. However, legal education is far broader than just the law degree. It encompasses teaching and learning law in schools and colleges, vocational training for the legal profession and continuing professional development for practitioners. Each of these is also likely to change to embrace digital technology. For example, schools and colleges may begin to teach students about the law and citizenship using examples drawn from digital technology (such as the use of social media, discussed in Chapter 5). Bespoke courses may be developed by vocational training providers for specific roles within the legal profession, such as legal engineers and legal project managers (see Chapter 12). Individuals working in existing legal roles may be required to learn new practical skills to enable them to effectively use emerging technology or may be required to undergo more fundamental retraining as the workplace changes.

Skills

The importance of developing and adapting skills is likely to increase, rather than decrease, over the next 30 years. Competition for jobs and increases in precarious models of employment (such as fixed-term or zero-hour contracts) mean that individuals must focus on enhancing their employability skills as much as possible. Although there remains a digital divide and areas of digital poverty (see Chapter 4), there will increasingly be an expectation that individuals within any role (legal or non-legal) have at least a basic level of digital literacy. For example, a receptionist at a law firm is likely to use a computer system to organise room bookings and schedule meetings.

As new models of lawyering emerge, law firms and other employers will want to recruit people who can show they understand the importance of a broad skill set. Skills that are currently seen as "soft skills" or "non-legal skills" will increasingly become a part of accepted skills and competencies frameworks within legal roles; for example, being creative, innovative and entrepreneurial in approaches to problem-solving. This will impact on the notion of professionalism and ideas of what being a legal professional involves. The cartoon stereotypes of lawyers in 30 years may well replace the individual in a suit at a desk surrounded by shelves of law books with someone who has digital devices stashed all over their person working at a "hot desk" with a technologist sat next door. These changes in expectations around skills will also impact on legal education, as law schools (and others) seek to accommodate new visions of the legal profession into their curriculum.

TAKING DIGITAL LAWYERING INTO THE FUTURE

If you are reading this textbook, it is quite possible that you will be a part of the future of digital lawyering. In fact, as someone studying the topic, you are already contributing to the shaping of its future development. We hope that this textbook also empowers you to continue to do so in future. It is impossible to predict all the new developments that will arise, both in digital technology and in legal practice, or to say with 100% certainty where emerging fields of interest will lead. However, that is one of the appeals of digital lawyering: It is about engaging with and contributing to dynamic, innovative and creative solutions to key problems and issues within society and the workplace. As authors, we sincerely hope that you continue your digital lawyering journey, whether as a practitioner, a researcher or an interested observer. In doing so, you will be a part of a vibrant, exciting and impactful community with a shared passion for digital lawyering. Whether considering your local town, your wider jurisdiction, or even space, digital technology and law are intertwined and increasingly pervasive.

REFERENCES

ABA Comment to the Model Rules of Professional Conduct <https://www.americanbar.org/groups/professional_responsibility/publications/model_rules_of_professional_conduct/rule_1_1_competence/comment_on_rule_1_1.html.> accessed 7 December 2020.

ABA Commission on Ethics 20/20, 'Introduction and Overview' <americanbar.org> accessed 1 December 2020.

Abdeen M and others, 'Automatic Generation of Mind Maps from Text with M2Gen' (2009) Science and Technology for Humanity (TIC-STH) 95.

Acosta D, 'The Lawyer's Dilemma: Challenges for Law Firms Adopting Legal Tech' (*Legal Technologist*, October 2020) <https://www.legaltechnologist.co.uk/the-lawyers-dilemma-challenges-for-law-firms-adopting-legal-tech> accessed 21 April 2021.

Allen LE, 'Symbolic Logic: A Razor-Edged Tool for Drafting and Interpreting Legal Documents' (1957) 66 Yale Law Journal 6 <https://digitalcommons.law.yale.edu/fss_papers/4519/>

Allen & Overy, 'Tech Innovation' (2020) <https://www.allenovery.com/en-gb/global/expertise/advanced_delivery/tech_innovation>.

Ambrogi R, '39 States Have Adopted the Duty of Technology Competence' (*Law Sites*, n.d.) <https://www.lawsitesblog.com/tech-competence> accessed 29 April 2021.

American Bar Association, '2020–2021 Standards and Rules of Procedure for Approval of Law Schools' <https://www.americanbar.org/groups/legal_education/resources/standards/> accessed 26 November 2020.

American Bar Association, 'Model Rules of Professional Conduct' <https://www.americanbar.org/groups/professional_responsibility/publications/model_rules_of_professional_conduct/> accessed 30 April 2021.

Antwi-Boasiako A and Venter H, 'A Model for Digital Evidence Admissibility Assessment' in G Peterson and S Shenoi (eds), *Advances in Digital Forensics XIII*, 511. DigitalForensics IFIP Advances in Information and Communication Technology (Springer, 2017) <https://doi.org/10.1007/978-3-319-67208-3_2>

Artess J and others, 'Employability: A Review of the Literature 2012 to 2016 A Report for the Higher Education Academy' 17 <https://www.advance-he.ac.uk/knowledge-hub/employability-review-literature-2012-2016> accessed 26 November 2020.

The Association of Chief Police Officers, 'ACPO Good Practice Guide for Digital Evidence' (2012) <https://www.digital-detective.net/digital-forensics-documents/ACPO_Good_Practice_Guide_for_Digital_Evidence_v5.pdf> accessed 30 April 2021.

Aveni C, 'Alexa, How Private Is My Home?' (*Litigation News*, 2 December 2018) <https://www.cpmlaw.com/alexa-how-private-is-my-home> accessed 30 April 2021.

The Bar Standards Board Handbook, 'Social Media Guidance' (2019) <https://www.barstandardsboard.org.uk/resources/resource-library/social-media-pdf.html> accessed 29 April 2021.

BBC, 'Paris Brown: Kent Youth PCC Resigns after Twitter Row' (*BBC News*, 9 April 2013) <https://www.bbc.co.uk/news/uk-england-22083032> accessed 14 April 2021.

BBC News, 'Bitcoin Consumes "More Electricity than Argentina"' (*BBC News*, 10 February 2021) <https://www.bbc.com/news/technology-56012952>

BBC News, 'General Election 2019: Labour Pledges Broadband for All' (*BBC News*, 15 November 2019) <https://www.bbc.co.uk/news/election-2019-50427369> accessed 19 April 2021.

BBC News, 'Lawyer Gets Stuck with Cat Filter During Virtual Court Case' (*BBC News*, 9 February 2021) <https://www.bbc.co.uk/news/av/world-us-canada-56005428> accessed 22 March 2021.

BBC News, 'TikTok Sued for Billions Over Use of Children's Data' (*BBC News*, 21 April 2021) <https://www.bbc.com/news/technology-56815480> accessed 29 April 2021.

BBC Tech News Reports, 'Fitbit Data Used to Charge US Man with Murder' (*BBC News*, 4 October 2018) <https://www.bbc.co.uk/news/technology-45745366>

Belshaw D, 'The Essential Elements of Digital Literacies [pdf]' (Self-published, 2014), 11–12 <https://dougbelshaw.com/blog/2016/06/27/ebook-now-free/> accessed 26 November 2020.

Berne Convention Texts at the World Intellectual Property Organization <https://www.wipo.int/treaties/en/ip/berne/>

Blakeley V and others, 'Social Media Evidence in Family Law: What Can Be Used and Its Probative Value' (2015) 5 Family Law Review 81–101.

Bowcott O, '77 More Courts in England and Wales to Close' (*Guardian*, September 2019) <https://www.theguardian.com/law/2019/sep/13/77-more-courts-in-england-and-wales-to-close> accessed 26 April 2021.

Bowditch K and Williams A, 'The Verdict: Social Media in the Legal Sector' (*FTI Consulting*, 2016) <https://www.fticonsulting-emea.com/~/media/Files/emea--files/insights/reports/legal-sector-social-media.pdf> accessed 14 April 2021.

Bradney A, *Conversations, Choices and Chances the Liberal Law School in the Twenty-First Century* (Hart Publishing, 2003).

Britten A, 'Graduate Employability: One in Five UK Graduates Not Workplace-ready' *University Business* <https://universitybusiness.co.uk/news/graduate-employability/> accessed 26 November 2020.

Brooks S, 'Fostering Wholehearted Lawyers: Practical Guidance for Supporting Law Students' Professional Identity Formation' (2018) 14 University of St Thomas Law Journal 412.

Brown CC, 'Professional Identity Formation: Working Backwards to Move the Profession Forward' (2015) 61 Loyola Law Review 313, 314.

Butler S and others, 'The Utah Online Dispute Resolution Platform: A Usability Evaluation, and Report' (September 2020) <http://law.arizona.edu/sites/default/files/i4J_Utah_ODR_Report.pdf> accessed 19 April 2021.

Byrom N and others, 'Rapid Review: The Impact of COVID-19 on the Civil Justice System' (2020) <https://www.judiciary.uk/wp-content/uploads/2020/06/FINAL-REPORT-CJC-4-June-2020.v2-accessible.pdf>

Cabinet Office and Government Digital Service, 'Government Transformation Strategy: Background Published 9 February 2017' <https://www.gov.uk/government/publications/government-transformation-strategy-2017-to-2020>

Cambridge University, 'Helping Police Make Custody Decisions Using Artificial Intelligence' (*Cambridge University Research*, 26 February) <https://www.cam.ac.uk/research/features/helping-police-make-custody-decisions-using-artificial-intelligence>

Canadian Bar Association, 'The Future of Legal Services in Canada: Trends and Issues' <https://www.cba.org/CBAMediaLibrary/cba_na/PDFs/CBA%20Legal%20Futures%20PDFS/trends-isssues-eng.pdf> accessed 16 March 2021.

Cappellino A, 'The Amazon Echo: Expert Witness in a Murder Trial?' (*Expert Institute*, 17 February 2021) <https://www.expertinstitute.com/resources/insights/amazon-echo-expert-witness-murder-trial/> accessed 21 April 2021.

Carnegie Mellon University, 'Carnegie Mellon and Facebook AI Beats Professionals in Six-Player Poker' (*Carnegie Mellon University*, July 11) <https://www.cmu.edu/news/stories/archives/2019/july/cmu-facebook-ai-beatspoker-pros.html>

Citizens Advice, 'Future of Advice: Our Strategic Framework 2019–22' <https://www.citizensadvice.org.uk/about-us/future-of-advice-our-strategic-framework-2019-22/> accessed 26 April 2021.

Civil Resolution Tribunal, 'Annual Report 2019/2020' <https://civilresolutionbc.ca/wp-content/uploads/2020/07/CRT-Annual-Report-2019-2020.pdf> accessed 25 April 2021.

Civin D, 'Explainable AI Could Reduce the Impact of Biased Algorithms' (*VentureBeat*, May 2018); European Commission, White Paper on Artificial Intelligence: A European Approach to Excellence (COM 2020 65).

Clementi D, 'Review of the Regulatory Framework for Legal Services in England and Wales' (December 2004) <https://www.avocatsparis.org/Presence_Internationale/Droit_homme/PDF/Rapport_Clementi.pdf> accessed 10 October 2019.

Cohen MA, 'The Golden Age of the Legal Entrepreneur—Why Now and Why It Matters' (*Forbes*) <https://www.forbes.com/sites/markcohen1/2018/06/01/the-golden-age-of-the-legal-entrepreneur-why-now-and-why-it-matters/?sh=5a4496447803> accessed 29 April 2021.

Cohen MA, 'Why Is Law so Slow to Use Data?' (*Forbes*) <https://www.forbes.com/sites/markcohen1/2019/06/24/why-is-law-so-slow-to-use-data/> accessed 8 September 2021.

Committee on Artificial Intelligence, 'AI in the UK: Ready, Willing, and Able?' (HL 2017–19, 100).

Crown Prosecution Service, 'The Criminal Procedure Rules 2020, Part 19, Expert Evidence' (updated 10 September 2019) <https://www.cps.gov.uk/legal-guidance/expert-evidence#:~:text=The%20duty%20of%20an%20expert%20witness%20is%20to%20help%20the,to%20matters%20within%20their%20expertise> accessed 27 August 2021.

Crown Prosecution Service, 'Cybercrime—Prosecution Guidance' (2020) <https://www.cps.gov.uk/legal-guidance/cybercrime-prosecution-guidance> accessed 27 August 2021.

Cuckier K and Mayer-Schonberger V, 'The Dictatorship of Data' (*MIT Technology Review*, 31 May 2013) <https://www.technologyreview.com/2013/05/31/178263/the-dictatorship-of-data/> accessed 31 January 2021.

Cueto E, 'Online Court Pilot Gets Low Marks Ahead of Wider Launch' (*Law 360*, 13 September 2020) <https://www.law360.com/access-to-justice/articles/1309437/online-court-pilot-gets-low-marks-ahead-of-wider-launch?nl_pk=77322a31-1bbc-4e35-8532-8a4ef2d22451&utm_source=newsletter&utm_medium=email&utm_campaign=access-to-justice&read_more=1> accessed 19 April 2021.

Cunningham A and others, 'Disruptive Technologies & Legal Service Provision in the UK: A Preliminary Study' (7 December 2018) <https://ssrn.com/abstract=3297074> accessed 16 March 2021.

Davenport TH and Patil DJ, 'Data Scientist: The Sexiest Job of the 21st Century' (*Harvard Business Review*, 1 October 2012) <https://hbr.org/2012/10/data-scientist-the-sexiest-job-of-the-21st-century>

Davies C and Dodd V, 'CPS Chief Apologises Over Disclosure Failings in Rape Cases' (*theguardian.com*, 5 June 2018) <https://www.theguardian.com/law/2018/jun/05/scores-of-uk-sexual-offence-cases-stopped-over-evidence-failings> accessed 14 April 2021.

De La Garza E, 'Charges Dropped in Amazon Echo Murder Case' (*Courthouse News Service*, 29 November 2017) <https://www.courthousenews.com/charges-dropped-in-amazon-echo-murder-case/>

Deloitte Legal, 'A Changing World Requires a New Approach to Law' (2017) <https://www2.deloitte.com/content/dam/Deloitte/global/Documents/Legal/dttl-legal-deloitte-approach-legal-management-consulting.pdf> accessed 12 October 2018.

Deloitte Legal, 'Developing Legal Talent: Stepping into the Future Law Firm' (February 2016) <https://www2.deloitte.com/content/dam/Deloitte/uk/Documents/audit/deloitte-uk-developing-legal-talent-2016.pdf> accessed 27 August 2021.

Department for International Development, 'Digital Strategy 2018–2020 Doing Development in a Digital World' (2018) <https://assets.publishing.service.gov.uk/government/uploads/system/uploads/attachment_data/file/701443/DFID-Digital-Strategy-23-01-18a.pdf>accessed 12 November 2019.

Design your Delta, 'Developing the Delta Model' <https://www.designyourdelta.com/about> accessed 27 August 2021.

Dickens C, *Bleak House* (Bradbury and Evans, 1853).

Douglas-Henry JP and Sanderson B, 'Empirical Evidence from Our Global Experience: Virtual Hearings' (2020) <https://www.dlapiper.com/~/media/files/insights/publications/2020/05/virtual-hearings-report.pdf?la=en&hash=9917A7A0EC9368965CFC25932075237514284C4F> accessed 19 April 2021.

Duhigg C, 'How Companies Learn Your Secrets (Published 2012)' (*New York Times*, 16 February 2012), sec. Magazine <https://www.nytimes.com/2012/02/19/magazine/shopping-habits.html> accessed 27 August 2021.

The Economist, 'The World's Most Valuable Resource is No Longer Oil, But Data' (*The Economist*, 2017) <https://www.economist.com/leaders/2017/05/06/the-worlds-most-valuable-resource-is-no-longer-oil-but-data> accessed 30 April 2021.

Enriquez J, "Your Online Life, Permanent as a Tattoo' (*Ted2013*, February 2013) <https://www.ted.com/talks/juan_enriquez_how_to_think_about_digital_tattoos#t-338590> accessed 3 February 2021.

European Network of Forensic Science Institute, 'Best Practice Manual for the Forensic Examination of Digital Technology' (ENFSI-BPM-FIT-01, 2015) <http://enfsi.eu/wp-content/uploads/2016/09/1._forensic_examination_of_digital_technology_0.pdf> accessed 27 August 2021.

European Parliament, 'Digital Agenda for Europe' (2008) <https://www.europarl.europa.eu/registre/docs_autres_institutions/commission_europeenne/sec/2008/2629/COM_SEC(2008)2629_EN.pdf>; <https://ec.europa.eu/digital-single-market/en/europe-2020-strategy> accessed 27 August 2021.

FisherBroyles, 'Distributed Disruption' (2021) <https://www.fisherbroyles.com/distributed-disruption> accessed 19 February 2021.

Forensic Capability Network, 'Digital Forensic Science Strategy' (2020), 12 <https://www.fcn.police.uk/sites/default/files/2020-07/Digital%20Forensic%20Science%20Strategy%20EMAIL%20VERSION%20ONLY.pdf> accessed 27 August 2021.

Forensic Science Regulator, 'Legal Obligations' (2020) <https://assets.publishing.service.gov.uk/government/uploads/system/uploads/attachment_data/file/882074/FSR_Legal_Obligations_-_Issue_8.pdf> accessed 27 August 2021.

Forensic Science Regulator, 'Newsletter' (2015), 3 <https://assets.publishing.service.gov.uk/government/uploads/system/uploads/attachment_data/file/470526/FSR_Newsletter_26__October_2015.pdf> accessed 27 August 2021.

Franqueira VN and Horsman G, 'Towards Sound Forensic Arguments: Structured Argumentation Applied to Digital Forensics Practice' (2020) 32 Forensic Science International Digital Investigation 300923.

Furlong F, 'Why Law Firms Need R&D Investment' (*L21 Blog*, 2014) <https://www.law21.ca/2014/08/law-firms-need-rd-investment/> accessed 12 October 2018.

Giancaspro M, 'The Consideration Myth About Smart Contracts' (2020) 1 ANU Journal of Law and Technology 11.

Gilster P, *Digital Literacy* (Wiley, 1997).

Goleman D, *Emotional Intelligence* (Bloomsbury, 1996).

Goodison SE and others, *Digital Evidence, and the US Criminal Justice System. Identifying Technology and Other Needs to More Effectively Acquire and Utilize Digital Evidence. Priority Criminal Justice Needs Initiative* (Rand Corporation, 2015).

Government Office for Science, 'Future of Skills and Lifelong Learning' 5 <https://assets.publishing.service.gov.uk/government/uploads/system/uploads/attachment_data/file/727776/Foresight-future-of-skills-lifelong-learning_V8.pdf> accessed 26 November 2020.

Grother P and others, 'Face Recognition Vendor Test (FRVT) Part 3: Demographic Effects' *NISTIR 8280* (Washington, DC, National Institute of Standards and Technology, 2019) <https://doi.org/10.6028/NIST.IR.8280> accessed 27 August 2021.

Gurin J, *Open Data Now* (McGraw-Hill Education, 2014).

Hagan M, 'Design Thinking About Law: A Perfect Match' (*Open Law Lab*, January 2014) <https://www.openlawlab.com/2014/01/16/design-thinking-law-perfecr-match> accessed 27 August 2021.

Hagan M, 'Law by Design' (2014) <https://www.lawbydesign.co/en/legal-design/> accessed 27 August 2021.

Hagan M, 'The User Experience of the Internet as a Legal Help Service' (2016) 20 Virginia Journal of Law & Technology 394, 465.

Hall W and Pesenti J, 'Growing the Artificial Intelligence Industry in the UK' (*Department for Digital, Culture, Media and Sport and Department for Business, Energy, and Industrial Strategy*, 2017) <https://www.gov.uk/government/publications/growing-the-artificial-intelligence-industry-in-the-uk> accessed 27 August 2021.

Her Majesty Courts and Tribunal Service and the Good Things Foundation, 'HMCTS Digital Support Service: Implementation Review' (2020) <https://www.goodthingsfoundation.org/sites/default/files/research-publications/digital_support_service_implementation_review_evaluation_report_-_september_2020.pdf> accessed 19 April 2021.

Her Majesty Government, 'Online Harms White Paper' (*Gov.uk*, April 2019) <https://assets.publishing.service.gov.uk/government/uploads/system/uploads/attachment_data/file/973939/Online_Harms_White_Paper_V2.pdf> accessed 14 April 2021.

Hill K, 'How Target Figured Out a Teen Girl Was Pregnant Before Her Father Did' (*Forbes*, n.d.) <https://www.forbes.com/sites/kashmirhill/2012/02/16/how-target-figured-out-a-teen-girl-was-pregnant-before-her-father-did/> accessed 1 January 2021.

Hill K, 'Wrongfully Accused by an Algorithm' (*New York Times*, 24 June 2020) <https://www.nytimes.com/2020/06/24/technology/facial-recognition-arrest.html> accessed 27 August 2021.

Hinton T, 'What Is a Lawyer?' (25 June 2019) <https://www.addleshawgoddard.com/en/insights/insights-briefings/tech-talks/what-is-a-lawyer/> accessed 19 February 2021.

Holmes V and others, 'Practising Professionalism: Observations from an Empirical Study of New Australian Lawyers' (2012) 15 (1) Legal Ethics 29.

Home Office, 'eDiscovery in Digital Forensic Investigations' (2014) <https://assets.publishing.service.gov.uk/government/uploads/system/uploads/attachment_data/file/394779/ediscovery-digital-forensic-investigations-3214.pdf> accessed 27 August 2021.

Home Office, 'Forensic Science Strategy' (2016) <https://assets.publishing.service.gov.uk/government/uploads/system/uploads/attachment_data/file/506683/54493_Cm_9217_Forensic_Science_Strategy_Print_ready.pdf> accessed 27 August 2021.

Horsman G, 'Can We Continue to Effectively Police Digital Crime?' (2017) 57 (6) Science & Justice 448–54.

Horsman G, 'The Collectors Ranking Scale for "At-scene" Digital Device Triage' (2021) 66 (1) Journal of Forensic Sciences 179–89.

Horsman G, 'Raiders of the Lost Artefacts: Championing the Need for Digital Forensics Research' (2019) 1 Forensic Science International: Reports 100003.

Horsman G, 'Tool Testing and Reliability Issues in the Field of Digital Forensics' (2019) 28 Digital Investigation 163–75.

Horswill I, 'Polly: A Vision-based Artificial Agent' *Proceedings of the National Conference on Artificial Intelligence* (AAAI, 1993).

House Committee on Oversight and Government Reform (2017) <https://www.fbi.gov/news/testimony/law-enforcements-use-of-facial-recognition-technology> accessed 27 August 2021.

House of Commons, Science and Technology and House of Commons Science and Technology Committee, 'Robotics and Artificial

Intelligence Fifth Report of Session 2016–17' (*House of Commons*, 2016) <https://publications.parliament.uk/pa/cm201617/cmselect/cmsctech/145/145.pdf> accessed 27 August 2021.

The House of Lords Library, 'The Criminal Procedure and Investigations Act 1996' (Code of Practice) Order 2020 <https://lordslibrary.parliament.uk/the-criminal-procedure-and-investigations-act-1996-code-of-practice-order-2020/> accessed 27 August 2021.

House of Lords Select Committee on Artificial Intelligence, 'Artificial Intelligence Committee—Publications' (*UK Parliament*, 2018) <https://www.parliament.uk/business/committees/committees-a-z/lords-select/ai-committee/publications/> accessed 27 August 2021.

House of Lords Select Committee on Digital Skills, *Make or Break: The UK's Digital Future* (February 2015), Chapter 3.

Huaixiu Z, 'COTA: Improving Uber Customer Care with NLP & Machine Learning' (*Uber Engineering*, 3 January 2018) <https://eng.uber.com/cota/> accessed 27 August 2021.

Hussain A, 'Two Months into Her Training Contract and Eve Cornwell Reveals What Magic Circle Trainee Life is Like' (*Legal Cheek*, 19 November 2019) <https://www.legalcheek.com/2019/11/two-months-into-her-training-contract-and-eve-cornwell-reveals-what-magic-circle-trainee-life-is-like/> accessed 29 April 2021.

Ibarra H, 'Provisional Selves: Experimenting with Image and Identity in Professional Adaptation' (1999) 44 Administrative Science Quarterly 764, 765.

IBM Cloud Education, 'What is AI' (*IBM*, 3 June 2020) <https://www.ibm.com/cloud/learn/what-is-artificial-intelligence> accessed 25 April 2021.

ICO, 'Mobile Phone Data Extraction by Police Forces in England and Wales Investigation Report' (2020) <https://ico.org.uk/media/about-the-ico/documents/2617838/ico-report-on-mpe-in-england-and-wales-v1_1.pdf> accessed 27 August 2021.

Institute for the Future (IFF), 'Future Work Skills 2020' (*University of Phoenix Research Institute*, 2011).

Institute for the Future for Dell Technologies, 'The Next Era of Human Machine Partnerships' (2017), 14 <https://www.delltechnologies.com/content/dam/delltechnologies/assets/perspectives/2030/pdf/SR1940_IFTFforDellTechnologies_Human-Machine_070517_readerhigh-res.pdf> accessed 3 October 2018.

International Council for Online Dispute Regulation, 'ICODR Standards' <https://icodr.org/standards/> accessed 18 April 2021.

International Institute of Legal Project Management, '4-Phase LPM Framework' <https://www.iilpm.com/wp-content/uploads/2020/05/IILPM-LPM-Framework-English-Version_2020.png> accessed 26 March 2021.

Ito J and others, 'The Blockchain Will Do to the Financial System What the Internet Did to Media' (*Harvard Business Review*, 2017) <https://hbr.org/2017/03/the-blockchain-will-do-to-banks-and-law-firms-what-the-internet-did-to-media> accessed 27 August 2021.

James C, 'Lawyers' Wellbeing and Professional Legal Education' (2008) 42 (1) The Law Teacher 85–97.

James C, 'Solicitor Reprimanded for Email Calling Opponent a Plonker' (18 August 2015) <https://www.lawgazette.co.uk/practice/solicitor-reprimanded-for-email-calling-opponent-a-plonker/5050611.article> accessed 18 October 2019.

Jisc, Developing Digital Literacies <https://www.jisc.ac.uk/full-guide/developing-digital-literacies> accessed 26 November 2020.

Johnson CA and Donnelly B, 'If Only We Knew What We Know' (2013) 88 Chicago-Kent Law Review 729.

Jones E, 'Digital Lawyering and the Growing Importance of the Human Touch: Implications for Wellbeing' (October 2019) 7 The Legal Technologist 25.

Jones E, 'Making Practice More Affective: Emotional Intelligence as a Legal Meta-competency' (2018) 24 (1) European Journal of Current Legal Issues.

Jones E and others, *Mental Health and Wellbeing in the Legal Profession* (Bristol University Press, 2020).

JP Morgan, 'Could Blockchain Have as Great an Impact as the Internet?' <https://www.jpmorganchase.com/news-stories/could-blockchain-have-great-impact-as-internet> accessed 27 August 2021.

Karol K and Zdonek D, 'Analytics Maturity Models: An Overview' (2020) 11 (3) Information 142.

Katsh E and Rabinovich-Einy O, *Digital Justice* (OUP, 2017).

Katsh E and Rule C, 'What We Know and Need to Know About Online Dispute Resolution' (2016) 67 SCL Rev 329, 343.

Kemp S, Digital 2021, 'Global Overview Report' (*Datareportal*, 27 January 2021) <https://datareportal.com/reports/digital-2021-global-overview-report> accessed 14 April 2021.

Kolb D, *Experiential Learning: Experience as the Source of Learning and Development* (Vol. 1, Prentice-Hall, 1984).

Kronman AT, *The Lost Lawyer: Failing Ideals of the Legal Profession* (Harvard University Press, 1993).

Lamport L and others, 'The Byzantine Generals Problem' (1982) 4 ACM Transactions on Programming Languages and Systems 382.

Law Commission, 'Evidence in Criminal Proceedings: Hearsay and Related Topics' (1997) Law Commission Report 245.

Law for Life, 'LASPO Implementation Review Consultation Response' (September 2018) <https://www.lawforlife.org.uk/wp-content/uploads/LASPO-Implementation-Review-Consultation-Law-for-Life-Advicenow-response-Final-Sept-2018.pdf> accessed 30 April 2021.

Law Geex, 'Comparing the Performance of Artificial Intelligence to Human Lawyers in the Review of Standard Business Contracts' (*Law-Geex*, 2018) <https://images.law.com/contrib/content/uploads/documents/397/5408/lawgeex.pdf> accessed 27 August 2021.

Law Geex, 'How the Platform Works' <https://www.lawgeex.com/platform/>

The Law Society, 'Horizon Scanning: Future Skills for Law' (2018) <https://www.lawsociety.org.uk/support-services/research-trends/horizon-scanning/future-skills-for-law/> accessed 27 August 2021.

The Law Society, 'Introduction to LawTech 2019' <https://tlsprd-sitecore.azureedge.net/-/media/files/campaigns/lawtech/introduction-to-lawtech-october-2019.pdf?rev=fc0013791e0c474198da aabd648a304d&hash=F030B90541BF66B22233A9702F4B22A5> accessed 30 April 2021.

The Law Society, 'Social Media: Practice Note' (*lawsociety.org.uk*, 5 December 2019) <https://www.lawsociety.org.uk/topics/business-management/social-media> accessed 14 April 2021.

The Law Society of England and Wales, 'Annual Statistics Report 2018' <https://www.lawsociety.org.uk/support-services/research-trends/annual-statistics-report-2018/> accessed 7 October 2019.

Law Society of England and Wales, 'Phishing Email Scam' (24 April 2014) <https://www.ft.com/content/4da1117e-756c-11e9-be7d-6d846537acab> accessed 18 October 2019 <https://www.lawsociety.org.uk/support-services/advice/articles/phishing-email-scam/> accessed 15th October 2019.

The Law Society of England and Wales, 'Unbundling Civil Legal Service's' (4 April 2016) <https://www.lawsociety.org.uk/support-services/advice/practice-notes/unbundling-civil-legal-services/> accessed 18 October 2019.

The Law Society of New South Wales, 'The Future of Law and Innovation in the Profession' 78 <https://www.lawsociety.com.au/sites/default/files/2018-03/1272952.pdf> accessed 30 November 2020.

Lawton D and others, 'eDiscovery in digital forensic investigations' (*UK Home Office*, 2014) CAST Publication Number 32/14 <https://assets.publishing.service.gov.uk/government/uploads/system/uploads/attachment_data/file/394779/ediscovery-digital-forensic-investigations-3214.pdf> accessed 27 August 2021.

The Lawyer, 'The Watson Glaser and BCAT Critical Thinking Tests' (*The Lawyer*, 28 April 2015) <https://www.thelawyer.com/watson-glaser-test/> accessed 29 April 2021.

Lawyer Monthly, 'Robots and AI: Giving Robots "Personhood" Status"' (*Lawyer Monthly*, 3 March 2017) <https://www.lawyer-monthly.com/2017/02/robots-and-ai-giving-robots-personhood-status/> accessed 27 August 2021.

Lawyers Defence Group, 'The Impact of Ransomware on Law Firms' (28 November 2017) <https://www.lawyersdefencegroup.org.uk/ransomware/> accessed 15 October 2019.

Leering MM, 'Conceptualizing Reflective Practice for Legal Professionals' (2014) 23 Journal of Law and Social Policy 83.

Leering MM, 'Integrated Reflective Practice: A Critical Imperative for Enhancing Legal Education and Professionalism' (2017) 95 The Canadian Bar Review 47.

Legal Cheek, 'Revealed: The Best Law Firms for Tech 2020' (*Legal Cheek*, 6 March 2020) <https://www.legalcheek.com/2020/03/revealed-the-best-law-firms-for-tech-2020/> accessed 18 February 2021.

Legal Design Lab, 'Legal FAQ' <https://legalfaq.org/> accessed 12 April 2021.

Legal Design Lab, 'Stanford Legal Design Lab' <https://www.legaltechdesign.com/> accessed 12 April 2021.

Legal Education and Training Review, 'Setting Standards. The Future of Legal Services Education and Training Regulation in England and Wales' (2013) <https://letr.org.uk/index.html> accessed 27 November 2020.

Legal Insights, 'When Big Data Meets Big Law' (*Legal Insights Europe*, 20 September 2019) <https://blogs.thomsonreuters.com/legal-uk/2019/09/20/when-big-data-meets-big-law/> accessed 27 August 2021.

Legal Services Board, 'Technology and Innovation in Legal Services—Main Report' (November 2018) <https://research.legalservicesboard.org.uk/wp-content/media/Innovation-survey-2018-report-FINAL-2.pdf> accessed 7 October 2019.

Legal Services Consumer Panel, 'Tracker Survey 2019. Briefing Note: How Consumers Are Using Legal Services' <https://www.legalservicesconsumerpanel.org.uk/wp-content/uploads/2019/07/2019-07-25-How-consumers-are-using-2019-FINAL.pdf> accessed 18 October 2019.

Legal Services Corporation, 'Justice Gap Report: Measuring the Civil Legal Needs of Low-income Americans' (2017) <https://www.lsc.gov/media-center/publications/2017-justice-gap-report> accessed 19 April 2021.

The Legal Technologist, 'Why Lawyers Should Learn to Code, But Not for the Reasons You Think' (25 November 2020) <https://www.legaltechnologist.co.uk/why-lawyers-should-learn-to-code-but-not-for-the-reasons-you-think/> accessed 22 March 2021.

Lesk M, 'Automatic Sense Disambiguation Using Machine Readable Dictionaries: How to Tell a Pinecone from an Ice Cream Cone' *SIGDOC'86: Proceedings of the 5th Annual International Conference on Systems Documentation* (June 1986), 24–26 <https://doi.org/10.1145/318723.318728>

Li W and others, 'Law Is Code: A Software Engineering Approach to Analysing the United States Code' (2015) 10 Journal of Business & Technology Law 297 <http://digitalcommons.law.umaryland.edu/jbtl/vol10/iss2/6> accessed 27 August 2021.

Lloyds Bank UK Customer Digital Index 2020, <https://www.lloydsbank.com/assets/media/pdfs/banking_with_us/whats-happening/lb-consumer-digital-index-2020-report.pdf> accessed 22 April 2021

Lord Chancellor, the Lord Chief Justice and the Senior President of Tribunals, 'Transforming Our Justice System' (2016) <https://assets.publishing.service.gov.uk/government/uploads/system/uploads/attachment_data/file/553261/joint-vision-statement.pdf> accessed 19 April 2021.

Lord Chief Justice, 'Coronavirus (COVID-19): Message from the Lord Chief Justice to Judges in the Civil and Family Courts' (*Judiciary.Gov*, 19 March 2020) <https://www.judiciary.uk/announcements/coronavirus-covid-19-message-from-the-lord-chief-justice-to-judges-in-the-civil-and-family-courts/> accessed 19 April 2021.

Macdonald C and Liberatore S, 'The Robot that Could Get You Off a Parking Ticket: DoNotPay System Has Won 160,000 Disputes in London and New York' (*Daily Mail*, 28 June 2016) <https://www.dailymail.co.uk/sciencetech/article-3664413/The-Robot-parking-ticket-DoNotPay-created-student-won-160-000-disputes-London-New-York.html> accessed 26 April 2021.

Mak E, *The T-shaped Lawyer and Beyond: Rethinking legal professionalism and legal education for contemporary societies* (The Hague, Eleven International Publishing, 2017).

Mann WC and Thompson SA, 'Rhetorical Structure Theory: Toward a Functional Theory of Text Organization' (1981) 8 (3) Text & Talk 243–81.

Manyika J and others, *Big Data: The Next Frontier for Innovation, Competition, and Productivity* (McKinsey Global Institute, 2011).

Marr B, 'Really Big Data At Walmart: Real-Time Insights From Their 40+ Petabyte Data Cloud' (*Forbes*, n.d.) <https://www.forbes.com/sites/bernardmarr/2017/01/23/really-big-data-at-walmart-real-time-insights-from-their-40-petabyte-data-cloud/> accessed 2 January 2021.

Maslen K, 'Teaching Law with Technology Prize 2020—Finalists Announced' (*Thomson Reuters*, 6 March 2020) <https://blogs.thomsonreuters.com/legal-uk/2020/03/06/teaching-law-with-technology-prize-2020-finalists-announced/> accessed 16 March 2021.

McAffee A and Brynjolfsson E, 'Big Data: The Management Revolution' (*Harvard Business Review*, 2012) <https://hbr.org/2012/10/big-data-the-management-revolution> accessed 27 August 2021.

McCormick D, 'Legal IT Insider Newsletter' (2018) <https://www.legaltechnology.com/wp-content/uploads/2018/09/Sept-Insider316.pdf> accessed 13 October 2018.

McFaul H and FitzGerald E, 'A Realist Evaluation of Student Use of a Virtual Reality Smartphone Application in Undergraduate Legal Education' (2020) 51 (3) British Journal of Educational Technology 572.

McFaul H and others, 'A Mobile App for Public Legal Education: A Case Study of Co-designing with Students' (2020) 28 Research in Learning Technology.

Mendez E, 'Dropping Dropbox in Your Law Practice to Maintain Your Duty of Confidentiality' (2013) 36 Campbell Law Review 175.

Mohler GO and others, 'Randomized Controlled Field Trials of Predictive Policing' [2016] Journal of the American Statistical Association

<https://amstat.tandfonline.com/doi/full/10.1080/01621459.2015.1077710> accessed 27 August 2021.

Molag T, 'The Complete Guide to Social Media for Lawyers' (*Clio.com*, 23 February 2021) <https://www.clio.com/resources/digital-marketing-lawyers/social-media-lawyers/> accessed 12 April 2021.

Monash University, 'Legal Tech Studio' <https://www.monash.edu/study/courses/find-a-course/2021/legal-tech-studio-pdl1031> accessed 12 April 2021.

Moore GE, 'The Future of Integrated Electronics' (1965) 38 Electronics 4.

Morse J, 'Amazon Announces New Employee Tracking Tech, and Customers Are Lining Up, Mashable UK' (2 December 2020) <https://mashable.com/article/amazon-aws-panorama-worker-customer-tracking-technology-smart-cameras/?europe=true>

My Virtual Lawyer, 'About Our Team' (2021) <https://myvirtual.lawyer/our-team/> accessed 19 February 2021.

My Virtual Lawyer, 'You Should Become a Virtual Lawyer: Here's Why and How to Begin Your Law Firm' (2021) <https://myvirtual.lawyer/why-and-how-to-become-a-virtual-lawyer/> accessed 19 February 2021.

Nakamoto S, 'Bitcoin: A Peer-to-Peer Electronic Cash System' (31 October 2008) <https://bitcoin.org/en/bitcoin-paper> accessed 27 August 2021.

National Centre for Education Statistics, 'A Description Of U.S. Adults Who Are Not Digitally Literate' <https://nces.ed.gov/pubs2018/2018161.pdf> accessed 26 November 2020.

The National Center for Technology and Dispute Resolution, 'Ethical Principles for Online Dispute Resolution' (2016) <http://odr.info/ethics-and-odr/> accessed 18 April 2021.

Naughton J, 'Is Blockchain the Most Important IT Invention of Our Age?' (*Guardian*, 24 January 2016) <https://www.theguardian.com/commentisfree/2016/jan/24/blockchain-bitcoin-technology-most-important-tech-invention-of-our-age-sir-mark-walport> accessed 27 August 2021.

NBC News, 'Fitbit Murder Case: Richard Dabate Pleads Not Guilty in Wife's Death' (29 April 2017) <https://www.nbcnews.com/news/us-news/fitbit-murder-case-richard-dabate-pleads-not-guilty-wife-s-n752526> accessed 27 August 2021.

Nicolson D, 'Calling, Character and Clinical Legal Education: A Cradle-to-grave Approach to Inculcating a Love for Justice' (2013) 16 (1) Legal Ethics 36.

Nieto A and others, 'IoT-forensics Meets Privacy: Towards Cooperative Digital Investigations' (2018) 18 (2) Sensors 492.

OED, *Oxford Dictionary* (OUP, 2021).

OFCOM, 'Connected Nations 2020 UK Report' (2020) <https://www.ofcom.org.uk/__data/assets/pdf_file/0024/209373/connected-nations-2020.pdf> accessed 19 April 2021.

Office for National Statistics, 'Exploring the UK's Digital Divide' (2019) <https://www.ons.gov.uk/peoplepopulationandcommunity/householdcharacteristics/homeinternetandsocialmediausage/articles/exploringtheuksdigitaldivide/2019-03-04> accessed 19 April 2021.

Office for National Statistics, 'Internet Access, Households and Individuals, Great Britain: 2020' (*ONS.Gov*, 7 August 2020) <https://www.ons.gov.uk/peoplepopulationandcommunity/householdcharacteristics/homeinternetandsocialmediausage/bulletins/internetaccesshouseholdsandindividuals/2020> accessed 14 April 2021.

Office for Students, 'Supply of Higher Skills Levels' <https://www.officeforstudents.org.uk/advice-and-guidance/skills-and-employment/supply-of-higher-level-skills/> accessed 26 November 2020.

Office of Lawyer Regulation Complainant v Kristine a Peshek [2011] WI 47 <https://www.wicourts.gov/sc/opinion/DisplayDocument.pdf?content=pdf&seqNo=66464> accessed 27 August 2021.

O'Kane S, 'A Second Apple Employee Was Charged with Stealing Self-driving Car Project' (*The Verge*, 2019) <https://www.theverge.com/2019/1/30/18203718/apple-self-driving-trade-secrets-china-titan> accessed 27 August 2021.

O'Leary DL, '"Smart Lawyering": Integrating Technology Competence into the Legal Practice Curriculum' (2020) <https://ssrn.com/abstract=3671632> accessed 21 February 2021.

The Open University, 'Digital Forensics' (2020) <https://www.open.edu/openlearn/science-maths-technology/digital-forensics/content-section-4.2#:~:text=Until%20the%20late%201990s%2C%20what,and%20Response%20Team%20(CART)> accessed 27 August 2021.

The Open University, 'Digital Justice' <https://www.open.ac.uk/open-justice/public-understanding-law/digital-justice> accessed 15 April 2021.

The O Shaped Lawyer, 'The O Shaped Lawyer Programme' <https://www.oshapedlawyer.com/about> accessed 27 August 2021.

Oswald and others, 'Algorithmic Risk Assessment Policing Models: Lessons from the Durham HART Model and "Experimental" Proportionality' (2018) 27 (2) Information & Communications Technology Law 223–50.

Ozenc K and Hagan M, *Rituals for Work* (John Wiley & Sons, 2019).

Palfrey J and Gasser U, *Born Digital, Understanding the First Generation of Digital Natives* (Basic Books, 2008), ii.

Pleasance P, '"Legal Need" and Legal Needs Surveys: A Background Paper' (*Open Society Foundations*, 2016) <https://namati.org/wp-content/uploads/2016/11/OSJI-Legal-Needs-Surveys-Background-Materials-1-An-Introduction-to-Legal-Needs-Surveys-1-v3.6-2016-06-22-web_Pascoe.pdf> accessed 2 October 2019.

The Police Foundation, 'Digital Forensics: The Next Steps' (2020) <https://www.police-foundation.org.uk/project/the-next-steps-for-digital-forensics/> accessed 27 August 2021.

'PredPol Operational Review—Initial Findings' (*Kent Police*, 2013) <https://www.statewatch.org/docbin/uk-2013-11-kent-police-pp-report.pdf> accessed 27 August 2021.

Preston CB, 'Lawyers' Abuse of Technology' (2018) 118 Cornell Law Review 881.

Puiu T, 'Smartphone Is Millions of Times Faster than NASA's 1960s Computers' (*ZME Science*, 11 February 2020) <https://www.zmescience.com/science/news-science/smartphone-power-compared-to-apollo-432/> accessed 20 April 2021.

Purtill V, 'Lawtech: Standards for the Lawyers of the Future' <https://www.regulationmatters.uk/features/legal-tech-for-the-lawyers-of-the-future/> accessed 22 February 2021.

Quality Assurance Agency, 'Subject Benchmark Statement Law November' <https://www.qaa.ac.uk/docs/qaa/subject-benchmark-statements/subject-benchmark-statement-law.pdf?sfvrsn=b939c881_16> accessed 30 November 2020.

Queensland Association of Independent Legal Services Inc., 'Queensland Community Legal Centres Use of Technology Literature Review and Discussion Paper' (2014).

Reith M and others, 'An Examination of Digital Forensic Models' (2002) 1 (3) International Journal of Digital Evidence 1.

Reyburn S, 'The $69 Million Beeple NFT Was Bought with Cryptocurrency' (*New York Times*, 12 March 2021) <https://www.nytimes.com/2021/03/12/arts/beeple-nft-buyer-ether.html> accessed 20 March 2021.

Reyes E, 'Who's Afraid of Computer Generation?' (28 October 2010) <https://www.lawgazette.co.uk/analysis/whos-afraid-of-computer-generation-/57836.article> accessed 12 November 2019.

Ritter C, 'Reach More Users: 4 Tips for Designing Accessible Apps and Websites' (2018) <https://www.thinkwithgoogle.com/marketing-strategies/app-and-mobile/website-app-accessibility-guidelines/> accessed 28 April 2021.

Rogers S, 'What is a Data Scientist?' (*Guardian*, 2012) <https://www.theguardian.com/news/datablog/2012/mar/02/data-scientist> accessed 12 October 2018.

Romm T and Lerman R, 'Amazon Suspends Parler, Taking pro-Trump Site Offline Indefinitely' (*Washington Post*, 2021) <https://www.washingtonpost.com/technology/2021/01/09/amazon-parler-suspension/> accessed 27 August 2021.

Rose N, 'Lewis Case: "Wishing Death on Neo-Nazis" Went too Far' (*Legal Futures*, 17 December 2018) <https://www.legalfutures.co.uk/latest-news/lewis-case-wishing-death-on-neo-nazis-went-too-far> accessed 29 April 2021.

Roux C and others, 'The End of the (Forensic Science) World as We Know It? The Example of Trace Evidence' (2015) 370 (1674) Philosophical Transactions of the Royal Society B: Biological Sciences 20140260.

Royal Geographical Society, 'Digital Divide in the UK' (*Royal Geographical Society*, n.d.) <https://21stcenturychallenges.org/what-is-the-digital-divide/> accessed 28 April 2021.

Rule C, 'Is ODR ADR?' (2016) 8 Online Dispute Resolution 8

Ryan F, 'A Virtual Law Clinic: A Realist Evaluation of What Works for Whom, Why, How and in What Circumstances?' (2020) 54 (2) The Law Teacher 237.

Salovey P and Mayer JD, 'Emotional Intelligence' (1990) 9 (3) Imagination, Cognition and Personality 185.

Sandefur R, *Accessing Justice in the Contemporary USA: Findings from the Community Needs and Services Study* (American Bar Foundation, 2014).

Sandefur R, 'Legal Tech for Non-Lawyers: Report on the Survey of US Legal Technologies' (2019) <americanbarfoundation.org> accessed 27 August 2021.

Schön DA, *Educating the Reflective Practitioner: Toward a New Design for Teaching and Learning in the Professions* (Jossey-Bass, 1987).

Scientific Working Group on Digital Evidence, 'SWGDE Multimedia and Digital Evidence Glossary' Ver 3.0 (June 2016), 6 <https://swgde.org/documents/Current%20Documents/Select> accessed 27 August 2021.

The Seattle Times, 'Soaring Bitcoin Prices Put Central Washington Electrical Utilities on Alert' (*The Seattle Times*, 9 January 2021) <https://www.seattletimes.com/business/technology/sunday-buzz-soaring-bitcoin-prices-put-central-washington-electrical-utilities-on-alert/> accessed 22 March 2021.

Select Committee on Artificial Intelligence, 'Report of Session 2017–19 AI in the UK: Ready, Willing and Able?' (*House of Lords*, 2018) HL Paper 100 <https://publications.parliament.uk/pa/ld201719/ldselect/ldai/100/100.pdf> accessed 8 September 2021.

Sergot MJ and others, 'The British Nationality Act as a Logic Program' (1986), 29:5 Communications of the ACM.

Siegel DJ, 'Ethics Corner: 12 Rules for Ethically Dealing with Social Media' (*ABA*, 16 February 2017) <https://www.americanbar.org/groups/business_law/publications/blt/2017/02/ethics_corner/> accessed 11 April 2021

Sky News, 'Mitesh Patel: Gay Pharmacist Jailed for Murdering Wife to Be with Boyfriend' (*Sky News*, 2018) <https://news.sky.com/story/mitesh-patel-pharmacist-who-murdered-wife-jailed-for-30-years-11572248> accessed 27 August 2021.

Smith A and Hutchinson T, 'Building Legal Project Management Skills and Organisational Capability' (2017) <https://gallery.mailchimp.com/ef0907072acfd9dfa8857ea40/files/d4eb13ae-8896-4b27-81ca-3ad6cf48e5ad/Building_LPM_Skills_Organisational_Capability.pdf> accessed 27 August 2021.

Solicitors Regulation Authority, 'SRA Code of Conduct for Solicitors' <https://www.sra.org.uk/solicitors/standards-regulations/> accessed 30 April 2021.

Solicitors Regulation Authority, 'Statement of Solicitor Competence' <https://www.sra.org.uk/solicitors/resources/cpd/competence-statement/> accessed 30 November 2020.

Solicitors Regulation Authority, 'Technology and Legal Services' (*Solicitors Regulatory Authority*, 11 December 2018) <https://www.sra.org.uk/risk/risk-resources/technology-legal-services/> accessed 30 April 2021.

Solicitors Regulation Authority, 'Use of Social Media and Offensive Communications' (25 November 2019) <https://www.sra.org.uk/sra/corporate-strategy/sra-enforcement-strategy/enforcement-practice/social-media-offensive-communications/> accessed 29 April 2021.

Sommerlad H, 'Researching and Theorising the Process of Professional Identity Formation' (2007) 34 (2) Journal of Law and Society 190.

South China Morning Post, 'Bitcoin Mining in Northern Chinese Province to Be Halted Amid Energy-Saving Push' <https://www.scmp.com/economy/china-economy/article/3123633/bitcoin-mining-northern-chinese-province-be-halted-amid> accessed 22 March 2021.

Srivastava M, 'WhatsApp Voice Calls Used to Inject Israeli Spyware on Phones' (*Financial Times*, 13 May 2019) <https://www.ft.com/content/4da1117e-756c-11e9-be7d-6d846537acab> accessed 30 April 2021.

Staff C, 'Big Data' (2017) 60 (6) Communications of the ACM 25 <https://doi.org/10.1145/3079064> accessed 27 August 2021.

Statista, 'Number of Smartphone Users Worldwide from 2016 to 2023' (undated), <https://www.statista.com/statistics/330695/number-of-smartphone-users-worldwide/> accessed 12 May 2021.

Statista, 'Social Media—Statistics and Facts' (undated) <https://www.statista.com/topics/1164/social-networks/#dossierSummary> accessed 12 May 2021.

Stubbings C, 'Foreword' in Price Waterhouse Cooper, 'The Workforce of the Future. The Competing Forces Shaping 2030' (2018) <https://www.pwc.com/gx/en/services/people-organisation/workforce-of-the-future/workforce-of-the-future-the-competing-forces-shaping-2030-pwc.pdf> accessed 17 October 2018.

Susskind R, *The End of Lawyers? Rethinking the Nature of Legal Services* (OUP, 2010).

Susskind R, *Online Courts and the Future of Justice* (OUP, 2019).

Susskind R, *Tomorrow's Lawyers: An Introduction to Your Future* (OUP, 2017).

Sweeney M, 'Lord McAlpine Settles Libel Action with Alan Davies over Twitter Comment' (*Guardian*, 24 October 2013) <https://www.theguardian.com/media/2013/oct/24/lord-mcalpine-libel-alan-davies> accessed 14 April 2021.

Tech Nation, 'The LawtechUK Panel' (*Tech Nation*, n.d.) <https://technation.io/lawtechukpanel/> accessed 21 March 2021.

TechTerms, 'Binary' (2020) <https://techterms.com/definition/binary> accessed 27 August 2021.

Thanaraj A, 'Making the Case for a Digital Lawyering Framework in Legal Education' (2017) (3) International Review of Law 17.

Thomas JB and others, 'Measuring Australia's Digital Divide: The Australian Digital Inclusion Index 2020, RMIT and Swinburne University of Technology, Melbourne, for Telstra' (2020), 6 <https://apo.org.au/sites/default/files/resource-files/2020-10/apo-nid308474.pdf> accessed 26 November 2020.

Thomson Reuters, 'Digital General Counsel are Transforming the Corporate Legal Department' (2020), 3 <https://legalsolutions.thomsonreuters.co.uk/content/dam/ewp-m/documents/legal-uk/en/pdf/reports/tr1135788-transforming-the-corporate.pdf> accessed 18 February 2021.

Thornton JI, 'The General Assumptions and Rationale of Forensic Identification' in DL Faigman, DH Kaye, MJ Saks and J Sanders (eds), *Modern Scientific Evidence: The Law and Science of Expert Testimony* (West Publishing Company, 1997).

Tiku N and others, 'Twitter Bans Trump's Account, Citing Risk of Further Violence' (*Washington Post*, 9 January 2021) <https://www.washingtonpost.com/technology/2021/01/08/twitter-trump-dorsey/> accessed 30 April 2021.

Tilstone WJ and others, *Forensic science: An Encyclopaedia of History, Methods, and Techniques* (ABC-CLIO, 2006).

United Nations, 'UN E-Government Survey 2016' (2016) <https://publicadministration.un.org/egovkb/en-us/reports/un-e-government-survey-2016> accessed 12 May 2021.

University of York, 'LLB (Hons) Law' <https://www.york.ac.uk/study/undergraduate/courses/llb-law/> accessed 28 April 2021.

US National Institute of Justice, 'Digital Evidence in the Courtroom: A Guide For Law Enforcement and Prosecutors' (2006) <https://www.ojp.gov/pdffiles1/nij/211314.pdf> accessed 30 April 2021.

Wexler C, 'The Changing Nature of Crime and Criminal Investigations' (2018) <https://www.policeforum.org/assets/ChangingNatureofCrime.pdf> accessed 30 April 2021.

WIRED, 'This Site Posted Every Face from Parler's Capitol Hill Insurrection Videos' (*Ars Technica*, 23 January 2021) <https://arstechnica.com/tech-policy/2021/01/this-site-posted-every-face-from-parlers-capitol-hill-insurrection-videos/> accessed 30 April 2021.

Woebbeking MK, 'The Impact of Smart Contracts on Traditional Concepts of Contract Law' (2019) 10 JIPITEC 8.

World Bank Live, 'Closing the Digital Divide' (*World Bank*, 2020) <https://live.worldbank.org/closing-the-digital-divide> accessed 28 April 2021.

Wright A and De Filippi P, 'Decentralized Blockchain Technology and the Rise of Lex Cryptographia' (2015) Social Science Research Network, SSRN Scholarly Paper ID 2580664 <https://papers.ssrn.com/abstract=2580664> accessed 21 March 2021.

Zhang L, 'Regulation of Cryptocurrency' (June 2018) <https://www.loc.gov/law/help/cryptocurrency/china.php> accessed 14 March 2021.

GLOSSARY

A number of key terms within this book are considered in detail within its chapters (e.g. digital lawyering). Others have short definitions next to them within the relevant sentences and paragraphs. This glossary contains a range of words used frequently within the legal profession and/or legal technology that may be less familiar to some readers than others.

Access to justice A basic principle, underpinning the rule of law, that everyone should have access to the courts and legal representation.

Adjudicator A person or body that makes a decision in a formal dispute.

Affordances Referring to user interfaces, the properties or features which give indications of a way to interact with the system or object, in order to achieve a specific outcome.

Algorithm A description of a computation or mathematical method, reduced to documentation or a software code executable by a computer.

Ambient A quality of computer interaction in which computer devices supporting a human-machine interaction are well-integrated into the experience, to the extent that the presence of the computing devices is not novel or noticed by the user and requires no additional cognitive load on the part of the user to accomplish the desired goal or task.

Analytics Systematic methods of processing and analysis for data or statistics.

App A vernacular shorthand for application, most often referring to those on mobile devices.

Application A computer programme or programmes packaged in such a way as to provide a ready-to-use object on a computer or mobile device.

Arbitration The settling of a dispute between parties by a mutually agreed other party outside a court of law.

Artificial intelligence (AI) The discipline concerned with the development of computer systems able to perform tasks normally performed by humans, requiring certain capabilities normally associated with humans such as decision-making, language translation, and visual perception.

Attacker A malicious actor attempting to infiltrate a computer system or network to steal information, deny access to others, etc.

Attorney A term used in the United States to refer to a lawyer.

Audit trail A record of a step-by-step process where the data can be tracked to its source.

Automated The use of technology to replicate a process with limited human involvement.

(The) Bar The collective term for barristers.

Barrister A type of legal professional in common law jurisdictions whose work is often focused upon advocacy (representing clients in court).

Big Data A body of data that is too large to store and process using the capabilities of traditional single computer systems.

Billable hours The amount of time billed to the client as a result of a legal professional's chargeable hours.

Bitcoin A market-leading cryptocurrency.

Block A unit of data on a blockchain that is introduced through a certain protocol and accepted using the blockchain's specified consensus mechanism.

Blockchain A distributed ledger technology duplicated and distributed to a network of participating computer systems, relying on a sequential series of data blocks created and managed according to a specific set of protocols for creating, validating and recording new blocks.

BYOD "Bring Your Own Device", a practice allowing business applications and communications to take place on employee-owned devices.

Chargeable hour Unit of time recorded by a legal professional when working on a particular issue.

Chartered legal executive A role in the legal profession within England and Wales, similar to that of a solicitor.

Client care The way in which a legal professional looks after and supports a client (similar to the more general term "customer service").

Client management system Software system that supports lawyers in tracking and managing the contact data of their clients, and in some cases including detailed collections of information, files and other supporting electronic documents related to specific matters for those clients.

Cloud A reference to the Internet as a ubiquitous computing environment.

Cloud computing The provision and use of computing resources accessible via the Internet in well-defined increments of resources for specified periods of time.

Coding See Programming.

Commodity computing Computers available at low unit cost, driving them to essentially interchangeable units, to be used and billed for use as utilities.

Common law jurisdiction A jurisdiction modelled on the English legal system which places a large reliance upon case law.

Communication The projecting of information to some destination or recipient over a distance.

Communications network A collection of two or more devices (computers, transmitters, receivers, radios, etc.) that can send and/or receive information, usually using electromagnetic signals carried by wire or wirelessly.

Computer vision A sub-discipline of AI concerned with the processing of image and video data.

Conditional fee agreement An agreement between the legal representative and their client in which legal fees are only paid in certain circumstances, normally if the client wins the case.

Consensus algorithm A mechanism by which new blocks are validated and accepted for incorporation into a blockchain.

Counterparties In a transaction, one or more other parties participating in that transaction.

Cryptocurrency A digital currency or means of facilitating exchange relying on cryptographic methods and often a blockchain for recording transactions and issuing units.

Cryptographic See Cryptography.

Cryptographic hash A large number of fixed size computed from a data input (e.g. a password or some other credential) used instead of storing the source value, as a means of authentication or validation in a secure computing system.

Cryptographic suites Collections of computer programs and reusable code containing implementations of cryptography that are used to secure communications and data storage from unauthorised access and use.

Cryptography The discipline of securing or protecting communications and data using certain mathematical methods and algorithms.

Curriculum Topics and subjects included in a programme, module or course.

Cyberattack A planned attempt by a hacker or an organisation to harm a computer system or network.

Dark web A collection of sites connected to the Internet that require special software, configurations, and techniques to access. Often referring to secret resources on the Internet hosting or supporting illicit or controversial activity.

Data collection Accumulation and storage of data for specific (and sometimes non-specific) purposes.

Data custody The act of holding and maintaining bodies of data.

Data protection officer A person designated in an organisation who is responsible for advising and guiding that organisation's compliance to the General Data Protection Regulation (GDPR).

Data set A collection of discrete records collected for analysis and the support of some activity such as the delivery of a service or the delivery of information to support a decision.

Demographic shift A change in population that impacts society.

Desktop-as-a-service A form of virtual desktop interface allowing a user to see and use a desktop computer system in a physically separate, sometimes more secure location. Used to enhance security or to control costs in spending on desktop computing resources.

Digital presence How individuals or businesses appear online; what is found when people search on web pages, blogs and social media.

Digital rights management A body of tools and practices to restrict the distribution and access to digital media to paid or licensed users.

Distributed ledger A technology that supports the secure functioning of a decentralized database.

DRM See Digital Rights Management.

Due diligence The steps reasonable to take to ensure everything is as it appears.

Electronic signature A signature attached to a document which may involve either a graphical marking, a cryptographically supported annotation or both.

Encoding One of a range of methods for representing information in digital format.

Encrypted at rest The characteristic of data that is secured and stored in encrypted form, requiring decryption with an appropriate key or other secret before reading.

Encryption Security technology incorporating methods that scramble data into random, unreadable data using mathematical functions that can be reversed using other, complementary mathematical functions, requiring specific secret inputs that act as keys.

Ethereum A blockchain and smart contract platform supporting the creation of general-purpose applications.

Exculpatory evidence Evidence that establishes the innocence of a defendant.

Execution The running of a programme on a computer (e.g. running a smart contract's code on a node on a blockchain distributed application network).

Expert system A computer system programmed with knowledge of a specific domain to emulate the decisions that would be made by a human in a well-defined set of conditions.

Fungible token A cryptocurrency unit that represents an asset or right which can be exchanged for a like asset or right.

Gas A unit of cryptocurrency for paying transaction fees related to applications built and run on the Ethereum blockchain.

GDPR The General Data Protection Regulation of the European Union. May also refer to the UK General Data Protection Regulation, depending on the context.

Generation Y Sometimes also known as Millennials, referring to people born from the late 1980s to 1990s.

Generation Z People born between the mid to late 1990s and the early 2010s, often known as the tech savvy generation because they were born into a time of fast digitally growth.

Globalisation The way in which the world has become increasing more interconnected and interdependent.

Hansard The records of a legislative body in jurisdictions following the British legal tradition.

Hardware technologies Physical components in computing systems including computers, storage, displays, networks, and electrical power supplies.

HMCTS Her Majesty's Court and Tribunal Service.

HMCTS Reform Programme A reform of the court service to introduce new working practices and technology.

HTML Hyper Text Markup Language, a language used to create pages readable in a web browser, with rich formatting and multimedia, including graphics and video.

ICO See Initial Coin Offering.

Immutability The property of data in certain systems that renders data unchangeable once accepted, whether for processing or storage.

Inculpatory evidence Evidence that shows a defendant's involvement in a crime.

Information retrieval The science of extracting information from bodies of data, including text and other forms of media.

Infrastructure Hardware and software that are assembled and managed together, to provide such services as processing, storage and communications for applications.

In-house Refers to an individual employed within a company or other organisation.

Initial coin offering An event where cryptocurrency units or tokens (coins) are purchased and issued to participants on a blockchain application network.

Input Data provided to a computer system by some means of interaction.

Instruct A client asking a legal professional to represent or advise them.

Interdisciplinary A combination of different disciplines (e.g. law and technology) within one activity.

Interfaces A hardware connection where two or more devices connect to each other.

Interlocutory hearing A hearing between the parties and the judge to decide procedural matters in a case.

Intermediary A party that acts as a carrier and conveyor of physical or virtual goods between two or more parties in a transaction.

Internet telephony Voice communications converted for transmission over the Internet. Compare with traditional telephony, which uses analogue signals carried over wires.

Internetwork A network connecting smaller networks. The largest example of an internetwork is the Internet itself.

Investigating authority An authority that is authorized to conduct investigations.

JSON JavaScript Object Notation, a standard text-based format for the encoding of data for reading by a machine.

Jurisdiction A defined set of boundaries, usually geographic, within which certain laws apply, or in which a court or other competent body may make a ruling.

Known file matching This is the process of identifying known relevant files on a device using computational hashing and comparison methods. A digital forensics practitioner may maintain a "HashSet" containing the hashes of files known to be evidential (a common practice for IIoC cases). When a suspect device is scanned, any files which have the same hash value as those in the practitioner's HashSet must be the same (subject to collision caveats) and are therefore likely to be flagged for attention.

Law enforcement The term refers to the police as an authorised body empowered by the state to investigate and detect crime and prevent civil disorder.

Lawyer-client privilege A doctrine protecting the communications between a lawyer and a client from compelled disclosure.

Lawyers A collective term for legal professionals. Although commonly associated with the US legal profession, it is used in this book to refer to legal professionals generally.

Legal aid If you cannot afford to pay for legal advice, you might be entitled to help to meet the costs of advice and representation through support provided by the government.

Legal brief A document that sets out the arguments in a legal case.

Legal executive A type of legal professional in England and Wales who performs similar work to a solicitor.

Legal practice The work undertaken by legal professionals.

Legal services The provision of legal advice and/or representation.

Legaltech A common vernacular term for legal technology, an emerging discipline at the intersection of legal practice and technology.

Litigation The legal process for resolving a dispute in a court of law.

Log parsing The systematic decomposition of events recorded in the log files of a software system for the purpose of extracting a usable data set describing the activity of that system or the users it serves for a specific period of time covered by those log files.

Machine learning A branch of AI that focuses on the development of computer systems that act without explicit programming, instead using data from previous experience to develop and improve models for action.

Machine learning tools Software and processes to support the training, evaluation, and improvement of mathematical models incorporated in the construction and maintenance of machine learning systems.

Malware Malicious software designed to infiltrate and damage devices.

Marketing The promotion and selling of goods or services, often using advertising in various forms.

Mediation The act of resolving a dispute with the assistance of a neutral third party.

Metadata Data describing transactions or a larger body of data.

Microchip A small wafer of semiconductor material, usually silicon, containing extremely small electrical circuits.

Microcomputer A computer with power and capacity that fits on a desktop package.

Microgrid network A local electrical power generation and distribution system, usually associated with renewable energy initiatives, often supported by blockchain-powered applications for measurement and billing.

Millennial Sometimes also known as Generation Y, referring to people born from the late 1980s to 1990s.

Mining The act of competitively verifying transactions to be incorporated into a blockchain, with a reward in cryptocurrency given to those who successfully complete validating a block, according to a certain selection protocol.

Mobile device A portable hand-sized device, usually (but not always) providing the capabilities of a mobile telephone and in many cases a general computing platform for running applications that use the communications capability of the device, such as voice, messaging, and Internet connectivity.

Moore's law An observation by the American engineer Gordon Moore that the number of transistors in a dense integrated circuit doubles every 18–24 months.

Natural language processing A discipline combining knowledge and methods from linguistics, computer science, and artificial intelligence, concerned with developing computer systems to process and analyse data in the form of text or spoken word.

Network A collection of computers connected and able to communicate with each other using wired or wireless links.

Networked A state of being connected over a communications network.

NFT See Non-Fungible Token.

NLP See Natural Language Processing.

Nodes Usually a single computer on a network, as in an application node for a network of computers servicing a blockchain application.

Non-fungible token A cryptocurrency unit that represents an asset or right which is in some way unique and cannot be exchanged for a like asset or right. Unique pieces of art or property are often exchanged using NFTs build with blockchain technology.

Non-repudiation The characteristic of certain systems where actions can neither be undone nor the records of such actions denied.

NoSQL database A database that supports the storage of data without requiring predefined definitions for the structure of that data. NoSQL databases are considered by technologists to provide more freedom for rapid development of solutions but can be more difficult to grow and maintain, given the lower requirements for structure.

Notarisation The act of certifying the authenticity of a legal instrument, often for the purpose of making that agreement legally binding according to the requirements of a jurisdiction governing the matter contained or described in that instrument.

Ontologies The practice of identifying, naming and categorising concepts, data and relationships as a means of facilitating of analysis, discourse and the creation of derivative works such as computer systems.

Open data Bodies of data available for public examination, copying, processing and redistribution, usually provided by a government or other large organization as a means of providing transparency and accountability to citizens or other stakeholders.

Open source software Software provided with source code and licenses that allow the viewing, modification and some permitted, possibly restricted forms of redistribution of the original and/or modified versions.

Optimisation In technological systems, the seeking of the shortest, most economical path for accomplishing a goal or delivering a service consuming the least amount of resources.

Output Data received from a computer system following some defined operation.

Paralegal A legal role often found in larger law firms. Sometimes viewed as a stepping stone to training as a lawyer.

Pattern recognition A branch of machine learning that exploits the mathematical characteristics of recurrent phenomena in data.

PBFT See Practical Byzantine Fault Tolerance.

PC A personal computer, referring to a desktop computer or laptop computing device, usually owned or provided for the use of a single individual.

Physical trace evidence Evidence that is found at the scene of a crime (e.g. fibres, hairs, gunshot residue) which is collected by the police for forensic examination.

PII Personally identifiable information.

PoS See Proof of Stake.

PoW See Proof of Work.

Place-shifting Use of a digital asset or capability held or provided in one place by a user physically located in another location, possibly in a different jurisdiction.

Practical Byzantine fault tolerance (PBFT) A characteristic of distributed computer systems that allows them to tolerate failure under conditions of imperfect information, such that they can continue to operate by reaching consensus. Blockchain consensus mechanisms incorporate PBFT.

Principal (of a law firm) A leader of a law firm, with strategic or fiduciary responsibility to the partners or shareholders.

Private practice Legal professionals who work for profit-making firms or other organisations rather than within the public sector.

Pro bono A lawyer who provides legal advice or representation free of charge.

Processing The manipulation of data according to some specification.

Programming The creation of instructions for computer systems to execute and perform specific computations or tasks.

Proof of stake (PoS) A consensus mechanism for validating blocks on a blockchain that requires participants to show proof of investment or tenure on the network.

Proof of work (PoW) A consensus mechanism for validating blocks on a blockchain that requires the expenditure of a certain amount of computing resources in addition to a result shared by other participants in the network.

Pseudonymisation A personal data protection practice in which PII is obfuscated using masking or encryption when exposing data for allowed purposes in which the PII is present.

Quantum computing A branch of computing technology focused on building computing systems based on the characteristics of interactions between atomic and subatomic particles.

Queen's Speech The Queen's Speech sets out the government's agenda for the next session of Parliament and covers what legislation will be brought.

Regression A mathematical technique that determines the best-fitting mathematical function that describes a set of given data points.

Retainer A fee paid to a legal professional by a client in return for legal advice and/or representation.

Rhetorical structure theory A theory in linguistics that describes the relationships between parts of text.

Rule of law The principle that the law applies equally to everyone and we are all subject to the same laws.

SaaS Software as a service, a way of delivering computing services over the Internet.

Scarcity of resources The demand for resources exceeds supply.

Search Retrieving specific data from a larger body of data based on certain characteristics, including keywords or metadata.

Self-represented litigants Sometimes also known as litigants in person, individuals who are representing themselves in legal proceedings.

Semantic analysis The practice of decomposing text into its underlying syntactic structures and determining their individual relationships to other structures and to the underlying text, allowing computers to interpret and act upon spoken or written text. A critical sub-discipline of natural language processing.

Server In hardware, usually a high-capacity computer providing the processing power, storage and network communications for a software programme providing services for an application. In software, a programme that contains the code implementation allowing a computer to provide services for an application communicating with remote devices over a network.

Smart contract A programme that is part of a blockchain-based application that incorporates to a certain extent an agreement between two or more parties, and which may also take an active agency role in the execution and validation of the conditions specified in that agreement.

Smartphone A portable handheld device, providing mobile telephony capabilities (voice, short messaging, and Internet connectivity) and a general-purpose computing platform for running applications and Internet browsing.

Social Credit System A system assigning a score to an individual based on observations of activity collected using mass surveillance and other methods of data collection mandated by the central government in the People's Republic of China.

Solicitor The most common type of legal professional in the UK who advises and represents clients on legal issues.

Solicitors Regulation Authority The independent regulatory body for solicitors in England and Wales.

Solidity A programming language for the authoring of smart contracts on the Ethereum blockchain.

Storage The reposing of data on an electronic medium for later retrieval and use.

Summarisation algorithms Certain classes of natural language processing techniques that extract a subset of data or text providing a capsule description of a body of underlying text.

Sync The act of connecting a device such as mobile phone to another device, such as a computer, to update and exchange data between the devices, such that the resulting copies are identical.

Telecommunications Communication over a distance, using electrical signals carried over a wire or electromagnetic waves such as radio.

Text mining The practice of using natural language processing methods and algorithms on large bodies of text to compute certain text characteristics such as word usage frequencies, relevant passages, etc.

Token A unit of cryptocurrency issued for the purpose of representing and facilitating the negotiation and exchange in assets or rights connected to the token.

Training A stage in setting up a machine learning or AI system whereby a set of example data, called training data, is used to compute parameters for a model addressing a given problem or problem domain.

Transistor component density A measure of the level of miniaturisation on a microchip, usually measured in transistor units per square millimetre. In general, the higher the density, the higher the capability and speed of the circuits on the microchip.

Transmission The projection of information to a destination or recipient at a distance, using an electronic means of communication.

Triage The sorting and allocation of legal cases.

Ubiquitous computing A state in which one's daily environment and lifestyle is supported by a range of computing devices.

Validation The act of verifying and certifying the data contained in a block to be incorporated into a blockchain.

Variables Data variables are things that can be changed and are used to store information on a computer programme.

Virtual assistants A human person or digital assistant who provides support services to business from a remote location.

Virtual learning environment Online space designed for teaching and learning.

Virtual reality A computer-generated environment to create an authentic simulated experience.

Virus A unit of malicious code or a programme which can infiltrate and harm devices.

Wallet A software application or hardware device built for the purpose of storing and managing units of cryptocurrency.

INDEX

Note: Page numbers in italics indicate a figure on the corresponding page.

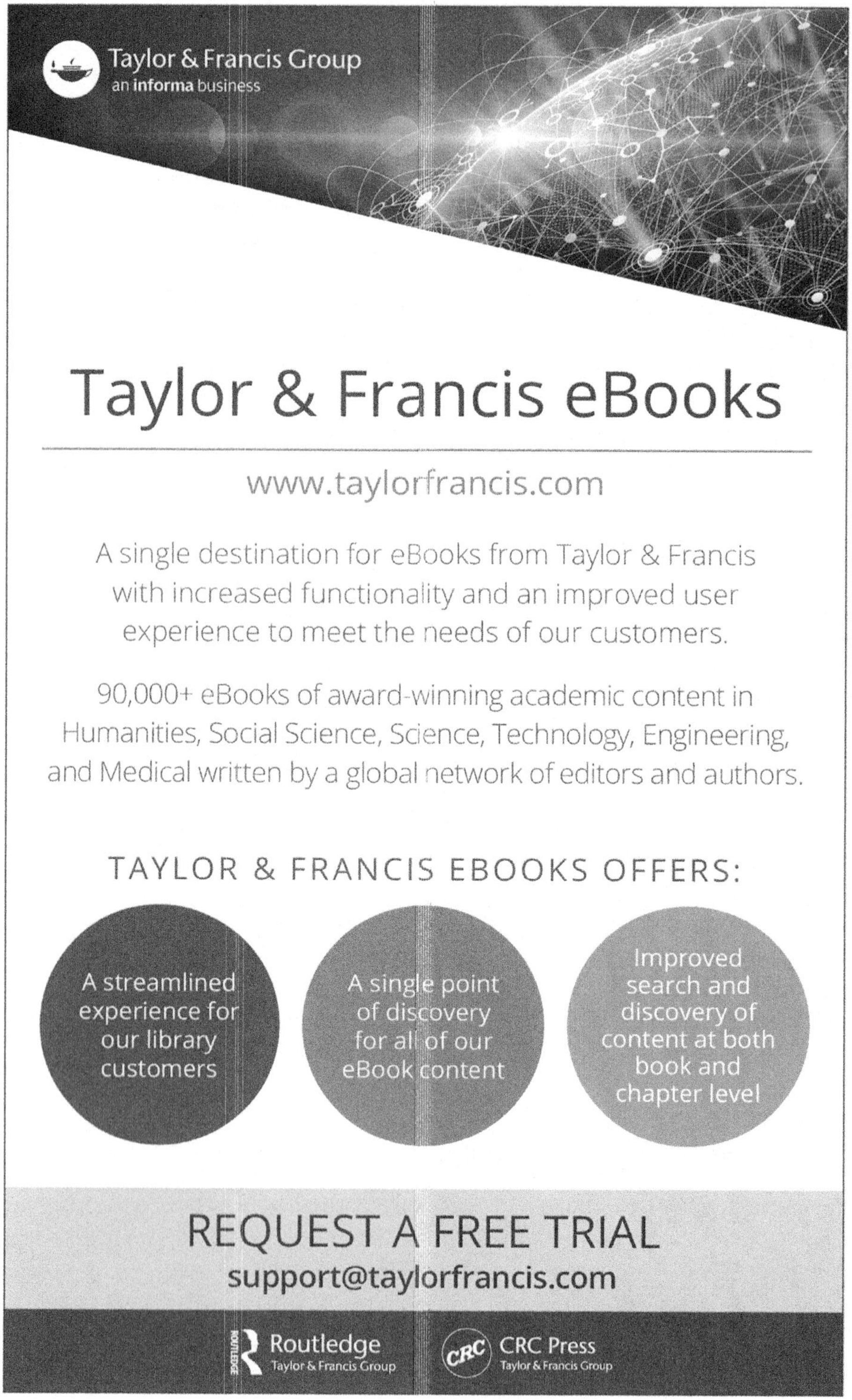
Taylor & Francis Group
an informa business
Taylor & Francis eBooks
www.taylorfrancis.com
A single destination for eBooks from Taylor & Francis with increased functionality and an improved user experience to meet the needs of our customers.
90,000+ eBooks of award-winning academic content in Humanities, Social Science, Science, Technology, Engineering, and Medical written by a global network of editors and authors.
TAYLOR & FRANCIS EBOOKS OFFERS:
A streamlined experience for our library customers
A single point of discovery for all of our eBook content
Improved search and discovery of content at both book and chapter level
REQUEST A FREE TRIAL
support@taylorfrancis.com
Routledge
Taylor & Francis Group
CRC Press
Taylor & Francis Group

Made in the USA
Coppell, TX
04 March 2022

74423340R10286